LONDON'S UNDERWORLD

Charles Booth.

LONDON'S UNDERWORLD

Edited by

Peter Quennell

BEING SELECTIONS FROM
'THOSE THAT WILL NOT WORK'
THE FOURTH VOLUME OF
'LONDON LABOUR AND THE LONDON POOR'
BY

HENRY MAYHEW

SPRING BOOKS
LONDON

The fourth volume of *London Labour and The London Poor* was first published in 1862. The first three appeared in 1851, and Peter Quennell's two volumes of selections from them are entitled *Mayhew's London* and *Mayhew's Characters*.

This edition first published 1950
Second impreisson 1959
Third impression 1960
Fourth impression 1962
Fifth impression 1965
Published by

SPRING BOOKS

WESTBOOK HOUSE · FULHAM BROADWAY · LONDON
Printed in Czechoslovakia by PZ, Bratislava

T 1431

CONTENTS

CONTENTS

CONTENTS

LIST OF
ILLUSTRATIONS

INTRODUCTION
by PETER QUENNELL

One of the most expressive of Victorian anecdotal pictures is a canvas by Holman Hunt entitled *The Awakened Conscience*. Hunt was a prodigiously high-minded artist, with little of Millais' underlying worldliness and no trace of Rossetti's easy-going southern cynicism. He planned each picture as a moral campaign; and to the story that he meant to tell, or to the message that he wished to propagate, every detail, down to the very smallest, must make some contribution. Finished in 1853, *The Awakened Conscience* was designed to form a pendant to *The Light of the World* (which Ruskin had acclaimed, partly because he enjoyed the striking religious allegory, partly, as he afterwards confessed, because the nettles in the foreground were admirably painted) and was intended to show in terms of modern existence the "manner in which the appeal of the spirit of heavenly love calls a soul to abandon a lower life." A young woman with abundant dishevelled hair has just leapt from the knee of her foxy-whiskered gallant, touched to the heart by the associations of a tune that, in an incautious moment, his fingers have been strumming out. His piano-playing and her career of shame are simultaneously interrupted. Across her distraught features breaks the dawn of conscience, depicted with a realism so vivid and poignant that the original purchaser induced Holman Hunt to re-paint her expression less disturbingly. Hunt's heroine is, of course, a "fallen woman"; and, determined that his representation of her surroundings should be scrupulously accurate, while he was portraying them he paid several visits to houses in St. John's Wood where no other consideration could have persuaded him to set foot.

Thus his canvas provides an accurate record of the professional setting of a mid-Victorian *demi-mondaine*—gay and opulent and over-crowded, with a rose-wood upright piano, a cheerful Turkey carpet, a gilded clock beneath a glass bell and a gold-framed looking-glass which reflects through the open window a glimpse of sunny back-garden. All the furniture is new and expensive but, at least from a Pre-Raphaelite point of view, embarrassingly

tasteless. Here is a "gilded cage"—similar to many cages, gilded
and lacquered, that lined the northern suburbs—from which
a "soiled dove," roused by some echo of her innocent past, now
spreads her wings for freedom. To what refuge she may aspire
the modern audience cannot guess; but our acquaintanceship
with Victorian stories and poems assures us that the process of
redemption will be neither swift nor easy. The doors of the
wholly respectable world are for ever closed against her: she
must be content perhaps with a quiet country refuge, there under
an assumed name to pass her remaining days in piety and good
works. A fallen woman was permanently fallen—a judgment,
strangely enough, that Byron also sponsored. If she fluttered
back to the domestic dovecote, it was always as a crippled
supplicant. And yet the pitilessness of Victorian moralists
reveals not so much their lack of humanity as the sensations
of extreme anxiety that moral problems caused them.

Those sensations are constantly re-echoed in nineteenth-century
art and literature; and we need not go very far afield to assemble
a long list of revelatory references. We think at once of Hood's
lugubrious ballad:

> "One more Unfortunate,
> Weary of breath,
> Rashly importunate,
> Gone to her death!"

and of the drawings and verses of Rossetti, who certainly frequented the *demi-monde*, though he dropped poetic tears upon it—
Found, in which he depicts a woman of the streets being recognised and reclaimed by an honest farmer parent, and *Jenny*, in
which the life of the prostitute takes on a more romantic colour-
ing. Jenny is the predestined victim of masculine lust, which
lurks always beneath the thin shell of respectable society:

> "Like a toad within a stone
> Seated while Time crumbles on;
> Which sits there since earth was curs'd
> For Man's transgression at the first;
> Which, living through all centuries,
> Not once has seen the sun arise...
> Which always—whitherso the stone
> Be flung—sits there, deaf, blind, alone; —

Aye, and shall not be driven out
Till that which shuts him round about
Break at the very Master's stroke,
And the dust thereof vanish as smoke,
And the seed of Man vanish as dust: —
Even so within this world is Lust."

But the most rhetorical description of the effects of sin is contained in *David Copperfield*, where Mr. Peggotty wanders across Europe in search of his deluded niece and eventually catches up with her in a shabby street near Golden Square. She is discovered thanks to the assistance of Martha, a good-hearted but demoralised girl who, when David and Peggotty track her down, is hesitating on the brink of suicide:

"As if she were a part of the refuse it had cast out, and left to corruption and decay, the girl we had followed strayed down to the river's brink, and stood in the midst of this night-picture, lonely and still, looking at the water... I think she was talking to herself. I am sure, although absorbed in gazing at the water, that her shawl was off her shoulders, and that she was muffling her hands in it, in an unsettled and bewildered way, more like the action of a sleep-walker than a waking person. I know, and never can forget, that there was that in her wild manner which gave me no assurance but that she would sink before my eyes, until I had her arm within my grasp...
"We carried her away from the water to where there were some dry stones, and there laid her down, crying and moaning. In a little while she sat among the stones holding her wretched head with both her hands.
" 'Oh, the river!' she cried passionately. 'Oh, the river!' "

Martha, naturally, is past hope. But Little Emily herself does not collapse motionless and unconscious into her forgiving uncle's arms before she has been upbraided and reviled and reminded of her abject condition by the vindictive Rosa Dartle; and even then her rescuers agree that she cannot remain on English soil. Worthy Ham shrinks from the sight of Steerforth's one-time mistress; and an emigrant ship bound for Australia becomes her dismal refuge, while her seducer meets a Byronic end in the tremendous closing storm-scape.

Such was the intensity of feeling with which the Victorians regarded unlicensed sexual pleasures and such the literary symbolism into which they translated an underlying sense of guilt. In the history of English morals, the fourth volume of Mayhew's great compilation, *London Labour and the London Poor*, seems to possess a double interest. It helps to explain that sense of guilt and anxiety by illustrating the conditions that appalled Victorian social critics, and it reveals an attitude of mind towards those conditions measurably in advance of most contemporary standards. For Henry Mayhew and his industrious collaborators, though they did not dissent from the contemporary moral code and were insistent that the way of the transgressor could only end in misery, believed that any attempt at reformation must be firmly founded on investigation. Organised vice had a historical background; and the volume begins with an enormous chapter (for the sake of clarity and brevity omitted from the present reprint) in which they trace the profession of the prostitute back to the very earliest times and show her at work in many different settings, from the lupanars of ancient Rome to the brothels and dancing-halls of nineteenth-century Paris. They strive to present her as a social phenomenon—not merely as an object for repulsion or false sentiment—and by doing so to clear the air of some unhealthy prejudices.

It must be admitted that they did not completely succeed, since they were by no means entirely emancipated from the influence of their social period. Prostitution being an unmitigated evil, they could not afford to devote much attention to sit psychological basis; still less could they allow it to appear that the spectacle afforded by its ministrants might now and then be fascinating. For them there could be no "flowers of evil"—none of the perverse dignity and distorted beauty that Charles Baudelaire and his companion, Constantin Guys, discovered in the descending circles of the Parisian underworld. Baudelaire's superb essay, *Le Peintre de la Vie Moderne*, a tribute to the genius of Guys, was published during the same decade—though written in the late 'fifties, it did not appear till 1863—and the section entitled *Les Femmes et les Filles* might well be studied in conjunction with the massive English survey. Here is a similar spectacle viewed through an artist's eyes and endowed with that imaginative beauty which only an artist's eyes could lend it. The prostitute acquires an almost legendary grandeur:

"She moves forward, glides, dances, sweeps on with her weight of embroidered skirts which serve her both as pedestal and balance; she darts her glances from beneath the brim of her hat like a portrait from within its frame. She is an apt type of the savagery of civilisation. She has the beauty that is bred of Evil, for ever devoid of spiritual grace, yet sometimes tinged with an air of fatigue that apes the air of melancholy. Her gaze is fixed on the horizon, as if she were a beast of prey: the same wild look, the same indolent distraction and, at times, the same attentive fixity. She typifies the bohemian roaming the frontiers of an established social universe; the triviality of her life, which is a life of ruse and struggle, is fatally apparent through the trappings which envelop her."

Baudelaire is writing of the prosperous *demi-monde*, and of resorts also described by Mayhew's band of students, where raffish elegance and a certain degree of youth still showed to advantage beneath the flaring gaslamps. The *Valentinos, Casinos* and *Prados*, which he visited with Constantin Guys, must have closely resembled the Argyll Rooms and the Holborn and "nighthouses" of the Haymarket explored by Mayhew's henchmen. There, too, was exhibited on parade the *femme galante* in her first flower, emulous of patrician airs and graces, insolently conscious of her beauty and her luxury, advancing a pointed toe and with two gloved fingers delicately lifting her undulatory crinoline, besides older and humbler women whose hold upon prosperity and luxury was becoming less self-confident. Finally Baudelaire reaches the ultimate depths; but even in those forlorn abysmal regions, among veterans of the wars of Venus, seated with arms akimbo astride a chair or lolling on sofas as they puff their cigarettes, "heavy, gloomy, brutish, fantastic-looking," their skirts ruffled in monstrous disorder, "their eyes filmed with spirits, their foreheads appearing to bulge with animal stupidity," he notes poses of an audacity and a nobility that might enchant the most fastidious sculptor." Such were the denizens of the lowest circles surveyed in Mayhew's volume—the "soldiers' women," for example, and the forlorn and diseased vagrants who hung about the London parks: witnesses to the "savagery of civilisation" as eloquent and pathetic as the "mud-larks" and the "pure-finders" whom in his previous volumes he had already viewed and catalogued.

The Parisian nether regions that Baudelaire knew can scarcely have surpassed in squalor their mid-Victorian London counterpart. London, it may be, during the 'fifties and 'sixties had yet grimmer and more sordid aspects, since not only do the Anglo-Saxon races take their pleasures sadly, but, as foreign visitors have often commented, they wear their vices awkwardly, with few attempts to confer upon dissipation any aesthetic grace or social charm. In a land of strongly puritan traditions, organised vice is both insolent and shamefaced; its commercialism is largely undisguised; its ministrants are not so much priestesses of an ancient, if disreputable, cult as tired and hurried businesswomen. Elsewhere, for instance in modern Japan, an elaborate ceremonial surrounds the satisfaction of naked sexual impulses, and we observe a hierarchy of prostitution, with rites and customs appropriate to each successive level. Thus, in contemporary Tokyo the indentured servant of the licensed brothel district (herself by several degrees superior to the least expensive prostitutes, who inhabit separate tiny rooms arranged about a courtyard, diminutive hutches containing a single mat which the client enters on his knees) is presented amid surroundings of fastidious antique elegance, against screens in the traditional taste, upon smooth-glistening *tatami* and discreetly patterned floor-cushions. Nor can she be approached without ceremonious parley. Her clothes are in multiple silken layers, while her make-up, with its violent white and red, increases her resemblance to a costly doll or cult-object. In the more aristocratic houses of assignation, the air of ceremony and artificiality is carried even further; and the *geisha* (who at her best is akin to the *hetaira* of Athens rather than to the courtesan of modern Europe) combines a knowledge of music and conversation with the professional arts of love-making, and wears an immense coiffure which suggests a towering lacquered helmet, and which it is said that she preserves unruffled through the wildest amorous forays. Some *geisha* may be hired at will, though the purchase price does not necessarily include permission to make love to them; but there are others whose national renown puts them beyond the reach of all but the richest and most distinguished suitors. Nor does their reputation decline with the passage of years; a *geisha* is thought to mature like some celebrated vintage; and in the early 'thirties there existed a member of the profession who owed her fame and popularity, which were still entirely undimmed, to a well-advertised youthful connection with one of the chief heroes of the Russo-Japanese War.

In France, during the Second Empire, a similar nation-wide prestige attached to the most successful *cocottes*. They were a manifestation of imperial wealth and taste; and every detail of the state they maintained—the *hôtels* they built, the carriages they kept, the clothes they wore, and the succession of opulent lovers, domestic and exotic, whom they accepted and exploited—were subjects of eager discussion and not a little national pride. Readers of the Goncourts' journals will remember how, among their other industrious efforts to give a comprehensive account of the period they lived in, they bribed the maid of a famous *cocotte* to show them the magnificent Valenciennes lace *déshabille*, just designed for her at prodigious cost, which she intended to wear while receiving specially favoured visitors. The names of Hortense Schneider, star of *La Belle Hélène*, of La Païva and Anna Deslions in one generation, of Liane de Pougy, Emilienne d'Alençon and Cléo de Mérode in the generation that succeeded it, were repeated not only in Paris but in every European capital city. National institutions beyond the reach of praise or blame, when they appeared in their carriages beneath the trees of the Bois, each carriage a triumph of art that far outshone the array of "respectable" equipages by which it was surrounded, they seem to float high over the heads of the admiring onlookers…

Across the English Channel, however, the idea of the great courtesan has never taken firm hold. Yet during the second half of the nineteenth century, at a moment when the reign of decorum was most solidly established in the realms of art and literature, the London *demi-monde* produced a large number of well-known, well-loved personages, some of whom emigrated to Paris, like Cora Pearl and Miss Howard (imported by Louis Napoleon, who had known her in his exile), while others, perhaps wisely, preferred their native hunting grounds. That informative volume of scandalous gossip, *London in the 'Sixties*, mentions, for example, an "undisputed Queen of Beauty," Sweet Nelly Fowler. "This beautiful girl (relates the anonymous author) had a natural perfume, so delicate, so universally admitted, that love-sick swains paid large sums for the privilege of having their handkerchiefs placed under the Goddess's pillow, and sweet Nelly pervaded—in spirit, if not in the flesh—half the clubs and drawing-rooms of London." Bracketed with Nelly Fowler was " 'Skittles,' celebrated for her ponies." But "Skittles" was also celebrated for having enslaved and nearly married the elder son of an English ducal family. Bought off by his relations, she retreated for a while to Paris; and it was there that she earned her nickname by her displays of skill in a skittles alley popular among young men of the British diplomatic service, and met the handsome and gifted Wilfred Scawen Blunt, minor poet, adventurer and traveller, who made her the heroine of his finest poetic production, *Love Sonnets of Proteus*. Later, she returned to London, where, according to Blunt's biographer, her "Sunday parties in Chesterfield Street and afterwards in South Street, Park Lane, were frequented by the Prince of Wales... Even Gladstone, to the delight of Blunt and of 'Skittles' herself, 'came along to take tea with her, having sent her beforehand twelve pounds of Russian tea.' In public she was to be seen rolling-skating with inimitable grace in the new, fashionable rinks of London and Tunbridge Wells, driving the prancing ponies of her phaeton in Hyde Park, or riding in Rotten Row a horse that had run second in the Grand National and that no one else could ride. The tale is famous of her larking over the eighteen feet wide water-jump at the National Hunt Steeplechase in Northamptonshire."*

"Skittles," in fact—or, to give her her real name, Catherine Walters, latterly Mrs. Bailey—was a courtesan in the grand tradition, companion as well as concubine, the friend of poets, musicians and painters, and possibly the last English represent-ative of the aristocracy of the half-world. Her progress began during the 'sixties; and she too must have graduated from the resorts described in Mayhew's volume. Here Mayhew's notes are confirmed by an equally zealous social critic, Dr. William Acton, the first edition of whose massive and rather alarming work, *Prostitution Considered in its Moral, Social, and Sanitary Aspects in London and Other Large Cities and Garrison Towns*, was pub-lished in 1857, while a second edition, containing much new mat-erial, appeared in 1869. Acton himself was a pioneer, who believed that the main evils attending prostitution could only be checked once its existence had been officially recognised, as had already been done in most cities of the Continent; that the causes of prostitution were preponderantly economic; and that the army of prostitutes would "lessen or decrease according as the causes...

---

* See *Wilfred Scawen Blunt*, by Edith Finch. Jonathan Cape, 1938. "Skittles" survived, full of honours and surrounded by friends, till 1920.

are removed or neglected." Acton's picture of conditions in London should be studied side by side with that of Mayhew. Both write of the Haymarket as a focus of urban depravity; and Acton quotes from an article in *Household Words*, which, though originally printed in 1857, was in 1860 "still to a great extent applicable":

> "About the top of this thoroughfare is diffused, every night, a very large part of what is blackguard, ruffianly, and deeply dangerous in London. If Piccadilly may be termed an artery of the metropolis, most assuredly that strip of pavement between the top of the Haymarket and the Regent Circus is one of its ulcers... It is always an offensive place to pass, even in the daytime; but at night it is absolutely hideous, with its sparring snobs, and flashing satins, and sporting gents, and painted cheeks, and brandy-sparkling eyes, and bad tobacco, and hoarse horse-laughs, and loud indecency... From an extensive continental experience of cities, I can take personally an example from three quarters of the globe; but I have never anywhere witnessed such open ruffianism and wretched profligacy as rings along those Piccadilly flagstones any time after the gas is lighted."

At this point the anonymous chronicler of *London in the 'Sixties* may be allowed to take up the story. The Haymarket he had known in his youth had "literally blazed with light" throughout the hours of darkness, "from such temples as the Blue Posts, Barnes's, The Burmese, and Barron's Oyster Rooms... The decorous Panton Street of to-day was another very sink of iniquity. Night-houses abounded, and Rose Burton's and Jack Percival's were sandwiched between hot baths of questionable respectability and abominations of every kind." Nearby were the notorious night-houses known as Mott's and Kate Hamilton's, the latter being approached by a long and closely guarded passage, leading to a saloon where the mistress of the establishment sat enthroned among her favourites, a formidable figure who must have weighed at least twenty stone, and had as hideous a physiognomy as any weather-beaten Deal pilot. Seated on a raised platform, with a bodice cut very low, Kate Hamilton "sipped champagne steadily from midnight until daylight, and shook like a blancmange every time she laughed." It was to the Haymarket

and neighbouring streets that the dissipated part of the metropolis resorted after the midnight closing of "casinos, music-halls,
and similar places," of which the most prominent were the Argyll
Rooms and the Holborn:

> "Formerly (writes Acton) there was a striking difference
> between these two places, the one receiving the upper, the
> other the under, current of the fast life of London; now,
> however, there is little of this distinction... The visitor, on
> passing the doors, finds himself in a spacious room, the
> fittings of which are of a most costly description, while
> brilliant gas illuminations, reflected by numerous mirrors,
> impart a fairy-like aspect to the scene. The company is...
> mixed... The women are of course all prostitutes. They are
> for the most part pretty, and quietly, though expensively
> dressed, while delicate complexions, unaccompanied by the
> pallor of ill-health, are neither few nor far between. This
> appearance is doubtless due in many cases to the artistic
> manner of the make-up by powder and cosmetics, on the
> employment of which extreme care is bestowed."

On a level with the Argyll and the Holborn were London's
various pleasure-gardens. The Cremorne Gardens in Chelsea,
which remained open, growing more disreputable, till 1877,
were by general consent the most attractive. Their daytime
population was steady and sober enough; but, on a summer
evening, "as calico and merry respectability tailed off eastward
by penny steamers, the setting sun brought westward Hansoms
freighted with demure immorality in silk and fine linen. By about
ten o'clock, age and innocence... had seemingly all retired..."
The amusements they provided were sometimes boisterous.
"A Derby night without a row (we learn) was, in those days, an
impossibility"; "to pass the private boxes was to run the gauntlet
of a quartern loaf or a dish of cutlets at one's head"; and the
occasion usually ended with a free-fight and general panic-
stricken stampede towards the safety of the King's Road. Yet
the tone of the Gardens was on the whole extremely quiet; and
Acton, when he visited Cremorne, was somewhat disappointed:

> "A jolly burst of laughter now and then came bounding
> through the crowd that fringed the dancing-floor and roved

about the adjacent sheds in search of company; but that gone by, you heard very plainly the sigh of the poplar, the surging gossip of the tulip-tree, and the plash of the little embowered fountain that served two plaster children for an endless shower-bath. The *gratus puellae risus* was put in a corner with a vengeance, under a colder shade than that of chastity itself, and the function of the very band appeared to be to drown not noise, but stillness."

So far Acton has been concerned with the lighter and less forbidding aspects of the problem that absorbed him. But around these centres of fashionable and expensive pleasure, frequented by courtesans in the ascendant or kept women whose star was only gradually declining, he also observed pestiferous outer territories—"Langham Place, portions of the New Road, the Quadrant, the Peristyle of the Haymarket Theatre, the City Road, and the purlieus of the Lyceum" — until recent years haunted by "rouged and whitewashed creatures, with painted lips and eyebrows, and false hair," the occupants of nearby "dress houses" or brothels, from which they were sent out to ply their trade under the escort of a "person of their own sex, employed purposely to prevent the abstraction of the lodging-house finery, and clandestine traffic with men. These wretched women, virtually slaves... were restricted, for the convenience of the real proprietors, to certain parades or beats... If their solicitations proved unsuccessful, their exertions were stimulated by the proprietor in person, who would sally forth from her den to aid the canvass, to admonish and swear; and sometimes by the sentinel in charge, who assumed for the time being these functions of authority." Women of this type, Acton concludes, "may still be observed in some of the principal streets of London, but... a great improvement has taken place... during the last twelve years." Indeed, one of the salutary changes—and there were not many—that he notes as having occurred since the publication of his first edition was a considerable decrease both in the quantity of brothels and houses where prostitutes lodged and resorted, and in the number of prostitutes pursuing their trade openly. According to figures furnished from police records in the year 1857, brothels and similar establishments then numbered 2,825, and professional prostitutes 8,600; whereas police returns for 1868 showed 2,119 suspect establishments, and 6,515 prostitutes of

one type and another. Yet Acton agrees that the student of urban
conditions must not be unduly optimistic, since the figures he has
provided give "but a faint idea of the grand total of prostitution
by which we are oppressed"; and although brothels seemed to
have become less numerous, "in the western and eastern districts
...are to be found a great number of lodging-houses crowded
together, in certain neighbourhoods of no fair fame... From
houses in St. John's Wood, Brompton, and Pimlico, to the
atrocious slums of Blackfriars and Whitechapel, there are, of
course, many steps, and with the rent at which the proprietors
offer their apartments varies, of course, the style of the sub-
tenants. In point of morality, there is, naturally, no difference..." Of privacy there was very little; all the inmates of such
an establishment drifted sooner or later into the common kitchen:

> "They are usually during the day, unless called upon by
> their followers, or employed in dressing, to be found dishev-
> elled, dirty, slipshod and dressing-gowned, in this kitchen,
> where the mistress keeps her *table d'hôte*. Stupid from beer,
> or fractious from gin, they swear and chatter brainless
> stuff all day, about men and millinery, their own schemes
> and adventures, and the faults of others of the sisterhood.
> As a heap of rubbish will ferment, so surely will a number
> of unvirtuous women thus collected deteriorate, whatever
> their antecedents or good qualities previously... From such
> houses issue the greater number of the dressy females
> with whom the public are familiar as the frequenters of
> the Haymarket and the night-houses. Here they seem to
> rally... when the general society, and the most decent as
> well as the lowest classes of prostitutes, are alike housed for
> the night. Here they throw the last allures of fascination
> to the prowler and the drunkard..."

Enough has been said—it may be, more than enough—to
emphasise the magnitude of the problem with which Victorian
reformers were confronted, and to explain the state of anxious
tension that underlay the apparent mercilessness of the Victorian
moral code. Any form of intolerance, sexual, racial or political,
is almost always an answer to a threat—as in this instance a very
real threat, but now and then a threat more than half imaginary;

the anger it betrays is bred of fear, just as the self-righteousness into which it overflows has very often a backing of secret shame and self-reproach. Not without reason the Victorian Age was secretly ashamed of many features of the universe it had created —the slums of its mighty industrial cities and the brutalised population which lived and bred and died there. Economists of the school attacked by Ruskin (whose eloquent protest against *laissez-faire* economics, *Unto This Last*, began to appear in the summer months of 1860) might suggest that widespread poverty and misery were "the result of Nature's simplest laws," and merely the price which had to be paid for the furious rate of modern progress; but the Victorian generation was scrupulous and sensitive as well as adventurous and hard-headed; and phenomena of the kind described by Mayhew and Acton were difficult to dismiss with the help of an economic theory.

The contemporary response was two-fold. On the one hand, Victorian moralists, stiffened by the Evangelical creed they had inherited from their fathers, assumed an attitude of aggressive puritanism in every question that affected the commerce of the sexes, and made a fetish of feminine purity to which novelists, poets and painters, willingly or unwillingly, were obliged to pay lip-service. On the other, they became practical reformers, preaching, proselytising, "rescuing," coaxed labourers into "workmen's colleges," herded children into "ragged schools," and chased prostitutes, as the opportunity offered, into Magdalen asylums and refuges for fallen women, where boredom, piety and religious discipline proved poor substitutes for the bohemian laxity and relative independence of the life that they had left behind. It is to the credit of Mayhew and Acton that they attempted, not unsuccessfully, to keep their surveys matter-of-fact, to banish contemporary phobias, and to study their subject as scientists rather than as moralists or sentimentalists. They agree in deploring a social evil: but Mayhew's collaborator goes so far as to admit that prostitution is a career to which certain women seem psychologically well suited, and that not every prostitute is as deeply discontented with her lot as Dickens' wretched Martha; while Acton asserts that, contrary to the current belief, many women who have "fallen" do ultimately rise again. " ...By far the larger number of women who have resorted to prostitution for a livelihood, return sooner or later to a more or less regular course of life"; they were frequently sought in marriage; and "I repeat (Acton continues) that prostitution is a transitory state, through which an untold number of British women are ever on their passage. Until preventive measures... shall have been... adopted... it is the duty, and it should be the business of us all... to see these women through that state, so as to save harmless as much as may be of the bodies and souls of them."

Together with the sections on prostitutes, Mayhew's book includes sections, scarcely less interesting and revelatory, on beggars, thieves and swindlers. Outcasts like the prostitute, they too "typified the bohemian roaming the frontiers of an established social universe"; and for them, as for her, the respectable world could provide no remedy, since it was powerless to remove the underlying social causes. The Victorian penal system was still chaotic. Though it had been shorn of some of its eighteenth-century rigours, public executions did not disappear till 1868, and the majority of London prisons were ancient, insanitary and hideously overcrowded. Thus Coldbath Fields Prison, which had been rebuilt as a model gaol at the instigation of John Howard, is described as having reached a state of "hopeless congestion" by 1861. Newgate was a populous school of criminals; and Bridewell, originally built as a royal residence during the reign of Henry VIII, in the words of the Inspector of Prisons, "answered no object save that of custody"; it did not "correct, alter, nor reform"; segregation was quite impossible, and daily association with others of his kind quickly counteracted "any efforts that can be made for moral and religious improvement of the prisoner." Conscious that gaols were usually nurseries of crime, Victorian reformers introduced the ghastly Silent System. Not only cut off from speech with his fellows, the prisoner was deprived of his proper name and reduced to the condition of a numbered and uniformed automaton, condemned to perform so many hours of entirely useless work upon the crank or treadmill. At exercise the prisoner was sometimes masked. But neither the sociable squalor of Newgate nor the segregated gloom of the prisons that had been reformed and remodelled could check the rapid expansion of the criminal and vagrant classes. The criminal and the beggar were always at hand, beneath the gas-lamps of Piccadilly and among the carriages in Hyde Park—the threatening army of the homeless and dispossessed, a constant reproach to the civilisation that had produced them, which had purchased progress at the cost of poverty and moral refinement at the price of prostitution. The underworld that Mayhew described in detail is to be felt, if not distinctly seen, looming in the troubled background of much Victorian literature. Mayhew's *magnum opus* is a work of curious information to be studied for its own sake. It is also a book of reference that admirers of the great Victorian novelists will find immensely valuable.

FOREWORD

I ENTER upon this part of my subject with a deep sense of the misery, the vice, the ignorance, and the want that encompass us on every side—I enter upon it after much grave attention to the subject, observing closely, reflecting patiently, and generalising cautiously upon the phenomena and causes of the vice and crime of this city—I enter upon it after a thoughtful study of the habits and character of the "outcast" class generally—I enter upon it, moreover, as forming an integral and most important part of the task I have imposed upon myself. Further, I am led to believe that I can contribute some new facts concerning the physics and economy of vice and crime generally, that will not only make the solution of the social problem more easy to us, but, setting more plainly before us some of its latent causes, make us look with more pity and less anger on those who want the fortitude to resist their influence; and induce us, or at least the more earnest among us, to apply ourselves steadfastly to the removal or alleviation of those social evils that appear to create so large a proportion of the vice and crime that we seek by punishment to prevent.

HENRY MAYHEW.

PROSTITUTION IN LONDON
GENERAL REMARKS

THE liberty of the subject is very jealously guarded in England, and so tenacious are the people of their rights and privileges that the legislature has not dared to infringe them, even for what by many would be considered a just and meritorious purpose. Neither are the magistracy or the police allowed to enter improper or disorderly houses, unless to suppress disturbances that would require their presence in the most respectable mansion in the land, if the aforesaid disturbances were committed within their precincts. Until very lately the police had not the power of arresting those traders who earned an infamous livelihood by selling immoral books and obscene prints. It is to the late Lord Chancellor Campbell that we owe this salutary reform, under whose meritorious exertions the disgraceful trade of Holywell Street and kindred districts has received a blow from which it will never again rally.

If the neighbours choose to complain before a magistrate of a disorderly house, and are willing to undertake the labour, annoyance, and expense of a criminal indictment, it is probable that their exertions may in time have the desired effect; but there is no summary conviction, as in some Continental cities whose condition we have studied in another portion of this work.

To show how difficult it is to give from any data at present before the public anything like a correct estimate of the number of prostitutes in London*, we may mention (extracting from the work of Dr. Ryan) that while the Bishop of Exeter asserted the number of prostitutes in London to be 80,000, the City Police stated to Dr. Ryan that it did not exceed 7,000 to 8,000. About the year 1793 Mr. Colquhoun, a police magistrate, concluded, after tedious investigations, that there were 50,000 prostitutes in this metropolis. At that period the population was one

---

* We rely for certain facts, statistics, etc., upon Reports of the Society for the Suppression of Vice; information furnished by the Metropolitan Police; Reports of the Society for the Prevention of Juvenile Prostitution; Returns of the Registrar-General; Ryan, Duchatelet, M. les Docteurs G. Richelot, Léon Faucher, Talbot, Acton, etc., etc.; and figures, information, facts, etc., supplied from various quarters; and lastly, on our own researches and investigations.

million, and as it is now more than double we may form some
idea of the extensive ramifications of this insidious vice.

In 1857, according to the best authorities, there were 8,600
prostitutes known to the police, but this is far from being even
an approximate return of the number of loose women in the
metropolis. It scarcely does more than record the circulating
harlotry of the Haymarket and Regent Street. Their actual
numerical strength is very difficult to compute, for there is an
amount of oscillatory prostitution it is easy to imagine, but
impossible to substantiate. One of the peculiarities of this class
is their remarkable freedom from disease. They are in the generality of cases notorious for their mental and physical elasticity.
Syphilis is rarely fatal. It is an entirely distinct race that suffer
from the ravages of the insidious diseases that the licence given
to the passions and promiscuous intercourse engender. Young
girls, innocent and inexperienced, whose devotion has not yet
bereft them of their innate modesty and sense of shame, will
allow their systems to be so shocked, and their constitutions
so impaired, before the aid of the surgeon is sought for, that
when he does arrive his assistance is almost useless.

We have before stated the assumed number of prostitutes in
London to be about 80,000, and large as this total may appear,
it is not improbable that it is below the reality rather than above
it. One thing is certain—if it be an exaggerated statement—
that the real number is swollen every succeeding year, for
prostitution is an inevitable attendant upon extended civilisation
and increased population.

We divide prostitutes into three classes. First, those women
who are kept by men of independent means; secondly, those
women who live in apartments, and maintain themselves by the
produce of their vagrant amours; and thirdly, those who dwell
in brothels.

The state of the first of these is the nearest approximation to
the holy state of marriage, and finds numerous defenders and
supporters. These have their suburban villas, their carriages,
horses, and sometimes a box at the opera. Their equipages are
to be seen in the park, and occasionally through the influence
of their aristocratic friends they succeed in obtaining vouchers
for the most exclusive patrician balls.

Houses in which prostitutes lodge are those in which one or
two prostitutes occupy private apartments; in most cases with

the connivance of the proprietor. These generally resort to night-houses, where they have a greater chance of meeting with customers than they would have were they to perambulate the streets.

Brothels are houses where speculators board, dress, and feed women, living upon the farm of their persons. Under this head we must include introducing houses, where the women do not reside, but merely use the house as a place of resort in the daytime. Married women, imitating the custom of Messalina, whom Juvenal so vividly describes in his Satires, not uncommonly make use of these places. A Frenchwoman in the habit of frequenting a notorious house in James Street, Haymarket, said that she came to town four or five times in the week for the purpose of obtaining money by the prostitution of her body. She loved her husband, but he was unable to find any respectable employment, and were she not to supply him with the necessary funds for their household expenditure they would sink into a state of destitution, and anything, she added, with simplicity, was better than that. Of course her husband connived at what she did. He came to fetch her home every evening about ten o'clock. She had no children. She didn't wish to have any.

Seclusives, or Those Who Live In Private Houses and Apartments

Two classes of prostitutes come under this denomination—first, kept mistresses, and, secondly, prima donnas or those who live in a superior style. The first of these is perhaps the most important division of the entire profession, when considered with regard to its effects upon the higher classes of society. Laïs, when under the protection of a prince of the blood; Aspasia, whose friend is one of the most influential noblemen in the kingdom; Phryne, the *chère amie* of a well-known officer in the Guards, or a man whose wealth is proverbial on the Stock Exchange and the city — have all great influence upon the tone of morality extant amongst the set in which their distinguished protectors move, and indeed the reflex of their dazzling profligacy falls upon and bewilders those who are in a lower condition of life, acting as an incentive to similar deeds of licentiousness though on a more limited scale. Hardly a parish in London is free from this impurity. Wherever the neighbourhood possesses peculiar charms, wherever

the air is purer than ordinary, or the locality fashionably distinguished, these tubercles on the social system penetrate and
abound. Again quoting from Dr. Ryan, although we cannot
authenticate his statements — "It is computed that £8,000,000
are expended annually on this vice in London alone. This is
easily proved: some girls obtain from twenty to thirty pounds
a week, others more, whilst most of those who frequent theatres,
casinos, gin palaces, music halls, etc., receive from ten to twelve
pounds. Those of a still lower grade obtain about four or five
pounds, some less than one pound, and many not ten shillings.
If we take the average earnings of each prostitute at £100 per
annum, which is under the amount, it gives the yearly income
of eight millions.

"Suppose the average expense of 80,000 amounts to £20 each,
£1,600,000 is the result. This sum deducted from the earnings
leaves £6,400,000 as the income of the keepers of prostitutes, or
supposing 5,000 to be the number, above £1,000 per annum each
—an enormous income for men in such a situation to derive
when compared with the resources of many respectable and
professional men."

Literally every woman who yields to her passions and loses
her virtue is a prostitute, but many draw a distinction between
those who live by promiscuous intercourse, and those who
confine themselves to one man. That this is the case is evident
from the returns before us. The metropolitan police do not concern
themselves with the higher classes of prostitutes; indeed, it would
be impossible, and impertinent as well, were they to make the
attempt. Sir Richard Mayne kindly informed us that the latest
computation of the number of public prostitutes was made on
the 5th of April, 1858, and that the returns then showed a total
of 7,261.

It is frequently a matter of surprise amongst the friends of a
gentleman of position and connection that he exhibits an in-
vincible distaste to marriage. If they were acquainted with his
private affairs their astonishment would speedily vanish, for
they would find him already to all intents and purposes united
to one who possesses charms, talents, and accomplishments,
and who will in all probability exercise the same influence over
him as long as the former continue to exist. The prevalence of
this custom, and the extent of its ramifications, is hardly dreamed
of, although its effects are felt, and severely. The torch of Hymen

burns less brightly than of yore, and even were the blacksmith of Gretna still exercising his vocation, he would find his business diminishing with startling rapidity year by year.

It is a great mistake to suppose that kept mistresses are without friends and without society; on the contrary, their acquaintance, if not select, is numerous, and it is their custom to order their broughams or their pony carriages, and at the fashionable hour pay visits and leave cards on one another.

They possess no great sense of honour, although they are generally more or less religious. If they take a fancy to a man they do not hesitate to admit him to their favour. Most kept women have several lovers who are in the habit of calling upon them at different times, and as they are extremely careful in conducting these amours they perpetrate infidelity with impunity, and in ninety-nine cases out of a hundred escape detection. When they are unmasked, the process, unless the man is very much infatuated, is of course summary in the extreme. They are dismissed probably with a handsome *douceur*, and sent once more adrift. They do not remain long, however, in the majority of cases, without finding another protector.

A woman who called herself Lady —— met her admirer at a house in Bolton Row that she was in the habit of frequenting. At first sight Lord —— became enamoured, and proposed *sur le champ*, after a little preliminary conversation, that she should live with him. The proposal with equal rapidity and eagerness was accepted, and without further deliberation his lordship took a house for her in one of the terraces overlooking the Regent's Park, allowed her four thousand a year, and came as frequently as he could, to pass his time in her society. She immediately set up a carriage and a stud, took a box at the opera on the pit tier, and lived, as she very well could, in excellent style. The munificence of her friend did not decrease by the lapse of time. She frequently received presents of jewellery from him, and his marks of attention were constant as they were various. The continual contemplation of her charms instead of producing satiety added fuel to the fire, and he was never happy when out of her sight. This continued until one day he met a young man in her *loge* at the opera, whom she introduced as her cousin. This incident aroused his suspicions, and he determined to watch her more closely. She was surrounded by spies, and in reality did not possess one confidential attendant, for they were all bribed to betray her. For a time, more by accident than precaution or care on her part, she succeeded in eluding their vigilance, but at last the catastrophe happened; she was surprised with her paramour in a position that placed doubt out of the question, and the next day his lordship, with a few sarcastic remarks, gave her her *congé* and five hundred pounds.

These women are rarely possessed of education, although they undeniably have ability. If they appear accomplished you may rely that it is entirely superficial. Their disposition is volatile and thoughtless, which qualities are of course at variance with the existence of respectability. Their ranks too are recruited from a class where education is not much in vogue. The fallacies about clergymen's daughters and girls from the middle classes forming the majority of such women are long ago exploded; there may be some amongst them, but they are few and far between. They are not, as a rule, disgusted with their way of living; most of them consider it a means to an end, and in no measure degrading or polluting. One and all look forward to marriage and a certain state in society as their ultimate lot. This is their bourne, and they do all in their power to travel towards it.

"I am not tired of what I am doing," a woman once answered me, "I rather like it. I have all I want, and my friend loves me to excess. I am the daughter of a tradesman at Yarmouth. I learned to play the piano a little, and I have naturally a good voice. Yes, I find these accomplishments of great use to me; they are, perhaps, as you say, the only ones that could be of use to a girl like myself. I am three and twenty. I was seduced four years ago. I tell you candidly I was as much to blame as my seducer; I wished to escape from the drudgery of my father's shop. I have told you they partially educated me; I could cypher a little as well, and I knew something about the globes; so I thought I was qualified for something better than minding the shop occasionally, or sewing, or helping my mother in the kitchen and other domestic matters. I was very fond of dress, and I could not at home gratify my love of display. My parents were stupid, easy-going old people, and extremely uninteresting to me. All these causes combined induced me to encourage the addresses of a young gentleman of property in the neighbourhood, and without much demur I yielded to his desires. We then went to London, and I have since that time lived with four different men. We got tired of one another in six months, and I was as eager to leave him as he was to get rid of me, so we mutually accommodated one another by separating. Well, my father and mother don't exactly know where I am or what I am doing, although if they had any penetration they might very well guess. Oh, yes! they know I am alive, for I keep them pleasantly aware of my existence by occasionally sending them money. What do I think will become of me? What an absurd question. I could marry to-morrow if I liked."

This girl was a fair example of her class. They live entirely for the moment, and care little about the morrow until they are actually pressed in any way, and then they are fertile in expedients.

We now come to the second class, or those we have denominated prima donnas. These are not kept like the first that we have just been treating of, although several men who know and admire them are in the habit of visiting them periodically. From these they derive a considerable revenue, but they by no means rely entirely upon it for support. They are continually increasing the number of their friends, which indeed is imperatively necessary, as absence and various causes thin their ranks considerably. They are to be seen in the parks, in boxes at the theatres, at concerts, and in almost every accessible place where fashionable people congregate; in fact, in all places where admission is not secured by vouchers, and in some cases those apparently insuperable barriers fall before their tact and address. At night their favourite rendezvous is in the neighbourhood of the Haymarket, where the hospitality of Mrs. Kate Hamilton is extended to them after the fatigues of dancing at the Portland Rooms, or the excesses of a private party. Kate's may be visited not only to dissipate ennui, but with a view to replenishing an exhausted exchequer; for as Kate is careful as to whom she admits into her rooms—men who are able to spend, and come with the avowed intention of spending five or six pounds, or perhaps more if necessary—these supper-rooms are frequented by a better set of men and women than perhaps any other in London. Although these are seen at Kate's they would shrink from appearing at any of the cafés in the Haymarket, or at the supper-rooms with which the adjacent streets abound, nor would they go to any other casino than Mott's. They are to be seen between three and five o'clock in the Burlington Arcade, which is a well-known resort of Cyprians of the better sort. They are well acquainted with its Paphian intricacies, and will, if their signals are responded to, glide into a friendly bonnet shop, the stairs of which leading to the coenacula or upper chambers are not innocent of their well-formed "bien chaussée" feet. The park is also, as we have said, a favourite promenade, where assignations may be made or acquaintances formed. Equestrian exercise is much liked by those who are able to afford it, and is often as successful as pedestrian, often more so. It is difficult to say what position in life the parents of these women were in, but generally their standing in society has been inferior. Principles of lax morality were early inculcated, and the seed that has been sown has not been slow to bear its proper fruit.

It is true that a large number of milliners, dressmakers, furriers, hat-binders, silk-binders, tambour-makers, shoe-binders, slop-women, or those who work for cheap tailors, those in pastry-cooks, fancy and cigar shops, bazaars, servants to a great extent, frequenters of fairs, theatres, and dancing-rooms, are more or less prostitutes and patronesses of the numerous brothels London can boast of possessing; but these women do not swell the ranks of the class we have at present under consideration. More probably they are the daughters of tradesmen and of artisans, who gain a superficial refinement from being apprenticed, and sent to shops in fashionable localities, and who becoming tired of the drudgery sigh for the gaiety of the dancing-saloons, freedom from restraint, and amusements that are not in their present capacity within their reach.

Loose women generally throw a veil over their early life, and you seldom, if ever, meet with a woman who is not either a seduced governess or a clergyman's daughter; not that there is a word of truth in such an allegation—but it is their peculiar whim to say so.

THE PROSTITUTES OF THE HAYMARKET

A STRANGER on his coming to London, after visiting the Crystal Palace, British Museum, St. James's Palace, and Buckingham Palace, and other public buildings, seldom leaves the capital before he makes an evening visit to the Haymarket and Regent Street. Struck as he is with the dense throng of people who crowd

A Night House—Kate Hamilton's

The Haymarket—Midnight

along London Bridge, Fleet Street, Cheapside, Holborn, Oxford
Street, and the Strand, perhaps no sight makes a more striking
impression on his mind than the brilliant gaiety of Regent Street
and the Haymarket. It is not only the architectural splendour of
the aristocratic streets in that neighbourhood, but the brilliant
illumination of the shops, cafés, Turkish divans, assembly halls,
and concert rooms, and the troops of elegantly dressed courtesans,
rustling in silks and satins, and waving in laces, promenading
along these superb streets among throngs of fashionable people,
and persons apparently of every order and pursuit, from the
ragged crossing-sweeper and tattered shoe-black to the high-bred
gentleman of fashion and scion of nobility.

Not to speak of the first class of kept women, who are supported by men of opulence and rank in the privacy of their own
dwellings, the whole of the other classes are to be found in the
Haymarket, from the beautiful girl with fresh blooming cheek,
newly arrived from the provinces, and the pale, elegant, young
lady from a milliner's shop in the aristocratic West End, to the
old, bloated women who have grown grey in prostitution, or
become invalid through venereal disease.

We shall first advert to the highest class who walk the Haymarket, which in our general classification we have termed the
second class of prostitutes.

They consist of the better educated and more genteel girls,
some of them connected with respectable middle-class families.
We do not say that they are well-educated and genteel, but
either well-educated or genteel. Some of these girls have a fine
appearance, and are dressed in high style, yet are poorly educated,
and have sprung from an humble origin. Others, who are more
plainly dressed, have had a lady's education, and some are not so
brilliant in their style, who have come from a middle-class home.
Many of these girls have at one time been milliners or sewing
girls in genteel houses in the West End, and have been seduced
by shopmen, or by gentlemen of the town, and after being ruined
in character, or having quarrelled with their relatives, may have
taken to a life of prostitution; others have been waiting-maids
in hotels, or in service in good families, and have been seduced
by servants in the family, or by gentlemen in the house, and
betaken themselves to a wild life of pleasure. A considerable
number have come from the provinces to London, with unprincipled young men of their acquaintance, who after a short

time have deserted them, and some of them have been enticed
by gay gentlemen of the West End, when on their provincial
tours. Others have come to the metropolis in search of work, and
been disappointed. After spending the money they had with them,
they have resorted to the career of a common prostitute. Others
have come from provincial towns, who had not a happy home,
with a stepfather or stepmother. Some are young milliners and
dressmakers at one time in business in town, but, being unfortunate, are now walking the Haymarket. In addition to these, many
of them are seclusives turned away or abandoned by the persons
who supported them, who have recourse to a gay life in the West
End. There are also a considerable number of French girls, and
a few Belgian and German prostitutes, who promenade this
locality. You see many of them walking along in black silk cloaks
or light grey mantles—many with silk paletots and wide skirts,
extended by an ample crinoline, looking almost like a pyramid,
with the apex terminating at the black or white satin bonnet,
trimmed with waving ribbons and gay flowers. Some are to be
seen with their cheeks ruddy with rouge, and here and there a
few rosy with health. Many of them looking cold and heartless;
others with an interesting appearance. We observe them walking up and down Regent Street and the Haymarket, often by
themselves, one or more in company, sometimes with a gallant
they have picked up, calling at the wine-vaults or restaurants to
get a glass of wine or gin, or sitting down in the brilliant coffee-
rooms, adorned with large mirrors, to a cup of good bohea or
coffee. Many of the more faded prostitutes of this class frequent
the Pavilion to meet gentlemen and enjoy the vocal and instrumental music over some liquor. Others of higher style proceed
to the Alhambra Music Hall, or to the Argyle Rooms, rustling in
splendid dresses, to spend the time till midnight, when they
accompany the gentlemen they have met there to the expensive
supper-rooms and night-houses which abound in the neighbourhood.

In the course of the evening, we see many of the girls proceeding
with young and middle-aged and sometimes silverheaded frail
old men, to Oxenden Street, Panton Street, and James Street,
near the Haymarket, where they enter houses of accommodation,
which they prefer to going with them to their lodgings. Numbers
of French girls may be seen in the Haymarket, and the neighbourhood of Tichbourne Street and Great Windmill Street,

many of them in dark silk paletots and white or dark silk bonnets, trimmed with gay ribbons and flowers, or walking up Regent Street in the neighbourhood of All Souls' Church, Langham Place, and Portland Place, or coming down Regent Street to Waterloo Place and Pall Mall, and hovering near the palatial mansions or the Clubs; or they might be seen decoying gents to their apartments in Queen Street, off Regent's Quadrant, from which locality they were lately forcibly ejected by the police. Most of these French girls have bullies, or what they term by a softer term "fancy men," who cohabit with them. These base wretches live on the prostitution of these miserable girls—hang as loafers in their houses or about the streets, and many of them, as we might expect, are gamblers and swindlers. Several of them, we blush to say, are political refugees, exiles for fighting at the barricades of Paris, for the liberty of their country; while they live here with courtesans in the purlieus of Haymarket, in the most infamous and degrading of all bondage.

The generality of the girls of the Haymarket have no bullies, but live in furnished apartments—one or more—in various localities of the metropolis. Many live in Dean Street, Soho, Gerrard Street, Soho, King Street, Soho, and Church Street, Soho, in Tennison Street, Waterloo Road, at Pimlico and Chelsea, several of the streets leading into Fitzroy Square, and other neighbourhoods, and pay a weekly rent varying from seven shillings to a guinea, which has to be regularly paid on the day it is due. In many cases little forbearance is shown by their heartless landladies. Many of these girls have gentlemen who stately visit them at their lodgings, some of whom are married men. Most of them are very thoughtless and extravagant, with handfuls of money to-day, and in poverty and miserable straits to-morrow, driven to the necessity of pawning their dresses. Hence there are many changes in their life. At one time they are in splendid dress, and at another time in the humblest attire; occasionally they are assisted by men who are interested in them, and restored to their former position, when they get their clothes out of the hands of the pawnbroker. Their living is very precarious, and many of them are occasionally exposed to privation, degradation, and misery, as they are very improvident. They are frequently treated to splendid suppers in the Haymarket and its vicinity, where they sit surrounded with splendour, partaking of costly viands amid lascivious smiles; but the scene is changed when you follow them to their own apartments in Soho or Chelsea, where you find them during the day, lolling drowsily on their beds, in tawdry dress, and in sad dishabille, with dishevelled hair, seedy-looking countenance, and muddy, dreary eyes—their voices frequently hoarse with bad humour and misery.

Large sums of money are spent in luxurious riot in the Haymarket; but it has not been so much frequented by the gentry and nobility for several years past, although considerable numbers are to be seen in the summer and winter seasons.

Strange midnight scenes were wont to be seen occasionally in Queen Street, Regent Street, where the French girls reside. Let us take an illustration. Some fast man—young or middle-aged—goes with them to the cafés and music halls, perhaps proceeds to the supper rooms, and after an expensive supper, retires with them to their domicile in Queen Street. Meantime their bully keeps out of sight, or sneaks behind the bedroom door. In many cases, not contented with the half-guinea or guinea given them, their usual hire for prostitution, they demand more money from their victim. On his declining to give it, they refuse to submit to his pleasure, and will not return him his money. The bully is then called up, and the silly dupe is probably unceremoniously turned out of doors.

There are few felonies committed by this class of prostitutes, as such an imputation would be fatal to their mode of livelihood in this district, where they are generally known, and can be easily traced.

The second class of prostitutes, who walk the Haymarket—the third class in our classification—generally come from the lower orders of society. They consist of domestic servants of a plainer order, the daughters of labouring people, and some of a still lower class. Some of these girls are of a very tender age—from thirteen years and upwards. You see them wandering along Leicester Square, and about the Haymarket, Tichbourne Street, and Regent Street. Many of them are dressed in a light cotton or merino gown, and ill-suited crinoline, with light grey, or brown cloak, or mantle. Some with pork-pie hat, and waving feather—white, blue, or red; others with a slouched straw-hat. Some of them walk with a timid look, others with effrontery. Some have a look of artless innocence and ingenuousness, others very pert, callous, and artful. Some have good features and fine figures, others are coarse-looking and dumpy, their features and accent indicating that they are Irish cockneys. They prostitute themselves for a lower price, and haunt those disreputable coffee-shops in the neighbourhood of the Haymarket and Leicester Square, where you may see the blinds drawn down, and the lights burning dimly within, with notices over the door that "beds are to be had within."

Many of those young girls—some of them good-looking—cohabit with young pickpockets about Drury Lane, St. Giles's, Gray's Inn Lane, Holborn, and other localities—young lads from fourteen to eighteen, groups of whom may be seen loitering about the Haymarket, and often speaking to them. Numbers of these girls are artful and adroit thieves. They follow persons into the dark by-streets of these localities, and are apt to pick his pockets, or they rifle his person when in the bedroom with him in low coffee-houses and brothels. Some of these girls come even from Pimlico, Waterloo Road, and distant parts of the metropolis, to share in the spoils of fast life in the Haymarket. They occasionally take watches, purses, pins, and handkerchiefs from their silly dupes who go with them into those disreputable places, and frequently are not easily traced, as many of them are migratory in their character.

The third and lowest class of prostitutes in the Haymarket—the fourth in our classification—are worn-out prostitutes or other degraded women, some of them married, yet equally degraded in character.

These faded and miserable wretches skulk about the Haymarket, Regent Street, Leicester Square, Coventry Street, Panton Street and Piccadilly, cadging from the fashionable people in the street and from the prostitutes passing along, and sometimes retire for prostitution into dirty low courts near St. James Street, Coventry Court, Long's Court, Earl's Court, and Cranbourne Passage, with shop boys, errand lads, petty thieves, and labouring men, for a few paltry coppers. Most of them steal when they get an opportunity. Occasionally a base coloured woman of this class may be seen in the Haymarket and its vicinity, cadging from the gay girls and gentlemen in the streets. Many of the poor girls are glad to pay her a sixpence occasionally to get rid of her company, as gentlemen are often scared away from them by the intrusion of this shameless hag, with her thick lips, sable black skin, leering countenance and obscene disgusting tongue, resembling a lewd spirit of darkness from the nether world.

Numbers of the women kept by the wealthy and the titled may occasionally be seen in the Haymarket, which is the only centre in the metropolis where all the various classes of prostitutes meet. They attend the Argyle Rooms and the Alhambra, and frequently indulge in the gaieties of the supper-rooms, where their broughams are often seen drawn up at the doors. In the more respectable circles they may be regarded with aversion, but they here reign as the prima-donnas over the fast life of the West End.

Occasionally genteel and beautiful girls in shops and work-rooms in the West End, milliners, dressmakers, and shop girls, may be seen flitting along Regent Street and Pall Mall, like bright birds of passage, to meet with some gentleman *on the sly*, and to obtain a few quickly-earned guineas to add to their scanty salaries. Sometimes a fashionable young widow, or beautiful young married woman, will find her way in those dark evenings to meet with some rickety silver-headed old captain loitering about Pall Mall. Such things are not wondered at by those acquainted with high life in London.

We next come to the consideration of convives, or those who live in the same house with a number of others, and we will commence with those who are independent of the mistress of the house. These women locate themselves in the immediate vicinity of the Haymarket, which at night is their principal scene of action, when the hospitable doors of the theatres and casinos are closed. They are charged enormously for the rooms they occupy, and their landlords defend themselves for their extortionate demands, by alleging that, as honesty is not a leading feature in the characters of their lodgers, they are compelled to protect their own interest by exacting an exorbitant rent. A drawing-room floor in Queen Street, Windmill Street, which is a favourite part on account of its proximity to the Argyle Rooms, is worth three, and sometimes four, pounds a week, and the other étages in proportion. They never stay long in one house, although some will remain for ten or twelve months in a particular lodging. It is their principle to get as deeply into debt as they are able, and then to pack up their things, have them conveyed elsewhere by stealth, and defraud the landlord of his money. The houses in some of the small streets in the neighbourhood of Langham Place are let to the people who underlet them for three hundred a year, and in some cases at a higher rental. This class of prostitutes do not live together on account of a gregarious instinct, but simply from necessity, as their trade would necessarily exclude them from respectable lodging-houses. They soon form an acquaintance with the girls who inhabit the same house, and address one another as "my dear," an unmeaning but very general epithet, an hour or two after their first meeting. They sometimes prefer the suburbs to reside in, especially while Cremorne is open; but some live at Brompton and Pimlico all the year round. One of their most remarkable characteristics is their generosity, which perhaps is unparalleled by the behaviour of any others, whether high or low in the social scale. They will not hesitate to lend one another money if they have it, whether they can spare it or not, although it is seldom that they can, from their innate recklessness and acquired improvidence. It is very common, too, for them to lend their bonnets and their dresses to their friends. If a woman of this description is voluble and garrulous, she is much sought after by the men who keep the cafés in the Haymarket, to sit decked out in gorgeous attire behind the counters, so that by her interesting appearance and the esprit she displays, the habitués of those places, but more usually those who pay only a casual visit, may be entrapped into purchasing some of the wares and fancy articles that are retailed at ten times their actual value. In order to effect this they will exert all their talents, and an inexperienced observer would imagine that they indeed entertain some feeling of affection or admiration for their victim, by the cleverness with which they simulate its existence. The man whose vanity leads him to believe that he is selected by the beautiful creature who condescends to address him, on account of his personal appearance, would be rather disgusted if he were to perceive the same blandishments lavished upon the next comer, and would regret the ten shillings he paid with pleasure for a glove-box, the positive market value of which is hardly one-fifth of the money he gave for it.

There is a great abandonment of everything that one may strictly speaking denominate womanly. Modesty is utterly annihilated, and shame ceases to exist in their composition. They all more or less are given to habits of drinking.

"When I am sad I drink," a woman once said to us. "I'm very often sad, although I appear to be what you call reckless. Well! we don't fret that we might have been ladies because we never

had a chance of that, but we have forfeited a position nevertheless, and when we think that we have fallen, never to regain that
which we have descended from, and in some cases sacrificed everything for a man who has ceased to love and deserted us, we get
mad. The intensity of this feeling does wear off a little after the
first; but there's nothing like gin to deaden the feelings. What are
my habits? Why, if I have no letters or visits from any of my
friends, I get up about four o'clock, dress (*"en dishabille"*) and
dine; after that I may walk about the streets for an hour or two,
and pick up any one I am fortunate enough to meet with, that
is if I want money; afterwards I go to the Holborn, dance a little,
and if any one likes me I take him home with me, if not I go to
the Haymarket, and wander from one café to another, from
Sally's to the Carlton, from Barn's to Sam's, and if I find no one
there I go, if I feel inclined, to the divans. I like the Grand Turkish best, but you don't as a rule find good men in any of the
divans. Strange things happen to us sometimes; we may now and
then die of consumption; but the other day a lady friend of mine
met a gentleman at Sam's, and yesterday morning they were
married at St. George's, Hanover Square. The gentleman had
lots of money, I believe, and he started off with her at once for the
Continent. It is very true this is an unusual case; but we often do
marry, and well too; why shouldn't we, we are pretty, we dress
well, we can talk and insinuate ourselves into the hearts of men
by appealing to their passions and their senses."

This girl was shrewd and clever, perhaps more so than those of
her rank in the profession usually are; but her testimony is sufficient at once to dissipate the foolish idea that ought to have been
exploded long ago, but which still lingers in the minds of both
men and women, that the harlot's progress is short and rapid, and
that there is no possible advance, moral or physical; and that
once abandoned she must always be profligate.

Another woman told us she had been a prostitute for two years;
she became so from necessity; she did not on the whole dislike
her way of living; she didn't think about the sin of it; a poor girl
must live; she wouldn't be a servant for anything; this was much
better. She was a lady's maid once, but lost her place for staying
out one night with the man who seduced her; he afterwards
deserted her, and then she became bad. She was fonder of dress
than anything. On an average she had a new bonnet once a week,
dresses not so often; she liked the casinos, and was charmed with

Cremorne; she hated walking up and down the Haymarket, and seldom did it without she wanted money very much. She liked the Holborn better than the Argyll, and always danced.

Board Lodgers

BOARD lodgers are those who give a portion of what they receive to the mistress of the brothel in return for their board and lodging. As we have had occasion to observe before, it is impossible to estimate the number of brothels in London, or even in particular parishes, not only because they are frequently moving from one district to another, but because our system so hates anything approaching to espionage, that the authorities do not think it worth their while to enter into any such computation. From this it may readily be understood how difficult the task of the statistician is. Perhaps it will be sufficient to say that these women are much more numerous than may at first be imagined; although those who give the whole of what they get in return for their board, lodging, and clothes are still more so. In Lambeth there are great numbers of the lowest of these houses, and only very recently the proprietors of some eight or ten of the worst were summoned before a police magistrate, and the parish officers who made the complaint bound over to prosecute at the sessions. It is much to be regretted that in dealing with such cases the method of procedure is not more expeditious and less expensive. Let us take for example one of the cases we have been quoting. A man is openly accused of keeping a ruffianly den filled with female wretches, destitute of every particle of modesty and bereft of every atom of shame, whose actual occupation is to rob, maltreat, and plunder the unfortunate individuals who so far stultify themselves as to allow the decoys to entrap them into their snares, let us hope, for the sake of humanity, while in a state of intoxication or a condition of imbecility. Very well; instead of an easy inexpensive process, the patriotic persons who have devoted themselves to the exposure of such infamous rascality, find themselves involved in a tedious criminal prosecution, and in the event of failure lay themselves open to an action. Mysterious disappearances, Waterloo Bridge tragedies, and verdicts of "found drowned" are common enough in this great city. Who knows how many of these unfathomable affairs may have been originated, worked out, and consummated in some disgusting rookery in the worst parts of our most demoralised metropolitan parishes; but it is with the better class of these houses we are more particularly engaged at present. During the progress of these researches we met a girl residing at a house in a street running out of Langham Place. Externally the house looked respectable enough; there was no indication of the profession or mode of life of the inmates, except that, from the fact of some of the blinds being down in the bedrooms, you might have thought the house contained an invalid. The rooms, when you were ushered in, were well, though cheaply furnished; there were coburg chairs and sofas, glass chandeliers, and handsome green curtains. The girl with whom we were brought into conversation was not more than twenty-three; she told us her age was twenty, but statements of a similar nature, when made by this class, are never to be relied on. At first she treated our inquiries with some levity, and jocularly inquired what we were inclined to stand, which we justly interpreted into a desire for something to drink; we accordingly "stood" a bottle of wine, which had the effect of making our informant more communicative. What she told us was briefly this. Her life was a life of perfect slavery, she was seldom if ever allowed to go out, and then not without being watched. Why was this? Because she would "cut it" if she got a chance, they knew that very well, and took very good care she shouldn't have much opportunity. Their house was rather popular, and they had lots of visitors; she had some particular friends who always came to see her. They paid her well, but she hardly ever got any of the money. Where was the odds, she couldn't go out to spend it? What did she want with money, except now and then for a train of white satin. What was white satin? Where had I been all my life to ask such a question? Was I a dodger? She meant a parson. No; she was glad of that, for she hadn't much idea of them, they were a canting lot. Well, white satin, if I must know, was gin, and I couldn't say she never taught me anything. Where was she born? Somewhere in Stepney. What did it matter where; she could tell me all about it if she liked, but she didn't care. It touched her on the raw—made her feel too much. She was 'ticed when she was young, that is, she was decoyed by the mistress of the house some years ago. She met Mrs. —— in the street, and the woman began talking to her in a friendly way. Asked her who her father was (he was a journeyman carpenter), where he lived, extracted all about her family, and finally asked her to come home to tea with her. The child, delighted at making the acquaintance of so kind and so well-dressed a lady, willingly acquiesced, without making any demur, as she never dreamt of anything wrong, and had not been cautioned by her father. She had lost her mother some years ago. She was not brought direct to the house where I found her? Oh! no. There was a branch establishment over the water, where they were broken in as it were. How long did she remain there? Oh! perhaps two months, maybe three; she didn't keep much account how time went. When she was conquered and her spirit broken, she was transported from the first house to a more aristocratic neighbourhood. How did they tame her? Oh! they made her drunk and sign some papers, which she knew gave them great power over her, although she didn't exactly know in what the said power consisted, or how it might be exercised. Then they clothed her and fed her well, and gradually inured her to that sort of life. And now, was there anything else I'd like to know particularly, because if there was, I'd better look sharp about asking it, as she was getting tired of talking, she could tell me. Did she expect to lead this life till she died? Well, she never did, if I wasn't going to preachify. She couldn't stand that—anything but that.

I really begged to apologise if I had wounded her sensibility; I wasn't inquiring from a religious point of view, or with any particular motive. I merely wished to know, to satisfy my own curiosity.

Well, she thought me a very inquisitive old party, anyhow. At any rate, as I was so polite she did not mind answering my questions. Would she stick to it till she was a stiff 'un? She supposed she would; what else was there for her? Perhaps something might turn up; how was she to know? She never thought, she would go mad if she did; she lived in the present, and never went blubbering about as some did. She tried to be as jolly as she could; where was the fun of being miserable?

This is the philosophy of most of her sisterhood. This girl possessed a talent for repartee, which accomplishment she endeavoured to exercise at my expense, as will be perceived by the foregoing, though for many reasons I have adhered to her own vernacular. That her answers were true I have no reason to question, and that this is the fate of very many young girls in London there is little doubt; indeed, the reports of the Society for the Protection of Young Females sufficiently prove it. Female virtue in great cities has innumerable assailants, and the moralist should pity rather than condemn. We are by no means certain that meretricious women who have been in the habit of working before losing their virtue, at some trade or other, and are able to unite the two together, are conscious of any annoyance or a want of self-respect at being what they are. This class have been called the "amateurs", to contradistinguish them from the professionals, who devote themselves to it entirely as a profession. To be unchaste amongst the lower classes is not always a subject of reproach. The commerce of the sexes is so general that to have been immodest is very seldom a bar to marriage. The depravity of manners amongst boys and girls begins so very early, that they think it rather a distinction than otherwise to be unprincipled. Many a shoe-black, in his uniform and leathern apron, who cleans your boots for a penny at the corners of the streets, has his sweetheart. Their connection begins probably at the low lodging-houses they are in the habit of frequenting, or, if they have a home, at the penny gaffs and low cheap places of amusement, where the seed of so much evil is sown. The precocity of the youth of both sexes in London is perfectly astounding. The drinking, the smoking, the blasphemy, indecency, and immorality that does not ever call a blush is incredible, and charity schools and the spread of education do not seem to have done much to abate this scourge. Another very fruitful source of early demoralisation is to be looked for in the quantities of penny and halfpenny romances that are sold in town and country. One of the worst of the most recent ones is denominated "Charley Wag, or the New Jack Shepherd, a history of the most successful thief in London." To say that these are not incentives to lust, theft, and crime of every description is to cherish a fallacy. Why should not the police, by act of Parliament, be empowered to take cognizance of this shameful misuse of the art of printing? Surely some clauses could be added to Lord Campbell's Act, or a new bill might be introduced that would meet the exigencies of the case, without much difficulty.

Men frequent the houses in which women board and lodge for many reasons, the chief of which is secrecy; they also feel sure that the women are free from disease, if they know the house, and it bears an average reputation for being well conducted. Men in a certain position avoid publicity in their amours beyond all things, and dread being seen in the neighbourhood of the Haymarket or the Burlington Arcade at certain hours, as their professional reputation might be compromised. Many serious, demure people conceal the iniquities of their private lives in this way.

Another woman told me a story, varying somewhat from that of the first I examined, which subsequent experience has shown me is slightly stereotyped. She was the victim of deliberate cold-blooded seduction; in course of time a child was born; up to this time her seducer had treated her with affection and kindness, but he now, after presenting her with fifty pounds, deserted her. Thrown on her own resources, as it were, she did not know what to do; she could not return to her friends, so she went into lodgings at a very small rental, and there lived until her money was expended. She then supported herself and her child by doing machine-work for a manufacturer, but at last bad times came, and she was thrown out of work; of course, the usual amount of misery consequent on such a catastrophe ensued. She saw her child dying by inches before her face, and this girl, with tears in her eyes, assured me she thanked God for it. "I swear," she added, "I starved myself to nourish it, until I was nothing but skin and bone, and little enough of that; I knew from the first the child must die if things didn't improve, and I felt they wouldn't. When I looked at my little darling I knew well enough he was doomed, but he was not destined to drag on a weary existence as I was, and I was glad of it. It may seem strange to you, but while my boy lived, I couldn't go into the streets to save his life or my own—I couldn't do it. If there had been a foundling hospital, I mean as I hear there is in foreign parts, I would have placed him there, and worked somehow, but there wasn't, and a crying shame it is too. Well, he died at last, and it was all over. I was half mad and three parts drunk after the parish burying, and I went into the streets at last; I rose in the world—(here she smiled sarcastically)—and I've lived in this house for years, but I swear to God I haven't had a moment's happiness since the child died, except when I've been dead drunk or maudlin."

Although this woman did not look upon the death of her child as a crime committed by herself, it was in reality none the less her doing; she shunned the workhouse, which might have done something for her and saved the life, at all events, of her child; but the repugnance evinced by every woman who has any proper feeling for a life in a workhouse or a hospital can hardly be imagined by those who think that, because people are poor, they must lose all feeling, all delicacy, all prejudice, and all shame.

Her remarks about a foundling hospital are sensible; in the opinion of many it *is* a want that ought to be supplied. Infanticide is a crime much on the increase, and what mother would kill her offspring if she could provide for it in any way?

The analysis of the return of the coroners' inquests held in London, for the five years ending in 1860, shows a total of 1,130 inquisitions on the bodies of children under two years of age, all of whom had been murdered. The average is 226 yearly.

Here we have 226 children killed yearly by their parents: this either shows that our institutions are defective, or that great depravity is inherent amongst Englishwomen. The former hypothesis is much more likely than the latter, which we are by no means prepared to indorse. This return, let it be understood, does not, indeed cannot, include the immense number of embryo children who are made away with by drugs and other devices, all of whom we have a right to suppose would have seen the light if adequate provision could have been found for them at their birth.

A return has also been presented to Parliament, at the instance of Mr. Kendal, M.P., from which we find that 157,485 summonses in bastardy cases were issued between the years 1845 and 1859 inclusive, but that only 124,218 applications against the putative fathers came on for hearing, while of this number orders for maintenance were only made in 107,776 cases, the remaining summonses, amounting to 15,981, being dismissed. This latter fact gives a yearly average of 1,141 illegitimate children thrown back on their wretched mothers. These statistics are sufficiently appalling, but there is reason to fear that they only give an approximate idea of the illegitimate infantile population, and more especially of the extent to which infanticide prevails.

Those Who Live In Low Lodging-Houses

IN order to find these houses it is necessary to journey eastwards, and leave the artificial glitter of the West End, where vice is pampered and caressed. Whitechapel, Wapping, Ratcliff Highway, and analogous districts are prolific in the production of these infamies. St. George's-in-the-East abounds with them, kept, for the most part, by disreputable Jews, and if a man is unfortunate enough to fall into their clutches he is sure to become the spoil of Israel. We may, however, find many low lodging-houses without penetrating so far into the labyrinth of east London.

There are numbers in Lambeth; in the Waterloo Road and contiguous streets; in small streets between Covent Garden and the Strand, some in one or two streets running out of Oxford Street. There is a class of women technically known as "bunters", who take lodgings, and after staying some time run away without paying their rent. These victimise the keepers of low lodging-houses successfully for years. A "bunter" whose favourite promenade, especially on Sundays, was the New Cut, Lambeth, said "she never paid any rent, hadn't done it for years, and never meant to. They was mostly Christ-killers, and chousing a Jew was no sin; leastways, none as she cared about committing. She boasted of it: had been known about town this ever so long as Swindling Sal. And there was another, a great pal of her'n, as went by the name of Chousing Bett. Didn't they know her in time? Lord bless me, she was up to as many dodges as there was men in the moon. She changed places, she never stuck to one long; she never had no things for to be sold up, and, as she was handy with her mauleys, she got on pretty well. It took a considerable big man, she could tell me, to kick her out of a house, and then when he done it she always give him something for himself, by way of remembering her. Oh! they had a sweet recollection of her, some on 'em. She'd crippled lots of the —— crucifiers." "Did she never get into a row?" "Lots on 'em, she believed me. Been quodded no end of times. She knew every beak as sat on the cheer as well as she knew Joe the magsman, who, she *might* say, wor a very perticaler friend of her'n." "Did he pay her well?"

This was merely a question to ascertain the amount of remuneration that she, and others like her, were in the habit of receiving; but it had the effect of enraging her to a great extent. My informant was a tall, stout woman, about seven-and-twenty, with a round face, fat cheeks, a rather wheezy voice, and not altogether destitute of good looks. Her arms were thick and muscular, while she stood well on her legs, and altogether appeared as if she would be a formidable opponent in a street quarrel or an Irish row.

"Did he pay well? Was I a-going to insult her? What was I asking her sich a 'eap of questions for? Why, Joe was good for a — sight more than she thought I was! Would she take a drop of summut? Well, she didn't mind if she did."

An adjournment to a public-house in the immediate vicinity, where "Swindling Sal" appeared very much at home, mollified and appeased her.

The "drop of summut short, miss," was responded to by the young lady behind the bar by a monosyllabic query, "Neat?" The reply being in the affirmative, a glass of gin was placed upon the marble counter, and rapidly swallowed, while a second, and a third followed in quick succession, much, apparently, to the envy of a woman in the same compartment, who, my inform- ant told me in a whisper, was "Lushing Lucy," and a stunner— whatever the latter appellation might be worth. But her added "Me an' 'er 'ad a rumpus," was sufficient to explain the fact of their not speaking.

"What do you think you make a week?" at last I ventured to ask.

"Well, I'll tell yer," was the response: "one week with another I makes nearer on four pounds nor three—sometimes five. I 'ave done eight and ten. Now Joe, as you 'eered me speak on, he does it 'ansome, he does: I mean, you know, when he's in luck. He give me a fiver once after cracking a crib, and a nice spree me an' Lushing Loo 'ad over it. Sometimes I get three shillings, half-a- crown, five shillings, or ten occasionally, accordin' to the sort of man. What is this Joe as I talks about? Well, I likes your cheek, howsomever, he's a 'ousebreaker. I don't do anything in that way, never did, and shan't; it ain't safe, it ain't. How did I come to take to this sort of life? It's easy to tell. I was a servant gal away down in Birmingham. I got tired of workin' and slavin' to make a livin', and getting a —— bad one at that; what o' five pun' a year and yer grub, I'd sooner starve, I would. After a bit I went to Coventry, cut Brummagem, as we calls it in those parts, and took up with the soldiers as was quartered there. I soon got tired of them. Soldiers is good—soldiers is—to walk with and that, but they don't pay; cos why, they ain't got no money; so I says to myself, I'll go to Lunnon, and I did. I soon found my level there. It is a queer sort of life, the life I'm leading, and now I think I'll be off. Good night to yer. I hope we'll know more of one another when we two meets again."

When she was gone I turned my attention to the woman I have before alluded to. "Lushing Loo" was a name uneuphemistic, and calculated to prejudice the hearer against the possessor. I had only glanced at her before, and a careful scrutiny surprised me, while it impressed me in her favour. She was lady-like in appearance, although haggard. She was not dressed in flaring colours and meretricious tawdry. Her clothes were neat, and evi-

denced taste in their selection, although they were cheap. I spoke
to her; she looked up without giving me an answer, appearing
much dejected. Guessing the cause, which was that she had been
very drunk the night before, and had come to the public-house
to get something more, but had been unable to obtain credit,
I offered her half-a-crown, and told her to get what she liked with
it. A new light came into her eyes: she thanked me, and, calling
the barmaid, gave her orders, with a smile of triumph. Her taste
was sufficiently aristocratic to prefer pale brandy to the usual
beverage dispensed in gin-palaces. A "drain of pale", as she termed
it, invigorated her. Glass after glass was ordered, till she had
spent all the money I gave her. By this time she was perfectly
drunk, and I had been powerless to stop her. Pressing her hand to
her forehead, she exclaimed, "Oh, my poor head!" I asked what
was the matter with her, and for the first time she condescended,
or felt in the humour to speak to me. "My heart's broken,"
she said. "It has been broken since the twenty-first of May.
I wish I was dead; I wish I was laid in my coffin. It won't be long
first. I am doing it. I've just driven another nail in, and 'Lushing
Loo', as they call me, will be no loss to society. Cheer up; let's
have a song. Why don't you sing?" she cried, her mood having
changed, as is frequently the case with habitual drunkards, and
a symptom that often precedes delirium tremens. "Sing, I tell
you," and she began,

> The first I met a cornet was
> In a regiment of dragoons,
> I gave him what he didn't like,
> And stole his silver spoons.

When she had finished her song, the first verse of which is all
I can remember, she subsided into comparative tranquillity.
I asked her to tell me her history.

"Oh, I'm a seduced milliner," she said, rather impatiently;
"anything you like."

It required some inducement on my part to make her speak,
and overcome the repugnance she seemed to feel at saying anything about herself.

She was the daughter of respectable parents, and at an early
age had imbibed a fondness for a cousin in the army, which in
the end caused her ruin. She had gone on from bad to worse after

his desertion, and at last found herself among the number of low
transpontine women. I asked her why she did not enter a refuge,
it might save her life.

"I don't wish to live," she replied. "I shall soon get D.T., and
then I'll kill myself in a fit of madness.'

Nevertheless I gave her the address of the secretary of the
Midnight Meeting Association, Red Lion Square, and was going
away when a young Frenchman entered the bar, shouting a
French song, beginning

Vive l'amour, le vin, et le tabac,

and I left him in conversation with the girl whose partiality for
the brandy bottle had gained her the suggestive name I have
mentioned above.

The people who keep the low lodging-houses where these women
live are rapacious, mean, and often dishonest. They charge enormously for their rooms in order to guarantee themselves against
loss in the event of their harbouring a "bunter" by mistake, so
that the money paid by their honest lodgers covers the default
made by those who are fraudulent.

Sailors' Women

MANY extraordinary statements respecting sailors' women have
at different times been promulgated by various authors; and
from what has gone forth to the world, those who take an interest
in such matters have not formed a very high opinion of the class
in question.

The progress of modern civilisation is so rapid and so wonderful, that the changes which take place in the brief space of a few
years are really and truly incredible.

That which ten, fifteen, or twenty years ago might have been said
with perfect truth about a particular district, or an especial denomination, if repeated now would, in point of fact, be nothing but
fiction of the grossest and most unsubstantial character. Novelists
who have never traversed the localities they are describing so
vividly, or witnessed the scenes they depict with such graphic
distinctness, do a great deal more to mislead the general public
than a casual observer may at first think himself at liberty to
believe.

The upper ten thousand and the middle-classes as a rule have to combat innumerable prejudices, and are obliged to reject the traditions of their infancy before they thoroughly comprehend the actual conditions of that race of people, which they are taught by immemorial prescription to regard as immensley inferior, if not altogether barbarous.

It is necessary to make these prefatory remarks before declaring that of late years everything connected with the industrious classes has undergone as complete a transformation as any magic can effect upon the stage. Not only is the condition of the people changed, but they themselves are as effectively metamorphosed. I shall describe the wonders that have been accomplished in a score or two of years in and about St. Giles's by a vigilant and energetic police-force, better parochial management, schools, washhouses, mechanics' institutes, and lodging-houses that have caused to disappear those noisome, pestilential sties that pigs would obstinately refuse to wallow in.

The spread of enlightenment and education has also made itself visible in the increased tact and proficiency of the thief himself; and this is one cause of the amelioration of low and formerly vicious neighbourhoods. The thief no longer frequents places where the police know very well how to put their hands upon him. Quitting the haunts where he was formerly so much at home and at his ease, he migrates westwards, north, south, anywhere but the exact vicinity you would expect to meet him in. Nor is the hostility of the police so much directed against expert and notorious thieves. They of course do not neglect an opportunity of making a capture, and plume themselves when that capture is made, but they have a certain sort of respect for a thief who is professionally so; who says, "It is the way by which I choose to obtain my living and were it otherwise I must still elect to be a thief for I have been accustomed to it from my childhood. My character is already gone, no one would employ me, and, above all, I take a prde in thieving skilfully, and setting your detective skill at defiance."

It is indeed the low petty thief, area-sneak, and that genus that more especially excites the spleen and rouses the ire of your modern policeman. The idle, lazy scoundrel who will not work when he can obtain it at the docks and elsewhere, who goes cadging about because his own inherent depravity and naturally based instints deprive him of a spark of inteligence, an atom of onest feeling, to point to a better and diferent goal. Emigration is a thing unexisting to them; they live a life of turpitude, preying upon society; they pass half their days in a prison, and they die prematurely unregretted and unmourned.

Whitechapel has always been looked upon as a suspicious, unhealthy locality. To begin, its population is a strange amalgamation of Jews, English, French, Germans, and other antagonistic elements that must clash and jar, but not to such an extent as has been surmised and reported. Whitechapel has its theatres, its music-halls, the cheap rates of admission to which serve to absorb numbers of the inhabitants, and by innocently amusing them soften their manners and keep them out of mischief and harm's way.

The Earl of Effingham, a theatre in Whitechapel Road, has been lately done up and restored, and holds three thousand people. It has no boxes; they would not be patronized if they were in existence. Whitechapel does not go to the play in kid-gloves and white ties. The stage of the Effingham is roomy and excellent, the trapwork very extensive, for Whitechapel rejoices much in pyrotechnic displays, blue demons, red demons, and vanishing Satans that disappear in a cloud of smoke through an invisible hole in the floor. Great is the applause when gauzy nymphs rise like so many Aphrodites from the sea, and sit down on apparent sunbeams midway between the stage and the theatrical heaven. The Pavilion is another theatre in the Whitechapel Road, and perhaps ranks higher than the Effingham. The Pavilion may stand comparison, with infinite credit to itself and its architect, with more than one West-end theatre. People at the West-end who never in their dreams travel farther east than the dividend and transfer department of the Bank of England in Threadneedle Street, have a vague idea that East-end theatres strongly resemble the dilapidated and decayed Soho in Dean Street, filled with a rough, noisy set of drunken thieves and prostitutes. It is time that these ideas should be exploded. Prostitutes and thieves of course do find their way into theatres and other places of amusement, but perhaps if you were to rake up all the bad characters in the neighbourhood they would not suffice to fill the pit and gallery of the Pavilion.

On approaching the playhouse you observe prostitutes standing outside in little gangs and knots of three or four, and you will also see them inside, but for the most part they are accompanied by their men. Sergeant Prior, of the H division, for whose services I am indebted to the courtesy of Superintendent White, assured me that when sailors landed in the docks, and drew their wages, they picked up some women to whom they considered themselves married pro tem., and to whom they gave the money they had made by their last voyage. They live with the women until the money is gone (and the women generally treat the sailors honourably). They go to sea again, make some more, come home, and repeat the same thing over again. There are perhaps twelve or fifteen public-houses licensed for music in St. George's Street and Ratcliff Highway: most of them a few years ago were thronged, now they can scarcely pay their expenses; and it is anticipated that next year many of them will be obliged to close.

This is easily accounted for. Many sailors go further east to the K division, which includes Wapping, Bluegate, etc.; but the chief cause, the *fons et origo* of the declension is simply the institution of sailors' savings banks. There is no longer the money to be spent that used to be. When a sailor comes on shore, he will probably go to the nearest sailors' home, and place his money in the bank. Drawing out again a pound or so, with which he may enjoy himself for a day or two, he will then have the rest of the money transmitted to his friends in the country, to whom he will himself go as soon as he has had his fling in town; so that the money that used formerly to be expended in one centre is spread over the entire country, *ergo* and very naturally the public-house keepers feel the change acutely. To show how the neighbourhood has improved of late years, I will mention that six or eight years ago the Eastern Music Hall was frequented by such ruffians that the proprietor told me he was only too glad when twelve o'clock came, that he might shut up the place, and turn out his turbulent customers, whose chief delight was to disfigure and ruin each other's physiognomy.

Mr. Wilton has since then rebuilt his concert-room, and erected a gallery that he sets apart for sailors and their women. The body of the hall is filled usually by tradesmen, keepers of tally-shops, etc., etc.

And before we go further a word about tally-shops. Take the New Road, Whitechapel, which is full of them. They present a respectable appearance, are little two-storied houses, clean, neat, and the owners are reputed to have the Queen's taxes ready when the collectors call for them. The principle of the tally business is this.—A man wants a coat, or a woman wants a shawl a dress, or some other article of feminine wearing apparel. Being somewhat known in the neighbourhood, as working at some trade or other, the applicant is able to go to the tally-shop, certain of the success of his or her application.

She obtains the dress she wishes for, and agrees to pay so much a week until the whole debt is cleared off. For instance, the dress costs three pounds, a sum she can never hope to possess in its entirety. Well, five shillings a week for three months will complete the sum charged; and the woman by this system of accommodation is as much benefited as the tally-man.

The British Queen, a concert-room in the Commercial Road, is a respectable, well conducted house, frequented by low prostitutes, as may be expected, but orderly in the extreme, and what more can be wished for? The sergeant remarked to me, if these places of harmless amusement were not licensed and kept open, much evil would be sown and disseminated throughout the neighbourhood, for it may be depended something worse and ten times lower would be substituted. People of all classes must have recreation. Sailors who come on shore after a long cruise will have it; and, added the sergeant, we give it them in a way that does no harm to themselves or anybody else. Rows and disturbances seldom occur, although, of course, they may be expected now and then. The dancing-rooms close at twelve—indeed their frequenters adjourn to other places generally before that hour, and very few publics are open at one. I heard that there had been three fights at the Prussian Eagle, in Ship Alley, Wellclose Square, on the evening I visited the locality; but when I arrived I saw no symptoms of the reported pugnacity of the people assembled, and this was the only rumour of war that reached my ears.

Ship Alley is full of foreign lodging-houses. You see written on a blind an inscription that denotes the nationality of the keeper and the character of the establishment; for instance *Hollandsche lodgement* is sufficient to show a Dutchman that his own language is spoken, and that he may have a bed if he chooses.

That there are desperate characters in the district was sufficiently evidenced by what I saw when at the station-house. Two women, both well-known prostitutes, were confined in the cells, one of whom had been there before no less than *fourteen times*, and had only a few hours before been brought up charged with nearly murdering a man with a poker. Her face was bad, heavy, and repulsive; her forehead, as well as I could distinguish by the scanty light thrown into the place by the bull's-eye of the policeman, was low; her nose was short and what is called podgy, having the nostrils dilated; and she abused the police for disturbing her when she wished to go to sleep, a thing, from what I saw, I imagined rather difficult to accomplish, as she had nothing to recline upon but a hard sort of locker attached to the wall, and running all along one side and at the bottom of the cell.

The other woman, whose name was O'Brien, was much better looking than her companion in crime; her hand was bandaged up, and she appeared faint from loss of blood. The policeman lifted her head up, and asked her if she would like anything to eat. She replied she could drink some tea, which was ordered for her. She had met a man in a public-house in the afternoon, who was occupied in eating some bread and cheese. In order to get into conversation with him, she asked him to give her some, and on his refusing she made a snatch at it, and caught hold of the knife he was using with her right hand, inflicting a severe wound: notwithstanding the pain of the wound, which only served to infuriate her, she flew at the man with a stick and beat him severely over the head, endangering his life; for which offence she was taken by the police to the station-house and locked up.

There are very few English girls who can be properly termed sailors' women; most of them are either German or Irish. I saw numbers of German, tall brazen-faced women, dressed in gaudy colours, dancing and pirouetting in a fantastic manner in a dancing-room in Ratcliff Highway.

It may be as well to give a description of one of the dancing-rooms frequented by sailors and their women.

Passing through the bar of the public-house you ascend a flight of stairs and find yourself in a long room well lighted by gas. There are benches placed along the walls for the accommodation of the dancers, and you will not fail to observe the orchestra, which is well worthy of attention. It consists, in the majority of cases, of four musicians, bearded shaggy-looking foreigners, probably German, including a fiddle, a cornet, two fifes or flutes. The orchestra is usually penned up in a corner of the room, and placed upon a dais or raised desk, to get upon which you ascend two steps; the front is boarded up with deal, only leaving a small door at one end to admit the performers, for whose convenience either a bench is erected or chairs supplied. There is a little ledge to

place the music on, which is as often as not embellished with
pewter pots. The music itself is striking in the extreme, and at all
events exhilarating in the highest degree. The shrill notes of the
fifes, and the braying of the trumpet in very quick time, rouses
the excitement of the dancers, until they whirl round in the waltz
with the greatest velocity.

I was much struck by the way in which the various dances
were executed. In the first place, the utmost decorum prevailed,
nor did I notice the slightest tendency to indecency. Polkas and
waltzes seemed to be the favourites, and the steps were marvel-
lously well done, considering the position and education of the
company. In many cases there was an exhibition of grace and
natural ease that no one would have supposed possible; but this
was observable more amongst foreigners than English. The generality of the women had not the slightest idea of dancing. There
was very little beauty abroad that night, at least in the neighbourhood of Ratcliff Highway. It might have been hiding under
a bushel, but it was not patent to the casual observer. Yet I must
acknowledge something prepossessing about the countenances of
the women, which is more than could be said of the men. It might
have been a compound of resignation, indifference, and recklessness, through all of which phases of her career a prostitute must
go; nor is she thoroughly inured to her vocation until they have
been experienced, and are in a manner mingled together. There
was a certain innate delicacy about those women, too, highly
commendable to its possessors. It was not the artificial refinement
of the West-end, nothing of the sort, but genuine womanly feeling.
They did not look as if they had come there for pleasure exactly,
they appeared too business-like for that; but they did seem as if
they would like, and intended, to unite the two, business and
pleasure, and enjoy themselves as much as the circumstances
would allow. They do not dress in the dancing-room, they attire
themselves at home, and walk through the streets in their
ball costume, without their bonnets, but as they do not live
far off this is not thought much of. I remarked several women
unattached sitting by themselves, in one place as many as half-
a-dozen.

The faces of the sailors were vacant, stupid and beery. I could
not help thinking one man I saw at the Prussian Eagle a perfect
Caliban in his way. There was an expression of owlish cunning
about his heavy-looking features that, uniting with the drunken

leer sitting on his huge mouth, made him look but a "very indifferent monster."

I noticed a sprinkling of coloured men and a few thorough negroes scattered about here and there.

The sergeant chanced to be in search of a woman named Harrington, who had committed a felony, and in the execution of his duty he was obliged to search some notorious brothels that he thought might harbour the delinquent.

We entered a house in Frederick Street (which is full of brothels, almost every house being used for an immoral purpose). But the object of our search was not there, and we proceeded to Brunswick Street, more generally known in the neighbourhood and to the police as "Tiger Bay"; the inhabitants and frequenters of which place are very often obliged to enter an involuntary appearance in the Thames police court. Tiger Bay, like Frederick Street, is full of brothels and thieves' lodging houses. We entered No. 6, accompanied by two policemen in uniform, who happened to be on duty at the entrance to the place, as they wished to apprehend a criminal whom they had reason to believe would resort for shelter, and the night's debauch, to one of the dens of the Bay. We failed to find the man the police wanted, but on descending to the kitchen, we discovered a woman sitting on a chair, evidently waiting up for some one.

"That woman," said the sergeant, "is one of the lowest class we have; she is not only a common prostitute herself, and a companion of ruffians and thieves, but the servant of prostitutes and low characters as debased as herself, with the exception of their being waited upon by her."

We afterwards searched two houses on the opposite side of the way. The rooms occupied by the women and their sailors were more roomy than I expected to find them. The beds were what are called "four-posters," and in some instances were surrounded with faded, dirty-looking, chintz curtains. There was the usual amount of cheap crockery on the mantelpieces, which were surmounted with a small looking-glass in a rosewood or gilt frame. When the magic word "Police" was uttered, the door flew open, as the door of the robbers' cave swung back on its hinges when Ali Baba exclaimed "Sesame". A few seconds were allowed for the person who opened the door to retire to the couch, and then our visual circuit of the chamber took place. The sailors did not evince any signs of hostility at our somewhat unwarrantable intrusion, and we in every case made our exit peacefully, but without finding the felonious woman we were in search of; which might cause sceptical people to regard her as slightly apocryphal, but in reality such was not the case, and in all probability by this time justice has claimed her own.

A glance at the interior of the Horse and Leaping Bar concluded our nocturnal wanderings. This public-house is one of the latest in the district, and holds out accommodation for man and beast until the small hours multiply themselves considerably.

Most of the foreign women talk English pretty well, some excellently, some of course imperfectly; their proficiency depending upon the length of their stay in the country. A German woman told me the following story: —

"I have been in England nearly six years. When I came over here I could not speak a word of your language; but I associated with my own countrymen. Now I talk the English well, as well as any, and I go with the British sailor. I am here to-night in this house of dancing with a sailor English, and I have known him two week. His ship is in docks, and will not sail for one month from this time I am now speaking. I knew him before, one years ago and a half. He always lives with me when he come on shore. He is nice man and give me all his money when he land always. I take all his money while he is with me, and not spend it quick as some of your English women do. If I not to take care, he would spend all in one week. Sailor boy always spend money like rain water; he throw it into the street and not care to pick it up again, leave it for crossing-sweeper or errand-boy who pass that way. I give him little when he want it; he know me well and have great deal confidence in me. I am honest, and he feel he can trust me. Suppose he have twenty-four pound when he leave his ship, and he stay six week on land, he will spend with me fifteen or twenty, and he will give me what left when he leave me, and we amuse ourself and keep both ourself with the rest. It very bad for sailor to keep his money himself; he will fall into bad hands; he will go to ready-made outfitter or slop-seller, who will sell him clothes dreadful dear and ruin him. I know very many sailors— six, eight, ten, oh! more than that. They are my husbands. I am not married, of course not, but they think me their wife while they are on shore. I do not care much for any of them; I have a lover of my own, he is a waiter in a lodging and coffee house;

Germans keep it; he is German and comes from Berlin, which is my town also. I is born there.''

Shadwell, Spitalfields, and contiguous districts are infested with nests of brothels as well as Whitechapel. To attract sailors, women and music must be provided for their amusement. In High Street, Shadwell, there are many of these houses, one of the most notorious of which is called The White Swan, or, more commonly, Paddy's Goose; the owner of which is reported to make money in more ways than one. Brothel-keeping is a favourite mode of investing money in this neighbourhood. Some few years ago a man called James was prosecuted for having altogether thirty brothels; and although he was convicted, the nuisance was by no means in the slightest degree abated, as the informer, by name Brooks, has them all himself at the present time.

There are two other well-known houses in High Street, Shadwell—The Three Crowns and The Grapes, the latter not being licensed for dancing.

Paddy's Goose is perhaps the most popular house in the parish. It is also very well thought of in high quarters. During the Crimean war, the landlord, when the Government wanted sailors to man the fleet, went among the shipping in the river, and recruited a number of men. His system of recruiting was very successful. He went about in a small steamer with a band of music and flags, streamers and colours flying. All this rendered him popular with the Admiralty authorities, and made his house extensively known to the sailors, and those connected with them.

Inspector Price, under whose supervision the low lodging-houses in that part of London are placed, most obligingly took me over one of the lowest lodging-houses, and one of the best, forming a strange contrast, and both presenting an admirable example of the capital working of the most excellent Act that regulates them. We went into a large room, with a huge fire blazing cheerfully at the furthest extremity, around which were grouped some ten or twelve people, others were scattered over various part of the room. The attitudes of most were listless; none seemed to be reading; one was cooking his supper; a few amused themselves by criticising us, and canvassing as to the motives of our visit, and our appearance altogether. The inspector was well known to the keeper of the place, who treated him with the utmost civility and respect. The greatest cleanliness prevailed everywhere. Any one was admitted to this house who could

command the moderate sum of threepence. I was informed those
who frequented it were, for the most part, prostitutes and thieves.
That is thieves and their associates. No questions were asked
of those who paid their money and claimed a night's lodging
in return. The establishment contained forty beds. There were
two floors. The first was divided into little boxes by means of
deal boards, and set apart for married people, or those who
represented themselves to be so. Of course, as the sum paid for
the night's lodging was so small, the lodgers could not expect
clean sheets, which were only supplied once a week. The sheets
were indeed generally black, or very dirty. How could it be
otherwise? The men were often in a filthy state, and quite un-
accustomed to anything like cleanliness, from which they were
as far as from godliness. The floors and the surroundings were
clean, and highly creditable to the management upstairs; the
beds were not crowded together, but spread over the surface
in rows, being a certain distance from one another. Many of them
were already occupied, although it was not eleven o'clock, and
the house is generally full before morning. The ventilation was
very complete, and worthy of attention. There were several venti-
lators on each side of the room, but not in the roof—all were
placed in the side.

The next house we entered was more aristocratic in appearance.
You entered through some glass doors, and going along a small
passage found yourself in a large apartment, long and narrow,
resembling a coffee-room. The price of admission was precisely
the same, but the frequenters were chiefly working men, sometimes men from the docks, respectable mechanics, etc. No suspicious characters were admitted by the proprietor on any pretence,
and he by this means kept his house select. Several men were
seated in the compartments reading newspapers, of which there
appeared to be an abundance. The accommodation was very
good, and everything reflected great credit upon the police,
who seem to have the most unlimited jurisdiction, and complete
control over the low people and places in the East-end of London.

Bluegate Fields is nothing more or less than a den of thieves,
prostitutes, and ruffians of the lowest description. Yet the police
penetrate unarmed without the slightest trepidation. There
I witnessed sights that the most morbid novelist has described,
but which have been too horrible for those who have never been
on the spot to believe. We entered a house in Victoria Place,

running out of Bluegate, that had no street-door, and penetrating a small passage found ourselves in a kitchen, where the landlady was sitting over a miserable fire; near her there was a girl, haggard and woebegone. We put the usual question. Is there anyone upstairs? And on being told that the rooms were occupied, we ascended to the first floor, which was divided into four small rooms. The house was only a two-storied one. The woman of the place informed me, she paid five shillings a week rent, and charged the prostitutes who lodged with her four shillings a-week for the miserable apartments she had to offer for their accommodation; but as the shipping in the river was very slack just now, times were hard with her.

The house was a wretched tumble-down hovel, and the poor woman complained bitterly that her landlord would make no repairs. The first room we entered contained a Lascar, who had come over in some vessel, and his woman. There was a sickly smell in the chamber, that I discovered proceeded from the opium he had been smoking. There was not a chair to be seen; nothing but a table, upon which were placed a few odds-and-ends. The Lascar was lying on a paliasse placed upon the floor (there was no bedstead), apparently stupefied from the effects of the opium he had been taking. A couple of old tattered blankets sufficed to cover him. By his bedside sat his woman, who was half idiotically endeavouring to derive some stupefaction from the ashes he had left in his pipe. Her face was grimy and unwashed, and her hands so black and filthy that mustard-and-cress might have been sown successfully upon them. As she was huddled up with her back against the wall she appeared an animated bundle of rags. She was apparently a powerfully made woman, and although her face was wrinkled and careworn, she did not look exactly decrepit, but like one more thoroughly broken down in spirit than in body. In all probability she was diseased; and the disease communicated by the Malays, Lascars, and Orientals generally is said to be the most frightful form of lues to be met with in Europe. It goes by the name of the Dry ———, and is much dreaded by all the women in the neighbourhood of the docks. Leaving this wretched couple, who were too much overcome with the fumes of opium to answer any questions, we went into another room which should more correctly be called a hole. There was not an atom of furniture in it, nor a bed, and yet it contained a woman. This woman was lying on the floor, with not even a bundle of straw beneath her, wrapped up in what appeared to be a shawl, but which might have been taken for the dress of a scarecrow feloniously abstracted from a corn-field, without any great stretch of the imagination. She started up as we kicked open the door that was loose on its hinges, and did not shut properly, creaking strangely on its rusty hinges as it swung back. Her face was shrivelled and famine-stricken, her eyes bloodshot and glaring, her features disfigured slightly with disease, and her hair dishevelled, tangled, and matted. More like a beast in his lair than a human being in her home was this woman. We spoke to her, and from her replies concluded she was an Irishwoman. She said she was charged nothing for the place she slept in. She cleaned out the water-closets in the daytime, and for these services she was given a lodging gratis.

The next house we entered was in Bluegate Fields itself. Four women occupied the kitchen in the ground-floor. They were waiting for their men, probably thieves. They had a can of beer, which they passed from one to the other. The woman of the house had gone out to meet her husband, who was to be liberated from prison that night, having been imprisoned for a burglary three years ago, his term of incarceration happening to end that day. His friends were to meet at his house and celebrate his return by an orgie, when all of them, we were told, hoped to be blind drunk; and, added the girl who volunteered the information, "None of 'em didn't care a dam for police." She was evidently anticipating the happy state of inebriety she had just been predicting.

One of the houses a few doors off contained a woman well known to the police, and rather notorious on account of her having attempted to drown herself three times. Wishing to see her, the inspector took me to the house she lived in, which was kept by an Irishwoman, the greatest hypocrite I ever met with. She was intensely civil to the inspector, who had once convicted her for allowing three women to sleep in one bed, and she was fined five pounds, all which she told us with the most tedious circumstantiality, vowing, as "shure as the Almighty God was sitting on his throne," she did it out of charity, or she wished she might never speak no more. "These gals," she said, "comes to me in the night and swears (as I knows to be true) they has no place where to put their heads, and foxes they has holes, likewise birds of the air, which it's a mortial shame as they is better provided for and against than them that's flesh and blood Christians. And one night I let one in, when having no bed you see empty I bundled them in together. Police they came and I was fined five pounds, which I borrowed from Mrs. Wilson what lives close to—five golden sovereigns, as I'm alive, and they took them all, which I've paid back two bob a week since, and I don't owe no one soul not a brass farthing, which it's all as thrue as Christ's holiness, let alone his blessed gospel." The woman we came to see was called China Emma, or by her intimate associates Chaney Emm. She was short in stature, rather stout, with a pale face utterly expressionless; her complexion was blond. There was a look almost of vacuity about her, but her replies to my questions were lucid, and denoted that she was only naturally slow and stupid.

"My father and mother," she said, "kept a grocer's shop in Goswell Street. Mother died when I was twelve years old, and father took to drinking. In three years he lost his shop, and in a while killed himself, what with the drink and one thing and another. I went to live with a sister who was bad, and in about a year she went away with a man and left me. I could not get any work, never having been taught any trade or that. One day I met a sailor, who was very good to me. I lived with him as his wife, and when he went away drew his half-pay. I was with him for six years. Then he died of yellow fever in the West Indies, and I heard no more of him. I know he did not cut me, for one of his mates brought me a silver snuff-box he used to carry his quids in, which he sent me when he was at his last. Then I lived for a bit in Angel Gardens; after that I went to Gravel Lane; and now I'm in Bluegate Fields. When I came here I met with a Chinaman called Appoo. He's abroad now, but he sends me money. I got two pounds from him only the other day. He often sends me the needful. When he was over here last we lived in Gregory's Rents. I've lived in Victoria Place and New Court, all about Bluegate. Appoo only used to treat me badly when I got drunk. I always get drunk when I've a chance to. Appoo used to tie my legs and arms and take me into the street. He'd throw me into the gutter, and then he'd throw buckets of water over me till I was wet through; but that didn't cure; I don't believe anything would; I'd die for the drink; I must have it, and I don't care what I does to get it. I've tried to kill myself more than once. I have fits at times—melancholy fits—and I don't know what to do with myself. I wish I was dead, and I run to the water and throw myself in; but I've had no luck; I never had since I was a child—oh! ever so little. I'm always picked out. Once I jumped off a first-floor window in Jamaica Place into the river, but a boatman coming by hooked me up, and the magistrate give me a month. The missus here (naming the woman who kept the place) wants me to go to a refuge or a home, or something of that. P'raps I shall."

The Irishwoman here broke in, exclaiming: —

"And so she shall. I've got three or four poor gals into the refuge, and I'll get Chaney Emm, as shure as the Almighty God's sitting on his throne." (This was a favourite exclamation of hers.) "I keeps her very quiet here; she never sees no one, nor tastes a drop of gin, which she shouldn't have to save her blessed life, if it were to be saved by nothink else; leastways, it should be but a taste. It's ruined her has drink. When she got the money Appoo sent her the other day or two back, I took it all, and laid it out for her, but never a drop of the crater passed down Chaney Emm's lips."

This declaration of the avaricious old woman was easily credible, except the laying out the money for her victim's advantage. The gin, in all probability, if any had been bought, had been monopolized in another quarter, where it was equally acceptable. As to the woman's seeing no one, the idea was preposterous. The old woman's charity, as is commonly the case, began at home, and went very little further. If she was excluded from men's society she must have been much diseased.

I find the women who cohabit with sailors are not, as a body, disorderly, although there may be individuals who habitually give themselves up to insubordination. I take them to be the reverse of careful, for they are at times well off, but at others, through their improvidence and the slackness of the shipping, immersed in poverty. The supply of women is fully equal to the demand; but as the demand fluctuates so much, I do not think the market can be said to be overstocked. They are unintelligent and below the average of intellectuality among prostitutes, though perhaps on a par with the men with whom they cohabit.

Soldiers' Women

THE evil effects of the want of some system to regulate prostitution in England are perhaps more shown amongst the army than any other class. Syphilis is very prevalent among soldiers, although the disease is not so virulent as it was formerly. That is, we do not see examples of the loss of the palate or part of the cranium, as specimens extant in our museums show us was formerly the case. The women who are patronized by soldiers are, as a matter of course, very badly paid; for how can a soldier out of his very scanty allowance, generally little exceeding a shilling a day, afford to supply a woman with means adequate for her existence? It follows from the state of things, that a woman may, or more correctly must, be intimate with several men in one evening and supposing her to be tainted with the disease, as many men as she may chance to pick up during the course of her peregrinations will be incapacitated from serving her Majesty for several weeks.

A woman was pointed out to me in a Music Hall in Knightsbridge, who my informant told me he was positively assured had only yesterday had two buboes lanced; and yet she was present at that scene of apparent festivity, contaminating the very air, like a deadly upas tree, and poisoning the blood of the nation, with the most audacious recklessness. It is useless to say that such things should not be. They exist, and they will exist. The woman was nothing better than a paid murderess, committing crime with impunity. She was so well known that she had obtained the soubriquet of the "hospital," as she was so frequently an inmate of one, and as she so often sent others to a similar involuntary confinement.

Those women whom, for the sake of distinguishing them from the professionals, I must call amateurs, are generally spoken of as "Dollymops." Now many servant-maids, nursemaids who go with children into the Parks, shop girls and milliners who may be met with at the various "dancing academies," so called, are "Dollymops." We must separate these latter again from the "Demoiselle de Comptoir," who is just as much in point of fact a "Dollymop," because she prostitutes herself for her own pleasure, a few trifling presents of a little money now and then, and not altogether to maintain herself. But she will not go to casinos, or any similar places to pick up men; she makes their acquaintance in a clandestine manner; either she is accosted in the street early in the evening as she is returning from her place of business to her lodgings, or she carries on a flirtation behind the counter, which, as a matter of course, ends in an assignation.

Soldiers are notorious for hunting up these women, especially nurse-maids and those that in the execution of their duty walk in the Parks, when they may easily be accosted. Nursemaids feel flattered by the attention that is lavished upon them, and are always ready to succumb to the "scarlet fever". A red coat is all powerful with this class, who prefer a soldier to a servant, or any other description of man they come in contact with.

This also answers the soldier's purpose equally well. He cannot afford to employ professional women to gratify his passions, and if he were to do so, he must make the acquaintance of a very low set of women, who in all probability will communicate some infectious disease to him. He feels he is never safe, and he is only too glad to seize the opportunity of forming an intimacy with a woman who will appreciate him for his own sake, cost him nothing but the trouble of taking her about with him occasionally, and who, whatever else may do, will never by any chance infect. I heard that some of the privates in the Blues and the brigade of Guards often formed very reprehensible connections with women of property, tradesmen's wives, and even ladies, who supplied them with money, and behaved with the greatest generosity to them, only stipulating for the preservation of secrecy in their intrigues. Of course, numbers of women throng the localities which contain the Knightsbridge, Albany Street, St. George's, Portman and Wellington Barracks in Birdcage Walk. They may have come up from the provinces: some women have been known to follow a particular regiment from place to place, all over the country, and have only left it when it has been under orders for foreign service.

A woman whom I met with near the Knightsbridge barracks, in one of the beerhouses there, told me she had been a soldiers' woman all her life.

"When I was sixteen," she said, "I went wrong. I'm up'ards of thirty now. I've been fourteen or fifteen years at it. It's one of those things you can't well leave off when you've once took to it. I was born in Chatham. We had a small baker's shop there, and I served customers and minded the shop. There's lots of soldiers at Chatham, as you know, and they used to look in at the window in passing, and nod and laugh whenever they could catch my eye. I liked to be noticed by the soldiers. At last one young fellow, a recruit, who had not long joined, I think, for he told me he hadn't been long at the depot, came in and talked to me. Well, this went on, and things fell out as they

always do with girls who go about with men, more especially
soldiers, and when the regiment went to Ireland, he gave me
a little money that helped me to follow it; and I went about
from place to place, time after time, always sticking to the same
regiment. My first man got tired of me in a year or two, but that
didn't matter. I took up with a sergeant then, which was a cut
above a private, and helped me on wonderful. When we were
at Dover, there was a militia permanently embodied artillery
regiment quartered with us on the western heights, and I got
talking to some of the officers, who liked me a bit. I was a ———
sight prettier then than I am now, you may take your dying
oath, and they noticed me uncommon: and although I didn't
altogether cut my old friends, I carried on with these fellows all
the time we were there, and made a lot of money, and bought
better dresses and some jewellery, that altered me wonderfully.
One officer offered to keep me if I would come and live with him.
He said he would take a house for me in the town, and keep a
pony carriage if I would consent; but although I saw it would
make me rise in the world, I refused. I was fond of my old associates, and did not like the society of gentlemen; so, when
the regiment left Dover, I went with them, and I remained with
them till I was five-and-twenty. We were then stationed in
London, and I one day saw a private in the Blues with one of my
friends, and for the first time in my life I fell in love. He spoke
to me, and I immediately accepted his proposals, left my old
friends, and went to live in a new locality, among strangers; and
I've been amongst the Blues ever since, going from one to the
other, never keeping to one long, and not particular as long
as I get the needful. I don't get much—very little, hardly enough
to live upon. I've done a little needlework in the daytime. I don't
now, although I do some washing and mangling now and then
to help it out. I don't pay much for my bed-room, only six bob
a week, and dear at that. It ain't much of a place. Some of the
girls about here live in houses. I don't; I never could abear it.
You ain't your own master, and I always liked my freedom. I'm
not comfortable, exactly; it's a brutal sort of life this. It isn't the
sin of it, though, that worries me. I don't dare think of that much,
but I do think how happy I might have been if I'd always lived
at Chatham, and married as other women do, and had a nice
home and children; that's what I want, and when I think of all
that, I do cut up. It's enough to drive a woman wild to think that

she's given up all chance of it. I feel I'm not respected either. If I have a row with any fellow, he's always the first to taunt me with being what he and his friends have made me. I don't feel it so much now. I used to at first. One dovetails into all that sort of thing in time, and the edge of your feelings, as I may say, wears off by degrees. That's what it is. And then the drink is very pleasant to us, and keeps up our spirits; for what could a woman in my position do without spirits, without being able to talk and blackguard and give every fellow she meets as good as he brings?"

It is easy to understand the state of mind of this woman, who had a craving after what she knew she never could possess, but which the maternal instinct planted within her forced her to wish for. This is one of the melancholy aspects of prostitution. It leads to nothing—marriage of course excepted; the prostitute has no future. Her life, saving the excitement of the moment, is a blank. Her hopes are all blighted, and if she has a vestige of religion left in her, which is generally the case, she must shudder occasionally at what she has merited by her easy compliance when the voice of the tempter sounded so sweetly.

The happy prostitute, and there is such a thing, is either the thoroughly hardened, clever infidel, who knows how to command men and use them for her own purposes; who is in the best set both of men and women; who frequents the night-houses in London, and who in the end seldom fails to marry well; or the quiet woman who is kept by the man she loves, and who she feels is fond of her; who has a provision made for her to guard her against want and the caprice of her paramour.

The sensitive, sentimental, weak-minded, impulsive, affectionate girl, will go from bad to worse, and die on a dunghill or in a workhouse. A woman who was well known to cohabit with soldiers, of a masculine appearance but good features, and having a good-natured expression, was pointed out to me as the most violent woman in the neighbourhood. When she was in a passion she would demolish everything that came in her way, regardless of the mischief she was doing. She was standing in the bar of a public-house close to the barracks talking to some soldiers, when I had an opportunity of speaking to her. I did not allow it to pass without taking advantage of it. I told her I had heard she was very passionate and violent.

"Passionate!" she replied; "I believe yer. I knocked my father down and well-nigh killed him with a flat-iron before I wor twelve years old. I was a beauty then an' I ain't improved much since I've been on my own hook. I've had lots of rows with these 'ere sodgers, and they'd have slaughter'd me long afore now if I had not pretty near cooked their goose. It's a good bit of it self-defence with me now-a-days, I can tell yer. Why, look here; look at my arm where I was run through with a bayonet once three or four years ago."

She bared her arm and exhibited the scar of what appeared to have once been a serious wound.

"You wants to know if them rowses is common. Well, they is, and it's no good one saying they ain't and the sodgers is such —— cowards they think nothing of sticking a woman when they'se riled and drunk, or they'll wop us with their belts. I was hurt awful onst by a blow from a belt; it hit me on the back part of the head, and I was laid up weeks in St. George's Hospital with a bad fever. The sodger who done it was quodded, but only for a drag* and he swore to God as how he'd do for me the next time as he comed across me. We had words sure enough, but I split his skull with a pewter, and that shut him up for a time. You see this public; well, I've smashed up this place before now; I've jumped over the bar, because they wouldn't serve me without paying for it when I was hard up, and I've smashed all the tumblers and glass, and set the cocks a-going, and fought like a brick when they tried to turn me out, and it took two peelers to do it; and then I lamed one of the bobbies for life by hitting him on the shin with a bit of iron—a crow or summet, I forget what it was. How did I come to live this sort of life? Get along with your questions. If you give me any of your cheek, I'll —— soon serve you the same."

I may easily be supposed I was glad to leave this termagant, who was popular with the soldiers, although they were afraid of her when she was in a passion. There is not much to be said about soldiers' women. They are simply low and cheap; often diseased, and as a class do infinite harm to the health of the service.

Thieves' Women

THE metropolis is divided by the police into districts, to which letters are attached to designate and distinguish them. The

---

* Imprisoned for three months.

head-quarters of the F division are at Bow Street, and the jurisdiction of its constabulary extends over Covent Garden, Drury
Lane and St. Giles's, which used formerly to be looked upon as
most formidable neighbourhoods, harbouring the worst characters
and the most desperate thieves.

Mr. Durkin, the superintendent at Bow Street, obligingly allowed
an intelligent and experienced officer (Sergeant Bircher) to give
me any information I might require.

Fifteen or twenty years ago this locality was the perpetual
scene of riot and disorder. The public-houses were notorious for
being places of call for thieves, pick-pockets, burglars, thieving
prostitutes, hangers-on (their associates), and low ruffians, who
rather than work for an honest livelihood preferred scraping
together a precarious subsistence by any disreputable means,
however disgraceful or criminal they might be. But now this
is completely changed. Although I patrolled the neighbourhood
on Monday night, which is usually accounted one of the noisiest
in the week, most of the public houses were empty, the greatest
order and decorum reigned in the streets, and not even an Irish
row occurred in any of the low alleys and courts to enliven the
almost painful silence that everywhere prevailed. I only witnessed
one fight in a public-house in St. Martin's Lane. Seven or eight
people were standing at the bar, smoking and drinking. A disturbance took place between an elderly man, pugnaciously intoxicated, who was further urged on by a prostitute he had been
talking to, and a man who had the appearance of being a tradesman in a small way. How the quarrel originated I don't know, for
I did not arrive till it had commenced. The sergeant who accompanied me was much amused to observe among those in the bar
three suspicious characters he had for some time "had his eye on."
One was a tall, hulking hang-dog looking fellow; the second a
short, bloated, diseased, red-faced man, while the third was a
common-looking woman, a prostitute and the associate of the
two former. The fight went on until the tradesman in a small way
was knocked head over heels into a corner, when the tall, hulking
fellow obligingly ran to his rescue, kindly lifted him up, and
quietly rifled his pockets. The ecstasy of the sergeant as he
detected this little piece of sharp practice was a thing to remember. He instantly called my attention to it, for so cleverly and
skilfully had it been done that I had failed to observe it.

When we resumed our tour of inspection the sergeant, having

mentally summed up the three suspicious characters, observed:
"I first discovered them in Holborn three nights ago, when I was
on duty in plain clothes. I don't exactly yet know rightly what
their little game is; but it's either dog-stealing or 'picking-up.'
This is how they do it. The woman looks out for a 'mug,' that is
a drunken fellow, or a stupid, foolish sort of fellow. She then
stops him in the street, talks to him, and pays particular attention to his jewellery, watch, and everything of that sort, of which
she attempts to rob him. If he offers any resistance, or makes a
noise, one of her bullies comes up and either knocks him down
by a blow under the ear, or exclaims: 'What are you talking to
my wife for?' and that is how the thing's done, sir, that's exactly
how these chaps do the trick. I found out where they live yesterday. It's somewhere down near Barbican, Golden Lane; the
name's a bad, ruffianly, thievish place. They are being watched to-night, although they don't know it. I planted a man on
them." Two women were standing just outside the same public.
They were dressed in a curious assortment of colours, as the
low English invariably are, and their faces had a peculiar
unctuous appearance, somewhat Israelitish, as if their diet from
day to day consisted of fried fish and dripping. The sergeant
knew them well, and they knew him, for they accosted him.
"One of these women," he said, "is the cleverest thief out. I've
known her twelve years. She was in the first time for robbing
a public. I'll tell you how it was. She was a pretty woman—a
very pretty woman — then, and never knocked about at night
publics or any of those places: had been kept by a man who
allowed her £4 a week for some time. She was very quiet too,
never went about anywhere, but she got into bad company, and
was in for this robbery. She and her accomplices got up a row in
the bar, everything being concerted beforehand; they put out
the lights, set all the taps running, and stole a purse, a watch, and
some other things; but we nabbed them all, and, strange to say,
one of the women thieves died the next day from the effects of
drink. All these women are great gluttons, and when they get any
money, they go in for a regular drink and debauch. This one
drank so much that it positively killed her slick off."
    At the corner of Drury Lane I saw three women standing
talking together. They were innocent of crinoline, and the
antiquity of their bonnets and shawls was really wonderful,
while the durability of the fabric of which they were composed

was equally remarkable. Their countenances were stolid, and their skin hostile to the application of soap and water. The hair of one was tinged with silver. They were inured to the rattle of their harness; the clank of the chains pleased them. They had *grown grey* as prostitutes.

I learnt from my companion that "that lot was an inexpensive luxury; it showed the sterility of the neighbourhood. They would go home with a man for a shilling, and think themselves well paid, while sixpence was rather an exorbitant amount for the temporary accommodation their vagrant amour would require."

There were a good many of them about. They lived for the most part in small rooms at eighteen pence, two shillings, and half-a-crown a week, in the small streets running out of Drury Lane.

We went down Charles Street, Drury Lane, a small street near the Great Mogul public-house. I was surprised at the number of clean-looking, respectable lodging-houses to be seen in this street, and indeed in almost every street thereabouts. Many of them were well-ventilated, and chiefly resorted to by respectable mechanics. They are under the supervision of the police, and the time of a sergeant is wholly taken up in inspecting them. Visits are made every day, and if the Act of Parliament by the provisions of which they are allowed to exist, and by which they are regulated, is broken, their licences are taken away directly. Some speculators have several of these houses, and keep a shop as well, full of all sorts of things to supply their lodgers.

There is generally a green blind in the parlour window, upon which you sometimes see written, Lodgings for Travellers 3*d*. a night, or, Lodgings for Gentlemen; or Lodgings for Single Men. Sometimes they have Model Lodging-house written in large black letters on a white ground on the wall. There are also several little shops kept by general dealers, in contiguity, for the use of the lodging-houses, where they can obtain two pennyworth of meat and "a ha'porth" of bread, and everything else in proportion.

There are a great number of costermongers about Drury Lane and that district, and my informant assured me that they found the profession very lucrative, for the lower orders, and industrial classes, don't care about going into shops to make purchases. They infinitely prefer buying what they want in the open street from the barrow or stall of a costermonger.

What makes Clare Market so attractive, too, but the stalls and barrows that abound there?

There are many flower-girls who are sent out by their old gin-drinking mothers to pick up a few pence in the street by the sale of their goods. They begin very young, often as young as five and six, and go on till they are old enough to become prostitutes, when they either leave off costermongering altogether, or else unite the two professions. They are chiefly the offspring of Irish parents, or cockney Irish, as they are called, who are the noisiest, the most pugnacious, unprincipled and reckless part of the population of London. There is in Exeter Street, Strand, a very old established and notorious house of ill-fame, called the ———, which the police says is always honestly and orderly conducted. Married women go there with their paramours, for they are sure of secrecy, and have confidence in the place. It is a house of accommodation, and much frequented; rich tradesmen are known to frequent it. They charge ten shillings and upwards for a bed. A man might go there with a large sum of money in his pocket, and sleep in perfect security, for no attempt would be made to deprive him of his property.

There is a coffee-house in Wellington Street, on the Covent Garden side of the Lyceum Theatre, in fact adjoining the playhouse, where women may take their men; but the police cannot interfere with it, because it is a coffee-house, and not a house of ill-fame, properly so called. The proprietor is not supposed to know who his customers are. A man comes with a woman and asks for a bed-room; they may be travellers, they may be a thousand things. A subterranean passage, I am told, running under the Lyceum connects this with some supper rooms on the other side of the theatre, which belongs to the same man who is proprietor of the coffee and chop house.

We have before spoken of "dress-lodgers"; there are several to be seen in the Strand. Any one who does not understand the affair, and had not been previously informed, would fail to observe the badly-dressed old hag who follows at a short distance the fashionably-attired young lady, who walks so gaily along the pavement, and who only allows the elasticity of her step to subside into a quieter measure when stopping to speak to some likely-looking man who may be passing. If her overtures are successful she retires with her prey to some den in the vicinity.

The watcher has a fixed salary of so much per week, and never loses sight of the dress-lodger, for very plain reasons. The dress-lodger probably lives some distance from the immoral house by whose owner she is employed. She comes there in the afternoon badly dressed, and has good things lent her. Now if she were not watched she might decamp. She might waste her time in public-houses; she might take her dupes to other houses of ill-fame, or she might pawn the clothes she has on; the keeper could not sue her for a debt contracted for immoral purposes. The dress-lodger gets as much money from her man as she can succeed in abstracting, and is given a small percentage on what she obtains by her employer. The man pays usually five shillings for the room. Many prostitutes bilk their man; they take him into a house, and then after he has paid for a room leave him. The dupe complains to the keeper of the house, but of course fails to obtain any redress.

I happened to see an old woman in the Strand, who is one of the most hardened beggars in London. She has two children with her, but one she generally disposes of by placing her in some doorway. The child falls back on the step, and pretends to be asleep or half-frozen with the cold. Her naturally pale face gives her a half-starved look, which completes her pitiable appearance. Any gentleman passing by being charitably inclined may be imposed upon and induced to touch her on the shoulder. The child will move slowly and rub her eyes, and the man, thoroughly deceived, gives her alms and passes on, when the little deceiver again composes herself to wait for the next chance. This occurred while I was looking on; but unfortunately for the child's success the policeman on the beat happened to come up, and she made her retreat to a safer and more convenient locality.

Many novelists, philanthropists, and newspaper writers have dwelt much upon the horrible character of a series of subterranean chambers or vaults in the vicinity of the Strand, called the Adelphi Arches. It is by no means even now understood that these arches are the most innocent and harmless places in London, whatever they might once have been. A policeman is on duty there at night, expressly to prevent persons who have no right or business there from descending into their recesses.

They were probably erected in order to form a foundation for the Adelphi Terrace. Let us suppose there were no wharves, and no embankments, consequently the tide must have ascended and gone inland some distance, rendering the ground marshy, swampy and next to useless. The main arch is a very fine pile of masonry, something like the Box tunnel on a small scale, while the other, running here and there like the intricacies of catacombs, looks extremely ghostly and suggestive of Jack Sheppards, Blueskins, Jonathan Wilds, and others of the same kind, notwithstanding they are so well lighted with gas. There is a doorway at the end of a vault leading up towards the Strand, that has a peculiar tradition attached to it. Not so very many years ago this door was a back exit from a notorious coffee and gambling house, where parties were decoyed by thieves, blacklegs or prostitutes, and swindled, then drugged, and subsequently thrown from this door into the darkness of what must have seemed to them another world, and were left, when they came to themselves, to find their way out as best they could.

My attention was attracted, while in these arches, by the cries and exclamations of a woman near the river, and proceeding to the spot I saw a woman sitting on some steps, before what appeared to be a stable, engaged in a violent altercation with a man who was by profession a cab proprietor—several of his vehicles were lying about—and who, she vehemently asserted, was her husband. The man declared she was a common woman when he met her, and had since become the most drunken creature it was possible to meet with. The woman put her hand in her pocket and brandished something in his face, which she triumphantly said was her marriage-certificate. "That," she cried, turning on me, "that's what licks them. It don't matter whether I was one of Lot's daughters afore. I might have been awful, I don't say I wasn't, but I'm his wife, and this 'ere's what licks 'em."

I left them indulging in elegant invectives, and interlarding their conversation with those polite and admirable metaphors that have gained so wide-spread a reputation for the famous women who sell fish in Billingsgate; and I was afterwards informed by a sympathising bystander, in the shape of a stable-boy, that the inevitable result of this conjugal altercation would be the incarceration of the woman, by the husband, in a horse-box, where she might undisturbed sleep off the effects of her potations, and repent the next day at her leisure. "Nec dulces amores sperne puer."

Several showily-dressed if not actually well-attired women, who are to be found walking about the Haymarket, live in St. Giles's and about Drury Lane. But the lowest class of women, who prostitute themselves for a shilling or less, are the most curious and remarkable class in this part. We have spoken of them before as growing grey in the exercise of their profession. One of them, a woman over forty, shabbily dressed, and with a disreputable, unprepossessing appearance, volunteered the following statement for a consideration of a spirituous nature.

"Times is altered, sir, since I come on the town. I can remember when all the swells used to come down here-away, instead of going to the Market; but those times is past, they is, worst luck, but, like myself, nothing lasts for ever, although I've stood my share of wear and tear, I have. Years ago Fleet Street and the Strand, and Catherine Street, and all round there was famous for women and houses. Ah! those were the times. Wish they might come again, but wishing's no use, it ain't. It only makes one miserable thinking of it. I come up from the country when I was quite a gal, not above sixteen, I dessay. I come from Dorsetshire, near Lyme Regis, to see a aunt of mine. Father was a farmer in Dorset, but only in a small way—tenant farmer, as you would say. I liked being out at night when I could get the chance. One night I went up the area and stood looking through the railing, when a man passed by, but seeing me he returned and spoke to me something about the weather. I, like a child, answered him unsuspectingly enough, and he went on talking about town and country, asking me, among other things, if I had long been in London, or if I was born there. I not thinking told him all about myself; and he went away apparently very much pleased with me, saying before he went that he was very glad to have made such an agreeable acquaintance, and if I would say nothing about it he would call for me about the same time, or a little earlier, if I liked, the next night, and take me out for a walk. I was, as you may well suppose, delighted, and never said a word. The next evening I met him as he appointed, and two or three times subsequently. One night we walked longer than usual, and I pressed him to return, as I feared my aunt would find me out; but he said he was so fatigued with walking so far, he would like to rest a little before he went back again; but if I was very anxious he would put me in a cab. Frightened about him, for I thought he might be ill, I preferred risking being found out; and when he proposed that we should go into some house and sit down I agreed. He said all at once, as if he had just remembered something, that a very old friend of his lived near there, and we couldn't go to a better place, for she would give us everything we could wish.

We found the door half open when we arrived. 'How careless,' said my friend, 'to leave the street-door open; any one might get in.' We entered without knocking, and seeing a door in the passage standing ajar we went in. My friend shook hands with an old lady who was talking to several girls dispersed over different parts of the room, who, she said, were her daughters. At this announcement some of them laughed, when she got very angry and ordered them out of the room. Somehow I didn't like the place, and not feeling all right I asked to be put in a cab and sent home. My friend made no objection and a cab was sent for. He, however, pressed me to have something to drink before I started. I refused to touch any wine, so I asked for some coffee, which I drank. It made me feel very sleepy, so sleepy indeed that I begged to be allowed to sit down on the sofa. They accordingly placed me on the sofa, and advised me to rest a little while, promising, in order to allay my anxiety, to send a messenger to my aunt. Of course I was drugged, and so heavily I did not regain consciousness till the next morning. I was horrified to discover that I had been ruined, and for some days I was inconsolable, and cried like a child to be killed or sent back to my aunt.

"When I became quiet I received a visit from my seducer, in whom I had placed so much silly confidence. He talked very kindly to me, but I would not listen to him for some time. He came several times to see me, and at last said he would take me away if I liked, and give me a house of my own. Finally, finding how hopeless all was I agreed to his proposal and he allowed me four pounds a week. This went on for some months, till he was tired of me, when he threw me over for some one else. There is always as good fish in the sea as ever came out of it, and this I soon discovered.

"Then for some years—ten years, till I was six-and-twenty— I went through all the changes of a gay lady's life, and they're not a few, I can tell you. I don't leave off this sort of life because I'm in a manner used to it, and what could I do if I did? I've no character; I've never been used to do anything, and I don't see what employment I stand a chance of getting. Then if I had to sit hours and hours all day long and part of the night, too, sewing or anything like that, I should get tired. It would worrit me so; never having been accustomed, you see, I couldn't stand it. I lodge in Charles Street, Drury Lane, now. I did live in Nottingham Court once, and Earls Street. But, Lord, I've lived in a many places you wouldn't think, and I don't imagine you'd believe one half. I'm always a-chopping and a-changing like the wind as you may say. I pay half-a-crown a week for my bed-room; it's clean and comfortable, good enough for such as me. I don't think much of my way of life. You folks as has honour, and character, and feelings, and such, can't understand how all that's been beaten out of people like me. I don't feel. *I'm used to it.* I did once, more especial when mother died. I heard on it through a friend of mine, who told me her last words was of me. I did cry and go on then ever so, but Lor', where's the good of fretting? I aren't happy either. It isn't happiness, but I get enough money to keep me in victuals and drink, and it's the drink mostly that keeps me going. You've no idea how I look forward to my drop of gin. It's everything to me. I don't suppose I'll live much longer, and that's another thing that pleases me. I don't want to live, and yet I don't care enough about dying to make away with myself. I arn't got that amount of feeling that some has, and that's where it is. I'm kinder 'fraid of it.''

This woman's tale is a condensation of the philosophy of sinning. The troubles she had gone through, and her experience of the world, had made her oblivious of the finer attributes of human nature, and she had become brutal.

I spoke to another who had been converted at a Social Evil Meeting, but from a variety of causes driven back to the old way of living.

The first part of her story offered nothing peculiar. She had been on the town for fifteen years, when a year or so ago she heard of the Midnight Meeting and Baptist Noel. She was induced from curiosity to attend; and her feelings being powerfully worked upon by the extraordinary scene, the surroundings, and the earnestness of the preacher, she accepted the offer held out to her, and was placed in a cab with some others, and conveyed to one of the numerous metropolitan homes, where she was taken care of for some weeks, and furnished with a small sum of money to return to her friends. When she arrived at her native village in Essex, she only found her father. Her mother was dead; her sister at service, and her two brothers had enlisted in the army. Her father was an old man, supported by the parish, so it was clear he could not support her. She had a few shillings left, with which she worked her way back to town, returned to her old haunts, renewed her acquaintance with her vicious companions, and resumed her old course of life.

I don't insert this recital as a reflection upon the refuges and homes, or mean to asperse the Midnight Meeting movement, which is worthy of all praise. On the contrary, I have much pleasure in alluding to the subject and acknowledging the success that has attended the efforts of the philanthropic gentlemen associated with the Rev. Mr. Baptist Noel.

I have already described the condition of low and abandoned women in Spitalfields, Whitechapel, Wapping, and Shadwell, although I have not touched very closely upon those who cohabit with thieves and other desperate characters, whose daily means of obtaining a livelihood exposes them to the penalties the law inflicts upon those who infringe its provisions. Their mode of living, the houses they inhabit, and the way in which they pass their time, does not very materially differ from that of other prostitutes, with this exception, they are not obliged to frequent casinos, dancing rooms, and other places of popular resort, to make acquaintances that may be of service to them in a pecuniary way, although they do make use of such places for the purposes of robbery and fraud. Some women of tolerably good repute—that is, who are regarded as knowing a good set of men, who have admission to the night-houses in Panton Street and the Haymarket—I am informed, are connected with thieves. The night-houses and supper-rooms in the neighbourhood of the Haymarket are for the most part in the hands of a family of Jews. Kate Hamilton's in Princes Street, Leicester Square, belongs to one of this family. She is given a percentage on all the wine that she sells during the course of the evening, and as she charges twelve shillings a bottle for Moselle and sparkling wines, it may readily be supposed that her profits are by no means despicable. Lizzie Davis's, Sams's, Sally's, and, I believe, the Carlton, also belong to this family. One of these Jews, I am told, was some few years back imprisoned for two years on a charge of manslaughter. He was proprietor of a brothel in the vicinity of Drury Lane, and the manslaughter occurred through his instrumentality on the premises. I have been informed by the police that some of the proprietors of these night-houses are well-known receivers of stolen goods, and the assertion is easily credible. To exemplify this I will relate a story told me by a sergeant of the H division. Some two years ago a robbery was committed by a "snoozer," or one of those thieves who take up their quarters at hotels for the purpose of robbery. The robbery was committed at an hotel in Chester.

The thief was captured, and the Recorder sentenced him to be imprisoned. This man was a notorious thief, and went under the soubriquet of American Jack. He was said to have once been in a very different position. He was polished in his manners, and highly accomplished. He could speak three or four languages with facility, and was a most formidable and dexterous thief, causing much apprehension and trouble to the police. After being incarcerated for a few weeks he contrived in a clever manner to make his escape from one of the London prisons; it was supposed by the connivance of his gaolers, who were alleged to have been bribed by his friends without. Be this as it may, he effected his liberation, and was successfully concealed in London until the hue and cry was over, and then shipped off to Paris. But the night after he escaped he perpetrated the most audacious robbery. He was dressed by his friends, and having changed his prison attire went to B—— Hotel, a well-known place, not far from the Freemasons Tavern, where, singularly enough, the Recorder of Chester, who had sentenced him, chanced to be staying. American Jack had the presumption to enter into conversation with the Recorder, who fancied he had seen his face before, but could not recollect where. The visitors had not long retired to bed before American Jack commenced operations. He was furnished by his accomplice with a highly-finished instrument for housebreaking, which, when inserted in the lock, would pass through and grasp the key on the inside. This done, it was easy to turn the key and open the door. The thief actually broke into sixteen or seventeen rooms that night, and made his exit before daybreak loaded with booty of every description. The proprietors of the hotel would offer no reward, as they feared publicity. The Recorder of Chester, when the robbery was discovered, remembered that the person he had conversed with the night before was the man he had convicted and sentenced at the assizes. He repaired to Bow Street with his information, and the police were put on the scent; but it is well known if no reward is offered for the apprehension of an eminent criminal the police are not so active as they are when they have a monetary inducement to incite them to action. It was imagined that American Jack had taken refuge with his friends near the Haymarket. A waiter who had been discharged from one of the night-houses was known slightly to a sergeant of police, who interrogated him on the subject. This waiter confessed that he could point out the whereabouts of the thief, and would do so for twenty pounds, which reward no one concerned in the matter would offer; and, as I have already stated, the criminal soon after made his escape to Paris, where he continued to carry on his depredations with considerable skill, until one day he mixed himself up in a great jewel robbery, and was apprehended by the *gendarmes*, and sent to the galleys for some time, where he is now languishing.

This little history is suggestive—why should not Parliament vote every year a small sum of money to form a "Detective and Inquiry Fund," from which the Commissioners of Police at Whitehall and Old Jewry might offer rewards for the capture of offenders? Some spur and inducement surely might be given to our detectives, who take a great deal of trouble, and, if unsuccessful, are almost always out of pocket through their researches.

Cannot Sir Richard Mayne and Mr. Daniel Whittle Harvey improve on this idea?

The police enter the night-houses every evening to see if spirits are sold on the premises; but as there are bullies at all the doors, and a code of signals admirably concerted to convey intelligence of the approach of the officers to those within, everything is carefully concealed, and the police are at fault. They might if they chose detect the practices they very well know are commonly carried on; but they either are not empowered to go to extremities, or else they do not find it their interest to do so. I have heard, I know not with what truth, that large sums of money are paid to the police to insure their silence and compliance; but until this is established it must be received with hesitation, though circumstances do occur that seem strongly to corroborate such suspicions. The women who cohabit with thieves are not necessarily thieves themselves, although such is often the case. Most pickpockets make their women accomplices in their misdeeds, because they find their assistance so valuable to them, and indeed for some species of theft almost indispensable. There are numbers of young thieves on the other side of the water, and almost all of them cohabit with some girl or other. The depravity of our juvenile thieves is a singular feature in their character. It is not exactly a custom that they follow, but rather an inherent depravity on their part. They prefer an idle luxurious life, though one also of ignominy and systematic dishonour, to one of honesty and labour; and this is the cause of their malpractices, perhaps inculcated at first by the force of evil example and bad bringing up, and invigorated every day by independence brought about by the liberty allowed them, the consequence of parental neglect.

It is of course difficult to give the stories of any of these women, as they would only criminate themselves disagreeably by confessing their delinquencies; and it is not easy to pitch upon a thieves' woman without she is pointed out by the police, and even then she would deny the imputation indignantly.

Park Women, or Those Who Frequent The Parks At Night and Other Retired Places

PARK women, properly so called, are those degraded creatures, utterly lost to all sense of shame, who wander about the paths most frequented after nightfall in the Parks, and consent to any species of humiliation for the sake of acquiring a few shillings. You may meet them in Hyde Park, between the hours of five and ten (till the gates are closed) in winter. In the Green Park, in what is called the Mall, which is a nocturnal thoroughfare, you may see these low wretches walking about sometimes with men, more generally alone, often early in the morning. They are to be seen reclining on the benches placed under the trees, originally intended, no doubt, for a different purpose, occasionally with the head of a drunken man reposing in their lap. These women are well known to give themselves up to disgusting practices, that are alone gratifying to men of morbid and diseased imaginations. They are old, unsound, and by their appearance utterly incapacitated from practising their profession where the gas-lamps would expose the defects in their personal appearance, and the shabbiness of their ancient and dilapidated attire. I was told that an old woman, whose front teeth were absolutely wanting, was known to obtain a precarious livelihood by haunting the by-walks of Hyde Park, near Park Lane. The unfortunate women that form this despicable class have in some cases been well off, and have been reduced to their present condition by a variety of circumstances, among which are intemperance, and the vicissitudes natural to their vocation. I questioned one who was in the humour to be communicative, and she gave the subjoined replies to my questions: —

"I have not always been what I now am. Twenty years ago I was in a very different position. Then, although it may seem ludicrous to you, who see me as I now am, I was comparatively well off. If I were to tell you my history it would be so romantic you would not believe it. If I employ a little time in telling you, will you reward me for my trouble, as I shall be losing my time in talking to you? I am not actuated by mercenary motives exactly in making this request, but my time is my money and I cannot afford to lose either one or the other. Well, then, I am the daughter of a curate in Gloucestershire. I was never at school, but my mother educated me at home. I had one brother who entered the Church. When I was old enough I saw that the limited resources of my parents would not allow them to maintain me at home without seriously impairing their resources, and I proposed that I should go out as a governess. At first they would not hear of it; but I persisted in my determination, and eventually obtained a situation in a family in town. Then I was very pretty. I may say so without vanity or ostentation, for I had many admirers, among whom I numbered the only son of the people in whose house I lived. I was engaged to teach his two sisters, and altogether I gave great satisfaction to the family. The girls were amiable and tractable, and I soon acquired an influence over their generous dispositions that afforded great facilities for getting them on in their studies. My life might have been very happy if an unfortunate attachment to me had not sprung up in the young man that I have before mentioned, which attachment I can never sufficiently regret was reciprocated by myself.

"I battled against the impulse that constrained me to love him, but all my efforts were of no avail. He promised to marry me, which in an evil hour I agreed to. He had a mock ceremony performed by his footman, and I went into lodgings that he had taken for me in Gower Street, Tottenham Court Road. He used to visit me very frequently for the ensuing six months, and we lived together as man and wife. At the expiration of that time he took me to the sea-side, and we subsequently travelled on the Continent. We were at Baden when we heard of his father's death. This didn't trouble him much. He did not even go to England to attend the funeral, for he had by his conduct offended his father, and estranged himself from the remainder of his family. Soon letters came from a solicitor informing him that the provisions of the will discontinued the allowance of five hundred a year hitherto made to him, and left him a small sum of money sufficient to buy himself a commission in the army, if he chose to do so. This course he was strongly advised to take, for it was urged that he might support himself on his pay if he volunteered for foreign service. He was transported with rage when this communication reached him, and he immediately wrote for the legacy he was entitled to, which arrived in due course. That evening he went to the gaming table, and lost every farthing in the world. The next morning he was a corpse. His remains were found in a secluded part of the town, he having in a fit of desperation blown his brains out with a pistol. He had evidently resolved to take this step before he left me, if he should happen to be unfortunate, for he left a letter in the hands of our landlady to be delivered to me in the event of his not returning in the morning. It was full of protest-ations of affection for me, and concluded with an avowal of the fraud he had practised towards me when our acquaintance was first formed, which he endeavoured to excuse by stating his ob-jections to be hampered or fettered by legal impediments.

"When I read this, I somewhat doubted the intensity of the affection he paraded in his letter. I had no doubt about the fervour of my own passion, and for some time I was inconsolable. At length, I was roused to a sense of my desolate position, and to the necessity for action, by the solicitations and importunity of my landlady, and I sold the better part of my wardrobe to obtain sufficient money to pay my bills, and return to England. But fate ordered things in a different manner. Several of my husband's friends came to condole with me on his untimely decease; among whom was a young officer of considerable personal attractions, whom I had often thought I should have liked to love, if I had not been married to my friend's husband. It was this man who caused me to take the second fatal step I have made in my life. If I had only gone home, my friends might have forgiven everything. I felt they would, and my pride did not stand in my way, for I would gladly have asked and obtained their forgiveness for a fault in reality very venial, when the circumstances under which it was committed are taken into consideration.

"Or I might have represented the facts to the family; and while the mother mourned the death of her son, she must have felt some commiseration for myself.

"The officer asked me to live with him, and made the prospect he held out to me so glittering and fascinating that I yielded. He declared he would marry me with pleasure on the spot, but he would forfeit a large sum of money, that he must inherit in a few years if he remained single, and it would be folly not to wait until then. I have forgotten to mention that I had not any children. My constitution being very delicate, my child was born dead, which was a sad blow to me, although it did not seem to affect the man I regarded as my husband. We soon left Baden and returned to London, where I lived for a month very happily with my para- mour, who was not separated from me, as his leave of absence had not expired. When that event occurred he reluctantly left me to go to Limerick, where his regiment was quartered. There in all probability he formed a fresh acquaintance, for he wrote to me in about a fortnight, saying that a separation must take place be- tween us, for reasons that he was not at liberty to apprise me of, and he enclosed a cheque for fifty pounds, which he hoped would pay my expenses. It was too late now to go home, and I was driven to a life of prostitution, not because I had a liking for it, but as a means of getting enough money to live upon. For ten years I lived first with one man then with another, until at last I was infected with a disease, of which I did not know the evil effects if neglected. The disastrous consequence of that neglect is only too apparent now. You will be disgusted, when I tell you that it attacked my face, and ruined my features to such an extent that I am hideous to look upon, and should be noticed by no one if I frequented those places where women of my class most congre- gate; indeed, I should be driven away with curses and execra- tions."

This recital is melancholy in the extreme. Here was a woman endowed with a very fair amount of education, speaking in a superior manner, making use of words that very few in her posi- tion would know how to employ, reduced by a variety of circum- stances to the very bottom of a prostitute's career. In reply to my further questioning, she said she lived in a small place in West- minster called Perkins' Rents, where for one room she paid two shillings a week. The Rents were in Westminster, not far from Palace Yard. She was obliged to have recourse to her present way of living to exist; for she would not go to the workhouse, and she could get no work to do. She could sew, and she could paint in water-colours, but she was afraid to be alone. She could not sit hours and hours by herself, her thoughts distracted her, and drove her mad. She added, she once thought of turning Roman Catholic, and getting admitted into a convent, where she might make atone- ment for her way of living by devoting the rest of her life to penit- ence, but she was afraid she had gone too far to be forgiven. That was some time ago. Now she did not think she would live long, she had injured her constitution so greatly; she had some internal disease, she didn't know what it was, but a hospital surgeon told her it would kill her in time, and she had her moments, generally hours, of oblivion, when she was intoxicated, which she always was when she could get a chance. If she got ten shillings from a drunken man, either by persuasion or threats, and she was not scrupulous in the employment of the latter, she would not come to the Park for days, until all her money was spent; on an average, she came three times a week, or perhaps twice; always on Sunday, which was a good day. She knew all about the Refuges. She had been in one once, but she didn't like the system; there wasn't enough liberty, and too much preaching, and that sort of thing; and then they couldn't keep her there always; so they didn't know what to do with her. No one would take her into their service, because they didn't like to look at her face, which presented so dreadful an appearance that it frightened people. She always wore a long thick veil, that concealed her features, and made her interesting to the unsuspicious and unwise. I gave her the money I promised her, and advised her again to enter a Refuge, which she refused to do, saying she could not live long, and she would rather die as she was.

In the course of my peregrinations I met another woman, commonly dressed in old and worn-out clothes; her face was ugly and mature; she was perhaps on the shady side of forty. She was also perambulating the Mall. I knew she could only be there for one purpose, and I interrogated her, and I believe she answered my queries faithfully. She said: —

"I have a husband, and seven small children, the eldest not yet able to do much more than cadge a penny or so by carter-wheeling and tumbling in the street for the amusement of gents as rides outside 'busses. My husband's bedridden, and can't do nothink but give the babies a dose of 'Mother's Blessing' (that's laudanum, sir, or some sich stuff) to sleep 'em when they's squally. So I goes out begging all day, and I takes in general one of the kids in my arms and one as runs by me, and we sell hartifishal flowers, leastways 'olds 'em in our 'ands, and makes believe cos of the police, as is nasty so be as you 'as nothink soever, and I comes hout in the Parks, sir, at night sometimes when I've 'ad a bad day, and ain't made above a few pence, which ain't enough to keep us as we should be kept. I mean, sir, the children should have a bit of meat, and my ole man and me want some blue ruin to keep our spirits up; so I'se druv to it, sir, by poverty, and nothink on the face of God's blessed earth, sir, shouldn't have druv me but that for the poor babes must live, and who's they to look to but their 'ard-working but misfortunate mother, which she is now talking to your honour, and won't yer give a poor woman a hap'ny, sir? I've seven small children at home, and my 'usban's laid with the fever. You won't miss it, yer honour, only a 'apny for a poor woman as ain't 'ad a bit of bread between her teeth since yesty morning. I ax yer parding," she exclaimed, interrupting herself — "I forgot I was talking to yourself. I's so used though to this way of speaking, when I meant to ax you for summut I broke off into the old slang, but yer honour knows what I mean: ain't yer got ever a little sixpence to rejoice the heart of the widow?"

"You call yourself a widow now," I said, "while before you said you were married and had seven children. Which are you?"

"Which am I? The first I told you's the true. But Lor', I's up to so many dodges I gets what you may call confounded; sometimes I's a widder, and wants me 'art rejoiced with a copper, and then I's a hindustrious needlewoman thrown out of work and going to be druv into the streets if I don't get summut to do. Sometimes I makes a lot of money by being a poor old cripple as broke her arm in a factory, by being blowed hup when a steam-engine blowed herself hup, and I bandage my arm and swell it out hawful big, and when I gets home, we gets in some lush and 'as some frens, and goes in for a reglar blow-hout, and now as I have told yer honour hall about it, won't yer give us an 'apny as I observe before?"

It is very proper that the Parks should be closed at an early hour, when such creatures as I have been describing exist and practise their iniquities so unblushingly. One only gets at the depravity of mankind by searching below the surface of society; and for certain purposes such knowledge and information are useful and beneficial to the community. Therefore the philanthropist must overcome his repugnance to the task, and draw back the veil that is thinly spread over the skeleton.

THE DEPENDANTS OF PROSTITUTES

HAVING described the habits, etc., of different classes of prostitutes, I now come to those who are intimately connected with and dependent upon them. This is a very numerous class, and includes

"Bawds," or those who keep brothels, the followers of dress-lodgers, keepers of accommodation houses, procuresses, pimps, and panders, fancy men, and bullies.

Bawds

THE first head in our classification is "Bawds." They may be either men or women. More frequently they are the latter, though any one who keeps an immoral house, or bawdy-house, as it is more commonly called, is liable to that designation. Bawdy-houses are of two kinds. They may be either houses of accommodation, or houses in which women lodge, are boarded, clothed, &c., and the proceeds of whose prostitution goes in the pocket of the bawd herself, who makes a very handsome income generally by their shame.

We cannot have a better example of this sort of thing than the bawdy-houses in King's Place, St. James's, a narrow passage leading from Pall Mall opposite the "Guards Club" into King Street, not far from the St. James's theatre. These are both houses of accommodation and brothels proper. Men may take their women there, and pay so much for a room and temporary accommodation, or they may be supplied with women who live in the house. The unfortunate creatures who live in these houses are completely in the power of the bawds, who grow fat on their prostitution. When they first came to town perhaps they were strangers, and didn't know a soul in the place, and even now they would have nowhere to go to if they were able to make their escape, which is a very difficult thing to accomplish, considering they are vigilantly looked after night and day. They have nothing fit to walk about the streets in. They are often in bed all day, and at night dressed up in tawdry ball costumes. If they ever do go out on business, they are carefully watched by one of the servants: they generally end when their charms are faded by being servants of bawds and prostitutes, or else watchers, or perhaps both.

There are houses in Oxenden Street, too, where women are kept in this way.

A victim of this disgraceful practice told me she was entrapped when she was sixteen years old, and prostituted for some time to old men, who paid a high price for the enjoyment of her person.

"I was born at Matlock in Derbyshire," she began; "father was a stone-cutter, and I worked in the shop, polishing the blocks and things, and in the spring of '51 we heard of the Great Exhibition. I wished very much to go to London, and see the fine shops and that, and father wrote to an aunt of mine, who lived in London, to know if I might come and stay a week or two with her to see the Exhibition. In a few days a letter came back, saying she would be glad to give me a room for two or three weeks and go about with me. Father couldn't come with me because of his business, and I went alone. When I arrived, aunt had a very bad cold, and couldn't get out of bed. Of course, I wanted to go about and see things, for though I didn't believe the streets were paved with gold, I was very anxious to see the shops and places I'd heard so much about. Aunt said when she was better she'd take me, but I was so restless I would go by myself. I said nothing to aunt about it, and stole out one evening. I wandered about for some time, very much pleased with the novelty. The crowds of people, the flaring gas jets, and everything else, all was so strange and new, I was delighted. At last I lost myself, and got into some streets ever so much darker and quieter. I saw one door in the middle of the street open, that is standing a-jar. Thinking no harm, I knocked, and hearing no sound, and getting no answer, I knocked louder, when some one came and instantly admitted me, without saying a word. I asked her innocently enough where I was, and if she would tell me the way to Bank Place. I didn't know where Bank Place was, whether it was in Lambeth, or Kensington, or Hammersmith, or where; but I have since heard it is in Kensington. The woman who let me in, and to whom I addressed my questions, laughed at this, and said, 'Oh! yes, I wasn't born yesterday.' But I repeated, 'Where am I, and what am I to do?'

"She told me to 'ax,' and said she'd heard that before.

"I suppose I ought to tell you, before I go further," she explained, "that 'ax' meant ask, or find out.

"Just then a door opened, and an old woman came out of a room which seemed to me to be the parlour. 'Come in, my dear,' she exclaimed, 'and sit down.' I followed her into the room, and she pulled out a bottle of gin, asking me if I would have a drop of something short, while she poured out some, which I was too frightened to refuse. She said, 'I likes to be jolly myself and see others so. I'm getting on now. Ain't what I was once. But as I says, I likes to be jolly, and I always is. A old fiddle, you know, makes the best music.

" 'Market full, my dear,' she added, pushing the wine-glass of gin towards me. 'Ah! I s'pose not yet; too early, so it is. I's glad you've dropped in to see a body. I've noticed your face lots of times, but I thought you was one of Lotty's girls, and wouldn't condescend to come so far up the street, though, why one part should be better nor another, I'm sure, I can't make out.'

" 'Really you must make a mistake,' I interposed. 'I am quite a stranger in London; indeed I have only been three days in town. The fact is, I lost myself this evening, and seeing your door open, I thought I would come in and ask the way.'

"Whilst I was saying this, the old woman listened attentively. She seemed to drink in every word of my explanation, and a great change came over her features.

" 'Well, pet,' she replied, 'I'm glad you've come to my house. You must excuse my taking you for some one else; but you are so like a gal I knows, one Polly Gay. I couldn't help mistaking you. Where are you staying?'

"I told her I was staying with my aunt in Bank Place.

" 'Oh! really,' she exclaimed; 'well, that is fortunate, 'pon my word, that is lucky. I'm gladder than ever now you came to my shop—I mean my house—cos I knows your aunt very well. Me an' 'er's great frens, leastways was, though I haven't seen her for six months come next Christmas. Is she's took bad, is she? Ah! well, it's the weather, or somethink, that's what it is; we're all ill sometimes; and what is it as is the matter with her? Influenzy, is it? Now, Lor' bless us, the influenzy! Well, you'll stay with me to-night; you's ever so far from your place. Don't say No; you must, my dear, and we'll go down to aunt's to-morrow morning early; she'll be glad to see me, I know. She always was fond of her old friends.'

"At first I protested and held out, but at last I gave in to her persuasion, fully believing all she told me. She talked about my father, said she hadn't the pleasure of knowing him personally, but she'd often heard of him, and hoped he was quite well, more especially as it left her at that time. Presently she asked if I wasn't tired, and said she'd show me a room up-stairs where I should sleep comfortable no end. When I was undressed and in bed, she brought me a glass of gin and water hot, which she called a night-cap, and said would do me good. I drank this at her solicitation, and soon fell into a sound slumber. The 'night-cap' was evidently drugged, and during my state of insensibility my ruin was accomplished. The next day I was wretchedly ill and weak, but I need not tell you what followed. My prayers and entreaties were of no good, and I in a few days became this woman's slave, and have remained so ever since; though, as she has more than one house, I am occasionally shifted from one to the other. The reason of this is very simple. Suppose the bawd has a house in St. James's and one in Portland Place. When I am known to the habitués of St. James's, I am sent as something new to Portland Place, and so on."

If I were to expatiate for pages on bawds, I don't think I could give a better idea than this affords. Their characteristics are selfishness and avariciousness, combined with want of principle and the most unblushing effrontery.

Followers of Dress-Lodgers

I HAVE spoken before of dress-lodgers, and I now come to women who are employed by the keepers of the brothels in which the dress-lodgers live, to follow them when they are sent into the streets to pick up men. They are not numerous. They are only seen in the Strand and about the National Gallery. This species of vice is much magnified by people who have vivid imaginations. It might have assumed larger dimensions, but at the present time it has very much decreased. They follow the dress-lodgers for various reasons, which I have mentioned already. For the sake of perspicuity and putting things in their proper sequence, I may be excused for briefly recapitulating them. If they were not closely watched, they might, imprimis, make their escape with all the finery they have about them, which of course they would speedily dispose of for its market value to the highest-bidding Jew, and then take lodgings and set up on their own account. These unfortunate dress-lodgers are profoundly ignorant of the English law. If they were better acquainted with its provisions, they would know very well that the bawds would have no legal claim against them for money, board, or clothes, for if the bawds could prove any consideration, it would be an immoral one, and consequently bad in law. But the poor creatures think they are completely in the wretch's power, and dare not move hand or foot, or call their hair their own. Instances have been known of bawds cutting off the hair of their lodgers when it became long, and selling it if it was fine and beautiful for thirty shillings and two pounds.

There is a dress-lodger who perambulates the Strand every night, from nine, or before that even, till twelve or one, who is followed by the inseparable old hag who keeps guard over her to prevent her going into public-houses and wasting her time and money, which is the second reason for her being watched, and to see that she does not give her custom to some other bawdy-house, which is the third reason.

This follower is a woman of fifty, with grey hair, and all the peculiarities of old women, among which is included a fondness for gin, which weakness was mainly instrumental in enabling me to obtain from her what I know about herself and her class. She wore no crinoline, and a dirty cotton dress. Her bonnet was made of straw, with a bit of faded ribbon over it by way of trimming, fully as shabby and discreditable as the straw itself.

She told me by fits and starts, and by dint of cross questioning, the subjoined particulars.

"They call me 'Old Stock'; why I shan't tell you, though I might easy, and make you laugh too, without telling no lies; but it ain't no matter of your'n, so we'll let it be. They do say I'm a bit cracky, but that's all my eye. I'm a drunken old b——— if you like, but nothing worser than that. I was once the swellest woman about town, but I'm come down awful. And yet it ain't awful. I sometimes tries to think it is, but I can't make it so. If I did think it awful I shouldn't be here now; I couldn't stand it. But the fact is life's sweet, and I don't care how you live. It's as sweet to the w———, as it is to the hempress, and mebbe it's as sweet to me as it is to you. Yes, I was well known about some years ago, and I ain't got bad features now, if it wasn't for the wrinkles and the skin, which is more parchmenty than anything else, but that's all along of the drink. I get nothing in money for following this girl about, barring a shilling or so when I ask for it to get some liquor. They give me my grub and a bed, in return for which in the day-time I looks after the house, when I ain't drunk, and sweeps, and does the place up, and all that. Time was when I had a house of my own, and lots of servants, and heaps of men sighing and dying for me, but now my good looks are gone and I am what you see me. Many of the finest women, if they have strong constitutions, and can survive the continual racket, and the wear and tear of knocking about town, go on like fools without making any provision for themselves, and without marrying, until they come to the bad. They are either servants, or what I am, or if they get a little money given them by men, they set up as bawdy-house-keepers. I wish to God I had, but I don't feel what I am. I'm past that ever so long, and if you give me half a crown, or five bob, presently, you'll make me jolly for a week. Talking of giving a woman five bob reminds me of having fivers (£5 notes) given me. I can remember the time when I would take nothing but paper; always tissue, nothing under a flimsy. Ah! gay women see strange changes; wonderful ups and downs, I can tell you. We, that is me and Lizzie, the girl I'm watching, came out to-night at nine. It's twelve now, ain't it? Well; what do ye think we've done? We have taken three men home, and Lizzie, who is a clever little devil, got two pound five out of them for herself, which ain't bad at all. I shall get something when we get back. We ain't always so lucky. Some nights we go about and don't hook a soul. Lizzie paints a bit too much for decent young fellows who've got lots of money. They aren't our little game. We go in more for trades-men, shopboys, commercial travellers, and that sort, and men who are a little screwy, and although we musn't mention it, we hooks a white choker now and then, coming from Exeter Hall. Medical students are sometimes sweet on Lizzie, but we ain't in much favour with the Bar. Oh! I know what a man is directly he opens his mouth. Dress too has a great deal to do with what a man is—tells you his position in life as it were. 'Meds' ain't good for much; they're larky young blokes, but they've never much money, and they're fond of dollymopping. But talk of dollymopping—lawyers are the fellows for that. Those chambers in the Inns of Court are the ruin of many a girl. And they are so convenient for bilking, you've no idea. There isn't a good woman in London who'd go with a man to the Temple, not one. You go to Kate's, and take a woman out, put her in a cab, and say you were going to take her to either of the Temples, which are res-pectable and decent places when compared to the other inns which are not properly Inns of Court, except Gray's Inn and Lincoln's Inn, and she'd cry off directly. I mean Barnard's Inn, and Thavies' Inn, and New Inn, and Clement's Inn, and all those. I've been at this sort of work for six or seven years, and I suppose I'll die at it. I don't care if I do. It snits me. I'm good for nothing else."

I gave her some money in return for her story, and wished her good night. What she says about women who have once been

what is called "swell," coming down to the sort of thing I have
been describing, is perfectly true. They have most of them been
well-known and much admired in their time; but every dog has
its day. They have had theirs, and neglected to make hay while
the sun was shining. Almost all the servants of bawds and
prostitutes have fallen as it were from their high estate into the
slough of degradation and comparative despair.

As I have before stated, there are very few dress-lodgers now
who solicit in the streets, and naturally few followers of dress-
lodgers whose condition does not afford anything very striking or
peculiar, except as evidencing the vicissitudes of a prostitute's
career, and the end that very many of them arrive at.

Keepers of Accommodation Houses

THOSE who gain their living by keeping accommodation houses,
or what the French call *maisons de passé*, are of course to be
placed in the category of the people who are dependent on
prostitutes, without whose patronage they would lose their only
means of support.

When you speak of bawds you in a great measure describe
this class also, for their avocations are the same, and the system
they exist upon very similar. The bawds keep women in their
houses, and the others let out their rooms to chance comers,
and any one who chooses to take them. The keepers are generally
worn-out prostitutes, who have survived their good looks and
settled down, as a means of gaining a livelihood; in Oxenden
Street and similar places an enormous amount of money is made
by these people. The usual charge for rooms of course varies
according to the height and the size of the room engaged. A first-
floor room is worth seven or ten shillings, then the rooms on the
second-floor are five shillings, and three shillings, and so on.
The average gains of keepers of accommodation houses in
Oxenden Street and James Street, Haymarket, are from two
pounds to ten pounds a night; the amount depending a good
deal on the popularity of the house, its connection with women,
its notoriety amongst men, and its situation. More money is
made by bawdy-house keepers, but then the expenses are greater.
A story is told of a celebrated woman who kept a house of ill-fame
in the neighbourhood of May Fair. The several inmates of her
establishment were dilatory on one occasion, and she gave vent

to her anger and disappointment by exclaiming, "Twelve o'clock striking. The house full of noblemen, and not a —— girl painted yet." I introduce this anecdote merely to exemplify what I have been advancing, namely, that the best brothels in London, such as Mrs. C—'s in Curzon Street, and others that I could mention, are frequented by men who have plenty of money at their command, and spend it freely.

A Mrs. J—, who kept a house in James Street, Haymarket, where temporary accommodation could be obtained by girls and their paramours, made a very large sum of money by her house, and some time ago bought a house somewhere near Camberwell with her five-shilling pieces which she had the questionable taste to call "Dollar House". A woman who kept a house in one of the small streets near the Marylebone Road told me she could afford to let her rooms to her customers for eighteen pence for a short time, and three and sixpence for all night, and she declared she made money by it, as she had a good many of the low New Road women, and some of those who infest the Edgware Road, as well as several servants and dress-makers, who came with their associates. She added she was saving up money to buy the house from her landlord who at present charged her an exorbitant rent, as he well knew she could not now resist his extortionate demands. If he refused to sell it, she should go lower down in the same street for she was determined before long to be independent.

When we come to touch upon clandestine prostitution we shall have occasion to condemn these houses in no measured terms, for they offer very great facilities for the illicit intercourse of the not yet completely depraved portion of the sexes such as sempstresses, milliners, servant girls, etc., etc., etc., who only prostitute themselves occasionally to men they are well acquainted with, for whom they may have some sort of a partiality— women who do not lower themselves in the social scale for money but for their own gratification. They become, however, too frequently insensibly depraved, and go on from bad to worse, till nothing but the *pavé* is before them. The ruin of many girls is commenced by reading the low trashy wishy-washy cheap publications that the news shops are now gorged with, and by devouring the hastily-written, immoral, stereotyped tales about the sensualities of the upper classes, the lust of the aristocracy, and the affection that men about town—noble lords, illustrious dukes, and even princes of the blood—are in the habit of imbibing

for maidens of low degree "whose face is their fortune," shop girls, very often dressmakers and the rest of the tribe who may perhaps feel flattered by reading about absurd impossibilities that their untutored and romantic imaginations suggest may, during the course of a life of adventure, happen to themselves. Well, they wait day after day, and year after year for the duke or the prince of the blood, perfectly ready to surrender their virtue when it is asked for, until they open their eyes, regard the duke and the prince of the blood as apocryphal or engaged to somebody else more fortunate than themselves, and begin to look a little lower, and favourably receive the immodest addresses of a counter-jumper, or a city clerk, or failing those a ruffianly pot-boy may realize their dreams of the ideal; at all events, they are already demoralized by the trash that has corrupted their minds, and perfectly willing at the first solicitation to put money into the pockets of the keepers of accommodation houses.

Procuresses, Pimps and Panders

PROCURESSES are women who in most cases possess houses of their own, where they procure girls for men who employ them. These establishments are called "Introducing Houses", and are extremely lucrative to the proprietors. There are also men who go about for these people, finding out girls, and bringing them to the houses, where they may meet with men. The procuresses who keep introducing houses often take in women to lodge and board. But they are quite independent, and must be well-known about town, and kept by some one, or the procuress, if she is, comparatively speaking, in any position, will not receive them.

To show how the matter is accomplished let us suppose an introducing house of notoriety and good report in its way, somewhere in the neighbourhood of St. George's Road, Pimlico, a district which, I may observe, is prolific in loose women. A well-known professional man, a wealthy merchant, an M.P., or a rich landed proprietor, calls upon a lady of the house, orders some champagne, and enters into conversation about indifferent matters, until he is able delicately to broach the object he has in view. He explains that he wishes to meet with a quiet lady whose secrecy he can rely upon, and whom he can trust in every possible way. He would like her, we will imagine, to be vivacious, witty, and gay.

The lady of the house listens complacently, and replies that she knows some one who exactly answers the description the amorous M.P. has given, and says that she will send a message to her at once if he wishes, but he must take his chance of her being at home; if she is out, an appointment will be made for the next day. In the mean time a messenger is despatched to the lady in question, who in all probability does not reside at any great distance; perhaps in Stanley Street, or Winchester Street, which streets everybody knows are contiguous to St. George's Road, and inhabited by beauty that ridicules decorum and laughs at the virtuous restrictions that are highly conducive to a state of single blessedness and a condition of old-maidism. Some more champagne is ordered and consumed, every bottle of which costs the consumer fifteen shillings, making a profit to the vendor of at least seventy per cent. When the lady arrives, the introduction takes place, and the matter is finally arranged as far as the introducer is concerned. The woman so introduced generally gives half the money she obtains from the man to the keeper of the house for the introduction.

Sometimes these women will write to men who occupy a high position in society, who are well-known at the clubs, and are reputed to be well off, saying that they have a new importation in their houses from the country that may be disposed of for a pecuniary consideration of perhaps fifty or a hundred pounds. This amount of course is readily paid by men who are in search of artificial excitement, and the negotiation is concluded without any difficulty. A woman is usually seduced five or six times. By that I mean she is represented as a maid, and imposed upon men as a virgin, which fabrication, as it is difficult to disprove, is believed, more especially if the girl herself be well instructed, and knows how to carry out the fraud. The Burlington Arcade is a well-known resort of women on the long winter afternoons, when all the men in London walk there before dinner.

It is curious to notice how the places of meeting and appointment have sprung up and increased within the last few years. Not many years ago Kate Hamilton, if I am not misinformed, was knocking about town. Lizzie Davis's has only been open a year or two. Barns's very recently established, and the Oxford and Cambridge last season. The Café Riche three years ago used to be called Bignell's Café. Sam's I believe is the oldest of the night-houses about the Haymarket. The Café Royal, or Kate's, is the largest and the most frequented, but is not now so select as it used formerly to be. Mott's, or the Portland Rooms, used to be the most fashionable dancing place in London, and is now in very good repute. Formerly only men in evening dress were admitted, now this distinction is abolished, and every one indiscriminately admitted. This is beginning to have its effect, and in all likelihood Mott's will in a short time lose its prestige. It is always so with places of this description. Some peculiarity about the house, or some clever and notorious woman, presiding over its destinies, makes it famous; when these vanish or subside, then the place goes down gradually, and some other rival establishment takes its place.

Loose women, as I have before asserted, very often marry, and sometimes, as often as not, marry well. The other day one of the most well-known women about town, Mrs. S—, was married to a German count; a few weeks ago Agnes W— married a member of an old Norfolk family, who settled three thousand a year upon her. This case will most likely come before the public, as the family, questioning his sanity, mean to take out a writ of *de lunatico inquirendo*, when the facts will be elicited by counsel in a court of law. Indeed, so little was the gentleman himself satisfied with the match that a week after marriage he advertised his wife in the newspapers, saying he would not be held responsible for her further debts. These out of many others. A frequenter of the night-houses will notice many changes in the course of the year, although some well-known face will turn up now and then. The habitué may miss the accustomed laugh and unabashed impudence of the "nun," who always appeared so fascinating and piquante in her little "Jane Clarke" bonnet, and demure black silk dress. The "nun" may be far away with her regiment in Ireland, or some remote part of England; for be it known that ladies are attached to the service as well as men, and the cavalry rejoices more than the line in the softening influences of feminine society. Amongst the little scandals of the night, it may be rumoured within the sacred precincts of the Café Royal by "Suppers" of the Admiralty, who has obtained that soubriquet by his known unwillingness to stand these midnight banquets, that the "Baby" was seen at the Holborn with a heightened colour, rather the production of art than nature; *ergo*, the "Baby" is falling off, which remark it is fortunate for "Suppers" the "baby" does not overhear. Billy Valentine, of her Majesty's "horse and saddle" department of the Home Office, as is his usual custom, may be seen at Conney's, exchanging a little quiet chaff with "Poodle," whose hair is more crimped than ever, while the "Poodle" is dexterously extracting a bottle of Moselle out of him for the benefit of the establishment. There is a woman of very mature age who goes about from one night-house to another with her betting book in her hand, perhaps "cadging" for men. Then there is Madame S. S.—, who plays the piano in different places, and Dirty Dick, who is always in a state of intoxication; but who, as he spends his money freely, is never objected to.

But the night-houses are carrying me away from my subject.

Pimps are frequently spoken of, and pimping is a word very generally used, but I doubt very much whether many of them exist, at least of the male gender. The women do most of the pimping that is requisite to carry on the amours of London society, and pander is a word that merges into the other, losing any distinctive significance that it may possess for the eyes of a lexicographer. A woman when she introduces a man to a woman is literally pimping for him, or what I have said about keepers of introducing houses must apply generally to the panders and the pimps. I may add a story I heard of a bully attached to a brothel, who on one occasion acting as a pimp, went into the streets to pick up a woman who was required for the purposes of the establishment. He went some way without success, and at last met a "wandering beauty of the night," whom he solicited; she yielded to his entreaties, and followed him to his brothel. When they reached the light in the passage she raised her veil, when he was as horrified as a man in his position and with his feelings could be to perceive that he had brought his own sister to an immoral house: he had not seen her for some years. His profligacy had killed his father, had brought him to his present degraded position, and in a great measure occasioned his sister's fall and way of living.

Ex uno—the proverb says—a lesson may be taught a great many.

Fancy-Men

FANCY-MEN are an extremely peculiar class, and are highly interesting to those who take an interest in prostitutes and their associates. They are—that is the best of them—tolerably well-dressed and well-looking, and sufficiently gentlemanly for women

to like to be seen about with them. I am now speaking of those
who cohabit with the best women about town.

Parent Duchatelet asserts that it is a common thing for many
law students and medical students to be kept, or semi-supported,
by loose women in Paris. This is a state of things that I need
hardly say is never observed in England. Yet there is a class
who throw all their self-respect into the background, and allow
themselves to be partially maintained by loose women who have
imbibed a partiality for them. They frequent the night-houses
in Panton Street, and often hook gentlemen out of several sovereigns, or by tossing them for champagne make them pay for
several bottles in the course of the evening. The best of the
aristocracy of fancy-men, are for the most part on the turf. They
bet when they have money to bet with, and when they have not
they endeavour, without scruple, to procure it from their mistresses, who never hesitate a moment in giving it them if they have
it, or procuring it for them by some means, however degrading
such means may be. A fancy-man connected with a prostitute
who is acquainted with a good set of men will, as the evening
advances, be seen in one of the night-houses in Panton Street.
His woman will come in perhaps about one o'clock, accompanied
by one or two men. Whilst they are talking and drinking he will
come up and speak to the woman, as if she was an old flame of his,
and she will treat him in the same manner, though more as a
casual acquaintance. In the course of time he will get into conversation with her men, and they, taking him for a gentleman,
will talk to him in a friendly manner. After a while he will propose to toss them for a bottle of champagne or a Moselle cup.
Then the swindling begins. The fancy-man has an infallible recipe
for winning. He has in his hand a cover for the half-crown he
tosses with, which enables him to win, however the piece falls.
It is a sort of "heads I win, tails you lose," a principle with which
schoolboys of a speculative disposition bother their friends.
Sometimes the proprietor of the house will come up and begin
to talk to them, ask them to step upstairs to have supper, and
get them into a room where the victim may be legged more
quietly, and more at their leisure. The proprietor then says that
he must in his turn "stand" a bottle of champagne, but the
fancy-man, pretending to be indignant, interposes, and exclaims,
"No, let's toss": so they toss. The fancy-man loses the toss, pays
the proprietor at once with money, with which he has been

previously supplied, and the man is more completely gulled than
ever. He may be some man in the service up in town on leave for a
short while, and determined as long as he stays to go in for some
fun, no doubt well supplied with money, and careless how he
spends it. He would be very irate if he discovered how he was
being robbed, and in all likelihood smash the place up, and the
fancy-man into the bargain, for people are not very scrupulous
as to what they do in the night-houses. But the affair is managed
so skilfully that he loses his four or five pounds at tossing or at
some game or other with equanimity, and without a murmur,
for he thinks it is his luck which happens to be adverse, and never
dreams for one instant that his adversary is not playing on the
"square." The rows that take place in the night-houses never
find their way into the papers. It isn't the "little game" of the
proprietors to allow them, and the police, if they are called in,
are too well bribed to take any further notice, without they are
particularly requested. I was told of a disturbance that took
place in one of the night-houses in Panton Street, not more than
a year ago, which for brutality and savage ferocity I should think
could not be equalled by a scalping party of North American
Red Indians.

Two gentlemen had adjourned there after the theatre, and
were quietly drinking some brandy and soda, when a woman,
with a very large crinoline, came in and went up to one of them,
whom we will call A. She asked him for something to drink, and
he, perceiving she was very drunk already, chaffed her a little.
Angry at his persiflage, she leant over and seized his glass,
which she threw into a corner of the room, smashing it to atoms
and spilling its contents. While doing so her crinoline flew into
the air, and A. put out his hand to keep it down. She immediately
began to slang him and abuse him immoderately, declaring that he
had attempted to take indecent liberties with her, and attempting
finally to strike him; he good-humouredly held her hands, but
she got more furious every moment, and at last he had to push
her down rather violently into a chair. A man who was sitting
at an opposite table commented upon this in an audible and
offensive manner, which excessively annoyed A., who however
at first took no notice of his conduct. Presently he handed the
woman over to one of the waiters, who with some difficulty turned
her out. Then the man who had before spoken said, "D—d
plucky thing, by Jove, to strike a woman." A. made some reply

to this, and the other man got up, when A. flew at him and
knocked him down. Two waiters ran up and seized A. by either
arm, when the man got up from his recumbent position and
struck A., while he was being retained by the waiters, a tremendous blow in the face, which speedily covered him with blood.
A., exerting all his strength, liberated himself, and rushed at the
coward, knocking him over a table, jumping over after him,
seizing his head and knocking it against the floor in a frightful
manner. The door porters were then called in, and A. with great
difficulty turned out. A.'s friend had been waiting his opportunity,
which had not yet come. When A. was at the door the man he had
knocked down raised himself up. A.'s friend seized him by the
collar and by one of his legs, and threw him with all his force
along the table, which was covered with glass. The velocity with
which he was thrown drove everything before him until he fell
down on the top of the broken glass in a corner stunned and
bleeding. His assailant then put his head down and charged like
a battering-ram through the opposing throng, throwing them
right and left, till he joined his friend in the street.

Many low betting-men are partially kept by prostitutes—men
who frequent Bride Lane and similar places, who, when out of
luck, fall back upon their women. Many thieves, too, are fancy-
men, and almost all the ruffians who go about "picking up", as
the police call it, which I have explained before to be a species
of highway robbery. The prostitute goes up to a man, and while
she is talking to him the ruffians come up and plunder him. If the
victim is drunk so much the better. Most low prostitutes have
their fancy-men, such as waiters at taverns, labourers—loose
characters, half thieves half loafers. It is strange that such
baseness should find a place in a man, but experience proves
what I have said to be true; and there are numbers of men in the
metropolis who think nothing of being kept by a prostitute on
the proceeds of her shame and her disgrace.

Bullies

BULLIES are men attached to brothels and bawdy-houses; but
this remark must not be understood to apply to houses of a
superior description, for it would not pay them to extort money
from their customers, as they have a character and a reputation
to support.

The bullies attached to low bawdy-houses are ostensibly kept to perform the functions of door-keepers, but in reality to prevent men from going away without paying enough money; they are in many cases a necessary precaution against "bilking," or going away without paying anything. If a well-dressed man went into an immoral house in Spitalfields, Whitechapel, or Shadwell, he would assuredly be robbed, but not maltreated to any greater extent than was absolutely requisite to obtain his money, and other valuables he might chance to have about him, at the time the depredation was committed.

A man a little tipsy once found himself, he hardly knew how, on the transpontine side of Waterloo Bridge, not far from Stamford Street. It was past twelve, and on being accosted by a woman, he half unconsciously followed her to her rooms in Stamford Street, which were situated about half-way down, near Duke Street, Blackfriars. When upstairs he sent the servant out for some brandy and soda-water, and not having enough silver gave her half-a-sovereign for that purpose, telling her to bring him the change. She soon returned with a bottle of brandy, which she said cost eight shillings, and two bottles of soda-water, and keeping one shilling for herself, told him she had no change to give him; he put up with this extortion, for he was too tipsy to make any resistance. The time passed quickly, and he spent two or three hours in her society, until the soda-water somewhat sobered him, when he put on his hat and declared his intention of going away. The woman sprang up to stop him, and placed her back against the door, meantime calling some one with all her might. Being a strong powerful man, he seized her by the arm and flung her on a sofa. Opening the door, he heard some one rapidly coming up stairs; he rushed back to the room and laid hold of a chair, which he threw at the advancing figure; it missed it, but had the effect of causing it to retreat. Chair after chair followed until the room was nearly denuded of its furniture, the woman being all the time too frightened to take any part in the affray. The man next took the poker in one hand, the lamp in the other, and began to descend the stairs, which he did with some difficulty, as the chairs rather impeded his progress. He had no doubt his adversary was waiting for him at the bottom, and it was evident that it was there the real struggle would take place. He descended very cautiously until he was very near the head of the stairs, when he saw a tall strongly-built man awaiting him with a bludgeon in his hand. The gentleman carefully, in the short space he had, reconnoitred the exit to the street by throwing the light of the lamp full into the passage. The bully finding he was discovered began to curse and make demonstrations of hostility, but remained where he was, as he was possessed of the best position. The gentleman when he was within three or four steps of the ground, hurled the lamp with all his force at the bully, striking him on the forehead. The lamp was smashed to atoms, and everything directly plunged in darkness. After this he ran in the direction of the door, but he found the chain up: while he was unfastening this as well as he could in the dark, he heard his antagonist picking himself up and muttering threats of vengeance. In a moment or two he began to grope his way towards the door, but fortunately the gentleman had succeeded in undoing the chain, and flinging the door wide open, he emerged into the street and began to run in the direction of the Waterloo Road as fast as he could. He made his escape; but if he had not had presence of mind, and been strong and powerful enough to fight with the bully, the result might have been very different.

A man who would be a bully at a bawdy-house would stick at nothing. During the daytime they either sleep or lounge about smoking a short pipe, or go to the pawnshops for the women or else for the public or gin.

The men who used to keep the Cocoa in St. James's Street were two brothers, who when they were young, held a position of no great importance in their mother's house, which was nothing more than a house of ill fame. They might have degenerated into something the same sort, but they had a certain amount of talent and opportunities, and once being possessed of this gambling house, which was famous enough in its day, they made money quickly enough.

It is not men, though, who have been amongst these scenes when they are young, who take to this sort of life. It is generally returned convicts or gaol birds, who look upon themselves as victims, and get desperate, and do not care very much what they do as long as they can have an easy time of it and enough to eat and drink.

Sometimes, if they watch their opportunity, they may become proprietors of bawdy-houses themselves. Great events spring from little causes; and good management and a good locality will always make a bawdy-house remunerative; but bullies generally have no energy, and are wanting in administrative capability, and more often than not die of disease and excess in the gutter.

The Argyle Rooms were once a small public-house called the "Hall of Rome," where *tableaux vivants* and *poses plastiques* found a home and an audience, but energy and a combination of causes have made it the first casino in London.

A bully in a house on one of the streets near the Haymarket, who was loafing about a public-house, told me in return for some spirits I paid for, that he was a ticket-of-leave man— "he didn't mind saying it, why should he? he'd got his ticket of-leave, he had, and he'd show it me in two twos.

"When he comed back from Norfolk Island, which he'd been sent to for a term of seven years, he knew no one in town, his pals mostly was lagged by police, and his most hintimit friend was hanged by mistake at the Old Bailey—he know it was by mistake, as his friend was hincapable of such an act without he was riled extraordinary. Well, he took to the bullying dodge, which paid. He couldn't work, it wornt in his nature, and he took to bullying, kindly—it suited him, it just did, and that was all about it."

The bullies are the lowest ruffians going, and will not mind doing any act of iniquity, although they stand in great dread of the police, and generally manage so as to keep out of their clutches.

CLANDESTINE PROSTITUTES

THE next division of our subject is clandestine prostitution whose ramifications are very extensive. In it we must include: 1. Female operatives; 2. Maid-servants, all of whom are amateurs, as opposed to professionals, or as we have had occasion to observe before, more commonly known as "Dollymops"; 3. Ladies of intrigue, who see men to gratify their passions; and 4. Keepers of houses of assignation, where the last-mentioned class may carry on their amours with secrecy.

This in reality I regard as the most serious side of prostitution. This more clearly stamps the character of the nation. A thousand and one causes may lead to a woman's becoming a professional prostitute, but if a woman goes wrong without any very cogent reason for so doing, there must be something radically wrong in her composition, and inherently bad in her nature, to lead her to abandon her person to the other sex, who are at all times ready to take advantage of a woman's weakness and a woman's love.

There is a tone of morality throughout the rural districts of England, which is unhappily wanting in the large towns and the centres of particular manufactures. Commerce is incontestably demoralizing. Its effects are to be seen more and more every day. Why it should be so, it is not our province to discuss, but seduction and prostitution, in spite of the precepts of the Church, and the examples of her ministers, have made enormous strides in all our great towns within the last twenty years. Go through the large manufacturing districts, where factory hands congregate, or more properly herd together, test them, examine them, talk to them, observe for yourself, and you will come away with the impression that there is room for much improvement. Then cast your eye over the statistics of births and the returns of the Registrar General, and compare the number of legitimate with illegitimate births. Add up the number of infanticides and the number of deaths of infants of tender years—an item more alarming than any. Goldsmith has said that "honour sinks when commerce long prevails," and a truer remark was never made, although the animus of the poet was directed more against men than women.

Female Operatives

WHEN alluding casually to this subject before, I enumerated some of the trades that supplied women to swell the ranks of prostitution, amongst which are milliners, dress makers, straw bonnet makers, furriers, hat binders, silk-winders, tambour-workers, shoe-binders, slop-women, or those who work for cheap tailors, those in pastry-cook, fancy and cigar-shops, bazaars, and ballet-girls.

I have heard it asserted in more than one quarter, although of course such assertions cannot be authenticated, or made reliable, for want of data, that one out of three of all female operatives in London are unchaste, and in the habit of prostituting themselves when occasion offers, either for money or more frequently for their own gratification.

I met a woman in Fleet Street, who told me that she came into the streets now and then to get money not to subsist upon, but to supply her with funds to meet the debts her extravagance caused her to contract. But I will put her narrative into a consecutive form.

"Ever since I was twelve," she said, "I have worked in a printing office where a celebrated London morning journal is put in type and goes to press. I get enough money to live upon comfortably; but then I am extravagant, and spend a great deal of money in eating and drinking, more than you would imagine. My appetite is very delicate, and my constitution not at all strong. I long for certain things like a woman in the family way, and I must have them by hook or by crook. The fact is the close confinement and the night air upset me and disorder my digestion. I have the most expensive things sometimes, and when I can, I live in a sumptuous manner, comparatively speaking. I am attached to a man in our office, to whom I shall be married some day. He does not suspect me, but on the contrary believes me to be true to him, and you do not suppose that I ever take the trouble to undeceive him. I am nineteen now, and have carried on with my 'typo' for nearly three years now. I sometimes go to the Haymarket, either early in the evening, or early in the morning, when I can get away from the printing; and sometimes I do a little in the day-time. This is not a frequent practice of mine; I only do it when I want money to pay anything. I am out now with the avowed intention of picking up a man, or making an appointment with some one for to-morrow or some time during the week. I always dress well, at least you mayn't think so, but I am always neat, and respectable, and clean, if the things I have on ain't worth the sight of money that some women's things cost them. I have good feet too, and as I find they attract attention, I always parade them. And I've hooked many a man by showing my ankle on a wet day. I shan't think anything of all this when I'm married. I believe my young man would marry me just as soon if he found out I went with others as he would now. I carry on with him now, and he likes me very much. I ain't of any particular family; to tell the truth, I was put in the workhouse when I was young, and they apprenticed me. I never knew my father or my mother, although 'my father was, as I've heard say, a well-known swell of capers gay, who cut his last fling with great applause'; or, if you must know, I heard that he was hung for killing a man who opposed him when committing a burglary. Mother's words, he was 'a macing-cove what robs,' and I'm his daughter, worse luck, I used to think at first, but what

was the good of being wretched about it? I couldn't get over it
for some time because I was envious, like a little fool, of other
people, but I reasoned, and at last I did recover myself, and was
rather glad that my position freed me from certain restrictions.
I had no mother whose heart I should break by my conduct,
no father who could threaten me with bringing his grey hairs
with sorrow to the grave. I had a pretty good example to follow
set before me, and I didn't scruple to argue that I was not to be
blamed for what I did. Birth is the result of accident. It is the
merest chance in the world whether you're born a countess or
a washerwoman. I'm neither one nor t'other; I'm only a mot who
does a little typographing by way of variety. Those who have
had good nursing, and all that, and the advantages of a sound
education, who have a position to lose, prospects to blight, and
relations to dishonour, may be blamed for going on the loose,
but I'll be hanged if I think that priest or moralist is to come
down on me with the sledge-hammer of their denunciation.
You look rather surprised at my talking so well. I know I talk
well, but you must remember what a lot has passed through
my hands for the last seven years, and what a lot of copy I've
set up. There is very little I don't know, I can tell you. It's what
old Robert Owen would call the spread of education."

I had to talk some time to this girl before she was so communicative; but it must be allowed my assiduity was amply
repaid. The common sense she displayed was extraordinary for
one in her position; but, as she said, she certainly had had
superior opportunities, of which she had made the most. And her
arguments, though based upon fallacy, were exceedingly clever
and well put. So much for the spread of education amongst the
masses. Who knows to what it will lead?

The next case that came under my notice was one of a very
different description. I met a woman in Leadenhall Street, a
little past the India House, going towards Whitechapel. She
told me, without much solicitation on my part, that she was
driven into the streets by want. Far from such a thing being
her inclination, she recoiled from it with horror, and had there
been no one else in the case, she would have preferred starvation
to such a life. I thought of the motto Vergniaud the Girondist
wrote on the wall of his dungeon in his blood, "Potius mori quam
foedari," and I admired the woman whilst I pitied her. It is easy
to condemn, but even vice takes the semblance of virtue when

it has a certain end in view. Every crime ought to be examined
into carefully in order that the motive that urged to the
commission may be elicited, and that should be always thrown
into the scale in mitigation or augmentation of punishment.

Her father was a dock labourer by trade, and had been ever
since he came to London, which he did some years ago, when
there was great distress in Rochdale, where he worked in a cotton
factory; but being starved out there after working short time
for some weeks, he tramped with his daughter, then about
fourteen, up to town, and could get nothing to do but work in
the docks, which requires no skill, only a good constitution, and
the strength and endurance of a horse. This however, as every one
knows, is a precarious sort of employment, very much sought
after by strong, able-bodied men out of work. The docks are
a refuge for all Spitalfields and the adjacent parishes for men
out of work, or men whose trade is slack for a time. Some three
weeks before I met her, the girl's father had the misfortune to
break his arm and to injure his spine by a small keg of spirits
slipping from a crane near to which he was standing. They took
him to the hospital, where he then was. The girl herself worked as
a hat-binder, for which she was very indifferently paid, and even
that poor means of support she had lost lately through the
failure of the house she worked for. She went to see her father
every day, and always contrived to take him something, if it only
cost twopence, as a mark of affection on her part, which he was
not slow in appreciating, and no doubt found his daughter's
kindness a great consolation to him in the midst of his troubles.
She said, "I tried everywhere to get employment, and I couldn't.
I ain't very good with my needle at fine needlework, and the
slopsellers won't have me. I would have slaved for them though,
I do assure you, sir; bad as they do pay you, and hard as you
must work for them to get enough to live upon, and poor living,
God knows, at that. I feel very miserable for what I've done, but
I was driven to it; indeed I was, sir. I daren't tell father, for
he'd curse me at first, though he might forgive me afterwards:
for though he's poor, he's always been honest, and borne a good
name; but now—I can't help crying a bit, sir. I ain't thoroughly
hardened yet, and it's a hard case as ever was. I do wish I was
dead and there was an end of everything, I am so awfully sad
and heartbroken. If it don't kill me, I suppose I shall get used to it
in time. The low rate of wages I received has often put into my

head to go wrong; but I have always withstood the temptation, and nothing but so many misfortunes and trials coming together could ever have induced me to do it."

This, I have every reason to believe, was a genuine tale of distress told with all simplicity and truth, although everything that a woman of loose morals says must be received with caution, and believed under protest.

Ballet-girls have a bad reputation, which is in most cases well deserved. To begin with their remuneration—it is very poor. They get from nine to eighteen shillings. Columbine in the pantomime gets five pounds a week, but then hers is a prominent position. Out of these nine to eighteen shillings they have to find shoes and petticoats, silk stockings, etc., etc., so that the pay is hardly adequate to their expenditure, and quite insufficient to fit them out and find them in food and lodging. Can it be wondered at that, while this state of things exists, ballet-girls should be compelled to seek a livelihood by resorting to prostitution?

Many causes may be enumerated to account for the lax morality of our female operatives. Among the chief of which we must class—

1. Low wages inadequate to their sustenance.

2. Natural levity and the example around them.

3. Love of dress and display, coupled with the desire for a sweetheart.

4. Sedentary employment, and want of proper exercise.

5. Low and cheap literature of an immoral tendency.

6. Absence of parental care and the inculcation of proper precepts. In short, bad bringing up.

Maid-servants

MAID-SERVANTS seldom have a chance of marrying, unless placed in a good family, where, after putting by a little money by pinching and careful saving, the housemaid may become an object of interest to the footman, who is looking out for a public-house or when the housekeeper allies herself to the butler, and together they set up in business. In small families, the servants often give themselves up to the sons, or to the policeman on the beat, or to soldiers in the Parks; or else to shopmen, whom they may meet in the streets. Female servants are far from being a virtuous class. They are badly educated and are not well looked after by their mistresses as a rule, although every dereliction from the paths of propriety by them will be visited with the heaviest displeasure, and most frequently be followed by dismissal of the most summary description, without the usual month's warning, to which so much importance is usually attached by both employer and employed.

Marylebone was lately characterised by one of its vestrymen as being one of the seven black parishes in London. Half the women it is asserted who are sent from the workhouse, and have situations·procured for them by the parochial authorities, turn out prostitutes. I have no means of corroborating the truth of this declaration, but it has been made and sent forth to the world through the medium of the public press, though I believe it has been partially contradicted by one of the workhouse authorities; however this may be, there can be no doubt that the tone of morality among servant-maids in the metropolis is low. I will not speak in the superlative—I merely characterise it as low. I had an opportunity of questioning a maid-of-all-work, a simple-minded, ignorant, uneducated, vain little body, as strong physically as a donkey, and thoroughly competent to perform her rather arduous duties, for the satisfactory performance of which she received the munificent remuneration of eight pounds annually, including her board and lodging.

She said: "came from Berkshire, sir, near Windsor; father put me to service some years ago, and I've been in London ever since. I'm two and twenty now. I've lived in four or five different situations since then. Are followers allowed? No, sir, missus don't permit no followers. No, I ain't got no perleeceman. Have I got a young man? Well, I have; he's in the harmy, not a hoffisser, but a soldier. I goes out along of him on Sundays, leastways Sunday afternoons, and missus she lets me go to see an aunt of mine, as I says lives in Camberwell, only between you and me, sir, there ain't no aunt, only a soldier, which he's my sweetheart, as I says to you before, sir."

Maid-servants in good families have an opportunity of copying their mistress's way of dressing, and making themselves attractive to men of a higher class. It is a voluntary species of sacrifice on their part. A sort of suicidal decking with flowers, and making preparations for immolation on the part of the victim herself. Flattered by the attention of the eldest son, or some friend of his staying in the house, the pretty lady's maid will often yield to soft solicitation. Vanity is at the bottom of all this, and is one of the chief characteristics of a class not otherwise naturally vicious. The housemaids flirt with the footmen, the housekeeper with the butler, the cooks with the coachmen, and so on; and a flirtation often begun innocently enough ends in something serious, the result of which may be to blight the prospect of the unfortunate woman who has been led astray.

There are book-hawkers, who go about the country, having first filled their wallets from the filthy cellars of Holywell Street, sowing the seeds of immorality; servants in country houses will pay, without hesitation, large prices for improper books. This denomination of evil, I am glad to say, is much on the decrease now, since the Immoral Publications Act has come into operation.

Maid-servants live well, have no care or anxiety, no character worth speaking about to lose, for the origin of most of them is obscure, are fond of dress, and under these circumstances it cannot be wondered that they are as a body immoral and unchaste.

Ladies of Intrigue and Houses of Assignation

THE reader will find more information about "ladies of intrigue" in the annals of the Divorce Court and the pages of the *Causes Célèbres* than it is in my power to furnish him with. By ladies of intrigue we must understand married women who have connection with other men than their husbands, and unmarried women who gratify their passion secretly.

There is a house in Regent Street, I am told, where ladies, both married and unmarried, go in order to meet with and be introduced to gentlemen, there to consummate their libidinous desires. This sort of clandestine prostitution is not nearly so common in England as in France and other parts of the Continent, where chastity and faithfulness among married women are remarkable for their absence rather than their presence. As this vice is by no means common or a national characteristic, but rather the exception than the rule, it can only expect a cursory notice at our hands.

An anecdote was told me illustrative of this sort of thing that may not be out of place here.

A lady of intrigue, belonging to the higher circles of society, married to a man of considerable property, found herself unhappy in his society, and after some time unwillingly came to the conclusion that she had formed an alliance that was destined to make her miserable. Her passions were naturally strong, and she one day resolved to visit a house that one of her female acquaintances had casually spoken about before her some time before. Ordering a cab, she drove to the house in question, and went in. There was no necessity for her to explain the nature of her business, or the object with which she called. That was understood. She was shown into a handsome drawing-room, beautifully fitted up, for the house was situated in one of the best streets in May Fair, there to wait the coming of her unknown paramour. After waiting some little time the door opened, and a gentleman entered. The curtains of the room were partially drawn round the windows, and the blinds were pulled down, which caused a "dim religious light" to pervade the apartment, preventing the lady from seeing distinctly the features of her visitor. He approached her, and in a low tone of voice commenced a conversation with her about some indifferent subject.

She listened to him for a moment, and then with a cry of astonishment recognized her husband's voice. He, equally confused, discovered that he had accidentally met in a house of ill-fame the wife whom he had treated with unkindness and cruelty, and condemned to languish at home while he did as he chose abroad. This strange encounter had a successful termination, for it ended in the reconciliation of husband and wife, who discovered that they were mutually to blame.

From the Divorce Court emanate strange revelations, to which the press gives publicity. It reveals a state of immorality amongst the upper and middle classes that is deplorable; but although this unveils the delinquencies of ladies of intrigue, they are not altogether the class we have under discussion. Those who engross our attention are ladies who, merely to satisfy their animal instincts, intrigue with men whom they do not truly love. But though we could multiply anecdotes and stories, it is not necessary to do more than say, they are a class far from numerous, and scarcely deserve to form a distinctive feature in the category of prostitution in London.

COHABITANT PROSTITUTES

THE last head in our classification is "Cohabitant Prostitutes", which phrase must be understood to include—

1. Those whose paramours cannot afford to pay the marriage fees. This is a very small and almost infinitesimal portion of the community, as banns now cost so very little, that it is next to an absurdity to say "a man and woman" cannot get married because they have not money enough to pay the fees consequent upon publishing the banns, therefore this class is scarcely deserving of mention.

2. Those whose paramours do not believe in the sanctity of the ceremony.

There may be a few who make their religious convictions an objection to marriage, but you may go a very long journey before you will be able to discover a man who will conscientiously refuse to marry a woman on this ground. Consequently we may dismiss these with a very brief allusion.

3. Those who have married a relative forbidden by law. We know that people will occasionally marry a deceased wife's sister, notwithstanding the anathemas of mother church are sure to be hurled at them. Yet ecclesiastical terrors may have weight with a man who has conceived an affection for a sister-in-law, for whom he will have to undergo so many penalties.

Perhaps parliamentary agitation may soon legitimise these connections, and abolish this heading from our category of Cohabitant Prostitution.

4. Those who would forfeit their income by marrying—as officers' widows in receipt of pensions, and those who hold property only while unmarried.

This class is more numerous than any we have yet mentioned, but it offers nothing sufficiently striking or peculiar to induce us to dwell longer upon it, as it explains itself.

5. Those whose paramours object to marry them for pecuniary or family reasons. This is a subject on which it has been necessary to dilate; for it includes all the lorettes in London, and the men by whom they are kept. By lorettes, I mean those I have touched upon before as prima donnas, who are a class of women who do not call going to night-houses in Panton Street, walking the Haymarket, and feel much insulted if you so characterize their nocturnal wanderings. The best women go to three or four houses in Panton Street, where the visitors are more select than in the other places, where the door porters are less discriminating. Sometimes women who are violent, and make a disturbance, are kept out of particular houses for months.

Of course, the visits of kept women are made by stealth, as the men who keep them would not countenance their going to such places. Perhaps their men are out of town, and they may then go with comparative safety.

Women who are well kept, and have always been accustomed to the society of gentlemen, have an intense horror of the Haymarket women, properly so called, who promenade the pavement in order to pick up men.

And in reality there is a greater distinction between the two classes than would at first appear. Even if a good sort of woman has been thrown over by her man, and is in want of money, she will not pick up anyone at a night-house who may solicit her; on the contrary, she will select some fellow she has a liking for; while, on the other hand, the Haymarket woman will pick up any low wretch who she thinks will pay her. She will not even object to a foreigner, though all the best women have a great dislike to low foreigners.

Were I to dwell longer on this subject it is clear I should merely be recapitulating what I have already said in a former portion of this work.

The following narrative was given me by a girl I met in the Haymarket, when in search of information regarding the prostitution of the West-end of London. Her tale is the usual one of unsuspecting innocence and virtue, seduced by fraud and violence. The victim of passion became in time the mistress of lust, and sank from one stage to another, until she found herself compelled to solicit in the streets to obtain a livelihood. She was about twenty-one years of age, beneath the ordinary height, and with a very engaging countenance. She appeared to be a high-spirited intelligent girl, and gave her sad tale with candour and modesty.

NARRATIVE OF A GAY WOMAN AT THE WEST END OF THE METROPOLIS

"I WAS born in the county of ——, in England, where my father was an extensive farmer, and had a great number of servants. I have three brothers and one younger sister. I was sent to a boarding school at B——, where I was receiving a superior education, and was learning drawing, music, and dancing. During the vacations and once every quarter, I went home and lived with my parents, where one of my chief enjoyments was to ride out on a pony I had, over the fields, and in the neighbourhood, and occasionally to go to M———, a few miles distant. On these occasions we often had parties of ladies and gentlemen: when some of the best people in the district visited us. I had one of the happiest homes a girl could have.

"When I was out riding one day at M———, in passing through the town, my pony took fright, and threatened to throw me off, when a young gentleman who was near rode up to my assistance. He rode by my side till we came to a hotel in town, when we both dismounted. Leaving the horses with the hostlers, we had some refreshment. I took out my purse to pay the expenses, but he would not let me and paid for me. We both mounted and proceeded towards my home. On his coming to the door of the house, I invited him to come in, which he did. I introduced him to my papa and mamma, and mentioned the kind service he had done to me. His horse was put up in our stables, and he remained for some time, and had supper with us, when he returned to M———. He was very wealthy, resided in London, and only visited M——— occasionally with his servants.

"I was then attending a boarding-school at B———, and was about fifteen years of age. A few days after this I left home and returned to B———. We corresponded by letter for nearly twelve months.

"From the moment he rode up to me at M——— I was deeply interested in him, and the attachment increased by the correspondence. He also appeared to be very fond of me. He sometimes came and visited me at home during my school holidays for the next twelve months. One day in the month of May—in summer— he came to our house in his carriage, and we invited him to dinner. He remained with us for the night, and slept with one of my brothers. We were then engaged to each other, and were to be married, as soon as I was eighteen years of age.

"The next day he asked my parents if I might go out with him in his carriage. My mamma consented. She asked if any of our servants would go with us, but he thought there was no occasion for this, as his coachman and footman went along with us. We proceeded to B——— Railway Station. He left his carriage with the coachman and footman, and pressed me to go with him to London. He pretended to my parents he was only going out for a short drive. I was very fond of him, and reluctantly consented to go with him to London.

"He first brought me to Simpson's hotel in the Strand, where we had dinner, then took me to the opera. We went to Scott's supper rooms in the Haymarket. On coming out we walked up and down the haymarket. He took me to several of the cafés, where we had wine and refreshment. About four o'clock in the morning he called a hansom, and drove me to his house; and there seduced me by violence in spite of my resistance. I screamed out, but none of the servants in the house came to assist me. He told his servants I was his young wife he had just brought up from the country.

"I wanted to go home in the morning, and began to cry, but he would not let me go. He said I must remain in London with him. I still insisted on going home, and he promised to marry me. He then bought me a watch and chain, rings and bracelets, and presented me with several dresses. After this I lived with him in his house, as though I had been his wife, and rode out with him in his brougham. I often insisted upon being married. He promised to do so, but delayed from time to time. He generally drove out every day over the finest streets, thoroughfares, and parks of the metropolis; and in the evenings he took me to the Argyle Rooms and to the Casino at Holborn. I generally went there very well dressed, and was much noticed on account of my youthful appearance. We also went to the fashionable theatres in the West-end, and several subscription balls.

"I often rode along Rotten Row with him, and along the drives in Hyde Park. We also went to the seaside, where we lived in the best hotels.

"This lasted for two years, when his conduct changed towards me.

"One evening I went with him to the Assembly Rooms at Holborn to a masked ball. I was dressed in the character of a fairy queen. My hair was in long curls hanging down my back.

"He left me in the supper-room for a short time, when a well-dressed man came up to me. When my paramour came in he saw the young man sitting by my side speaking to me. He told him I was his wife, and inquired what he meant by it, to which he gave no reply. He then asked me if I knew him. I replied no. He asked the gentleman to rise, which he did, apologising for his seating himself beside me, and thereby giving offence. On the latter showing him his card, which I did not see, they sat down and had wine together.

"We came out of the supper-room, and we had a quarrel about the matter. We walked up and down the ball-room for some time, and at last drove home.

"When we got home he quarrelled again with me, struck me, and gave me two black eyes. I was also bruised on other parts of my body, and wanted to leave him that night, but he would not let me.

"In the morning we went out as usual after breakfast for a drive.

"Next evening we went to the Casino at Holborn. Many of the gentlemen were staring at me, and he did not like it. I had on a thick Maltese veil to conceal my blackened eyes.

"The gentleman who had accosted me the previous night came up and spoke to me and my paramour (whom we shall call S.), and had some wine with us. He asked the reason I did not raise my veil. S. said because I did not like to do it in this place. The gentleman caught sight of my eyes, and said they did not look so brilliant as the night before.

"S. was indignant, and told him he took great liberty in speaking of his wife in this manner. The other remarked that no one could help noticing such a girl, adding that I was too young to be his wife, and that he should not take me to such a place if he did not wish me to be looked at. He told him he ought to take better care of me than to bring me there.

"When we got home we had another quarrel, and he struck me severely on the side.

"We did not sleep in the same bed that night. On coming downstairs to breakfast next morning I was taken very ill, and a medical man was sent for. The doctor said I was in a fever, and must have had a severe blow or a heavy fall. I was ill and confined to my bed for three months. He went out every night and left me with a nurse and the servants, and seldom returned till three or four o'clock in the morning. He used to return home drunk; generally came into my bedroom and asked if I was better; kissed me and went downstairs to bed.

"When I got well he was kind to me, and said I looked more charming than ever. For three or four months after he took me out as usual.

"The same gentleman met me again in the Holborn one night while S. had gone out for a short time, leaving me alone. He came up and shook hands with me, said he was happy to see me, and wished me to meet him. I told him I could not. S. was meanwhile watching our movements. The gentleman asked me if I was married, when I said that I was. He admired my rings. Pointing to a diamond ring on his finger, he asked me if I would like it. I said no. He said your rings are not so pretty. I still refused it; but he took the ring off his finger and put it on one of mine, and said, 'See how well it looks,' adding, 'Keep it as a memento; it may make you think of me when I am far away.' He told me not to mention it to my husband.

"Meantime S. was watching me, and came up when the man had gone away, and asked what he had been saying to me. I told him the truth that the same man had spoken to me again. He asked me what had passed between us, and I told him all, with the exception of the ring.

"He noticed the ring on my finger, and asked me where I had got it. I declined at first to answer. He then said I was not true to him, and if I would not tell him who gave me the ring he would leave me. I told him the man had insisted on my having it.

"He thereupon rushed along the room after him, but did not find him. On coming back he insisted on my going home without him.

"He took me outside to his brougham, handed me in it, and then left me. I went home and sat in the drawing-room till he returned, which was about three o'clock in the morning. He quarrelled with me again for not being true to him. I said I was, and had never left his side for a moment from the time I rose in the morning till I lay down at night.

"I then told him I would go home and tell my friends all about it, and he was afraid.

"Soon after he said to me he was going out of town for a week and wished me to stop at home. I did not like to remain in the house without a woman, and wished to go with him. He said he could not allow me, as he was to be engaged in family matters.

"He was absent for a week. I remained at home for three nights, and was very dull and wearied, having no one to speak to. I went to my bedroom, washed and dressed, ordered the carriage to be got ready, and went to the Holborn. Who should I see there but this gentleman again. He was astonished to see me there alone. Came up and offered me his arm.

"I told him I was wearied at home in the absence of S., and came out for a little relaxation. He then asked to see me home, which I declined. I remained till the dancing was nearly over. He got into the brougham with me and drove to Sally's, where we had supper, after which he saw me home. He bade me 'good-bye' and said he hoped to see me at the Holborn again some other night.

"Meantime S. had been keeping watch over me, it appears, and heard of this. When he came home he asked me about it. I told him. He swore the gentleman had connexion with me. I said he had not. He then hit me in the face and shook me, and threatened to lock me up. After breakfast he went out to walk, and I refused to go with him.

"When he had gone away I packed up all my things, told the servant to bring a cab, wrote a note and left it on the table. I asked the cabman if he knew any nice apartments a long way from C———, where I was living. He drove me to Pimlico, and took me to apartments in ————— where I have ever since resided.

"When I went there I had my purse full of gold, and my dresses and jewellery, which were worth about £300.

"One evening soon after I went to the Holborn and met my old friend again, and told him what had occurred. He was astonished, and said he would write to my relations, and have S. pulled up for it.

"After this he saw me occasionally at my lodgings, and made me presents.

"He met S. one day in the City, and threatened to write to my friends to let them know how I had been treated.

"I still went to the Holborn occasionally. One evening I met S., who wished me to go home with him again, but I refused, after the ill-usage he had given me.

"I generally spent the day in my apartments, and in the evening went to the Argyle until my money was gone. I now and then got something from the man who had taken my part; but he did not give me so much as I had been accustomed to, and I used to have strange friends against my own wish.

"Before I received them I had spouted most of my jewellery and some of my dresses. When I lived with S. he allowed me £10 a week, but when I went on the loose I did not get so much.

"After I had parted with my jewellery and most of my clothes I walked in the Haymarket, and went to the Turkish divans, 'Sally's,' and other cafés and restaurants.

"Soon after I became unfortunate, and had to part with the

remainder of my dresses. Since then I have been more shabby in appearance, and not so much noticed."

CRIMINAL RETURNS

IT is very interesting to philanthropists and people who take an interest in seeing human nature improved, and to those who wish to see crime decrease, to notice the fluctuations of crime, its increase, its decrease, or its being stationary, especially among different classes.

Through the kindness of Sir Richard Mayne, and the obliging courtesy of Mr. Yardley, of the Metropolitan Police-Office. Whitehall, I am enabled to show the number of disorderly prostitutes taken into custody during the years 1850 to 1860, Mr. Yardley supplied me with the criminal returns of the Metropolitan Police for the last ten years, from which I have extracted much valuable and interesting information, besides what I have just mentioned.

NUMBER OF DISORDERLY PROSTITUTES taken into Custody during the years 1850 to 1860, and their Trades.

1850	—	—	2,502
1851	—	—	2,573
1852	—	—	3,750
1853	—	—	3,386
1854	—	—	3,764
1855	—	—	3,592
1856	—	—	4,303
1857	—	—	5,178
1858	—	—	4,890
1859	—	—	4,282
1860	—	—	3,734

After some search I have been enabled to give the trades and occupations of those women.

74	were	Hatters and trimmers.
418	,,	Laundresses.
646	,,	Milliners, etc.
400	,,	Servants.
249	,,	Shoemakers.
58	,,	Artificial flower-makers.
215	,,	Tailors.

33 were Brushmakers.
42 „   Bookbinders.
 8 „   Corkcutters.
 7 „   Dyers.
 2 „   Fishmongers.
 8 „   General and marine-store dealers.
24 „   Glovers.
18 „   Weavers.

The remainder described themselves as having no trade or occupation.

TRAFFIC IN FOREIGN WOMEN

ONE of the most disgraceful, horrible and revolting practices (not even eclipsed by the slave-trade) carried on by Europeans is the importation of girls into England from foreign countries to swell the ranks of prostitution. It is only very recently that the attention of Mr. Tyrrwhit, at the Marlborough Police Court, was drawn to the subject by Mr. Dalbert, agent to the "Society for the Protection of Women and Children."

It is asserted that women are imported from Belgium, and placed in houses of ill-fame, where they are compelled to support their keepers in luxury and idleness by the proceeds of their dishonour. One house in particular was mentioned in Marylebone; but the state of the law respecting brothels is so peculiar that great difficulty is experienced in extricating these unfortunate creatures from their dreadful position. If it were proved beyond the suspicion of a doubt that they were detained against their will, the Habeas Corpus Act might be of service to their friends, but it appears they are so jealously guarded, that all attempts to get at them have hitherto proved futile, although there is every reason to believe that energetic measures will be taken by the above-mentioned Society to mitigate the evil and relieve the victims.

As this traffic is clandestine, and conducted with the greatest caution, it is impossible to form any correct idea of its extent. There are numbers of foreign women about, but it is probable that many of them have come over here of their own free-will, and not upon false pretences or compulsion. One meets with French, Spanish, Italian, Belgian and other women.

The complaint made before the metropolitan magistrate a short while since was in favour of Belgian women. But the traffic is not confined to them alone. It would appear that the unfortunate creatures are deluded by all sorts of promises and cajolery, and when they arrive in this country are, in point of fact, imprisoned in certain houses of ill-fame, whose keepers derive considerable emolument from their durance. They are made to fetter themselves in some way or other to the trepanner, and they, in their simple-mindedness, consider their deed binding, and look upon themselves, until the delusion is dispelled, as thoroughly in the power of their keepers.

English women are also taken to foreign parts by designing speculators. The English are known to congregate at Boulogne, at Havre, at Dieppe, at Ostend, and other places. It is considered lucrative by the keepers of bawdy-houses at these towns to maintain an efficient supply of English women for their resident countrymen: and though the supply is inadequate to the demand, great numbers of girls are decoyed every year, and placed in the *"Maisons de passé,"* or *"Maisons de joie,"* as they are sometimes called, where they are made to prostitute themselves. And by the farm of their persons enable their procurers to derive considerable profit.

An Englishwoman told me how she was very nearly entrapped by a foreign woman. "I met an emissary of a French bawdy-house," she said, "one night in the Haymarket, and, after conversing with her upon various subjects, she opened the matter she had in hand, and, after a little manoeuvring and bush-beating, she asked me if I would not like to go over to France. She specified a town, which was Havre. 'You will get lots of money,' she added, and further represented, 'that I should have a very jolly time of it.' 'The money you will make will be equally divided between yourself and the woman of the house, and when you have made as much as you want, you may come back to England and set up a café or night-house, where your old friends will be only too glad to come and see you. You will of course get lots of custom, and attain a better future than you can now possibly hope for. You ought to look upon me as the greatest friend you have, for I am putting a chance in your way that does not occur every day, I can tell you. If you value your own comfort, and think for a moment about your future, you cannot hesitate. I have an agreement in my pocket, duly drawn up by a solicitor, so you may rely upon its being all on the square, and if you sign this—'

" 'To-night?' I asked.

" 'Yes, immediately. If you sign this, I will supply you with some money to get what you want, and the day after to-morrow you shall sail for Havre. Madame —— is a very nice sort of person, and will do all in her power to make you happy and comfortable, and indeed she will allow you to do exactly as you please.' "

Fortunately for herself my informant refused to avail herself of the flattering prospect so alluringly held out to her. The bait was tempting enough, but the fish was too wary.

Now let us hear the recital of a girl who, at an early age, had been incarcerated in one of these *"Maisons de passé."* She is now in England, has been in a refuge, and by the authorities of the charity placed in an occupation which enables her to acquire a livelihood sufficient to allow her to live as she had, up to that time, been accustomed to. Her story I subjoin:—

"When I was sixteen years old, my father, who kept a public-house in Bloomsbury, got into difficulties and became bankrupt. I had no mother, and my relations, such as they were, insisted upon my keeping myself in some way or other. This determination on their part thoroughly accorded with my own way of thinking, and I did not for an instant refuse to do so. It then became necessary to discover something by which I could support myself. Service suggested itself to me and my friends, and we set about finding out a situation that I could fill. They told me I was pretty, and as I had not been accustomed to do anything laborious, they thought I would make a very good lady's maid. I advertised in a morning paper, and received three answers to my advertisement. The first I went to did not answer my expectations, and the second was moderately good; but I resolved to go to the third, and see the nature of it before I came to my conclusion. Consequently I left the second open, and went to the third. It was addressed from a house in Bulstrode-street near Welbeck-street. I was ushered into the house, and found a foreign lady waiting to receive me. She said she was going back to France, and wished for an English girl to accompany her, as she infinitely preferred English to French women. She offered me a high salary, and told me my duties would be light; in fact by comparing her statement of what I should have to do with that of the others I had visited, I found that it was more to my advantage to live with her than with them. So after a little consultation with myself, I determined to accept her offer. No sooner had I told her so than she said in a soft tone of voice: —

" 'Then, my dear, just be good enough to sign this agreement between us. It is merely a matter of form—nothing more, *ma chère.*'

"I asked her what it was about, and why it was necessary for me to sign any paper at all.

"She replied, 'Only for our mutual satisfaction. I wish you to remain with me for one year, as I shall not return to England until then. And if you hadn't some agreement with me, to bind you as it were to stay with me, why, *mon Dieu*, you might leave me directly—oh! *c'est rien.* You may sign without fear or trembling.'

"Hearing this explanation of the transaction, without reading over the paper which was written on half a sheet of foolscap (for I did not wish to insult or offend her by so doing), I wrote my name.

"She instantly seized the paper, held it to the fire for a moment or two to dry, and folding it up placed it in her pocket.

"She then requested me to be ready to leave London with her on the following Thursday, which allowed me two days to make my preparations and to take leave of my friends, which I did in very good spirits, as I thought I had a very fair prospect before me. It remained for what ensued to disabuse me of that idea.

"We left the St. Katherine's Docks in the steamer for Boulogne, and instead of going to an hotel, as I expected, we proceeded to a private house in the Rue N— C—, near the Rue de l'Ecu. I have farther to tell you that three other young women accompanied us. One was a housemaid, one was a nursery governess, and the other a cook. I was introduced to them as people that I should have to associate with when we arrived at Madame's house. In fact they were represented to be part of the establishment; and they, poor things, fully believed they were, being as much deluded as myself. The house that Madame brought us to was roomy and commodious, and, as I afterwards discovered, well, if not elegantly, furnished. We were shown into very good bedrooms, much better than I expected would be allotted to servants; and when I mentioned this to Madame, and thanked her for her kindness and consideration, she replied with a smile:—

" 'Did I not tell you how well you would be treated? We do these things better in France than they do in England.'

"I thanked her again as she was going away, but she said, '*Tais toi, Tais toi*,' and left me quite enchanted with her goodness."

I need not expatiate on what subsequently ensued. It is easy to imagine the horrors that the poor girl had to undergo. With some difficulty she was conquered and had to submit to her fate. She did not know a word of the language, and was ignorant of the only method she could adopt to ensure redress. But this she happily discovered in a somewhat singular manner. When her way of living had become intolerable to her, she determined to throw herself on the generosity of a young Englishman who was in the habit of frequenting the house she lived in, and who seemed to possess some sort of affection for her.

She confessed her miserable position to him, and implored him to protect her or point out a means of safety. He at once replied, "The best thing you can do is to go to the British Consul and lay your case before him. He will in all probability send you back to your own country." It required little persuasion on her part to induce her friend to co-operate with her. The main thing to be managed was to escape from the house. This was next to impossible, as they were so carefully watched. But they were allowed occasionally, if they did not show any signs of discontent, to go out for a walk in the town. The ramparts surrounding the "*Haute Ville*" were generally selected by this girl as her promenade, and when this privilege of walking out was allowed her, she was strictly enjoined not to neglect any opportunity that might offer itself. She arranged to meet her young friend there, and gave him notice of the day upon which she would be able to go out. If a girl who was so privileged chanced to meet a man known to the *Bonne* or attendant as a frequenter of the house, she retired to a convenient distance or went back altogether. The plot succeeded, the consul was appealed to and granted the girl a passport to return to England, also offering to supply her with money to pay her passage home. This necessity was obviated by the kindness of her young English friend, who generously gave her several pounds, and advised her to return at once to her friends.

Arrived in England, she found her friends reluctant to believe the tale she told them, and found herself thrown on her own resources. Without a character, and with a mind very much disturbed, she found it difficult to do anything respectable, and at last had recourse to prostitution;—so difficult is it to come back to the right path when we have once strayed from it.

THIEVES AND SWINDLERS

INTRODUCTION

IN tracing the geography of a river it is interesting to go to its source, possibly a tiny spring in the cleft of a rock in some mountain glen. You follow its windings, observing each tributary which flows into its gathering flood until it discharges its water into the sea. We proceed in a similar manner to treat of the thieves and swindlers of the metropolis.

Thousands of our felons are trained from their infancy in the bosom of crime; a large proportion of them are born in the homes of habitual thieves and other persons of bad character, and are familiarised with vice from their earliest years; frequently the first words they lisp are oaths and curses.

One day, in going down a dark alley in the Borough, near Horsemonger Lane Gaol, we saw a little boy—an Irish cockney, who had been tempted to steal by other boys he was in the habit of associating with. He was stripped entirely naked, and was looking over a window on the first floor with a curious grin on his countenance. His mother had kept his clothes from him that day as a punishment for stealing, and to prevent him getting out of the house while she went out to her street-stall.

There are thousands of neglected children loitering about the low neighbourhoods of the metropolis, and prowling about the streets, begging and stealing for their daily bread. They are to be found in Westminster, Whitechapel, Shoreditch, St. Giles's, New Cut, Lambeth, the Borough, and other localities. Hundreds of them may be seen leaving their parents' homes and low lodging-houses every morning sallying forth in search of food and plunder. They are fluttering in rags and in the most motley attire. Some are orphans and have no one to care for them; others have left their homes and live in lodging-houses in the most improvident manner, never thinking of to-morrow; others are sent out by their unprincipled parents to beg and steal for a livelihood; others are the children of poor but honest and industrious people, who have been led to steal through the bad companionship of juvenile thieves.

These juvenile thieves find an ample field for plunder at the stalls and shop doors in Whitechapel, Shoreditch, Edgware Road and similar localities, where many articles are exposed for sale, which can be easily disposed of to some of the low fences. In this manner thousands of our felons are trained to be expert and daring in crime, and are frequently tried and convicted before the Police Courts.

This is the main source of the habitual felons of the metropolis. As these boys and girls grow up they commence a system of sneaking thefts over the metropolis, some purloining in shops, others gliding into areas and lobbies on various pretences, stealing articles from the kitchen, and when opportunity occurs carrying off the plate.

As these young felons advance in years they branch off into three different classes, determined partly by their natural disposition and personal qualities, and partly by the circumstances in which they are placed. Many of them continue through life to sneak as common thieves, others become expert pickpockets, and some ultimately figure as burglars.

A vast number of juvenile thieves as they grow up continue to carry on a system of petty felonies over the metropolis, and reside in the lowest neighbourhoods. Some pretend to sell laces and small wares to get a pretext to call at the houses of labouring people and tradesmen, and to go down the areas and enter the lobbies in fashionable streets. In addition to the paltry profits arising from these sales they get a livelihood by begging, and as a matter of course do not scruple to steal when they can find an opportunity.

These common thieves are of both sexes, and of various ages, and are often characterised by mental imbecility and low cunning. Many of them are lazy in disposition and lack energy both of body and mind. They go out daily in vast shoals over the metropolis picking up a miserable and precarious livelihood, sometimes committing felonies in the houses they visit of considerable value.

The pickpockets are of various ages and of different degrees of proficiency, from the little ragged urchin in St. Giles's stealing a handkerchief at the tail of a gentleman's coat, to the elegantly dressed and expert pickpocket promenading in the West-end and attending fashionable assemblies. Some are dressed as mechanics, others as clerks, some as smart business men, and others in fashionable attire. They are to be found on all public occasions, some of them clumsy and timid, others daring and most expert. Many of them continue to pursue this class of felonies in preference to any other. They receive a considerable accession to their numbers by young women, frequently servants who have been seduced, and cohabit with burglars, pickpockets, and others, and who are trained to this infamous profession, and in many cases are shoplifters.

Many are trained to commit house-breaking and burglaries from fourteen to fifteen years of age. Boys are occasionally employed to enter through fanlights and windows, and to assist otherwise in plundering dwellings and shops. Some of them commit burglaries of small value in working neighbourhoods, where comparatively little ingenuity and skill are required, others plunder shops and warehouses and fashionable dwellings, which is generally done with greater care and ingenuity, and where the booty is often of higher value.

In addition to the three classes we have named, the common thief, the pickpocket, and the burglar, there is another class of low ruffians who frequently cohabit with low women and prostitutes, and commit highway robberies. They often follow these degraded females on the streets, and attack persons who accost them, believing them to be prostitutes. At other times they garotte men on the street at midnight, or in the by-streets in the evening, and plunder them with violence. This class of persons are generally hardened in crime, and many of them are returned convicts.

THE SNEAKS, OR COMMON THIEVES

THE common thief is not distinguished for manual dexterity and accomplishment, like the pickpocket or mobsman, nor for courage, ingenuity, and skill, like the burglar, but is characterised by low cunning and stealth—hence he is termed the Sneak, and is despised by the higher classes of thieves.

There are various orders of Sneaks—from the urchin stealing an apple at a stall, to the man who enters a dwelling by the area or an attic window and carries off the silver plate.

In treating of the various classes of common thieves and their different modes of felony, we shall first treat of the juvenile thieves and their delinquencies, and notice the other classes in their order, according to the progressive nature and aggravation of their crime.

Stealing From Street Stalls

IN wandering along Whitechapel we see ranges of stalls on both sides of the street, extending from the neighbourhood of the Minories to Whitechapel church. Various kinds of merchandise are exposed to sale. There are stalls for fruit, vegetables, and oysters. There are also stalls where fancy goods are exposed for sale—combs, brushes, chimney-ornaments, children's toys, and common articles of jewellery. We find middle-aged women standing with baskets of firewood, and Cheap Johns selling various kinds of Sheffield cutlery, stationery, and plated goods.

It is an interesting sight to saunter along the New Cut, Lambeth, and to observe the street stalls of that locality. Here you see some old Irish woman, with apples and pears exposed on a small board placed on the top of a barrel, while she is seated on an upturned bushel smoking her pipe.

Alongside you notice a deal board on the top of a tressel, and an Irish girl of 18 years of age seated on a small three-legged stool, shouting in shrill tones "Apples, fine apples, ha'penny a lot!" You find another stall on the top of two tressels, with a larger quantity of apples and pears, kept by a woman who sits by with a child at her breast.

In another place you see a costermonger's barrow, with large green and yellow piles of fruit of better quality than the others, and a group of boys and girls assembled around him as he smartly disposes of pennyworths to the persons passing along the street.

THE NEW CUT—EVENING

ORANGE MART, DUKES'S PLACE—AN OBVIOUS TEMPTATION TO THIEVES

Outside a public-house you see a young man, humpbacked, with a basket of herrings and haddocks standing on the pavement, calling "Yarmouth herrings—three a-penny!" and at the door of a beershop with the sign of the "Pear Tree" we find a miserable looking old woman selling cresses, seated on a stool with her feet in an old basket.

As we wander along the New Cut during the day, we do not see so many young thieves loitering about; but in the evening when the lamps are lit, they steal forth from their haunts, with keen roguish eye, looking out for booty. We then see them loitering about the stalls or mingling among the throng of people in the street, looking wistfully on the tempting fruit displayed on the stalls.

These young Arabs of the city have a very strange and motley appearance. Many of them are only 6 or 7 years of age, others 8 or 10. Some have no jacket, cap, or shoes, and wander about London with their ragged trousers hung by one brace; some have an old tattered coat, much too large for them, without shoes and stockings, and with one leg of the trousers rolled up to the knee; others have an old greasy grey or black cap, with an old jacket rent at the elbows, and strips of the lining hanging down behind; others have an old dirty pinafore; while some have petticoats. They are generally in a squalid and unwashed condition, with their hair clustered in wild disorder like a mop, or hanging down in dishevelled locks—in some cases cropped close to the head.

Groups of these ragged urchins may be seen standing at the corners of the streets and in public thoroughfares, with blacking-boxes slung on their back by a leathern belt, or crouching in groups on the pavement; or we may occasionally see them running alongside of omnibuses, cabs, and hansoms, nimbly turning somersaults on the pavement as they scamper along, and occasionally walking on their hands with their feet in the air in our fashionable streets, to the merriment of the passers-by. Most of them are Irish cockneys, which we can observe in their features and accent—to which class most of the London thieves belong. They are generally very acute and ready-witted, and have a knowing twinkle in their eye which exhibits the precocity of their minds.

As we ramble along the New Cut in the dusk, mingled in the throng on the crowded street, chiefly composed of working people, the young ragged thieves may be seen stealing forth; their keen eye readily recognises the police-officers proceeding in their rounds, as well as the detective officers in their quiet and cautious movements. They seldom steal from costermongers, but frequently from the old women's stalls. One will push an old woman off her seat—perhaps a bushel basket, while the others will steal her fruit or the few coppers lying on her stall. This is done by day as well as by night, but chiefly in the dusk of the evening.

They generally go in a party of three or four, sometimes as many as eight together. Watching their opportunity, they make a sudden snatch at the apples or pears, or oranges or nuts, or walnuts, as the case may be, then run off, with the cry of "stop thief!" ringing in their ears from the passers-by. These petty thefts are often done from a love of mischief rather than from a desire for plunder.

When overtaken by a police-officer, they in general readily go with him to the police-station. Sometimes the urchin will lie down in the street and cry "let me go!" and the bystanders will take his part. This is of frequent occurrence in the neighbourhood of the New Cut and the Waterloo Road—a well-known rookery of young thieves in London.

By the petty thefts at the fruit-stalls they do not gain much money—seldom so much as to get admittance to the gallery of the Victoria Theatre, which they delight to frequent. They are particularly interested in the plays of robberies, burglaries, and murders performed there, which are done in melodramatic style. There are similar fruit-stalls in the other densely populated districts of the metropolis.

In the Mile End Road, and New North Road, and occasionally in other streets in different localities of London, common jewellery is exposed for sale, consisting of brooches, rings, bracelets, breast-pins, watch-chains, eye-glasses, ear-rings and studs, &c. There are also stalls for the sale of china, looking-glasses, combs, and chimney-ornaments. The thefts from these are generally managed in this way: —

One goes up and looks at some trifling article in company with his associates. The party in charge of the stall—generally a woman—knowing their thieving propensity, tells them to go away, which they decline to do. When the woman goes to remove him, another boy darts forward at the other end of the stall and steals some article of jewellery, or otherwise, while her attention is thus distracted.

These juvenile thieves are chiefly to be found in Lucretia Street, Lambeth; Union Street, Borough Road; Gunn Street, and Friars Street, Blackfriars Road; also at Whitechapel, St. Giles's, Drury Lane, Somers Town, Anderson Grove, and other localities.

The statistics connected with this class of felonies will be given when we come to treat on "Stealing from the doors and windows of shops."

Stealing From The Tills

THIS is done by the same class of boys, generally by two or three, or more, associated together. It is committed at any hour of the day, principally in the evening, and generally in the following way: One of the boys throws his cap into the shop of some greengrocer or other small dealer, in the absence of the persons in charge; another boy, often without shoes or stockings, creeps in on his hands and knees as if to fetch it, being possibly covered from without by one of the boys standing beside the shop-door, who is also on the look-out. Any passer-by seeing the cap thrown in would take no particular notice in most cases, as it merely appears to be a thoughtless boyish frolic. Meantime the young rogue within the shop crawls round the counter to the till, and rifles its contents.

If detected, he possibly says, "Let me go; I have done nothing. That boy who is standing outside and has just run away threw in my bonnet, and I came to fetch it." When discovered by the shopkeeper, the boy will occasionally be allowed to get away, as the loss may not be known till afterwards.

Sometimes one of these ragged urchins watches a favourable opportunity and steals from the till while his comrade is observing the movements of the people passing by and the police, without resorting to the ingenious expedient of throwing in the cap.

The shop tills are generally rifled by boys, in most cases by two or more in company; this is only done occasionally. It is confined chiefly to the districts where the working classes reside.

In some cases, though rarely, a lad of 17 or 19 years of age or upwards, will reach his hand over the counter to the till, in the absence of the person in charge of the shop.

These robberies are not very numerous, and are of small collective value.

Stealing From the Doors and Windows of Shops

In various shopping districts of London we see a great variety
of goods displayed for sale at the different shop-doors and
windows, and on the pavement in front of the shops of brokers,
butchers, grocers, milliners, &c.

Let us take a picture from the New Cut, Lambeth. We observe
many brokers' shops along the street, with a heterogeneous
assortment of household furniture, tables, chairs, looking-glasses,
plain and ornamental, cupboards, fire-screens, &c., ranged along
the broad pavement; while on tables are stores of carpenters'
tools in great variety, copper-kettles, brushes, and bright tin
pannikins, and other articles.

We see the dealer standing before his door, with blue apron,
hailing the passer-by to make a purchase. Upon stands on the
pavement at each side of his shop-door are cheeses of various
kinds and of different qualities, cut up into quarters and slices,
and rashers of bacon lying in piles in the open windows, or laid
out on marble slabs. On deal racks are boxes of eggs, "fresh from
the country," and white as snow, and large pieces of bacon,
ticketed as of "fine flavour," and "very mild."

Alongside is a milliner's shop with the milliner, a smart young
woman, seated knitting beneath an awning in front of her door.
On iron and wooden rods, suspended on each side of the doorway,
are black and white straw bonnets and crinolines, swinging in the
wind; while on the tables in front are exposed boxes of gay feathers,
and flowers of every tint, and fronts of shirts of various styles,
with stacks of gown-pieces of various patterns.

A greengrocer stands by his shop with a young girl of 17 by
his side. On each side of the door are baskets of apples, with
large boxes of onions and peas. Cabbages are heaped at the front
of the shop, with piles of white turnips and red carrots.

Over the street is a furniture ware-room. Beneath the canvas
awning before the shop are chairs of various kinds, straw-bot-
tomed and seated with green or puce-coloured leather, fancy
looking-glasses in gilt frames, parrots in cages, a brass mounted
portmanteau, and other miscellaneous articles. An active young
shopman is seated by the shop-door, in a light cap and dark
apron—with newspaper in hand.

Near the Victoria Theatre we notice a second-hand clothes
store. On iron rods suspended over the doorway we find trousers,

vests, and coats of all patterns and sizes, and of every quality, dangling in the wind; and on small wooden stands along the pavement are jackets and coats of various descriptions. Here are corduroy jackets, ticketed "15s. made to order." Corduroy trousers warranted "first rate," at 7s. 6d. Fustian trousers to order for 8s. 6d.; while dummies are ranged on the pavement with coats buttoned upon them, inviting us to enter the shop.

In the vicinity we see stalls of workmen's iron tools of various kinds—some old and rusty, others bright and new.

Thefts are often committed from the doors and windows of these shops during the day, in the temporary absence of the person in charge. They are often seen by passers-by, who take no notice, not wishing to attend the police court, as they consider they are insufficiently paid for it.

The coat is usually stolen from the dummy in this way: One boy is posted on the opposite side of the street to see if a police-officer is in sight, or a policeman in plain clothes, who might detect the depredation. Another stands two or three yards from the shop. The third comes up to the dummy, and pretends to look at the quality of the coat to throw off the suspicion of any bystander or passer-by. He then unfastens the button, and if the shopkeeper or any of his assistants come out, he walks away. If he finds that he is not seen by the people in the shop, he takes the coat off the dummy and runs away with it.

If seen, he will not return at that time, but watches some other convenient opportunity. When the young thief is chased by the shopkeeper, his two associates run and jostle him, and try to trip him up, so as to give their companion an opportunity of escaping. This is generally done at dusk, in the winter time, when thieving is most prevalent in those localities.

In stealing a piece of bacon from the shop-doors or windows, they wait till the shopman turns his back, when they take a piece of bacon or cheese in the same way as in the case alluded to. This is commonly done by two or more boys in company.

Handkerchiefs at shop-doors are generally stolen by one of the boys and passed to another who runs off with it. When hotly chased, they drop the handkerchief and run away.

These young thieves are the ragged boys formerly noticed, varying from 9 to 14 years of age, without shoes or stockings. Their parents are of the lowest order of Irish cockneys, or they live in low lodging-houses, where they get a bed for 2d.

or 3*d*. a night, with crowds of others as destitute as themselves.

There are numbers of young women of 18 years of age and upwards, Irish cockneys, belonging to the same class, who steal from these shop-doors. They are poorly dressed, and live in some of the lowest streets in Surrey and Middlesex, but chiefly in the Borough and the East End. Some of them are dressed in a clean cotton dress, shabby bonnet and faded shawl, and are accompanied by one or more men, costermongers in appearance. They steal rolls of printed cotton from the outside of linen drapers' shops, rolls of flannel, and of coarse calico, hearthrugs and rolls of oilskin and table-covers: and from brokers' shops they carry off rolls of carpet, fenders, fire-irons, and other articles, exposed in and around the shop-door. The thefts of these women are of greater value than those committed by the boys. They belong to the felon-class and are generally expert thieves.

The mode in which they commit these thefts is by taking advantage of the absence of the person in charge of the shop, or when his back is turned. It is done very quickly and dexterously, and they are often successful in carrying away articles such as those named without anyone observing them.

Another class of Sneaks, who steal from the outsides of shops, are women more advanced in life than those referred to—some middle-aged and others elderly. Some of them are thieves, or the companions of thieves, and others are the wives of honest, hard-working mechanics and labouring men, who spend their money in gin and beer at various public-houses.

These persons go and look over some pieces of bacon or meat outside of butchers' shops; they ask the price of it, sometimes buy a small piece and steal a large one, but more frequently buy none. They watch the opportunity of taking a large piece which they slip into their basket and carry to some small chandler's shop in a low neighbourhood, where they dispose of it at about a fourth of its value.

We have met some thieves of this order, basket in hand, returning from Drury Lane, who were pointed out to us by a detective officer.

The mechanics' and labourers' wives in many cases leave their homes in the morning for the purpose of purchasing their husbands' dinners. They meet with other women fond of drink like themselves. They meet, for example, outside the "Plum Tree," or such-like public-house, and join their money together to buy beer or gin. After partaking of it, they leave the house, and remain for some time outside conversing together. They again join their money and return to the public-house, and have some additional liquor, leave the house and separate. Some of them join with other parties fond of liquor as they did with the former. One says to the other: "I have no money, otherwise we would have a drop of gin. I have just met Mrs. So-and-so, and spent nearly all my money." The other may reply: "I have not much to get the old man's dinner, but we can have a quartern of gin." After getting the liquor, they separate. The tradesman's wife, finding that she has spent nearly the whole of her money, goes to a cheese-monger's or butcher's shop, and steals a piece of meat, or bacon, for the purpose of placing it before her husband for dinner, perhaps selling the remainder of the booty at shops in low neighbourhoods, or to lodging-houses.

Such cases frequently occur, and are brought before the police-courts.

These persons sometimes steal flat-irons for ironing clothes at the brokers' shop-doors, which they carry to other pawn-brokers if not detected. At other times they take them to the leaving-shop of an unlicensed pawnbroker. On depositing them, they get a small sum of money. These leaving-shops are in the lowest localities, and take in articles pawnbrokers would refuse. They are open on Sundays, and at other times when no business is done in pawnbrokers' shops.

These shops are well-known to the police, and give great assistance to these Sneaks in disposing of their stolen property.

A considerable number of depredations are committed at the doors of shoemakers' shops. They are committed by women of the lower orders, of all ages, some of them very elderly. They come up to the door as though they were shopping, attired generally in an old bonnet and faded shawl. The shoes are hanging inside the door, suspended from an iron rod by a piece of string, and are sometimes hanging on a bar outside the shop.

These parties are much of the same order of thieves already described, possibly many of them the mothers and some the grand-mothers of the ragged boys referred to. The greater number of them are Irish cockneys. They come up to the shop-door generally in the afternoon, as if to examine the quality of the shoes or boots, but seldom make any purchase. They observe how the articles are suspended and the best mode of abstracting them. They return in the dusk of the evening and steal them.

The shops from which these robberies are committed are to be found in Lambeth Walk, New Cut, Lower Marsh, Lambeth, Tottenham Court Road, Westminster, Drury Lane, the neighbourhood of St. Giles's, Petticoat Lane, Spitalfields, Whitcross Street, St. Luke's, and other localities.

Small articles are occasionally taken from shop windows in the winter evenings, by means of breaking a pane of glass in a very ingenious way. These thefts are committed at the shops of confectioners, tobacconists, and watchmakers, &c., in the quiet by-streets.

Sometimes they are done by the younger ragged-boys, but in most cases by lads of 14 and upwards, belonging to the fraternity of London thieves.

In the dark winter evenings we may sometimes see groups of these ragged boys, assembled around the windows of a small grocery-shop, looking greedily at the almond-rock, lollipops, sugar-candy, barley-sugar, brandy-balls, pies, and tarts, displayed in all their tempting sweetness and in all their gaudy tints. They insert the point of a knife or other sharp instrument into the corner or side of the pane, then give it a wrench, when the pane cracks in a semi-circular starlike form around the part punctured. Should a piece of glass large enough to admit the hand not be sufficiently loosened, they apply the sharp instrument at another place in the pane, when the new cracks communicate with the rents already made; on applying a sticking-plaster to the pane, the piece readily adheres to it, and is abstracted. The thief inserts his hand through an opening in the window, seizes a handful of sweets or other goods, and runs away, perhaps followed by the shopman in full chase. These thieves are termed star-glazers.

Such petty robberies are often committed by elder lads at the windows of tobacconists, when cigars and pipes are frequently stolen.

They cut the pane in the manner described, and sometimes get a younger boy to commit the theft, while they get the chief share of the plunder, without having exposed themselves to the danger of being arrested stealing the property.

Stealing From Children

CHILDREN are occasionally sent out by their mothers, with bundles of washing to convey to different persons, or they may be employed to bring clothes from the mangle. They are sometimes met by a man, at other times by a woman, who entices them to go to a shop for a halfpenny or a pennyworth of sweets, meanwhile taking care they leave their parcels or bundle, which they promise to keep for them till they return. On their coming out of the shop, they find the party has decamped, and seldom any clue can be got of them, as they belong to distant localities of the metropolis.

In other cases they go up to the children, when they are proceeding on their way, with a bundle or basket, and say: "You are going to take these things home. Do you know where you are going to take them?" The child being taken off her guard may say she is to carry them to "Mrs. So-and-so, of such a street." They will then say, "You are a good girl, and are quite right. Mrs. So-and-so sent me for them, as she is in a hurry and is going out." The child probably gives her the basket or bundle, when the thief absconds. A case of this kind occurred in the district of Marylebone about six months ago.

A girl was going with two silk-dresses to a lady in Devonshire Street, when she was met by a young woman, who said she was a servant of the lady, and was sent to get the dresses done or undone, and was very glad she had met her. The woman was an entire stranger to the lady. The larceny was detected on the Saturday night, and the lady was put to great inconvenience, as she had not a dress to go out with on the Sunday. Robberies of clothes sent out to be mangled, and of articles of linen, are very common. Milliners often send young girls on errands who are not old enough to see through the tricks of these parties prowling about the metropolis.

These larcenies are generally committed by vagrants decently dressed, and too lazy to work, who go sneaking about the streets and live in low neighbourhoods, such as St. Giles's, Drury Lane, Short's Gardens, Queen Street, and the Borough. They are in most cases committed in the evening, though sometimes during the day.

Child Stripping

THIS is generally done by females, old debauched drunken hags
who watch their opportunity to accost children in the streets,
tidily dressed with good boots and clothes. They entice them
away to a low or quiet neighbourhood for the purpose, as they
say, of buying them sweets, or with some other pretext. When
they get into a convenient place, they give them a halfpenny
or some sweets, and take off the articles of dress, and tell them
to remain till they return, when they go away with the booty.

This is done most frequently in mews in the West End, and
at Clerkenwell, Westminster, the Borough, and other similar
localities. These heartless debased women sometimes commit
these felonies in the disreputable neighbourhoods where they
live, but more frequently in distant places, where they are not
known and cannot be easily traced. This mode of felony is not
so prevalent in the metropolis as formerly. In most cases, it is
done at dusk in the winter evenings, from 7 to 10 o'clock.

Stealing From Drunken Persons

THERE is a very common low class of male thieves, who go
prowling about at all times of the day and night for this purpose.

They loiter about the streets and public-houses to steal from
drunken persons, and are called "Bug-hunters" and "mutchers."
You see many of them lounging about gin-palaces in the vicinity
of the Borough, near St. George's Church. We have met them
there in the course of our rambles over the metropolis, and at
Whitechapel and St. Giles's. They also frequent the Westminster
Road, the vicinity of the Victoria Theatre, Shoreditch, and
Somers Town. These low wretches are of all ages, and many of
them have the appearance of bricklayers', stonemasons' and
engineers' labourers. They pretend they are labourers out of
work, and are forward in intruding themselves on the notice of
persons entering those houses, and expect to be treated to liquor,
though entire strangers to them.

They are not unfrequently so rude as to take the pewter-pot
of another person from the bar, and pass it round to their
comrades till they have emptied the contents. If remonstrated
with, they return insulting language, and try to involve the
person in a broil.

You occasionally find them loafing about the tap-rooms. They watch for drunken people, whom they endeavour to persuade to treat them. They entice him to go down some court or slum, where they strip him of his watch, money, or other valuables he may have on his person. Or they sometimes rob him in the public-houses; but this seldom occurs, as they are aware it would lead to detection. They prefer following him out of the public-house. Many of these robberies are committed in the public urinals at a late hour at night.

These men have often abandoned women who cohabit with them, and assist them in these low depredations. They frequently dwell in low courts and alleys in the neighbourhood of gin-palaces, have no settled mode of life, and follow no industrious calling— living as loafers and low ruffians.

Some of them have wives, who go out washing and charing to obtain a livelihood for their children and themselves, as well as to support their brutal husbands, lazzaroni of the metropolis.

This class of persons are in the habit of stealing lead from houses, and copper boilers from kitchens and wash-houses.

There is another class of thieves, who steal from drunken persons, usually in the dusk of the evening, in the following manner: Two women, respectably dressed, meet a drunken man in the street, stop him and ask him to treat them. They adjourn to the bar of a public-house for the purpose of getting some gin or ale. While drinking at the bar, one of the women tries to rob him of his watch or money. A man who is called a "stickman," an accomplice and possibly a paramour of hers, comes to the bar a short time after them. He has a glass of some kind of liquor, and stands beside them. Some motions and signs pass between the two females and this man. If they have by this time secured the booty, it is passed to the latter, who thereupon slips away, with the stolen articles in his possession.

In some cases, when the property is taken from the drunken man, one of the women on some pretext steps to the door and passes it to the "stickman" standing outside, who then makes off with it. In other cases these robberies are perpetrated in the outside of the house, in some by-street.

Sometimes the man quickly discovers his loss, and makes an outcry against the women; when the "stickman" comes up and asks, "What is the matter?" the man may reply, "These two women have robbed me." The stickman answers, "I'll go and fetch a policeman." The property is passed to him by the women, and he decamps. If a criminal information is brought against the females, the stolen goods are not found in their possession, and the case is dropped.

These women seldom or never allow drunken men to have criminal connection with them, but get their living by this base system of plunder. They change their field of operation over the metropolis, followed by the sneaking "stickman."

Some of these females have been known in early life to sell oranges in the street.

The "stickman" during the day lounges about the parlours in quiet public-houses where thieves resort, and the women during the day are sometimes engaged in needlework—some of the latter have a fair education, which they may have learned in prison, and others are very illiterate.

Though respectable in dress and appearance, they generally belong to the felon class of Irish cockneys, with few exceptions.

They are to be found in Lisson Grove, Leicester Square, Portland Town, and other localities.

Females in respectable positions in society occasionally take too much intoxicating liquor, and are waylaid by old women, gin-drinkers, who frequent public-houses in low neighbourhoods. They introduce themselves to the inebriated woman as a friend, to see her to some place of safety until she has recovered from the effects of her dissipation—she may have been lying on the pavement, and unable to walk. They lift her up by the hand, and steal the gold ring from her finger.

At other times they take her into some by-court or street in low neighbourhoods, where doors may frequently be seen standing open; they rob her in some of these dark passages of her money, watch, and jewellery, and sometimes carry off her clothes.

If seen by persons in the neighbourhood, it is winked at, and no information given, as they generally belong to the same unprincipled class.

There is another low class of women who prowl about the streets at midnight, watching for any respectable-looking person who may be passing the worse of liquor. If they notice a drunken man, one comes and enters into conversation with him, and while thus engaged, another woman steps up, touches him under the chin, or otherwise distracts his attention. The person who first accosted him, with her companion, then endeavours to pick his pockets and plunder him of his property. A case of this kind occurred near the Marble Arch in August 1860.

They have many ingenious ways of distracting the attention of their victim, some of them very obscene and shameless.

They take care to see that no policeman is in sight, and generally endeavour to find out if the person they intend to victimise has something to purloin.

They may ask him for change, or solicit a few coppers to get beer, or inquire what o'clock it is, to see if he is in possession of a watch or money. They abstract the money from the pocket, or snatch the watch from the swivel, which they are adroit in breaking.

Such persons are often seen at midnight in the neighbourhood of Bloomsbury and Oxford Street, the Strand, Lower Thames Street, and other localities.

The most of those engaged in this kind of robbery in Oxford Street come from the neighbourhood of St. Giles's and Lisson Grove.

Stealing Linen, etc., Exposed To Dry

THIS is generally done by vagrants in the suburbs of the metropolis, from 7 to 11 o'clock in the evening; when left out all night, it is often done at midnight.

Linen and other clothes are frequently left hanging on lines or spread out on the grass in yards at the back of the house. Entrance is effected through the street-doors which may have been left open, or by climbing over the wall. In many cases these felonies are committed by middle-aged women. If done by a man, he is generally assisted by a female who carries off the property; were he seen carrying a bundle of clothes, he would be stopped by a vigilant officer, and be called to give an account of it which would possibly lead to his detection.

These felonies generally consist of sheets, counterpanes, shirts, table-covers, pinafores, towels, stockings, and such-like articles.

When any of them are marked, the female makes it her business to pick out the marks, in case it might lead to their detection. Such robberies are often traced by the police through the assistance of the pawnbrokers.

They are very common where there are gardens at the back of the house, such as Kensall Green, Camden Town, Kensington, Battersea, Clapham, Peckham, and Victoria Park.

The clothes are generally disposed of at pawnbrokers or the leaving-shops, commonly called "Dolly Shops." They leave them there for a small sum of money, and get a ticket. If they return for them in the course of a week, they are charged 3*d*. a shilling interest. If they do not return for them in seven days, they are disposed of to persons of low character. These wretches at the leaving-shops manage to get them into the hands of parties who would not be likely to give information—the articles, from their superior quality, being generally understood to be stolen.

These felonies are also committed by the female Sneaks who call at gentlemen's houses, selling small wares, or on some other similar errand. When they find the door open and a convenient opportunity, they often abstract the linen and other clothes from the lines, and dispose of them in the manner referred to.

They are also stolen by ragged juvenile thieves, who get into the yards by climbing over the wall. This is occasionally done in the Lambeth district, in the dusk of the evening, or early in the morning, and is effected in this way:—Some time previously they commence some boyish game, about half a dozen of them together. Then they pretend to quarrel, when one boy will take the other's cap off his head and place it on the garden wall. Another boy lifts him up to fetch it—the object being to reconnoitre the adjacent grounds, and see if there are any clothes laid out to dry, as well as to find out the best mode of stealing them.

When they discover clothes in a yard, they come back at dusk, or at midnight, and carry them off the lines.

They take the stolen property to the receiver's after having divided the clothes among the party. Some will go off in one direction, and others in another to get them disposed of, which is done to prevent suspicion on the part of the police.

The receiving-houses are open to them at night, as these low people are very greedy of gain. Sometimes they convey the stolen property to their lodgings, at other times they lodge it in concealment till the next day. These clothes are occasionally of trifling value, at other times worth several pounds, which on being sold bring the thief a very poor return—scarcely the price of his breakfast—the lion's share of the spoil being given to the unprincipled receiver.

They are often encouraged to commit these thefts by wretches in the low lodging-houses, who are aware of their midnight excursions.

Robberies From Carts and Other Vehicles

THERE are many depredations committed over the metropolis from carts, carriers' waggons, cabs, railway vans, and other vehicles. Many of those people have the appearance of porters at a warehouse, and are a peculiar order.

At one time they may have been porters at warehouses, or connected with railways, or carmen to large commercial firms. Some have corduroy or moleskin jacket and trousers, and cloth cap; others have a plain frock-coat and cap.

Many of the robberies from carts are done by the connivance of the carters. They are sent by business establishments to dispose of goods over the metropolis; some of them are connected with the worst class of thieves. They connive with those men in stealing their employers' property, and in rifling other carts, carry the booty away in their own, and always manage to secure a part of the prize.

These carters take thieves occasionally to railway stations to assist them with their work, and when an opportunity occurs, carry off goods from the railway platform, such as bales of bacon, cheese, bags of nails, boxes of tin and copper, and travellers' luggage, which they dispose of to marine-store dealers and at chandlers' shops. The wearing apparel in the trunks they sell at second-hand shops, kept by Jews and others in low neighbourhoods, such as Petticoat Lane, Lambeth, Westminster, and the Borough of Southwark.

Many carts are rifled by persons who represent themselves as hawkers or costermongers—men who have no steady industrious mode of livelihood, and are usually in the company of prostitutes and thieves of the worst description. The carter may have occasion to call at a city house, and to leave his horse and cart in the street, when they steal a whip, coat, or horsecloth, the reins from off the horse, or any portable article they can lay their hands on.

Numbers of hay, straw, and store carmen frequently steal a truss of hay, or clover, or straw, from their employer's cart, and dispose of it to some person who has a horse, or pony, or donkey, for a small sum of money. These dishonest practices are carried on to a far greater extent than the public are aware of, as it is only occasionally they are brought to public notice.

Robberies from cabs and carriages are sometimes effected in the following way:—They follow the cab or vehicle with a horse

and cart, driving along in its wake—two or three thieves generally in the cart. One of them jumps on the spring of the conveyance while the driver is sitting in front of his vehicle, pulls
down the trunk or box, and slips it into the cart, then drives
away with the booty.

At other times they run up, and leap on the spring of the
conveyance while the driver is proceeding along with his back
toward them; lower the trunk or other article from the roof,
and walk off with it. These trunks sometimes contain money,
silver plate, and other valuable property.

These depredations are always done at night, by experienced
thieves, and generally in the winter season. They are common
in the fashionable squares of the West End, at the East End,
toward the Commercial Road and St. George's-in-the-East, at
Ratcliffe Highway, the City, the Borough of Southwark, and
Lambeth, along the docks, and at the railway stations around
the metropolis.

There are a number of laundresses residing at Chelsea, Uxbridge,
Hampstead, Holloway, and other districts in the suburbs, who
wash large quantities of clothes for the gentry and nobility in
the fashionable streets and squares of the metropolis. After
washing and dressing the linen, they pack it up in large wicker
baskets, and generally convey it in their own carts to the residences of the owners.

A class of people are frequently on the look-out for these carts
to plunder them of their linen. The carts are under the management of a man or a woman. The thieves follow the vehicle to
a quiet street, one puts his shoulder under a basket while the
other cuts the cord which attaches it to the cart, when both
make off with the stolen property.

These thieves reside over London in low districts, such as St.
Giles's and Shoreditch, and are occasionally brought before the
police courts.

There is a class of robberies from gentlemen's carriages about
the West End of the metropolis. In going to the Opera, West
End theatres, or other fashionable places of amusement, the
gentleman frequently leaves his valuable overcoat or cloak in
the carriage. These thieves follow the conveyance to some quiet
street leading to the stables where the vehicle is to remain till the
gentleman returns from his evening's amusement. They let
down the window of the carriage and carry off any article which

is left. The theft is nimbly committed while the vehicle is on its way to the stables, or when it is returning to the Opera, and is done chiefly by young men, experienced thieves. They live in the low neighbourhoods already referred to.

There is a good deal of this mode of thieving carried on in the West End of London during the winter season.

Stealing Lead From House-tops, Copper From Kitchens, and Workmen's Tools, etc., in Dwelling-Houses

OF late this mode of thieving has been extensively carried on over the metropolis, chiefly at unoccupied houses. In some cases, a key is obtained by the thief, respectable in appearance, from the gentleman who lets the house, without his accompanying him to the empty dwelling, when he takes the opportunity of stealing the copper boiler from the washing-house, and the lead pipe from the butt or cistern. He passes the stolen property to some of his associates, and returns the key of the dwelling.

This is a peculiar class who make a livelihood by going round empty houses in different districts on similar errands. They do not give their name and address, are strangers in the neighbourhood, and cannot be easily tracked out by the police.

Lead is frequently stolen from the house-tops, by the loafing ruffians we have before described, who lounge about public-houses, robbing drunken men, and occasionally by boys. Sometimes these robberies are committed by plumbers' workmen and others engaged in repairing the houses.

Lead in most cases is stolen from those dwellings which are under repair, or have been unoccupied for some time. When a house is repaired, it frequently happens the roofs of the adjoining occupied houses are stripped and carried off by unprincipled workmen.

These depredations are often committed by the workmen themselves, or by their connivance. At other times they are done by persons climbing over low walls, and clambering up spouts to the roof, and cutting up the sheet lead. This is usually done under night by two or more in company; sometimes, though rarely, by boys. One keeps a look-out to see there is no person near to detect them. This person is termed a "crow". If anyone should be near, the "crow" gives a signal, and they decamp. Before commencing their depredations, they generally look out for the means of escape, seldom returning the same way they mounted the roof. They make their way out in another direction. If hard pressed, they sometimes hide themselves on the roof behind chimneys, or lie down in gutters or cisterns or any other likely place of concealment. These felonies are often done by bricklayers' labourers (Irish cockneys) during the winter, and in many cases, as we have said, with the connivance of the workmen engaged in repairing the houses.

There is another class of persons who engage in lead-stealing from the roofs of houses. They were formerly in the service of builders, plumbers, or carpenters, but are out of employment. They go to their late employer's customers, under the pretext that they were sent by him to repair the roof, and meanwhile plunder the sheet lead, which they generally roll up, convey down, and carry off by means of their accomplices, who are hovering in the neighbourhood. They have the appearance and dress of industrious workmen, and may have been lately seen employed in houses in the neighbourhood, so that they are more likely to deceive the unsuspecting people who admit them into their dwellings. This kind of lead-stealing has been lately of very frequent occurrence in the metropolis.

Copper is frequently stolen from the boilers in the kitchens and wash-houses by the same parties. Sometimes they enter by the area door or the window, which is left open. At other times they climb the garden wall at the back of the house, and enter by a window, left unfastened. They take the copper out of the brickwork in the wash-house, or from the kitchen, roll it up and carry it away. This is generally done in unoccupied houses. Sweeps employed cleaning the chimneys sometimes take away copper in like manner in their soot-bags.

In houses under repair, as well as in unfinished houses, they steal carpenters' tools, planes, saws, ploughs, squares, hammers, &c., left by the workmen.

They obtain access to the house by climbing over the wooden enclosure or over garden walls. This is generally done in the evening, between the hours of 9 and 12, and frequently by discharged workmen.

In many cases they are stopped on the way with the tools in their possession. If a proper account is not given, it often leads to the detection of the robbery, which generally puts a stop for the time to such depredations in that neighbourhood.

The stolen tools are taken to pawnbrokers or receiving-shops, and sold at an under price. In some cases the pawnbroker gives notice to the police, but in these other shops, this is seldom or never done.

The thieves generally go to some house where no watchman is employed.

Robberies By False Keys

THERE are many robberies committed in the metropolis by means of false keys, generally between the hours of seven and nine o'clock in the evening. After nine o'clock they would be considered burglaries. This class of robberies is generally committed by thieves of experience, and frequently, before depredations are committed, persons call at the house in the daytime, who take particular notice of the lock of the street-door, to know the key which opens it, whether a Bramah, Chubb, or other lock. These persons are termed "putters up of robberies," and supply the thieves with the requisite information, when they come in the evening and enter the house. In many cases they get clear off with the booty.

The houses entered are frequently respectable lodging-houses, or houses occupied by one family where there are likely to be no children about the upper rooms. In the case of entering these dwellings they make their way to the bedrooms above, their chief object being to steal the jewellery and dressing-case left on the dressing-table, often of great value. They also take clothes out of the drawers, and other articles. On coming out they often put on some of the apparel, such as an overcoat, and fill the pockets with stolen property.

In houses in the West End, single gentlemen, such as government clerks, officers in the army, and others, are often out dining in the evening, or at the clubs; and as the servant is generally engaged downstairs at this time, the thief is frequently not obstructed.

To elude suspicion from the police constables in the street they often have a carpet-bag to carry off the booty. If they meet one of them near the house, they generally ask him some question, such as the way to some street, to take him off his guard.

A case of this kind occurred early this year at the West End, where four men were engaged in a robbery. On their arriving at the corner of the street where the felony was committed they found two policemen there. They stepped up to them, and conversed for some time, when the constables left, having no suspicion, from their respectable appearance. Two of the thieves crossed the street to a house opposite. Meanwhile their movements were narrowly watched by a keen-eyed detective, who knew the parties, three of the four being returned convicts. Having arrived at the door of the house, they endeavoured to gain an entrance, which, after trying several keys, they effected. The other two confederates had taken up a position opposite the house, being what is termed "look-out," or outside men.

In a short time the two who had entered the house came out and closed the door behind them. They were perceived to have some bulky articles in their possession. The other two men remained for a few minutes in their place on the opposite side of the street, when they followed their companions. When at a short distance from the house, they rejoined them, and the property was divided among them. This was done in the dusk in the quiet street.

The detective officer saw two of the parties with Inverness capes, and carrying umbrellas in their hand they did not have before they entered the house. He went up to them, told them who he was, and arrested one of them; the other was captured a few yards off by another officer when in the act of throwing off the Inverness cape. The other two, meanwhile, escaped. On conducting the two men to the police-station the two capes were taken from them, and in their pockets were found a number of skeleton keys, a wax-taper, and silent lights, along with various small articles, evidently part of the robbery which had just been committed.

Two hours after this a gentleman drove up in a cab to the police-station, and gave information of the robbery, when he identified the articles taken from the prisoners as his property. The two thieves were tried at the sessions, and sentenced to six years' penal servitude. One of the two confederates who escaped was apprehended by the same detective, found guilty, and sentenced to the same punishment, which broke up a gang of thieves who had infested the neighbourhood for several months, and occasioned great alarm.

Robberies from gentlemen's houses by means of false keys are generally put up by some person acquainted with the house, and who may have frequented it under some pretext, such as by courting the servant girl, or by being acquainted with some of the men-servants. They rifle the valuables from wardrobes and drawing-rooms, such as watches, rings, purses, clothes, &c.

Attic thieves chiefly aim at abstracting jewels from ladies' bedrooms, generally on the second floor; but this class of skeleton-key thieves frequently carry away bundles of stolen goods, and are not so fastidious in their choice.

An instance of a skeleton-key robbery from a gentleman's house occurred lately at the West End of the metropolis. The two thieves had engaged a cab to carry off the stolen property (the driver of the cab being a confederate), and drove up to the house next door to where the robbery was to be committed. They were seen to leave the cab, to go up to the door of the house, to apply the key to the door, and to walk in. About ten minutes after, they left the house, and walked to the cab with large parcels in their hands, when it drove swiftly away.

On that evening the butler of the house discovered that the whole of his master's clothes had been stolen from his wardrobe, and his dressing-case, with costly articles, his gold watch and chain, and the whole of his linen. Information was given to a detective officer, who in two days after traced the robbery to two well-known thieves, one of them being singularly expert in the use of skeleton keys.

The manner in which it was detected was very ingenious, and reflected high credit on the officer.

On visiting a public-house near Tottenham Court Road, one Saturday night, he saw a middle-aged, intelligent man, like a respectable mechanic, conversing with a person at the bar over a pint of half-and-half. The sharp eye of the detective observed the former with a neckerchief which corresponded with one of the articles of this stolen property. The suspicion of the officer was aroused, and he followed him late at night, and saw where he resided. On the next morning he went with two officers to his house, and found him in bed with his paramour, and arrested him for the robbery. On searching his house a handkerchief was found marked with the crest of the nobleman to whom the property belonged. On a further search a quantity of other articles were found belonging to this robbery.

On his paramour getting out of bed she was perceived by the detective to conceal something under her petticoats. On being asked to produce it, she denied having anything. On being searched, another handkerchief was found on her person, bearing the nobleman's crest. This man was afterwards identified as one of the two persons who were seen to enter the house where the robbery was committed, and to leave with the cab. He was tried at the Sessions, and sentenced to seven years' penal servitude. This man had for some time been well-known to the police, and was suspected of committing a series of large robberies, but he was so dexterous in executing his felonies that his movements had not previously been traced.

Robberies By Lodgers

ROBBERIES are frequently committed by lodgers in various parts of the metropolis, in low as well as in middle-class localities.

A great many of these are committed in low neighbourhoods, by abandoned women, frequently young. They commit depredations in their own room, or in other rooms in the house in which they lodge, by entering open doors, or by turning the key when the door is locked, while the parties are out. Many of these are done by prostitutes of the lowest order, who sometimes steal the linen, bedding, wearing-apparel, and other property, and pawn or sell it.

Robberies of this kind are sometimes perpetrated by mechanics' wives, addicted to dissipated habits, who steal similar articles from dwelling-houses. Sometimes they are done by servants out of place, driven to steal by poverty and destitution; at other times by sewing girls, often toiling from 4 in the morning to 10 o'clock at night for about 8*d*. a day—many of whom commit suicide rather than resort to prostitution; and occasionally by clerks and shopmen—fast young men, when in poverty and distress; and by betting-men and skittle-sharps.

In March, 1861, two known prostitutes, lodging together in a house in Charlotte Street, were brought before the Lambeth police court for a felony committed in the room in which they lodged. They abstracted knives and forks, plates and spoons, along with two chairs, rifling the apartment of nearly all it contained. They were convicted and sentenced, the one to three months,' and the other to six months', imprisonment — the latter having been previously convicted.

Another felony occurred lately in Isabella Street, Lambeth,

where a mechanic's wife stole the bed-clothes and the feathers out of a bed in the house in which she lodged. Her husband was glad to pay the amount to prevent criminal prosecution.

There are many felonies committed by persons lodging in coffee-houses and hotels, some of them of considerable value. The hotel thieves assume the manner and air of gentlemen, dress well, and live in high style. They lodge for an evening or two in some fashionable hotel, frequently near the railway stations. They get up at night, when the house is quiet and business suspended, and commit robberies in the house. They have an ingenious mode of opening the doors, though locked in the inner side, by inserting a peculiar instrument and turning round the key. They go stealthily into the rooms, and abstract silver plate, articles of jewellery, watches, money, and other valuables.

These persons usually leave early in the morning, before the other gentlemen get up. Some of them are young, and others are middle-aged. They have generally some acquaintance with commercial transactions, and conduct themselves like active business men. They are birds of passage, and do not reside long in any one locality, as they would become known to the police.

A very extensive robbery of this kind occurred some time ago at a fashionable hotel in the metropolis, near the Great Northern Railway, to the amount of £700 or £800. The thief was apprehended at York, and committed for trial.

Robberies By Servants

THERE are a great number of felonies committed by servants over the metropolis, many of which might be prevented by prudent precautions on the part of their employers. On this subject we would wish to speak with discrimination. We are aware that many honest and noble-minded servants are treated with injustice by the caprice and bad temper of their employers, and many a poor girl is without cause dismissed from her situation, and refused a proper certificate of character. Being unable to get another place, she is often driven with reluctance from poverty and destitution to open prostitution on the street. On the other hand, many of our employers foolishly and thoughtlessly receive male and female servants into their service without making a proper inquiry into their character.

Many felonies are committed by domestic female servants who

have been only a month or six weeks in service. Some of them steal tea, sugar, and other provisions, which are frequently given to acquaintances or relatives out of doors. Others occasionally abstract linen and articles of wearing-apparel, or plunder the wardrobe of gold bracelets, rings, pearl necklaces, watch, chain, or other jewellery, or of muslin and silk dresses and mantles, which they either keep in their trunk, or otherwise dispose of.

Female domestic servants are often connected with many felonies committed in the metropolis. Two of the female servants in a gentleman's family are sometimes courted by two smartly-dressed young men, bedecked with jewellery, who visit them at the house occasionally. One of them may call by himself on a certain evening, and after sitting with them for some time in the kitchen, may pretend that he is going upstairs to the front door on some errand, such as to bring in some liquor. He goes alone, and opens the door to his companion whom he had arranged to meet him and who may be hovering in the street. He admits him into the house to rifle the rooms in the floors above. Meantime he comes in with the liquor, and proceeds downstairs, and remains there for some time to occupy the attention of the servants until his companion has plundered the house of money, jewels or other property.

On other occasions, two young men may remain downstairs with the servants, while a third party is committing a robbery in the apartments above.

Some respectable-looking young women, in the service of middle-class and fashionable families, are connected with burglars, and have been recommended to their places through their influence, or that of their acquaintances. Some of these females are usually not a fortnight or a month in service before a heavy burglary is committed in the house, and will remain for two or three months longer to prevent suspicion. They will then take another similar place in a gentleman's family, remain several months there, and by their conduct ingratiate themselves into the good graces of the master and mistress, when another burglary is committed through their connivance. The booty is shared between them and the thieves.

Some continue this system for a considerable time, as their employers have no suspicion of their villainy. They are often Irish cockneys, connected with the thieves, and have been trained with them from their infancy. They generally aim at stealing the silver plate, clothes, and other valuables. In these robberies they are always ready to give the "hue and cry" when a depredation has been committed.

There are often instances of these robberies brought before the police-courts and sessions, where the dishonesty of many servants is brought to light.

There are many felonies committed by the male servants in gentlemen's families; some of them of considerable value. Numbers of these are occasioned by betting on the part of the butlers, who have the charge of the plate. They go and bet on different horses, and pawn a certain quantity of plate which has not the crest of their employer on it, and expect to be able to redeem it as soon as they have got money when the horse has won. He may happen to lose. He bets again on some other horse he thinks will win — perhaps bets to a considerable amount, and thinks he will be able to redeem his loss; he again possibly loses his bet. His master is perhaps out of town, not having occasion to use the plate.

On his coming home there may be a dinner-party, when the plate is called for. The butler absconds, and part of the plate is found to be missing. Information is given to the police; some pawnbroker may be so honourable as to admit the plate is in his possession. The servant is apprehended, convicted, and sentenced possibly to penal servitude. Cases of this kind occasionally occur, and are frequently caused by such betting transactions.

Robberies occasionally are perpetrated by servants in shops and warehouses, clerks, warehousemen, and others, of money and goods of various kinds.

A remarkable case of robbery by a servant occurred lately. A young man, employed by a locksmith, near the West End of the metropolis, was frequently sent to gentlemen's houses on his master's business to pick locks. In many of the houses where he was employed, money and other property was found missing. He went to pick a lock at a jeweller's shop. After he was gone, the jeweller found a beautiful gold chain missing. As his son was a fast young man, he was afraid to charge the young locksmith with the robbery. Meantime the latter was sent to other houses, and in those places articles were found missing, and servants in the families were discharged on suspicion of committing the robberies.

He went to a solicitor's office to pick the locks of some boxes containing title-deeds and money. From one of the boxes, which he did not require to open, he stole £100 and locked it up again. The head clerk was then away on business for several days. On his return he found that one of the boxes in the office had been opened and £100 had been abstracted.

Information was given to Bow Street police office by the solicitor, who offered £5 as a reward to anyone who would give information regarding the robbery. Meantime he stated he would give no one into custody. His clerks had been with him a long time. He had one man employed in the office to pick some locks, but as he belonged to a respectable firm, he did not believe it to be him. Meantime the solicitor discharged his general clerks. His confidential clerk was so indignant at this that he gave in his resignation.

One of the most accomplished detective officers of the Bow Street police resolved to ferret out the matter. It was arranged the journeyman locksmith was to be sent to a certain house to pick a lock in an apartment where some money was placed which had been marked. The detective watched his movements from the next room. On this occasion also, he not only picked the lock as requested, but picked other locks in the room, and carried off part of the money which was marked.

When he went downstairs, he was detained till it was ascertained if the money had been tampered with. On inspecting it, part was missing. He was taken into custody, and the money got on his person. On searching his house a waggon load of stolen property was found, belonging to a series of robberies he had committed in the houses he had visited, amounting in value to £200. All the charges against him were not investigated. He was tried for nine acts of robbery at Clerkenwell, convicted, and sentenced to six years' penal servitude. He was one of the finest locksmiths in the world, and received from his employer higher wages than the other workmen in the establishment.

Area and Lobby Sneaks

THIS is a large, and variegated class of thieves, ranging from the little ragged boy of six years of age, to the old woman of threescore and ten. Some are hanging in rags and tatters in pitiable condition; others have a respectable appearance likely to disarm suspicion. Some are ignorant and obtuse; others are intelligent, and have got a tolerable education. Some are skulking and timid; others are so venturesome as to enter dwelling-houses through open windows, and conceal themselves in closets, waiting a favourable opportunity to skulk off, unobserved, with plunder.

Numbers of little ragged boys sneak around the areas of dwellings, where respectable tradesmen reside, as well as in the fashionable streets of the metropolis. We may see them loitering about half-naked, or fluttering in shreds and patches, sometimes alone, at other times in small bands, looking with skulking eye into the areas, as they move along. They are not permitted to beg at the houses, and some of them have no ostensible errand to visit those localities, and are hunted away by the police. During the day they generally sneak in the thoroughfares and quiet by-streets of London.

A few days ago we saw one of them skulking along Blackfriars Road. He was about 13 years of age, and had on an old ragged coat, much too large for him, hanging over his back in tatters, with a string to fasten it round his waist, and a pair of old trousers and grey cap. He had the air of an old man, as he lazily walked along, and looked a pitiable object. On seeing us eyeing him with curiosity, he suddenly laid aside his mendicant air, and with sharp keen eye and startled attitude, appeared to take us for a police officer in undress. We looked over our shoulder, as we moved on, and saw him stand for a time looking after us, when he resumed his former downcast appearance, and sauntered slowly along looking eagerly into the areas as he passed. He appeared to us a very good type of the young area sneak.

These area-divers go down into the areas, and open the safes where provisions are kept, such as roast and boiled beef, butter and bread, and fish, and carry off the spoil. If the door is open, they enter the kitchen, and steal anything they can find, such as clothes, wet and dry linen, and sometimes a copper kettle, and silver spoons; or they will take the blacking-brushes from the boothouse. Nothing comes amiss.

There is another class of area sneaks who make their daily calls at gentlemen's houses, ask the servants when they come in contact with them, if they have any kitchen stuff to sell, or old clothes or glass bottles. Should they not find the servant in the kitchen, they try to make their way to the butler's pantry, which generally adjoins the kitchen, and carry off the basket of plate.

These parties are men from 20 years of age and upwards.

There is a class of women who go down the areas, under pretence of selling combs, stay-laces, boot-laces and other trifling commodities. When they find a stealthy opportunity, many of them carry off articles from the kitchen, similar to those just described. These people are of all ages, some young, others tottering with old age. They generally belong to London, and go their regular rounds over the streets and squares. Many of them live in Westminster, St. Giles's and Kent Street in the Borough.

There are other sneaks who enter the lobbies of houses, and commit robberies, chiefly in the West End districts. These persons are of the same class with the area sneak, but perhaps a step higher in the thievish profession. Their depredations are generally committed in the morning between 7 and 8, when servants are busily engaged dusting furniture and sweeping the hall and rooms. These thieves are then seen loitering about watching a favourable opportunity to steal.

The mode of stealing is the same in the passages of the houses of middle-class people, and the entry halls of the elegant mansions of the gentry and aristocracy. Some of these thieves are men respectably dressed while others are in more shabby condition. They are young and middle-aged. You may see them in those quiet localities, generally in dark clothing, having the appearance of respectable mechanics, or warehousemen. Others are like men who hang about the streets to run messages and assist menservants.

They walk into the house, and pilfer any article they can find, such as articles of clothing, umbrellas, and walking-canes. Sometimes they take a coat off the knob and whip it under the breast of their coat, or put it on over their own. They frequently carry off a bundle of clothes, and sell them to some receiver of stolen property.

Such robberies are frequent in the neighbourhood of Brompton, Chelsea, Pimlico, Paddington, Stepney, Hackney, Bayswater, Camberwell, the Kent Road and other similar districts.

The lobby sneaks are the same class of persons as those who enter the areas, and contrive to get a livelihood in this way. They live in various parts of London, such as the dirty slums, alleys, and by-streets of Covent Garden, Drury Lane and St. Giles's, Somers Town, Westminster, the Borough, Whitechapel, and Walworth Common and other similar neighbourhoods.

Sometimes these men are seen in public-houses with large sums of money, no doubt got from the disposal of their plunder; and at other times lounge in low coffee-houses, without even the scanty means of paying for their bed, and are scarcely able to pay a penny for a cup of coffee. They often have to ask assistance from their companions, though a few days previous they may have been seen in possession of handfuls of cash.

They are usually unmarried, and live an uncomfortable, homeless life; often cohabiting with a low class of women, miserably clad, and generally wretched in appearance.

Middle-aged and elderly women are occasionally engaged in sneaking depredations from the dwelling-houses of labouring men. An old woman may observe a child standing at her mother's door, and ask if her mother is in. When the child answers "No," she will say, "I will mind the house, while you go and get a halfpenny worth of sweets," giving the little girl a halfpenny. On the child's return the woman has decamped carrying away with her money, or any other portable article she may have found in the house. This is the class of women we have noticed stealing from the shops of the butchers and cheesemongers.

It is a strange fact, that many of these common thieves, engaged in paltry sneaking thefts, have a more desperate and criminal appearance than most of the daring burglars and highwaymen. Their soft and timid natures feel more poignant misery in their debased and anxious life than the more stern and callous ruffians of a higher class, engaged in more extraordinary adventures.

Another class of larcenies in dwelling-houses are committed by means of false messages.

This is a very ingenious mode of thieving, and is done by means of calling at the house, and stating to the servants that they are sent from respectable firms in the neighbourhood for some article of dress to be repaired, or for lamps, fenders, glasses, or decanters to be mended, with other pretences of various descriptions.

Their object is to get the absence of the servant from the hall. While the servant is upstairs, telling a man has called, sent by such and such a firm, they walk into the dining-room on the first floor, and abstract any articles of plate that may be exposed, silver-mounted inkstands, books, or other property. If they don't succeed in this, and see no article of value, they will return to the hall, and clear the passages of the coats hanging on the knobs, and the umbrellas and walking-sticks from the stand, while an accomplice is generally outside to receive the property. Should the servant come down too soon, while he has only got a short distance off, no property is found upon his person. They seldom take hats, as these could be easily detected.

They have an endless variety of ingenious expedients to effect this object. A case of this kind occurred in the district of Marylebone a short time ago, where a gentleman was in quest of a lady's maid, and advertised in the "Times" newspaper, and at the same time answered a number of advertisements by anonymous persons. The next day his house was thronged by a number of people anxious to obtain the situation.

After all had left, a purse containing a large amount of money was missing, consisting partly of bank-notes; when he gave information to the police. Some days after, through the admirable ingenuity and tact of a detective officer at Marylebone, a person was traced out in the locality of Edgware Road, as having been guilty of the felony, and the stolen purse was found on her person. Her apprehension led to the discovery that she had been pursuing a system of robberies of this description over various parts of the metropolis, for twelve months previously. She was sentenced to three years' penal servitude, and while in Milbank Penitentiary, committed suicide about three months after.

These felonies abound chiefly in the West End of the metropolis, in the neighbourhood of Belgravia, Russell and Bedford Squares, Oxford Square, Gloucester Square, Seymour Street, Hyde Park Street, Gloucester Terrace, and other fashionable localities. They are often committed by servants of worthless character out of situation, also lads of respectable appearance, sent out by trainers of thieves who often begin their despicable life in this manner, and advance to picking of pockets and burglary.

Stealing by Lifting Up Windows or Breaking Glass

AREA-SNEAKS frequently lift up the kitchen windows to steal. Sometimes they cannot reach the articles through the iron bars, and have recourse to an ingenious expedient to effect their object. They tie two sticks together, and attach a hook to the end, and seize hold of any articles they can find and draw them through the bars; they frequently leave their sticks behind them, which are found by the police.

There is generally an iron fastening in the centre of the window

frame. The thief inserts a small thin knife or other sharp instrument in the opening of the frame, and forces back the iron catch.
In some instances a fastening or clasp in the inner side of the
window is pushed back by means of breaking a pane of glass.
These robberies are often committed in dwelling-houses in Queen
Street, Mitre Street, and Webber Street, near Blackfriars Road;
in Tower Street, Waterloo Road, and similar localities—generally
by a man and a young lad. This young lad is employed to enter
the window of the house to be robbed, which in these localities is
often a front parlour. The window is drawn up softly, not to
excite any alarm.

The man generally keeps watch while the lad enters the house
perhaps at the corner of the street, when both decamp with the
property.

In some instances they break the glass in the same way that
star-glazers do at shop-windows, as already described. This is
done either at the front or the back window. They prefer the back
window if there is a ready access to it. These robberies are committed in occupied houses as well as in houses while the inmates
are absent for a few days. They steal money, trinkets, linen, or
anything that is easily carried off.

Similar robberies are perpetrated by two or more persons at
the West End fashionable houses by the area or back windows,
when they steal money, jewels, mantelpiece clocks, clothes, linen
and other property.

Sometimes they enter by cutting the window with a diamond.
These felonies are often of considerable value.

The parlour windows are sometimes lifted up by young thieves
in the morning, when plate is laid on the table for breakfast; the
servant frequently leaves the dining-room window open for
ventilation, when they effect an entrance in this way:—one throws
a cap into the area by way of joke, or through the window into
the room; another mounts the railings and enters the window.
Should any of the inmates detect him, he will say that "a lad
had thrown his cap into the house, and he came in to fetch it."
If not disturbed, he carries off the silver plate, and often returns
through the window with the plunder without being observed.
These thieves take any article easily carried off, such as wearing
apparel, work-boxes, or fancy clocks, and are generally Irish
cockneys; they are to be found in considerable numbers in the
vicinity of King's Cross, Waterloo Road, and other localities.

They abstract any valuable property they find lying about, but their chief object is to get the silver plate.

There are few cases of larceny from back bedroom windows, as the servants and inmates are generally hovering about after breakfast. This is sometimes effected, though rarely, by the connivance of the servants.

At other times these robberies from the house are committed by means of breaking a pane of glass, when the thieves undo the fastening of the window and effect an entrance. This is often perpetrated during the temporary absence of the inmates.

The statistics in this class of robberies will be given when we come to treat on "Attic or Garret Thieves."

Attic or Garret Thieves

THESE are generally the most expert thieves in the metropolis. Their mode of operation is this:—They call at a dwelling-house with a letter, or have communication with some of the servants, for the purpose of discovering the best means of access, and to learn how the people in the house are engaged and the time most suitable for the depredation. They generally come to plunder the house in the evening, when one or two of their accomplices loiter about, watching the movements of the police, the other meanwhile proceeding to the roof of the house.

These attic robberies are generally effected through unoccupied houses—perhaps by the house next door, or some other on the same side of the street. They pass through the attic to the roof, and proceed along the gutters and coping to the attic window of the house to be robbed. They unfasten the attic window by taking the pane of glass out, or pushing the fastening back, and enter the dwelling. This is generally done about 7 or 8 o'clock in the evening, when the family are at dinner—the servants being engaged between the dining-room on the first floor and the kitchen below, serving up the dinner.

The thieves proceed to the bedroom on the second floor, and force open the wardrobe with a short jemmy which they carry, and try to find the jewel-case and any other articles of value. Their object is generally to get valuable jewels.

The dining-room is on the first floor, so that they have often full scope for their operations without being seen or obstructed, while the inmates are engaged below. They return the same way through the attic window on the roof, run along the gutters, and escape by the same house through which they entered.

A very remarkable robbery of this kind occurred in the beginning of 1861 at Lowndes Square, where the thieves entered through an attic and obtained jewels to the amount of £3,000.

On their return from the dwelling-house, it being a very windy night, a hat belonging to one of them was blown from the housetop upon one of the slanting roofs he could not reach, which afterwards led to his detection. A short time previously it was in the hands of a hatter for certain repairs, when he inserted a paper marked with his name within it. The thief was arrested, tried, and got ten years' penal servitude.

Some get to the roof by means of a ladder placed outside an unfinished house, or house under repair, and steal in the same manner.

An ingenious attempt at a jewel robbery occurred lately by means of a cab drawing up with a lady before a dwelling-house. The cabman, who was evidently in collusion with the thieves, dismounted, rang the bell, and told the butler who answered the door, that a lady wished to see him. On his coming to the cab, it being about ten or fifteen yards from the street-door, he was kept in conversation by a female. Meantime he observed a respectable-looking man steal into the house from the street, while thus engaged. He left the cab without taking any notice of what he saw, and entered the house, when the cab drove off at a rapid rate, which convinced him that there was something wrong. He made his way up into the bedroom on the second floor, and found a man of respectable appearance concealed in the apartment. An officer was called and the man was searched. There was found on his person a jemmy, a wax taper, and silent lights. He was taken into custody; but no trace of the cabman or woman could be found. He was afterwards committed for the offence.

These attic thieves generally live in Hackney Road and Kingsland Road. On one occasion a gang was discovered in a furnished house in Russell Square. They generally have apartments in respectable neighbourhoods to avoid suspicion, and have servants to attend them, who assist in disposing of the stolen property. The best attic thieves reside in Hackney and Kingsland Roads, and many are to be found in the neighbourhood of Shoreditch Church; a few of them are known to be residing in Waterloo Road, but not of so high a class as in the localities referred to.

The women connected with them have an abundance of jewellery; they live in high style, with plenty of cash, but not displayed to any great extent at the time any robbery is committed, as it would excite suspicion.

Many of them have a very gentleman-like appearance, and none but a detective officer would know them. When brought before the police courts for these felonies, it is usual to have constables brought from all the districts to see them and make them known, which very much annoys them.

They generally succeed in making off with their booty, and are seldom caught. Their robberies are skilfully planned, in the same experienced careful manner in which burglaries are effected. They have gone through all grades of thieving from their infancy— through sneaking and picking pockets.

This is a late system of robbery, and has been carried on rather extensively over the West End of the metropolis.

A VISIT TO THE ROOKERY OF ST. GILES AND ITS NEIGHBOURHOOD

In company with a police officer we proceeded to the Seven Dials, one of the most remarkable localities in London, inhabited by bird-fanciers, keepers of stores of old clothes and old shoes, costermongers, patterers, and a motley assemblage of others, chiefly of the lower classes. As we stood at one of the angles in the centre of the Dials we saw three young men—burglars— loitering at an opposite corner of an adjoining dial. One of them had a gentlemanly appearance, and was dressed in superfine black cloth and beaver hat. The other two were attired as mechanics or tradesmen. One of them had recently returned from penal servitude, and another had undergone a long imprisonment.

Leaving the Seven Dials and its dingy neighbourhood, we went to Oxford Street, one of the first commercial streets in London, and one of the finest in the world. It reminded us a good deal of the celebrated Broadway, New York, although the buildings of the latter are in some places more costly and splendid, and some of the shops more magnificent. Oxford Street is one of the main streets of London, and is ever resounding with the din of vehicles, carts, cabs, hansoms, broughams, and omnibuses driving along. Many of the shops are spacious and crowded with costly goods, and the large windows of plate-glass, set in massive brass frames, are gaily furnished with their various articles of merchandise.

On the opposite side of the street, we observed a jolly, comfortable-looking, elderly man, like a farmer in appearance, not at all like a London sharper. He was standing looking along the street as though he were waiting for someone. He was a magsman (a skittle-sharp), and no doubt other members of the gang were hovering near. He appeared to be as cunning as an old fox in his movements, admirably fitted to entrap the unwary.

A little farther along the street we saw a fashionably-dressed man coming towards us, arm-in-arm with his companion, among the throng of people. They were in the prime of life, and had a respectable, and even opulent appearance. One of them was good-humoured and social, as though he were on good terms with himself and society in general; the other was more callous and reserved, and more suspicious in his aspect. Both were bedecked with glittering watch chains and gold rings. They passed by a few paces, when the more social of the two, looking over his shoulder, met our eye directed towards him, turned back and accosted us, and was even so generous as to invite us into a gin-palace near by, which we courteously declined. The two magsmen (card-sharpers) strutted off, like fine gentlemen, along the street on the outlook for their victims.

Here we saw another young man, a burglar, pass by. He had an engaging appearance, and was very tasteful in his dress, very unlike the rough burglars we met at Whitechapel, the Borough and Lambeth.

Leaving Oxford Street we went along Holborn to Chancery Lane, chiefly frequented by barristers and attorneys, and entered Fleet Street, one of the main arteries of the metropolis, reminding us of London in the olden feudal times, when the streets were crowded together in dense masses, flanked with innumerable dingy alleys, courts and by-streets, like a great rabbit-warren. Fleet Street, though a narrow, business street, with its traffic often choked with vehicles, is interesting from its antique, historical and literary associations. Elbowing our way through the throng of people, we passed through one of the gloomy arches of Temple Bar, and issued into the Strand, where we saw two pickpockets, young, tall, gentlemanly men, cross the street from St. Clement's Church and enter a restaurant. They were attired in a suit of superfine black cloth, cut in fashionable style. They entered an elegant dining-room, and probably sat down to costly viands and wines.

Leaving the Strand, we went up St. Martin's Lane, a narrow street leading from the Strand to the Seven Dials. We here saw a young man, an expert burglar, of about twenty-four years of age and dark complexion, standing at the corner of the street. He was well dressed, in a dark cloth suit, with a billicock hat. One of his comrades was taken from his side about three weeks ago on a charge of burglary.

Entering a beershop in the neighbourhood of St. Giles, close by the Seven Dials, we saw a band of coiners and ringers of changes. One of them, a genteel-looking, slim youth, is a notorious coiner, and has been convicted. He was sitting quietly by the door over a glass of beer, with his companion by his side. One of them is a moulder; another was sentenced to ten years' penal servitude for coining and selling base coin. A modest-looking young man, one of the gang, was seated by the bar, also respectably dressed. He is generally supposed to be a subordinate connected with this coining band, looking out, while they are coining, that no officers of justice are near, and carrying the bag of base money for them when they go out to sell it to base wretches in small quantities at low prices. Five shillings' worth of base money is generally sold for tenpence. "Ringing the changes" is effected in this way:—A person offers a good sovereign to a shopkeeper to be changed. The gold piece is chinked on the counter, or otherwise tested, and is proved to be good. The man hastily asks back and gets the sovereign, and pretends that he has some silver, so that he does not require to change it. On feeling his pocket he finds he does not have it, and returns a base piece of money resembling it, instead of the genuine gold piece.

We returned to Bow Street, and saw three young pickpockets proceeding along in company, like three well-dressed coster-mongers, in dark cloth frock-coats and caps.

Being desirous of having a more thorough knowledge of the people residing in the rookery of St. Giles, we visited it with Mr. Hunt, inspector of police. We first went to a lodging-house in George Street, Oxford Street, called the Hampshire-Hog Yard. Most of the lodgers were then out. On visiting a room in the garret we saw a man, in mature years, making artificial flowers; he appeared to be very ingenious, and made several roses before us with marvellous rapidity. He had suspended along the ceiling bundles of dyed grasses of various hues, crimson, yellow, green, brown, and other colours to furnish cases of stuffed birds. He was a very intelligent man and a natural genius. He told us strong drink had brought him to this humble position in the garret, and that he once had the opportunity of making a fortune in the service of a nobleman. We felt, as we looked on his countenance and listened to his conversation, he was capable of moving in a higher sphere of life. Yet he was wonderfully contented with his humble lot.

We visited Dyott House, George Street, the ancient manor-house of St. Giles-in-the-Fields, now fitted up as a lodging-house for simple men. The kitchen, an apartment about fifteen feet square, is surrounded with massive and tasteful panelling in the olden style. A large fire blazing in the grate—with two boilers on each side—was kept burning night and day to supply the lodgers with hot water for their tea and coffee. Some rashers of bacon were suspended before the fire, with a plate underneath. There was a gas-light in the centre of the apartment, and a dial on the back wall. The kitchen was furnished with two long deal tables and a dresser, with forms to serve as seats. There were about fifteen labouring men present, most of them busy at supper on fish, and bread, and tea. They were a very mixed company, such as we would expect at a London lodging-house, men working in cab-yards assisting cabmen, some distributing bills in the streets, one man carrying advertising boards, and others jobbing at anything they can find to do in the neighbourhood. This house was clean and comfortable, and had the appearance of being truly a comfortable poor man's home. It was cheerful to look around us and to see the social air of the inmates. One man sat with coat off, enjoying the warmth of the kitchen; a boy was at his tea, cutting up dried fish and discussing his bread and butter. A young man of about nineteen sat at the back of the apartment, with a very sinister countenance, very unlike the others. There was something about him that indicated a troubled mind. We also observed a number of elderly men among the party, some in jackets, and others in velvet coats, with an honest look about them.

When the house was a brothel, about fifteen years ago, an unfortunate prostitute, named Mary Brothers, was murdered in this kitchen by a man named Connell, who was afterwards executed at Newgate for the deed. He had carnal connexion with this woman some time before, and he suspected that she had communicated to him the venereal disease with which he was afflicted. In revenge he took her life, having purchased a knife at a neighbouring cutler's shop.

We were introduced to the landlady, a very stout woman who came up to meet us, candle in hand, as we stood on the staircase. Here we saw the profile of the ancient proprietor of the house, carved over the panelling, set, as it were, in an oval frame. In another part of the staircase we saw a similar frame, but the profile had been removed or destroyed. Over the window that overlooks the staircase there are three figures, possibly likenesses of his daughters; such is the tradition. The balustrade along the staircase is very massive and tastefully carved and ornamented. The bed-rooms were also clean and comfortable.

The beds are furnished with a bed-cover and flock bed, with sufficient warm and clean bedding, for the low charge of 2s. a week, or 4d. a night. The first proprietor of the house is said to have been a magistrate of the city, and a knight or baronet.

Leaving George Street we passed on to Church Lane, a by-street in the rear of New Oxford Street, containing twenty-eight houses. It was dark as we passed along. We saw the street lamps lighted in Oxford Street, and the shop-windows brilliantly illuminated, while the thunder of vehicles in the street broke on our ear, rolling in a perpetual stream. Here a very curious scene presented itself to our view. From the windows of the three-storied houses in Church Lane were suspended wooden rods with clothes to dry across the narrow streets—cotton gowns, sheets, trousers, drawers, and vests, some ragged and patched, and others old and faded giving a more picturesque aspect to the scene, which was enhanced by the dim lights in the windows, and the groups of the lower orders of all ages assembled below, clustered around the doorways, and in front of the houses, or indulging in merriment in the street. Altogether the appearance of the inhabitants was much more clean and orderly than might be expected in such a low locality. Many women of the lower orders, chiefly of the Irish cockneys, were seated, crouching with their knees almost touching their chin, beside the open windows. Some men were smoking their pipes as they stood leaning against the walls of their houses, whom from their appearance we took to be evidently out-door labourers. Another labouring man was seated on the side of his window, in corduroy trousers, light-gray coat and cap

STREET-PERFORMERS ON STILTS

STREET ACROBATS PERFORMING

with an honest look of good-humour and industry. Numbers of young women, the wives of costermongers, sat in front of their houses in the manner we have described, clad in cotton gowns, with a general aspect of personal cleanliness and contentment. At the corners of the streets, and at many of the doorways, were groups of young costermongers, who had finished their hard day's work, and were contentedly chatting and smoking. They generally stood with their hands in their breeches pockets. Most of these people are Irish, or the children of Irish parents. The darkness of the street was lighted up by the street lamps as well as by the lights in the windows of two chandlers' shops and one public-house. At one of the chandlers' shops the proprietor was standing by his door with folded arms as he looked good-humouredly on his neighbours around his shopdoor. We also saw some of the young Arabs bareheaded and barefooted, with their little hands in their pockets, or squatted on the street, having the usual restless, artful look peculiar to their tribe.

Here a house was pointed out to us, No. 21, which was formerly let at a rent of £25 per annum to a publican that resided in the neighbourhood. He let the same in rooms for £90 a year, and these again receive from parties residing in them upwards of £120. The house is still let in rooms, but they are occupied, like all others in the neighbourhood, by one family only.

At one house as we passed along we saw a woman selling potatoes, at the window, to persons in the street. On looking into the interior we saw a cheerful fire burning in the grate and some women sitting around it. We also observed several bushel baskets and sacks placed round the room, filled with potatoes, of which they sell a large quantity.

In Church Lane we found lodging-houses, the kitchens of which are entered from the street by a descent of a few steps leading underground to the basement. Here we found numbers of people clustered together around several tables, some reading the newspapers, others supping on fish, bread, tea, and potatoes, and some lying half asleep on the tables in all imaginable positions. These, we were told, had just returned from hopping in Kent, had walked long distances, and were fatigued.

On entering some of these kitchens, the ceiling being very low, we found a large fire burning in the grate, and a general air of comfort, cleanliness and order. Such scenes as these were very homely and picturesque, and reminded us very forcibly of localities of London in the olden time. In some of them the inmates were only half dressed, and yet appeared to be very comfortable from the warmth of the apartment. Here we saw a number of the poorest imbeciles we had noticed in the course of our rambles through the great metropolis. Many of them were middle-aged men, others more elderly, very shabbily dressed, and some half naked. There was little manliness left in the poor wretches as they squatted drearily on the benches. The inspector told us they were chiefly vagrants, and were sunk in profound ignorance and debasement, from which they were utterly unable to rise.

The next kitchen of this description we entered was occupied by females. It was about fifteen feet square and belonged to a house of ten rooms, part of which was occupied as a low lodging-house. Here we found five women seated around a table, most of them young, but one more advanced in life. Some of them were good-looking, as though they had been respectable servants. They were busy at their tea, bread and butcher's meat. On the table stood a candle on a small candlestick. They sat in curious positions round the table, some of them with an ample crinoline. One sat by the fire with her gown drawn over her knees, displaying her white petticoat. As we stood beside them they burst out in a titter which they could not suppress. On looking round we observed a plate-rack at the back of the kitchen, and, as usual in these lodging-houses, a glorious fire burning brightly in the grate. An old chest of drawers, surmounted with shelves, stood against the wall. The girls were all prostitutes or thieves, but had no appearance of shame. They were apparently very merry. The old woman sat very thoughtfully, looking observant on, and no doubt wondering what errand could have brought us into the house.

We then entered another dwelling-house. On looking down the stairs we saw a company of young women, from seventeen to twenty-five years of age. A rope was hung over the fireplace, with stockings and shirts suspended over it, and clothes were drying on a screen. A young woman, with her hair netted and ornamented, sat beside the fire with a green jacket and striped petticoat with crinoline. Another good-looking young woman sat by the table dressed in a cotton gown and striped apron, with coffee-pot in hand, and tea-cups before her. Some pleasant-looking girls sat by the table with their chins leaning on their hands, smiling cheerfully, looking at us with curiosity. Another coarser featured dame lolled by the end of the table with her gown drawn over her head, smirking in our countenance; and one sat by, her shawl drawn over her head. Another apparently modest girl sat by cutting her nails with a knife. On the walls around the apartment were suspended a goodly assortment of bonnets, cloaks, gowns and petticoats.

Meantime an elderly little man came in with a cap on his head and a long staff in his hand, and stood looking on with curiosity. On the table lay a pack of cards beside the bowls, cups, and other crockery-ware. Some of the girls appeared as if they had lately been servants in respectable situations, and one was like a quiet genteel shop girl. They were all prostitutes, and most of them prowl about at night to plunder drunken men. As we looked on the more interesting girls, especially two of them, we saw the sad consequences of one wrong step, which may launch the young and thoughtless into a criminal career, and drive them into the dismal companionship of the most lewd and debased.

We then went to Short's Gardens, and entered a house there. On the basement underground we saw a company of men, women, and children of various ages, seated around the tables, and by the fire. The men and women had mostly been engaged in hopping, and appeared to be healthy, industrious, and orderly. Until lately thieves used to lodge in these premises.

As we entered Queen Street we saw three thieves, lads of about fourteen years of age, standing in the middle of the street as if on the outlook for booty. They were dressed in black frock-coats, corduroy, and fustian trousers, and black caps. Passing along Queen Street, which is one of the wings of the Dials, we went up to the central space between the Seven Dials. Here a very lively scene presented itself to our view; clusters of labouring men, and a few men of doubtful character, in dark shabby dress, loitered by the corners of the surrounding streets. We also saw groups of elderly women standing at some of the angles, most of them ragged and drunken, their very countenances the pictures of abject misery. The numerous public-houses in the locality were driving a busy traffic and were thronged with motley groups of people of various grades, from the respectable merchant and tradesman to the thief and the beggar.

Bands of boys and girls were gambolling in the street in wild frolic, tumbling on their head with their heels in the air, and shouting in merriment, while the policeman was quietly looking on in good humour.

Around the centre of the Dials were bakers' shops with large illuminated fronts, the shelves being covered with loaves, and the baker busy attending to his customers. In the window was a large printed notice advertising the "best wheaten bread at 6*d.*" a loaf. A druggist's shop was invitingly adorned with beautiful green and purple jars, but no customers entered during the time of our stay.

At the corner of an opposite dial was an old clothes store, with a large assortment of second-hand garments, chiefly for men, of various kinds, qualities, and styles, suspended around the front of the shop. There were also provision shops, which were well attended with customers. The whole neighbourhood presented an appearance of bustle and animation, and omnibuses and other vehicles were passing along in a perpetual stream.

The most of the low girls in this locality do not go out till late in the evening, and chiefly devote their attention to drunken men. They frequent the principal thoroughfares in the vicinity of Oxford Street, Holborn, Farringdon Street, and other bustling streets. From the nature of their work they are of a migratory character. The most of the men we saw in the houses we visited belong to the labouring class, men employed to assist in cleaning cabs and omnibuses, carriers of advertising boards, distributors of bills, patterers, chickweed sellers, ballad singers, and persons generally of industrious character. They are willing to work, but will steal rather than want.

The lodging-house people here have not been known of late years to receive stolen property, and the inhabitants generally are steadily rising in habits of decency, cleanliness and morality.

The houses we visited in George Street, and the streets adjacent, were formerly part of the rookery of St. Giles-in-the-Fields, celebrated as one of the chief haunts of redoubtable thieves and suspicious characters in London. Deserted as it comparatively is now, except by the labouring poor vagrants and low prostitutes, it was once the resort of all classes, from the proud noble to the beggar picking up a livelihood from door to door.

We have been indebted to Mr. Hunt, inspector of the lodging-houses of this district, for fuller information regarding the rookery of St. Giles and its inhabitants twenty years ago, before a number of these disreputable streets were removed to make way for New Oxford Street. We quote from a manuscript nearly in his own words:—"The ground covered by the Rookery was enclosed by

Great Russell Street, Charlotte Street, Broad Street, and High Street, all within the parish of St. Giles-in-the-Fields. Within this space were George Street (once Dyott Street), Carrier Street, Maynard Street, and Church Street, which ran from north to south, and were intersected by Church Lane, Ivy Lane, Buckeridge Street, Bainbridge Street, and New Street. These, with an almost endless intricacy of courts and yards crossing each other, rendered the place like a rabbit-warren.

"In Buckeridge Street stood the 'Hare and Hounds' public-house, formerly the 'Beggar in the Bush'; at the time of which I speak (1844) kept by the well-known and much-respected Joseph Banks (generally called 'Stunning Joe'), a civil, rough, good-hearted Boniface. His house was the resort of all classes, from the aristocratic marquis to the vagabond whose way of living was a puzzle to himself.

"At the opposite corner of Carrier Street stood Mother Dowling's, a lodging-house and provision shop, which was not closed nor the shutters put on for several years before it was pulled down, to make way for the improvements in New Oxford Street . . . The shop was frequented by vagrants of every class, including foreigners, who, with moustache, well-brushed hat and seedy clothes— consisting usually of a frock-coat buttoned to the chin, light trousers, and boots gaping at each lofty step—might be seen making their way to Buckeridge Street to regale upon cabbage, which had been boiled with a ferocious pig's head or a fine piece of salt beef. From 12 to 1 o'clock at midnight was chosen by these ragged but proud gentlemen from abroad as the proper time for a visit to Mrs. Dowling's.

"Most of the houses in Buckeridge Street were lodging-houses for thieves, prostitutes, and cadgers. The charge was fourpence a night in the upper rooms, and threepence in the cellars, as the basements were termed. If the beds were occupied six nights by the same parties, and all dues paid, the seventh night (Sunday) was not charged for. The rooms were crowded, and paid well. I remember seeing fourteen women in beds in a cellar, each of whom paid 3*d.* a night, which, Sunday free, amounted to 21*s.* per week. The furniture in this den might have originally cost the proprietor £7 or £8. At the time I last visited it, it was not worth more than 30*s.*

"Both sides of Buckeridge Street abounded in courts, particularly the north side, and these, with the connected backyards and

low walls in the rear of the street, afforded an easy escape to any
thief when pursued by officers of justice. I remember on one
occasion, in 1844, a notorious thief was wanted by a well-known
criminal officer (Restieaux). He was known to associate with
some cadgers who used a house in the rear of Paddy Corvan's,
near Church Street, and was believed to be in the house when
Restieaux and a sergeant entered it. They went into the kitchen
where seven male and five female thieves were seated, along with
several cadgers of the most cunning class. One of them made
a signal, indicating that someone had escaped by the back of the
premises, in which direction the officers proceeded. It was evident
the thief had gone over a low wall into an adjoining yard. The
pursuers climbed over, passed through the yards and back premises of eleven houses, and secured him in Jones Court. There
were about twenty persons present at the time of the arrest, but
they offered no resistance to the constables. It would have been
a different matter had he been apprehended by strangers.

"In Bainbridge Street, one side of which was nearly occupied
by the immense brewery of Meux and Co., were found some of the
most intricate and dangerous places in this low locality. The most
notorious of these was Jones Court, inhabited by coiners, utterers
of base coin, and thieves. In former years a bull terrier was kept
here, which gave an alarm on the appearance of a stranger, when
the coining was suspended till the course was clear. This dog was
at last taken away by Duke and Clement, two police officers, and
destroyed by an order from a magistrate.

"The houses in Jones Court were connected by roof, yard, and
cellar with those in Bainbridge and Buckeridge Streets, and with
each other in such a manner that the apprehension of an inmate
or refugee in one of them was almost a task of impossibility to
a stranger, and difficult to those well acquainted with the interior
of the dwellings. In one of the cellars was a large cess-pool, covered in such a way that a stranger would likely step into it. In the
same cellar was a hole about two feet square, leading to the next
cellar, and thence by a similar hole into the cellar of a house in
Scott's Court, Buckeridge Street. These afforded a ready means
of escape to a thief, but effectually stopped the pursuer, who
would be put to the risk of creeping on his hands and knees
through a hole two feet square in a dark cellar in St. Giles's
Rookery, entirely in the power of dangerous characters. Other
houses were connected in a similar manner. In some instances there

was a communication from one back window to another by means of large spike nails, one row to hold by, and another for the feet to rest on, which were not known to be used at the time we refer to.

"In Church Street were several houses let to men of an honest but poor class, who worked in omnibus and cab-yards, factories, and such other places as did not afford them the means of procuring more expensive lodgings. Their apartments were clean and their way of living frugal.

"Other houses of a less reputable character were very numerous. One stood at the corner of Church Street and Lawrence Street, occupied by the most infamous characters of the district. On entering the house from Lawrence Lane, and proceeding upstairs, you would find on each floor several rooms connected by a kind of gallery, each room rented by prostitutes. These apartments were open to those girls who had fleeced any poor drunken man who had been induced to accompany them to this den of infamy. When they had plundered the poor dupe, he was ejected without ceremony by the others who resided in the room; often without a coat or hat, sometimes without his trousers, and occasionally left on the staircase naked as he was born. In this house the grossest scenes of profligacy were transacted. In pulling it down a hole was discovered in the wall opening into a timber-yard which fronted High Street—a convenient retreat for any one pursued.

"Opposite to this was the 'Rose and Crown' public-house, resorted to by all classes of the light-fingered gentry, from the mobsman and his 'Amelia' to the lowest of the street thieves and his 'Poll.' In the tap-room might be seen Black Charlie the fiddler, with ten or a dozen lads and lasses enjoying the dance, and singing and smoking over potations of gin-and-water, more or less plentiful according to the proceeds of the previous night—all apparently free from care in their wild carousals. The cheek waxed pale when the policeman opened the door and glanced round the room, but when he departed the merriment would be resumed with vigour.

"The kitchens of some houses in Buckeridge Street afforded a specimen of life in London rarely seen elsewhere even in London, though some in Church Lane do so now on a smaller scale. The kitchen, a long apartment usually on the ground-floor, had a large coke fire, along with a sink, water-tap, one or two tables, several forms, a variety of saucepans, and other cooking utensils and was lighted with a gas jet. There in the evenings suppers were discussed by the cadgers an alderman might almost have envied— rich steaks and onions, mutton and pork chops, fried potatoes, sausages, cheese, celery, and other articles of fare, with abundance of porter, half-and-half and tobacco.

"In the morning they often sat down to a breakfast of tea, coffee, eggs, rashers of bacon, dried fish, fresh butter, and other good things which would be considered luxuries by working people, when each discussed his plans for the day's rambles, and arranged as to the exchange of garments, bandages, etc., con- sidered necessary to prevent recognition in those neighbourhoods recently worked.

"Their dinners were taken in the course of their rounds, con- sisting generally of the best of the broken victuals given them by the compassionate, and were eaten on one of the doorsteps of some respectable street, after which they would resort to some obscure public-house or beer-shop in a back street or alley to partake of some liquor.

"Heaps of good food were brought home and thrown, on a side-table, or into a corner, as unfit to be eaten by those 'pro- fessional' cadgers—food which thousands of the working men of London would have been thankful for. It was given to the children who visited these lodging-houses. The finer viands, such as pieces of fancy bread, rolls, kidneys, mutton and lamb, the gentlemen of the establishment reserved for their own more fastidious palates.

"On Sunday many of the cadgers stayed at home till night. They spent the day at cards, shove-halfpenny, tossing, and other amusements. Sometimes five or six shillings were staked on the table among a party of about ten of them at cards, although coppers were the usual stakes. . . . The life of a cadger is not in many instances a life of privation. I do not speak (says Mr. Hunt) of the really distressed, to whose wants too little attention is sometimes paid. I allude to beggars by profession, who prefer a life of mendicancy to any other. There are among them sailors, whose largest voyage has been to Tothill Fields prison, or to Gravesend on a pleasure trip. Cripples with their arms in slings, or feet, swathed in blood-stained rags, swollen to double the size, who may be seen dancing when in their lodging at their evening revels. You may see poor Irish with from five to thirty sovereigns in a bag hung round their necks or in the waistband of their trousers; women who carry hired babes, or it may be a bundle of clothing resembling a child, on their back or breast, and other such-like impostors.

"Between Buckeridge Street and Church Lane stood Ivy Lane, leading from George Street to Carrier Street, communicating with the latter by a small gateway. Clark's Court was on its left, and Rats' Castle on its right. The castle was a large dirty building occupied by thieves and prostitutes, and boys who lived by plunder. On the removal of these buildings, in 1845, the massive foundations of an hospital were found, which had been built in the 12th century by Matilda, Queen of Henry the First, daughter of Malcolm, King of Scotland, for persons afflicted with leprosy.

"At this place criminals were allowed a bowl of ale on their way from Newgate to Tyburn.

"Maynard Street and Carrier Street were occupied by coster-mongers and a few thieves and cadgers. George Street, part of which still stands, consisted of lodging-houses for tramps, thieves, and beggars, together with a few brothels."

From George Street to High Street runs a mews called Hamp-shire-Hog Yard, where there is an old established lodging-house for single men, poor but honest.

The portion of the rookery now remaining, consisting of Church Lane, with its courts, a small part of Carrier Street, and a smaller portion of one side of Church Street, is now more densely crowded than when Buckeridge Street and its neighbourhood were in exist-ence. The old Crown public-house in Church Lane, formerly the resort of the most notorious cadgers, was in 1851 inhabited by Irish people, where often from twelve to thirty persons lodged in a room. At the back of this public-house is a yard, on the right-hand side of which is an apartment then occupied by thirty-eight men, women and children, all lying indiscriminately on the floor.

Speaking of other houses in this neighbourhood in 1851, Mr. Hunt states: "I have frequently seen as many as sixteen people in a room about twelve feet by ten, these numbers being exceeded in larger rooms. Many lay on loose straw littered on the floor, their heads to the wall and their feet to the centre, and decency was entirely unknown among them."

Now, however, the district is considerably changed, the inhabit-ants are rapidly rising in decency, cleanliness, and order, and the Rookery of St. Giles will soon be ranked among the memories of the past.

NARRATIVE OF A LONDON SNEAK, OR COMMON THIEF

THE following narrative was given us by a convicted thief, who has for years wandered over the streets of London as a ballad singer, and has resided in the low lodging-houses scattered over its lowest districts. He was a poor wretched creature, degraded in condition, of feeble intellect, and worthless character, we picked up in a low lodging house in Drury Lane. He was shabbily dressed in a pair of old corduroy trousers, old brown coat, black shabby vest, faded grey neckerchief, an old dark cap and peak, and unwashed shirt. For a few shillings he was very ready to tell us the sad story of his miserable life.

"I was born at Abingdon, near Oxford, where my father was a bricklayer, and kept the N———n public-house. He died when I was fourteen years of age; I was sent to school and was taught to read, but not to write. At this time I was a steady, well-conducted boy. At fourteen years of age I went to work with my uncle, a basket-maker and rag merchant in Abingdon, and lived with my mother. I wrought there for three years, making baskets and cutting willows for them. I left my uncle then, as he had not got any more work for me to do, and was living idle with my mother. At this time I went with a Cheap John to the fairs, and travelled with him the whole of that season. He was a Lancashire man, between fifty and sixty years of age, and had a woman who travelled the country with him, but I do not think they were married. He was a tall, dark-complexioned man, and was a 'duffer,' very unprincipled in his dealings. He sold cutlery, books, stationery, and hardware.

"When we were going from one fair to another, we would stop on the road and make a fire, and steal fowls and potatoes, or any green-stuff that was in season. We sometimes travelled along with gipsies, occasionally to the number of fifty or sixty in a gang. The gipsies are a curious sort of people, and would not let you connect with any of them unless they saw you were to remain among them.

"I assisted Cheap John in the markets when selling his goods, and handed them to the purchasers.

"The first thing I ever pilfered was a pair of boots and a handkerchief from a drunken man who lay asleep at a fair in Reading, in Berks. He was lying at the back of a booth and no one near him. This was about dusk in September. I pawned the boots at

Windsor on the day of a fair for 3*s*., and sold the handkerchief for 1*s*.

"I was about seventeen years of age when I went with Cheap John, and remained with him about thirteen weeks, when I left, on account of a row I had with him. I liked this employment very well, got 2*s*. in the pound for my trouble, and sometimes had from £1 to 25*s*. a week. But the fairs were only occasional, and the money I earned was very precarious.

"I left Cheap John at Windsor, and came to Slough with a horse-dealer, where I left him. He gave me 2*s*. for assisting him. I then came up to London, where I have lived ever since in the lodging-houses in the different localities. I remember on coming to this great city I was much astonished at its wonders, and every street appeared to me like a fair. On coming to London I had no money, and had not any friend to assist me. I went to Kensington workhouse and got a night's lodging, and lived for about a fortnight at different workhouses in London. They used to give the lodgers a piece of bread at night, and another in the morning, and a night's lodging on straw and boards.

"I then went out singing ballads in the streets of London, and could get at an average from 2*s*. to 2*s*. 6*d*. a night, but when the evenings were wet, I could not get anything. In the winter I sang in the daytime, and in summer I went out in the evening. I have wandered in this way over many of the streets and thoroughfares of London. I sing in Marylebone, Somers Town, Camden Town, Paddington, Whitecross Street, City, Hammersmith, Commercial Road, and Whitechapel, and live at different lodgings, and make them my home as I move along. I sing different kinds of songs, sentimental and comic; my favourites are 'Gentle Annie,' 'She's reckoned a good hand at it,' 'The Dandy Husband,' 'The Week's Matrimony,' 'The Old Woman's Sayings,' and 'John Bull and the Taxes.' I often sing 'The Dark-eyed Sailor,' and 'The Female Cabin Boy.' For many years now I have lived by singing in the public street, sometimes by myself, at other times with a mate. I occasionally beg in Regent Street and Bond Street on the 'fly,' that is, follow people passing along, and sometimes in Oxford Street and Holborn. Sometimes I get a little job to do from people at various kinds of handiwork, such as turning the wheel to polish steel, and irons, etc., and do other kinds of job work. When hard up I pick pockets of handkerchiefs, by myself or with one or two mates. [In the course of our interview we saw he was very clumsy at picking pockets.] I sometimes go out with the dark-complexioned lad you saw down stairs, who is very clever at pocket picking, and has been often convicted before the criminal courts.

"I have spent many years living in the low lodging-houses of London. The worst I ever saw was in Keat Street, White-chapel, about nine years ago, before they were reformed and changed. Numbers were then crowded into the different rooms, and the floors were littered with naked people of all ages, and of both sexes, men and women, and boys and girls sleeping alongside indiscriminately. It was very common to see young boys and girls sleeping together. The conversations that passed between them, and the scenes that were transacted, were enough to contaminate the morals of the young.

"In the morning they used to go to their different haunts over the city, some begging, and others thieving.

"On Sunday evenings the only books read were such as 'Jack Sheppard,' 'Dick Turpin,' and the 'Newgate Calendar,' they got out of the neighbouring libraries by depositing 1s. These were read with much interest; the lodgers would sooner have these than any other books. I never saw any of them go to church on Sundays. Sometimes one or two would go to the ragged-school, such as the one in Field Lane near Smithfield.

"It often happened a man left his wife, and she came to the lodg-ing-house and got a livelihood by begging. Some days she would glean 2s. or 3s., and at other times would not get a half-penny.

"The thieves were seldom in the lodging-house, except to meals and at bedtime. They lived on better fare than the beg-gars. The pickpocket lives better than the sneaking thief, and the pickpocket is thought more of in the lodging-houses and prisons than the beggar.

"The lowest pickpockets often lived in these low lodging-houses, some of them young lads, and others middle-aged men. The young pickpockets, if clever, soon leave the lodging-houses and take a room in some locality, as at Somers Town, Marylebone, the Burgh, Whitechapel, or Westminster. The pickpockets in lodging houses, for the most part, are stock-buzzers, i.e., stealers of handkerchiefs.

"I have often seen the boys picking each others' pockets for diversion in the lodging-house, many of them from ten to eleven years of age.

"There are a great number of sneaks in the lodging-houses. Two of them go out together to the streets, one of them keeps a look-out while the other steals some article, shoes, vest, or coat, etc., from the shop or stall. I sometimes go out with a mate and take a pair of boots at a shop-door and sell them to the pawnbroker, or to a labouring man passing in the street.

"Sometimes I have known the lodgers make up a packet of sawdust and put in a little piece of tobacco to cover an opening, leaving only the tobacco to be seen looking through, and sell it to persons passing by in the street as a packet of tobacco.

"When I am hard up I have gone out and stolen a loaf at a baker's shop, or chandler's shop, and taken it to my lodging. I have often stolen handkerchiefs, silk and cambric, from gentlemen's pockets.

"I once stole a silver snuff-box from a man's coat-pocket, and on one occasion took a pocket-book with a lot of papers and postage-stamps. I burnt the papers and sold the stamps for about 1s. 6d.

"I never had clothes respectable enough to try purses and watches, and did not have nerve for it. I have seen young thieves encouraged by people who kept the lodging-houses, such as at Keat Street, Whitechapel, and at the Mint. They would ask the boys if they had anything, and wish them to sell it to them, which was generally done at an under-price. In these lodging-houses some lived very well, and others were starving. Some had steaks and pickles, and plenty of drink, porter and ale, eggs and bacon, and cigars to smoke. Some of the poorest go out and get a pennyworth of bread, halfpennyworth of tea, halfpennyworth of butter, and halfpennyworth of sugar, and perhaps not have a halfpenny left to pay for their lodging at night. When they do get money they often go out and spend it in drink, and perhaps the next night are starving again.

"I have been tried for stealing a quart pot and a handkerchief, at Bagnigge Wells police station, and was taken to Vine Street police station for stealing 2s. 6d. from a drunken woman respectably dressed. I took it out of her hand, and was seen by a policeman, who ran after me and overtook me, but the woman refused to prosecute me, and I was discharged. I was also brought before Marylebone police-court for begging.

"In my present lodging I am pretty comfortable. We spend our evenings telling tales and conversing to each other on our wanderings, and playing at games, such as 'hunt the slipper.' I have often been in great want, and have been driven to steal to get a livelihood."

PICKPOCKETS AND SHOPLIFTERS

IN tracing the pickpocket from the beginning of his career, in most cases we must turn our attention to the little ragged boys living by a felon's hearth, or herding with other young criminals in a low lodging-house, or dwelling in the cold and comfortless home of drunken and improvident parents. The great majority of the pickpockets of the metropolis, with few exceptions, have sprung from the dregs of society—from the hearths and homes of London thieves—so that they have no reason to be proud of their lineage. Fifteen or twenty years ago many of those accomplished pickpockets, dressed in the highest style of fashion, and glittering in gold chains, studs, and rings, who walk around the Bank of England and along Cheapside, and our busy thoroughfares, were poor ragged boys walking barefooted among the dark and dirty slums and alleys of Westminster and the Seven Dials, or loitering among the thieves' dens of the Borough and Whitechapel.

Step by step they have emerged from their rags and squalor to a higher position of physical comfort, and have risen to higher dexterity and accomplishment in their base and ignoble profession.

We say there are a few exceptions to the general rule, that the most of our habitual thieves have sprung from the loins of felon parents. We blush to say that some have joined the ranks of our London thieves, and are living callous in open crime, who were trained in the homes of honest and industrious parents, and were surrounded in early life with all those influences which are fitted to elevate and improve the mind. But here our space forbids us to enlarge.

The chief sources whence our pickpockets spring are from the low lodging-houses—from those dwellings in low neighbourhoods where their parents are thieves, and where improvident and drunken people neglect their children, such as Whitechapel, Shoreditch, Spitalfields, New Cut, Lambeth, the Borough, Clerkenwell, Drury Lane, and other localities. Many of them are the children of Irish parents, costermongers, bricklayers' labourers and others. They often begin to steal at six or seven years of age sometimes as early as five years, and commit petty sneaking thefts, as well as pick handkerchiefs from gentlemen's pockets. Many of these ragged urchins are taught to steal by their companions, others are taught by trainers of thieves, young men and women, and some middle-aged convicted thieves. They are learned to be expert in this way. A coat is suspended on the wall with a bell attached to it, and the boy attempts to take the handkerchief from the pocket without the bell ringing. Until he is able to do this with proficiency he is not considered well trained. Another way in which they are trained is this:—The trainer—if a man—walks up and down the room with a handkerchief in the tail of his coat, and the ragged boys amuse themselves abstracting it until they learn to do it in an adroit manner. We could point our finger to three of these execrable wretches, who are well known to train schools of juvenile thieves—one of them, a young man at Whitechapel; another, a young woman at Clerkenwell; and a third, a middle-aged man residing about Lambeth Walk. These base wretches buy the stolen handkerchiefs from the boys at a paltry sum. We have also heard of some being taught to pick pockets by means of an effigy; but this is not so well authenticated.

Great numbers of these ragged pickpockets may be seen loitering about our principal streets, ready to steal from a stall or shop-door when they find an opportunity. During the day they generally pick pockets two or three in a little band, but at dusk a single one can sometimes do it with success. They not only steal handkerchiefs of various kinds, but also pocket-books from the tails of gentlemen's coats. We may see them occasionally engaged at this work on Blackfriars Bridge and London Bridge, also along Bishopsgate, Shoreditch, Whitechapel, Drury Lane, and similar localities. They may be seen at any hour of the day, but chiefly from 10 to 2 o'clock. They are generally actively on the look-out on Saturday evening in the shopping streets where the labouring people get their provisions in for the Sunday. At this early stage the boys occasionally pick pockets, and go about cadging and sneaking (begging and committing petty felonies).

The next stage commences—we shall say—about fourteen years of age, when the stripling lays aside his rags, and dresses in a more decent way, though rather shabby. Perhaps in a dark or gray frock-coat, dark or dirty tweed trousers, and a cap with peak, and shoes. At this time many of them go to low neighbourhoods, or to those quieter localities where the labouring people reside, and pick the pockets of the wives and daughters of this class of persons; others steal from gentlemen passing along thoroughfares, while a few adroit lads are employed by men to steal from ladies' pockets in the fashionable streets of the metropolis. These young thieves seldom commit their depredations in the localities where they are known but prowl in different parts of the metropolis. They are of a wandering character, changing from one district to another, and living in different lodging houses—often leaving their parents' houses as early as ten years of age. Sometimes they are driven by drunken, loafing parents to steal, though in most cases they leave their comfortless homes and live in lodging houses.

When they have booty, they generally bring it to some person to dispose of, as suspicion would be aroused if they went to sell or pawn it themselves. In some cases they give it to the trainer of thieves, or they take it to some low receiving house, where wretches encourage them in stealing; sometimes to low coffee-houses, low hairdressers or tailors, who act as middlemen to dispose of the property, generally giving them but a small part of the value.

In the event of their rambling to a distant part of London, they sometimes arrange to get one of their number to convey the stolen goods to these parties. At other times they dispose of them to low wretches connected with the lodging houses, or other persons in disreputable neighbourhoods.

At this time many of them cohabit with girls in low lodging-houses; many of whom are older than themselves, and generally of the felon class.

These lads frequently steal at the "tail" of gentlemen's coats, and learn the other modes of picking pockets.

Stealing the handkerchief from the "tail" of a gentleman's coat in the street is generally effected in this way. Three or four usually go together. They see an old gentleman passing by. One remains behind, while the other two follow up close beside him, but a little behind. The one walking by himself behind is the looker out to see if there are any police or detectives near, or if anyone passing by or hovering around is taking notice of them. One of the two walking close by the gentleman adroitly picks his pocket, and coils the handkerchief up in his hand so as not to be seen, while the other brings his body close to him, so as not to let his arm be seen by any passer by.

If the party feel him taking the handkerchief from his pocket, the thief passes it quickly to his companion, who runs off with it. The looker out walks quietly on as if nothing had occurred, or sometimes walks up to the gentleman and asks him what is the matter, or pretends to tell him in what direction the thief has run, pointing him to a very different direction from the one he has taken.

They not only abstract handkerchiefs but also pocketbooks from the tail of gentlemen's coats, or any other article they can lay their fingers on.

This is the common way in which the coat pocket is picked when the person is proceeding along the street. Sometimes it happens that one thief will work by himself, but this is very seldom. In the case of a person standing, the coat tail pocket is picked much in the same manner.

These boys in most cases confine themselves to stealing from the coat pocket on the streets, but in the event of a crowd on any occasion, they are so bold as to steal watches from the vest-pocket. This is done in a different style, and generally in the company of two or three in this manner:—One of them folds his arms across his breast in such a way that his right hand is covered with his left arm. This enables him to use his hand in an unobserved way, so that he is thereby able to abstract the watch from the vest pocket of the gentleman standing by his side.

A police-officer informed us that when at Cremorne, about a fortnight ago, a large concourse of people was assembled to see the female acrobat, termed the "Female Blondin," cross the Thames on a rope suspended over the river, he observed two young men of about twenty-four years of age, and about the middle height, respectably dressed, whom he suspected to be pickpockets. They went up to a smart gentlemanly man standing at the riverside looking eagerly at the Female Blondin, then walking the rope over the middle of the river. As his attention was thus absorbed, the detective saw these two men go up to him. One of them placed himself close on the right hand side of him, and putting his right arm under his left, thus covered his right hand, and took the watch gently from the pocket of the gentleman's vest. The thief made two attempts to break the ring attached to the watch, termed the "bowl" or swivel, with his finger and thumb.

After two ineffective endeavours he bent it completely round and yet it would not break. He then left the watch hanging down in front of the vest, the gentleman meanwhile being unaware of the attempted felony. The detective officer took both the thieves into custody. They were brought before the Westminster police court and sentenced each to three months' imprisonment for an attempt to steal from the person.

The same officer informed us that about a month or six weeks ago, in the same place, on a similar occasion, he observed three persons, a man, a boy, and a woman, whom he suspected to be picking pockets. The man was about twenty-eight years of age, rather under the middle size. The woman hovered by his side. She was very good looking, about twenty-four years of age, dressed in a green coloured gown, Paisley shawl, and straw bonnet trimmed with red velvet and red flowers. The man was dressed in a black frock coat, brown trousers, and black hat. The boy, who happened to be his brother, was about fourteen years old, dressed in a brown shooting coat, corduroy trousers, and black cap with peak. The boy had an engaging countenance, with sharp features and smart manner. The officer observed the man touch the boy on the shoulder and point him towards an old lady. The boy placed himself on her right side, and the man and woman kept behind. The former put his left hand into the pocket of the lady's gown and drew nothing from it, then left her and went about two yards farther; there he placed himself by two other ladies, tried both their pockets and left them again. He followed another lady and succeeded in picking her pocket of a small sum of money and a handkerchief. The officer took them all to the police station with the assistance of another detective officer, when they were committed for trial at Clerkenwell sessions. The man was sentenced to ten years' penal servitude, the boy to two months' hard labour, and three months in a reformatory, and the woman was sentenced to two years' imprisonment, with hard labour, in the House of Correction at Westminster.

It appeared, in the course of the evidence at the trial, that this man had previously been four years in penal servitude, and since his return had decoyed his little brother from a situation he held, for the purpose of training him to pick pockets, having induced him to rob his employer before leaving service.

The *scarf pin* is generally taken from the breast in this way. The thief generally has a handkerchief in his hand, pretending to wipe his nose, as he walks along the street. He then places his right hand across the breast of the person he intends to rob, bringing his left hand stealthily under his arm. This conceals his movements from the eyes of the person. With the latter hand he

ASYLUM FOR THE HOUSELESS POOR, CRIPPLEGATE

Vagrants in the Casual Ward of Workhouse

snatches out the pin from the scarf. It is sometimes done with the right hand, at other times with the left, according to the position of the person, and is generally done in the company of one or more. The person robbed is rarely aware of the theft. Should he be aware, or should anyone passing by have observed the movement, the pin got from the scarf is suddenly passed into the hands of the other parties, when all of them suddenly make off in different directions, soon to meet again in some neighbouring locality.

At other times the thief drives the person with a push, in the street, bringing his hands to his breast as if he had stumbled against him, at the same time adroitly laying hold of the pin. This is done in such a way that the person is seldom aware of the robbery until he afterwards finds out the loss of the article.

The *trousers pocket* is seldom picked on the public street, as this is an operation of considerable difficulty and danger. It is not easy to slip the hand into the trousers pocket without being felt by the person attempted to be robbed. This is generally done in crowds where people are squeezed together, when they contrive to do it in this way:—They cut up the trousers with a knife or other sharp instrument, lay open the pocket, and adroitly rifle the money from it; or they insert the fingers or hand into it in a push, often without being observed, while the person's attention is distracted, possibly by some of the accomplices or stalls. They often occasion a disturbance in crowds, and create a quarrel with people near them, or have sham fights with each other, or set violently on the person they intend to rob. Many rough expedients are occasionally had recourse to, to effect this object.

Sometimes the pocket is picked in a crowd by means of laying hold of the party by the middle as if they had jostled against him, or by pressing on his back from behind, while the fingers or hand are inserted into the pocket of his trousers to snatch any valuables, money or otherwise, contained therein.

This mode of stealing is sometimes done by one person, at other times by the aid of accomplices. It is most commonly done in the manner now described.

By dint of long experience and natural skill, some attain great perfection in this difficult job, and accomplish their object in the most clever and effective manner. They are so nimble and accomplished that they will accost a gentleman in the street, and while speaking to him, and looking him in the face, will quietly insert their hand into his vest pocket and steal his watch.

In a crowd, the pin is sometimes stolen with dexterity by a person from behind inserting his hand over the shoulder. Sometimes the watch is stolen by a sudden snatch at the guard, when the thief runs off with his booty. This is not so often done in the thoroughfares, as it is attended with great danger of arrest. It is oftener done in quiet by-streets, or by-places, where there are many adjacent courts and alleys intersecting each other, through which the thief has an opportunity of escaping.

These are various modes by which gentlemen's pockets are generally picked.

A lady's pocket is commonly picked by persons walking by her side, who insert their hand gently into the pocket of her gown. This is often effected by walking alongside of the lady, or by stopping her in the street, asking the way to a particular place, or inquiring if she is acquainted with such and such a person. When the thief is accomplished, he can abstract the purse from her pocket in a very short space of time: but if he is not so adroit, he will detain her some time longer, asking further questions till he has completed his object. This is often done by a man and a woman in company.

A lady generally carries her gold or silver watch in a small pocket in front of her dress, possibly under one of the large flounces. It is often stolen from her by one or two, or even three persons, one of the thieves accosting her in the street in the manner described. They seldom steal the guard, but in most cases contrive to break the ring or swivel by which it is attached. Let us suppose that two pickpockets, a man and a woman, were to see a lady with a watch in the public street; they are possibly walking arm in arm; they make up to her, inquire the way to a particular place, and stand in front of her. One of them would ask the way while the other would meantime be busy picking her pocket. If they succeed, they walk off arm in arm as they came.

Sometimes two or three men will go up to a lady and deliberately snatch a parcel or reticule bag from her hand or arm, and run off with it.

At other times a very accomplished pickpocket may pick ladies' pockets without any accomplice, or with none to cover his movements.

Walking along Cheapside one day, toward the afternoon, we observed a well-dressed, good-looking man of about thirty years of age, having the appearance of a smart man of business, standing by the side of an elderly looking, respectably dressed lady at a jeweller's window. The lady appeared to belong to the country, from her dress and manner, and was absorbed looking into the window at the gold watches, gold chains, lockets, pins, and other trinkets glittering within. Meantime the gentleman also appeared to be engrossed looking at these articles beside her, while crowds of people were passing to and fro in the street, and the carts, cabs, omnibuses, and other vehicles were rumbling by, deadening the footsteps of the passers-by. Our eye accidentally caught sight of his left hand dropping by his side in the direction of the lady's pocket. We observed it glide softly in the direction of her pocket beneath the edge of her shawl with all the fascination of a serpent's movement. While the hand lay drooping, the fingers sought their way to the pocket. From the movement we observed that the fingers had found the pocket, and were seeking their way farther into the interior. The person was about to plunge his hand to abstract the contents when we instinctively hooked his wrist with the curve of our walking stick and prevented the robbery. With great address and tact he withdrew his hand from the lady's pocket, and his wrist from our grasp, and walked quietly away. Meantime a group of people had gathered round about us, and a gentleman asked if we had observed a pocket picked. We said nothing, but whispered to the lady, who stood at the window unaware of the attempted felony, that we had prevented her pocket being picked, and had just scared a thief with his hand in her pocket, then walked over to the other side of the street and passed on.

The more accomplished pickpockets are very adroit in their movements. A young lady may be standing by a window in Cheapside, Fleet Street, Oxford Street, or the Strand, admiring some beautiful engraving. Meantime a handsomely dressed young man, with gold chain and moustache, also takes his station at the window beside her, apparently admiring the same engraving. The young lady stands gazing on the beautiful picture, with her countenance glowing with sentiment, which may be enhanced by the sympathetic presence of the nice looking young man by her side, and while her bosom is thus throbbing with romantic emotion, her purse, meanwhile, is being quietly transferred to the pocket of this elegantly attired young man, whom she might find in the evening dressed as a rough costermonger, mingling among the low ruffians at the Seven Dials or Whitechapel, or possibly lounging in some low beershop in the Borough.

There are various ranks of pickpockets, from the little ragged boy, stealing the handkerchief from a gentleman's coat pocket, to the fashionable thief, promenading around the Bank, or strolling, arm in arm, with his gentlemanly looking companion along Cheapside.

The swell mob are to be seen all over London, in crowded thoroughfares, at railway stations, in omnibuses and steamboats. You find them pursuing their base traffic in the Strand, Fleet Street, Holborn, Parliament Street, and at Whitehall, over the whole of the metropolis, and they are to be seen on all public occasions looking out for plunder.

Some commence their work at 8 and 9 in the morning, others do not rise till 11 or 12. They are generally seen about 11 or 12 o'clock—sometimes till dusk. Some work in the evening, and not during the day, while others are out during the day, and do nothing in the evening. In times of great public excitement, when crowds are assembled, such as at the late fire at London Bridge, when those great warehouses were burnt down—they are in motion from the lowest to the highest. They are generally as busy in summer time as in the winter. When the gentry and nobility have retired to their country seats in the provinces, crowds of strangers and tourists are pouring into the metropolis every day.

They often travel into the country to attend races such as Ascot, the Derby at Epsom, and others in the surrounding towns. They go to the Crystal Palace, where the cleverest of them may be frequently seen, also to Cremorne, the Zoological Gardens, Regent's Park, the theatres, operas, ball-rooms, casinos and other fashionable places of amusement—sometimes to the great crowds that usually assemble at Mr. Spurgeon's new Tabernacle.

They also occasionally make tours in different parts of the United Kingdom and to Paris, and along the railways in all directions.

The most accomplished pickpockets reside at Islington, Hoxton, Kingsland Road, St. Luke's, the Borough, Camberwell, and Lambeth, in quiet, respectable streets, and occasionally change their lodging if watched by the police.

They have in most cases been thieves from their cradle; others are tradesmen's sons and young men from the provinces, who have gone into dissipated life and adopted this infamous course. These fast men are sometimes useful as stalls, though they rarely acquire the dexterity of the native born, trained London pickpocket.

There are a few foreign pickpockets, French and others. Some of them are bullies about the Haymarket. There are also some German pickpockets, but the foreigners are principally French. As a general rule, more of the latter are engaged in swindling than in picking pockets. Some of the French are considered in adroitness equal to the best of the English. There are also a few Scotch, but the great mass are Irish cockneys, which a penetrating eye could trace by their look and manner. Many of them have a restless look, as if always in dread of being taken, and generally keep a sharp look out with the side of their eye as they walk along.

They differ a good deal in appearance. The better class dress very fashionably; others in the lower class do not dress so well. The more dexterous they are, they generally dress in higher style, to get among the more respectable and fashionable people. Some of the female pickpockets also dress splendidly and have been heard to boast of frequently stealing from £20 to £30 a day in working on ladies' pockets. They are sometimes as adroit as the men in stealing ladies' purses, and are less noticed lingering beside them on the streets, by the shop windows, and in places of public resort.

Yet, though well dressed, there is a peculiarity about the look of most of the male and female pickpockets. The countenance of many of them is suspicious to a penetrating eye. Many of them have considerable mental ability, and appear to be highly intelligent.

The most dexterous pickpockets generally average from twenty to thirty-five years of age, when many of them become depressed in spirit, and "have the steel taken out of them" with the anxiety of the life and the punishments inflicted on them in the course of their criminal career. The restlessness and suspense of their life have the effect of dissipation upon a good many of them, so that, though generally comparatively temperate in the use of intoxicating liquors, they may be said to lead a fast life.

Some of them take a keen bold look, full into your countenance; others have a sneaking, suspicious, downcast appearance, showing that all is not right within.

They dress in various styles; sometimes in the finest of super-fine black cloth; at other times in fashionable suits, like the first gentlemen in the land, spangled with jewellery. Some of them would pass for gentlemen—they are so polite in their address. Others appear like a mock-swell, vulgar in their manner—which is transparent through their fine dress, and are debased in their conversation, which is at once observed when they begin to speak.

The female pickpockets dress in fashionable attire; sometimes in black satin dresses and jewellery. Some of them are very lady-like, though they have sprung originally from the lowest class. You may see very beautiful women among them, though vulgar in their conversation. The females are often superior in intellect to the men, and more orderly in their habits. They are seldom married, but cohabit with pickpockets, burglars, resetters, and other infamous characters. Their paramour is frequently taken from them, and they readily go with another man in the same illicit manner.

They are passionately fond of their fancy man in most cases; yet very capricious—so much so that they not infrequently leave the man they cohabit with for another sweetheart, and afterwards go back to their old lover again, who is so easy in his principles that he often welcomes her, especially if she is a good worker—that is, an expert pickpocket.

The greater part of these women have sprung from the class of Irish cockneys; others have been domestic servants and the daughters of labourers, low tradesmen, and others. This gives us a key to many of these house robberies, done with the collusion of servants—a kind of felony very common over the metropolis. These are not the more respectable genteel class of servants, but the humbler order, such as nursery girls and females in tradesmen's families. Many of them have come from the country, or from labouring people's families over the working neighbourhoods of the metropolis. They are soon taught to steal by the men they cohabit with, but seldom acquire the dexterity of the thief who has been younger trained. They seldom have the acuteness, tact, and dexterity of the latter.

They live very expensively on the best of poultry, butcher meat, pastry, and wines, and some of them keep their pony and trap; most of them are very improvident, and spend their money foolishly on eating and drinking—though few of them drink to excess—on dress, amusements, and gambling.

They do not go out every day to steal, but probably remain in the house till their money is nearly spent, when they commence anew their system of robbery to fill their purse.

The female pickpockets often live with the burglars. They have their different professions which they pursue. When the one is not successful in the one mode of plunder, they often get it in the other, or the women will resort to shoplifting. They must have money in either of these ways. The women do not resort to prostitution, though they may be of easy virtue with those they fancy. Some of them live with cracksmen in high style, and have generally an abundance of cash.

Female pickpockets are often the companions of skittle-sharps, and pursue their mode of livelihood as in the case of cohabiting with burglars. Their age averages from sixteen to forty-five.

The generality of the pickpockets confine themselves to their own class of robberies. Others betake themselves to card-sharping and skittle-sharping, while a few of the more daring eventually become dexterous burglars.

In their leisure hours they frequently call at certain beershops and public-houses, kept possibly by some old "pals" or connexions of the felon class, at King's Cross, near Shoreditch Church, Whitechapel, the Elephant and Castle, and Westminster, and are to be seen dangling about these localities.

Some of the swell-mobsmen have been well-educated men, and at one time held good situations; some have been clerks; others are connected with respectable families, led away by bad companions, until they have become the dregs of society, and after having been turned out of their own social circle, have become thieves. They are not generally so adroit as the young trained thief, though they may be useful to their gangs in acting as stalls.

Many of them are intelligent men, and have a fund of general information which enables them to act their part tolerably well when in society.

OMNIBUS PICKPOCKETS

THE most of this class of thieves are well-dressed women, and go out one or two together, sometimes three. They generally manage to get to the farthest seats in the interior of the omnibus, on opposite sides of the vehicle, next to the horses. As the lady passengers come in, they eye them carefully, and one of them seats herself on the right side of the lady they intend to plunder. She generally manages to throw the bottom of her cape or shawl over the lap of the lady, and works with her hand under it, so as to cover her movement.

Her confederate is generally sitting opposite to see that no one is noticing. In abstracting from a lady's pocket, the female thief has often to cut through the dress and pocket, which she does with a pocket-knife, pair of scissors, or other sharp instrument. So soon as she has secured her purse, or other booty, she and her companion leave the omnibus on the earliest opportunity often in their hurry giving the conductor more than his fare, which creates suspicion and frequently leads to their detection. Experienced conductors often inquire of the passengers on such occasions if they have lost anything, and if they find they have, they give chase to the parties to apprehend them.

It often happens the thief follows a lady into an omnibus from seeing the lady take out her purse, perhaps in some shop. If she could not pick her pocket in the street, she contrives to go into an omnibus and do it there. These robberies are committed in all parts of London. They generally work at some distance from where they live, so that they are not easily traced if detected at the time.

They invariably give false names and false addresses, when taken into custody. The same women who pick ladies' pockets in the street, perpetrate these felonies in omnibuses, and often travel by railway, pursuing this occupation—sometimes two women together, sometimes one along with a man.

Sometimes gentlemen's pockets are picked in omnibuses by male pickpockets, who also steal from the lady passengers when they find a suitable opportunity, especially at dusk.

RAILWAY PICKPOCKETS

THIS is the same class of persons who pick pockets on the public street as already described. They often visit the various railway stations and are generally smartly dressed as they linger there— some of them better than others. Some of the females are dressed like shopkeepers' wives, others like milliners, varying from nineteen to forty years of age, mostly from nineteen to twenty-five; some of them attired in cotton gowns, others in silks and satins.

At the railway stations they are generally seen moving restlessly about from one place to another, as if they did not intend to go by any particular railway train. There is an unrest about the most of them which to a discerning eye would attract attention.

They seldom take the train, but dangle among the throng around the ticket office, or on the platform beside the railway carriages on the eve of the train starting off, as well as when the train arrives. When they see ladies engaged in conversation they go up to them and plant themselves by their side, while the others cover their movements. There generally are two, sometimes three of them in a party. They place themselves on the right hand side of the ladies, next to their pocket, and work with the left hand. When the ladies move, the thieves walk along with them.

The female pickpockets generally carry a reticule on their right arm so as to take off suspicion, and walk up to the persons at the railway station, and inquire what time the train starts to such and such a place, to detain them in conversation and to keep them in their company.

The older female thieves generally look cool and weary, the younger ones are more restless and suspicious in their movements. They sometimes go into first and second class waiting rooms and sit by the side of any lady they suppose to be possessed of a sum of money, and try to pick her pocket by inserting their hand, or by cutting it with a knife or other sharp instrument. They generally insert the whole hand, as the ladies' pockets are frequently deep in the dress. They often have a large cape to cover their hands, and pick the pocket while speaking to the lady, or sitting by her side. The young pickpockets are generally the most expert.

They seldom take the brooch from the breast, but confine themselves to picking pockets.

After they take the purse, they generally run to some by-place and throw it away, so that it cannot be identified; sometimes they put it into a water-closet, at other times drop it down an area as they pass along.

After taking the purse, the thief hands it to her companion and they separate and walk away, and meet at some place appointed.

They occasionally travel with the trains to the Crystal Palace

and other places in the neighbourhood of London, and endeavour to plunder the passengers on the way. Frequently they take longer excursions—especially during the summer—journeying from town to town, and going to races and markets, agricultural shows, or any places where is a large concourse of people. Unless they are detected at the time they pick the pocket, they seldom leave any suspicion behind them, as they take care to lodge in respectable places, where no one would suspect them, and have generally plenty of money.

A considerable number of the male thieves also attend the railway stations, and pick pockets in the railway trains. They are generally well dressed, and many of them have an Inverness cape, often of a dark colour, and sometimes they carry a coat on their arm to hide their hand. There are commonly two or more of them together—sometimes women accompanying them. They are the same parties we have already so fully described, who commit such felonies in the streets, thoroughfares, and places of public resort in the metropolis, and their movements are in a great measure the same.

Number of felonies by picking pockets in the Metropolitan
districts for 1860 1,498
Ditto, ditto, in the City 380
                                                     ‾‾‾‾‾
                                                     1,878

Value of property thereby abstracted in the Metropolitan
districts £5,819
Ditto, ditto, in the City 375
                                                     ‾‾‾‾‾
                                                     £6,194

SHOPLIFTERS

THERE is a class of women who visit the shops in various parts of the metropolis, sometimes two and at other times three together. They vary their dress according to the locality they visit. Sometimes you find them dressed very respectably, like the wives of people in good circumstances in life; at other times they appear like servants. They often wear large cloaks, or shawls, and are to be found of different ages, from 14 to 60. They generally call into shops at busy times, when there are many persons standing around the counter, and will stand two or three together. They ask a look of certain articles, and will possibly say, after they have inspected them, that they do not suit them; they will say they are too high in price, or not the article they want, or not the proper colour. They will likely ask to see some other goods, and keep looking at the different articles until they get a quantity on the counter. When the shopman is engaged getting some fresh goods from the window, or from the shelves, one of them generally contrives to slip something under her cloak or shawl, while the other manages to keep his attention abstracted. Sometimes they carry a bag or a basket, and set it down on the counter, and while the shopman is busy they will get some article and lay it down behind their basket, such as a roll of ribbons, or a half dozen of gloves, or other small portable goods. While the shopman's back is turned, or his attention withdrawn, it is hidden under their shawl or cloak. We frequently find the skirt of their dress lined from the pocket downward, forming a large repository all around the dress, with an opening in front, where they can insert a small article, which is not observed in the ample crinoline. In stealing rolls of silk, or other heavier goods, they conceal them under their arm. Women who engage in shoplifting sometimes pick pockets in the shops. They get by the side of a lady engaged looking over articles, and under pretence of inspecting goods in the one hand, pick their pockets with the other.

We find more of these people living in the East End and on the Surrey side than in the West End of the metropolis. A great many live in the neighbourhood of Kingsland Road and Hackney Road. Some of them cohabit with burglars, others with magsmen (skittle-sharps).

We find ladies in respectable positions occasionally charged with shoplifting.

Respectably dressed men frequently go into the shops of drapers and others early in the morning, or at intervals during the day, or evening, to look at the goods, and often manage to abstract one or two articles and secrete them under their coats. They frequently take a bundle of neckties, a parcel of gloves, or anything that will go in a small compass, and perhaps enter a jeweller's shop, and in this way abstract a quantity of jewellery. On going there, they will ask a sight of some articles; the first will not suit them, and they will ask to look at more. When the shopman is engaged, they will abstract some gold rings or gold pins, or other property, sometimes a watch. Occasionally they will go so far as to leave a deposit on the article, promising to call again. They do this to prevent suspicion. After they are gone the shopman may find several valuables missing.

Sometimes they will ring the changes. On entering the shop they will bring patterns of rings and other articles in the window, which they have got made as facsimiles from metal of an inferior quality. On looking at the jewellery they will ring the changes on the counter, and keep turning them over, and in so doing abstract the genuine article and leave the counterfeit in its place.

The statistics applicable to this class of felonies are comprised under those given when treating on "stealing from the doors and windows of shops."

A VISIT TO THE DENS OF THIEVES IN SPITALFIELDS AND ITS NEIGHBOURHOOD

ONE afternoon, in company with a detective officer, we visited Spitalfields, one of the most notorious rookeries for infamous characters in the metropolis. Leaving Whitechapel, we went up a narrow alley called George Yard, where we saw four brothels of a very low description, the inmates being common thieves. On proceeding a little farther along the alley we passed eight or nine lodging-houses. Most of the lodgers were out prowling over the various districts of the metropolis, some picking pockets, others area-sneaking.

On entering into a public-house in another alley near Union Street we came to one of the most dangerous thieves' dens we have visited in the course of our rambles. As we approached the door of the house we saw a dissipated-looking man stealthily whispering outside the door to the ruffian-looking landlord, who appeared to be a fighting man, from his large coarse head and broken nose. The officer by our side hinted to us that the latter was a fence, or receiver of stolen property, and was probably speaking to his companion on some business of this nature. As we went forward they sneaked away, the one through a neighbouring archway, and the other into his house. We followed the latter into the public-house, and found two or three brutal-looking men loafing about the bar. We passed through a small yard behind the house, where we found a number of fighting dogs chained to their kennels. Some were close to our feet as we passed along, and others, kept in an outhouse beside them, could almost snap at our face. We went to another outhouse beyond, where between thirty and forty persons were assembled round a wooden enclosure looking on, while some of their dogs were killing rats. They consisted of burglars, pickpockets, and the associates of thieves, along with one or two receivers of stolen property. Many of them were coarse and brutal in their appearance, and appeared to be in their element as they urged on their dogs to destroy the rats, which were taken out one after another from a small wooden box. These men apparently ranged from twenty-two to forty years of age. Many of them had the rough stamp of the criminal in their countenances, and when inflamed with strong drink, would possibly be fit for any deed of atrocious villainy. Some of the dogs were strong and vigorous, and soon disposed of the rats as they ran round the wooden enclosure, surrounded by this redoubtable band of ruffians, who made the rafters ring with merriment when the dog caught hold of his prey, or when the rat turned desperate on its adversary. During the brief space of time we were present, a slim little half-starved dog killed several rats. When the rat was first let loose it was very nimble and vigorous in its movements, and the little dog kept for a time at a respectful distance, as the former was ready to snap at it. Sometimes the rat made as though it was to leap over the wooden fence to get away from the dog, but a dozen rough hands were ready to thrust it back. After it had got nearly exhausted with its ineffectual struggles to get away, the little dog seized it by the throat and worried it; when another rat was brought out to take its place, and another dog introduced to this brutal sport.

This is one of the most dangerous thieves' dens we have seen in London. Were any unfortunate man to be inveigled into it in the evening, or at midnight, when the desperadoes who haunt it are inflamed with strong drink, he would be completely in their power, even were he the bravest soldier in the British service, and armed with a revolver. Were he to fight his way desperately through the large ferocious gang in this outhouse, the fighting-dogs in the yard might be let loose on him, and were he to cleave his way through them, he would have to pass through the public-house frequented by similar low characters.

Leaving this alley we proceeded to Fashion Street and entered a skittle-ground attached to a low beershop, where we saw another gang of thieves, to the number of about twelve. Some of them, though in rough costermonger's dress, or in the dress of mechanics, are fashionable pickpockets, along with thieves of a coarser and lower description, who push against people in crowds and snatch away their watches and property. One of them, a tall athletic young man, was pointed out to us as a very expert pickpocket. He was dressed in a dark frock, dark trousers and cap, and was busy hurling the skittle-ball with great violence. On our standing by for a little, he slouched his cap sulkily over his eyes and continued at his game. He had an intelligent countenance, but with a callous, bronze-like forbidding expression. Some of his companions were standing at the other end of the skittle-ground engaged in the sport, while the rest of his "pals" sat on a seat alongside and looked on, occasionally eyeing us with considerable curiosity. Some of them were very expert thieves.

In passing through Church Lane we met two young lads dressed like costermongers, and a young woman by their side in a light dirty cotton dress and black bonnet. They were pointed out to us as those base creatures who waylay, decoy, and plunder drunken men at night. We proceeded to Wentworth Street and entered a large lodging-house of a very motley class of people consisting of men working at the docks, prostitutes, and area-sneaks. We called at a house in George Street, principally occupied by females from eighteen to thirty years of age, all prostitutes. In Thrall Street we entered a lodging-house where we saw about thirty persons of both sexes, and of different ages, assembled, consisting chiefly of area-sneaks and pickpockets. Here we saw one prostitute, with a remarkably beautiful child on her knee, seated at her afternoon meal. In the tap-room of a public-house in Church Street we found a large party of thieves, consisting of burglars, pickpockets, and area-sneaks, along with several resetters, one of them a Jew. On the walls of the room were pictures of notorious pugilists, Tom Cribb and others. Several of them had the appearance of pugilists, in their bloated and bruised countenances, and most of them had a rough aspect, which we found to be a general characteristic of the Whitechapel thieves as well as of most of the thieves we saw in the Borough, and at Lambeth. Two of the resetters, who appeared to be callous politic men, sneaked off upon our seating ourselves beside them. One of the band, as we found on similar occasions, stood between us and the door, flourishing a large clasp knife. We sat for some time over a glass of ale, and he slunk off to a corner and resumed his seat, finding his bullying attitude was of no avail. The Jewish resetter was very social and communicative as he sat on the table. The more daring of the band were also frank and good-humoured.

Being desirous to gain a more intimate acquaintance with the haunts of the London thieves, we were brought into communication with Mr. Price, inspector of the lodging-houses of this district, who accompanied us on several visits over the neighbourhood, one of the chief rookeries of thieves in London.

Before setting out on our inspection he gave us the following information:—

About twenty years ago a number of narrow streets, thickly populated with thieves, prostitutes, and beggars, were removed when New Commercial Street was formed, leading from Shoreditch in the direction of the London Docks, leaving a wide space in the midst of a densely populated neighbourhood, which is favourable to its sanitary condition, and might justly be considered one of the lungs of the metropolis. The rookery in Spitalfields we proposed to visit is comprised within a space of about 400 square yards. It is bounded by Church Street, Whitechapel, East Brick Lane, and West Commercial Street, and contains 800 thieves, vagabonds, beggars, and prostitutes, a large proportion of whom may be traced to the old criminal inhabitants of the now extinct Essex Street and old Rose Lane.

For instance, a man and woman lived for many years in George Yard, Whitechapel, a narrow, dirty and overcrowded street leading from Whitechapel into Wentworth Street. The man was usually seen among crowds of thieves, gambling and associating with them. As his family increased, in the course of time he took a beershop and lodging-house for thieves in Thrall Street. His family consisted of three boys and three girls. His wife usually addressed the young thieves as they left her lodging-house in the morning, in the hearing of her own children, in this manner: "Now, my little dears, do the best you can, and may God bless you!"

The following is a brief account of their children:—

The eldest son married a girl whose father died during his transportation. He and his wife gained their living by thieving, and were frequently in custody. At last he connected himself with burglars, was tried, convicted, and sentenced to six years' penal servitude. He is now at Gibraltar, ten months of his sentence being unexpired. His wife has been left with three young children; since his transportation she has been frequently in custody for robbing drunken men, and has had an illegitimate child since her husband left. Her eldest daughter was taken from her about twelve months ago by Mr. Ashcroft, secretary of the Refuge Aid Society, and placed in a refuge in Albert Street, Mile End New Town, where the Society maintains her. The girl is eleven years of age, and appeared pleased that she was taken away from her filthy abode and bad companions in George Street. The second son has been repeatedly in custody for uttering base coin, and was at last convicted and transported for four years. The eldest daughter married a man who also was transported, and is now a returned convict. She was apprehended, convicted, and sentenced to four years' penal servitude. While in Newgate jail she was delivered of twins, and received a reprieve, and has since been in custody for shoplifting.

We went with the inspector to Lower Keat Street, and entered a lodging house there. Most of the inmates were male thieves, from twelve to nineteen years of age and upwards. The husband of the woman who keeps the house is a returned convict and has been in custody for receiving stolen property from her lodgers.

We entered another lodging-house in this street, haunted by thieves of a lower class. An old woman was here employed as a deputy or servant, who formerly lived in Kent Street in the Borough, and kept a public house there, a resort of thieves. She lived with a man there for twenty years and upwards, keeping a brothel, and was then and is now an old fence. We found a number of low thieves in the house at the time of our visit. The landlord has been in custody for having stolen handkerchiefs in his possession, with the marks taken out.

Opposite to this house is a public-house resorted to by thieves.

We then went to Lower George Street, where we entered a registered lodging-house. In three rooms we saw about ninety persons of both sexes and of various ages, many of them thieves and vagrants. This house is not used as a brothel, but some of the lodgers cohabit together as man and wife, which is common in the low neighbourhoods.

We went to a lodging-house in Flower-and-Dean Street, the keeper of which has been recently in prison for receiving from his lodgers. We saw a number of wretched mendicants here. One man had his leg bound up with rags. Many of the inmates gain their livelihood by begging, and others by thieving. Few honest persons reside here.

We next went to a brothel in Wentworth Street, kept by a woman, a notorious character. She has been repeatedly in custody for robbing drunken men, and her husband is now in prison for felony. She is a strong coarse-looking woman, with her countenance bearing marked traces of unbridled passion—the type of person we would expect as the keeper of a low brothel. She had been stabbed on the cheek a few days previously by another woman, and bore the scar of the fresh wound at the time of our visit. The rooms of her house were wretchedly furnished, suitable to the low orgies transacted in this foul abode. One or two withered prostitutes were lounging about the kitchen.

We passed on to a lodging-house of a very different description, occupied by industrious honest working people, which we shall describe afterwards when we treat of an after visit.

In this locality we visited the elderly woman living in this neighbourhood whom we have referred to as having blessed the young thieves. She had a very plausible condoling manner, as she sat with her two daughters by her side—one a young auburn-haired girl of about fourteen, with engaging countenance and handsome form, plainly but neatly dressed; the other, an ordinary-looking young woman, with a child in her arms.

We made another visit to this rookery with the inspector of police, and made a more minute survey of this remarkable district.

We went into a lodging-house in George Yard. The kitchen was about 35 feet in length, and had originally consisted of two rooms, the partition between them being removed. There was a fireplace in each; a group of people, men, lads, and boys, were ranged along the long tables, many of them labourers at the docks.

The boys were better dressed than the wild young Arabs of the city, some of them in dark and brown coats and tartan and black caps. They sat on the forms along the sides of the tables, or lolled on seats by the fire. The apartments were papered, and ornamented with pictures. A picture of the Great Eastern steamship set in a frame was suspended over the mantelpiece; one boy sat with his head bound up, and another with his jacket off, and his white shirt sleeves exposed. The inmates consisted of beggars and dock-labourers seated around the ample kitchen, some busy at their different meals, and others engaged in conversation, which was suspended on our entrance. At the door we saw the deputy, a young man decently dressed. On our former visit we saw an old man with an ample unshorn beard, who works during the day as a crossing-sweeper. He had when young been engaged in sea-faring life, and has now become an admirable picture of Fagin the Jew, as pictured by Charles Dickens. The beds are let here at 3*d.* a night. The people who usually lodge here are crossing-sweepers, bone-pickers and shoe-blacks, etc.

We entered a house in Wentworth Street and passed through a chandler's shop into the kitchen, which is about 31 feet in length and 15 feet in breadth. There we found, as is usual in those lodging-houses, a large fire blazing in the grate. The room had a wooden floor, and clothes were suspended on lines beneath the rafters. There were two large boilers on each side of the fire to supply the lodgers with hot water for coffee or tea. Tables were ranged around the wall on each side, and a motley company were seated around them. Numbers of them were busy at supper—coffee, bread, fish, and potatoes. An elderly man sat in the corner of the room cobbling a pair of old shoes, with a candle nearly burned to the socket placed before him. Groups of elderly women were also clustered around the benches, some plainly but decently dressed, others in dirty tattered skirts and shabby shawls, with careworn, melancholy countenances. Some were middle-aged women, apparently the wives of some of the labourers there. A young man sat by their side, a respectable mechanic out of work.

Two young lads, vagrants, sat squatted by the fire, one of them equipped in dirty tartan trousers, a shabby black frock-coat sadly torn, and brown bonnet. The other sat in his moleskin trousers and shirt. At one of the tables several young women were seated at their tea, some good-looking, others very plain, with coarse features. An elderly woman, the servant of the establishment, stood by the fire with a towel over her bare brown arm.

The tables around were covered with plates, cups and other crockery; caps, jackets and other articles of dress.

While in this street the musical band of the ragged school at George Yard passed by, with the teacher at their head, and many of the scholars clustered around them, with other juveniles and people of the district. Knots of people were assembled in the streets as we passed along.

We entered several other lodging-houses in this locality, occupied by beggars, dock-labourers, prostitutes, and thieves, ballad-singers, and patterers of the lowest class.

We went into a house in George Street. The kitchen was also very large, about 36 feet long and 24 feet broad, and had two blazing fires to warm the apartment and cook the food. Tables were ranged round the room as in the other lodging-houses alluded to. There were about twenty-two people here, chiefly young of both sexes. There was one middle-aged bald-headed man among them. Many of them were sad and miserable. A young good-looking girl, not apparently above seventeen years of age, sat by the fire with a child in her arms. Many of the young women had a lowering countenance and dissipated look. Some of the young lads had a more pleasing appearance, dressed as costermongers.

The long tables were strewed with plates and bowls, cups and saucers. Some young men sat by reading the newspapers, others smoking their pipe and whiffing clouds of smoke around them. Some young women were sewing, others knitting; some busy at their supper, others lying asleep, crouching with their arms on the tables.

On going into another lodging-house we saw a number of people of both sexes, and of various ages, similar to those described. There we saw a woman about thirty, also engaged in knitting, and another reading Reynolds' *Miscellany*. A number of young lads of about seventeen years were smoking their pipe; another youth, a pickpocket, was reading a volume he had got from a neighbouring library. Most of the persons here were prostitutes, pickpockets, and sneaks. There were about fifteen present, chiefly young people.

On passing through Flower-and-Dean Street we saw a group of young lads and girls, all of them thieves, standing in the middle of the street.

We passed into another lodging-house, and entered the kitchen, which is about 30 feet long and 18 feet broad. A large fire was burning in the grate. On the one side of the kitchen were tables and forms, and the people seated around them at supper on bread and herring, tea and coffee. There were a number of middle-aged women among them. On the other side of the kitchen were stalls as in a coffee-shop. We saw several rough-looking men here. There was a rack on the wall covered with plates, ranged carefully in order. The tables were littered with heaps of bottles, jugs, books, bonnets, baskets, and shirts, like a broker's shop.

An old gray-headed man sat at one of the tables with his hand on his temples, a picture of extreme misery, his trousers old, greasy, and ragged, an old shabby ragged coat, and a pair of old torn shoes. His face was furrowed with age, care, and sorrow; his breast was bare, and his head bald in front. He had a long gray beard. His arms were thin and skinny, and the dark blue veins looked through the back of his hands. He was a poor vagrant, and told us he was eighty-eight years of age. There were about forty persons present of both sexes, and of various ages; many of them young, and others very old.

We passed on to Lower Keat Street, and on going into a low lodging-house there we saw a number of young prostitutes, pickpockets, and sneaks.

We visited another lodging house of the lowest description, belonging to an infamous man whom we have already referred to. We were shown upstairs to a large room filled with beds, by a coarse-featured hideous old hag with a dark moustache. Her hair was gray, and her face seamed and scarred with dark passions, as she stood before us with her protruding breasts and bloated figure. Her eyes were dark and muddy. She had two gold rings on one of her fingers, and was dressed in a dirty light cotton gown, sadly tattered, a red spotted soiled handkerchief round her neck, and a dirty light apron, almost black. On observing us looking at her, she remarked, "I am an old woman, and am not so young as I have been. Instead of enjoying the fruit of my hard-wrought life, some other person has done it."

On examining one of the beds in the room, we found the bedding to consist of two rugs, two sheets and a flock bed, with a pillow and pillow-case, let at 3*d*. a night. This house is registered for thirty lodgers. Young and middle-aged women, the lowest prostitutes, and thieves frequent this house; some with holes cut with disease into their brow. D—bl—n B—ll is the proprietor of this infamous abode. We saw him as we passed through the house: a sinister-looking, middle-aged man, about 5 feet 7 inches in height. On leaving the house, the old hag stood at the foot of the stair, with a candle in her hand, a picture of horrid misery.

In this locality we went into another infamous lodging-house, a haunt of prostitutes and thieves, mostly young. There was a very interesting boy here, respectably dressed, with a dark eye and well-formed placid countenance, a pickpocket. He told us his parents were dead, and he had no friends and no home. He did not show any desire to leave his disreputable life. Several of them were seated at their supper on herrings, plaice, butter, bread and coffee.

We visited several of the more respectable lodging-houses in George Yard, to have a more complete view of the dwellings of the poor in this locality. We entered one lodging-house, and passed into the kitchen, 33 feet long by 18 feet broad. There were tables and forms planted round the room, as in the other lodging-houses noticed, and on the walls were shelves for crockery ware. There was a sink in the corner of the kitchen for washing the dishes, and a gas-burner in the centre of the apartment. The kitchen was well ventilated at the windows. There was a large fire burning, with a boiler on each side of the fireplace. Over the mantelpiece was a range of bright coffee and tea pots. Coats were hung up on pegs against the wall, and a fender before the fire. Decent-looking men were seated around, some smoking, some writing, others eating a plain but comfortable supper, others lounging on the seat, exhausted with the labours of the day. In out-houses were ample washing accommodation, and water-closets. Attached to this lodging-house was a reading-room. We went to the bedrooms, and saw the accommodation and furniture. There were iron bedsteads with flock mattress and bed; on each bed were two sheets, one blanket, and a coverlet, a pillow-case, and a pillow. The bedrooms were ventilated by a flue.

There is here accommodation for eighty-nine persons at 3*d*. a night, and there are on an average sixty lodgers each night. The rector of Christ Church visits and supplies the lodgers with tracts and religious services. A register is kept of all the people who lodge here. In this house Karls was apprehended, concerned with another party in the murder of Mrs. Halliday at Kingswood Rectory.

We visited another lodging-house in the same neighbourhood. The kitchen was large, with spacious windows in front. There was a large fireplace, with boiler and oven with a large hotplate. The lodgers had a respectable appearance—some in blue guernseys, and others in respectable dark dresses. There was also a reading-room here, with a dial over the mantelpiece. Some of the men were reading, and others engaged in writing. There was accommodation for washing, water-closets, and excellent beds. This house belongs to the same proprietor as the one already described. It is closed at 12 o'clock, while the others are kept open all night, and is generally frequented by respectable lodgers.

We also inspected another lodging-house in Thrall Street of a superior kind, where beds are to be had at 3*d*. a night. There are two superior lodging-houses of the same character, kept by Mr. Wilmot and Mr. Argent, in Thrall Street and Osborne Place, at 3½d. and 4d. a night.

We thus find that alongside those low lodging-houses and brothels, in the very bosom of that low neighbourhood, there are respectable lodging-houses of different gradations in price and position, where working-people and strangers can be accommodated at 3d., 3½d. and 4d. a night, in which decency, cleanliness, and morality prevail.

In the course of our visits to Spitalfields we found two institutions of high value and special interest—a ragged school and a reformatory for young women. The ragged school was instituted by the Rev. Hugh Allen, the incumbent of St. Jude's, in 1853. There are at present 350 ragged children of both sexes attending it, averaging from four to fifteen years of age. They are taught by Mr. Holland, a most intelligent and devoted teacher, who is exercising a powerful influence for good in that dark and criminal locality.

A female reformatory was lately instituted by the Rev. Mr. Thornton, the present incumbent of St. Jude's, who labours with unwearied energy in this district. This asylum is in Wentworth Street, and is fitted to accommodate eighteen persons.

NARRATIVE OF A PICKPOCKET

THE following recital was given us by a young man who had till lately been an adroit pickpocket in various districts of London, but has now become a patterer for his livelihood. He is about the middle height, of sallow complexion, with a rich, dark, penetrating eye, a moustache and beard. He is a man of tolerably good education, and has a most intelligent mind, well furnished with reading and general information. At the time we met him he was rather melancholy and crushed in spirit, which he stated was the result of repeated imprisonments, and the anxiety and suspense connected with his wild criminal life, and the heavy trials he has undergone. The woman who cohabits with him was then in one of the London prisons, and he was residing in a low lodging-house in the West End of the metropolis. While giving us several exciting passages in his narrative, his countenance lightened up with intense interest and adventurous expression, though his general mien was calm and collected. As we endeavoured to inspire him with hope in an honest career, he mournfully shook his head as he looked forward to the difficulties in his path. He was then shabbily dressed in a dark frock-coat, dark trousers, and cap. We give his narrative almost verbatim:—

"I was born in a little hamlet, five miles from Shrewsbury, in the county of Shropshire, in October, 1830, and am now thirty-one years of age. My father was a Wesleyan minister, and died in 1854, after being subject to the yellow jaundice for five or six years, during which time he was not able to officiate. My mother was a Yorkshire woman, and her father kept a shoemaker's shop in the town of Full Sutton. I had two brothers, one of them older and the other younger than I, and a sister two years younger.

"I went to school to learn to write and cipher, and had before this learned to read at home with my father and mother. We had a very happy home, and very strict in the way of religion. I believe that my father would on no account tolerate such a thing as stopping out after nine o'clock at night, and have heard my mother often say that all the time she was wedded to him, she never had known him the worse of liquor. My father had family worship every night between 8 and 9 o'clock, when the curtains were drawn over the windows, the candle was lighted, and each of the children was taught to kneel separately at prayer. After reading the Bible and half an hour's conversation, each one retired to their bed. In the morning my father would get up and attend to a small pony he had, and when I was very young we had a stout girl who milked the cow and did the dairy and household work. The house we lived in was my grandfather's property, but being a man very fond of money, my father paid him the rent as if he had been a stranger.

"There were two acres of land attached to the house, as nearly as I can recollect; about half an acre was kept in cultivation as a garden, and the other was tilled and set apart for the pony and cow.

"Our people were much respected in the neighbourhood. If there were any bickerings among the neighbours, they came to my father to settle them, and anything he said they generally yielded to without a murmur. In the winter time, when work was slack among the poor labouring people, though my father had little himself to give, he got money from others to distribute among those who were the most deserving. I lived very happy and comfortable at home, but always compelled, though against my own inclination, to go twice to service on the Sunday, and twice during the week (Tuesday and Friday). I always seemed to have a rebellious nature against these religious services, and they were a disagreeable task to me, though my father took more pains with me than with my brothers and sister. I always rebelled against this in my heart, though I did not display it openly.

"I was a favourite with my father, perhaps more so than any of the others. For example, if Wombwell's menagerie would come to Shrewsbury for a short time, he would have taken me instead of my brothers to visit it, and would there speak of the wonders of God and of His handiwork in the creation of animals. Everything that he said and did was tinged with religion, and religion of an ascetic argumentative turn. It was a kind of religion that seemed to banish eternally other sects from happiness and from heaven.

"My mind at this time was injured by the narrow religious prejudices I saw around me. We often had ministers to dinner and supper at our house, and always after their meals the conversation would be sure to turn into discussions on the different points of doctrine. I can recollect as well now as though it were yesterday the texts used on the various sides of the question, and the stress laid on different passages to uphold their arguments. At this time I would be sitting there greedily drinking in every word, and as soon as they were gone I would fly to the Bible and examine the different texts of Scripture they had brought forward, and it seemed to produce a feeling in my mind that any religious opinions could be plausibly supported by it. The arguments on these occasions generally hinged on two main points, predestination and election. My father's opinions were those of the Wesleyan creed, the salvation of all through the blood of Christ.

"These continual discussions seemed to steel my heart completely against religion. They caused me to be very disobedient and unruly, and led to my falling out with my grandfather, who had a good deal of property that was expected to come to our family. Though I was young, he bitterly resented this. In 1839 he was accidentally drowned, and it was found when his will was opened that I was not mentioned in it. The whole of his property was left to my father, with the exception of four houses, which he had an interest in till my brothers and sister arrived at the age of twenty-one. Again the property that was left to my father for the whole of his life he had no power to will away at his death, as it went to a distant relative of my grandfather's.

"This was the first cause of my leaving home. It seemed to rankle in my boyish mind that I was a black sheep, something different from my brothers and sister.

"After being several time spoken to by my father about my quarrelsome disposition with my brothers and sister, I threatened, young as I was, to burn the house down the first opportunity I got. This threat, though not uttered in my father's hearing, came to his ear, and he gave me a severe beating for it, the first time he ever corrected me. This was in the summer of 1840, in the end of May. I determined to leave home, and took nothing away but what belonged to me. I had four sovereigns of pocket money, and the suit of clothes I had on, and a shirt. I walked to Shrewsbury and took the coach to London. When I got to London I had neither friend nor acquaintance. I first put up in a coffee-shop in the Mile End Road, and lodged there for seven weeks, till my money was nearly all spent.

"During this time my clothes had been getting shabby and dirty, having no one to look after me. After being there for seven weeks I went to a mean lodging-house at Field Lane, Holborn. There I met with characters I had never seen before, and heard language that I had not formerly heard. This was about July, 1840, and I was about ten years of age the ensuing October. I stopped there about three weeks doing nothing. At the end of that time I was completely destitute.

"The landlady took pity on me as a poor country boy who had been well brought up, and kept me for some days longer after my money was done. During these few days I had very little to eat, except what was given me by some of the lodgers when they got their own meals. I often thought at that time of my home in the country, and of what my father and mother might be doing, but I had never written to them since the day I had first left my home.

"I sometimes was almost tempted to write to them and let them know the position I was in, as I knew they would gladly send me up money to return home, but my stubborn spirit was not broke then. After being totally destitute for two or three days, I was turned out of doors, a little boy in the great world of London, with no friend to assist me, and perfectly ignorant in the ways and means of getting a living in London.

"I was taken by several poor ragged boys to sleep in the dark arches of the Adelphi. I often saw the boys follow the male passengers when the halfpenny boats came to the Adelphi stairs, i.e., the part of the river almost opposite to the Adelphi Theatre. I could not at first make out the meaning of this, but I soon found they generally had one or two handkerchiefs when the passengers left. At this time there was a prison-van in the Adelphi arches, without wheels, which was constructed different from the present prison-van, as it had no boxes in the interior. The boys used to take me with them into the prison-van. There we used to meet a man my companions called 'Larry'. I knew him by no other name for the time. He used to give almost what price he liked for the handkerchiefs. If they refused to give them at the price he named, he would threaten them in several ways. He said he would get the other boys to drive them away, and not allow them to get any more handkerchiefs there. If this did not intimidate them, he would threaten to give them in charge, so that at last they were compelled to take whatever price he liked to give them.

"I have seen handkerchiefs I afterwards found out to be of the value of four or five shillings, sold him lumped together at 9*d*. each.

"The boys, during this time, had been very kind to me, sharing what they got with me, but always asking why I did not try my hand, till at last I was ashamed to live any longer upon the food they gave me without doing something for myself. One of the boys attached himself to me more than the others, whom we used to call Joe Muckraw, who was afterwards transported, and is now in a comfortable position in Australia.

"Joe said to me, that when the next boat came in, if any man came out likely to carry a good handkerchief, he would let me have a chance at it. I recollect when the boat came in that evening: I think it was the last one, about nine o'clock. I saw an elderly gentleman step ashore, and a lady with him. They had a little dog, with a string attached to it, that they led along. Before Joe said anything to me, he had 'fanned' the gentleman's pocket, i.e., had felt the pocket and knew there was a handkerchief.

"He whispered to me, 'Now, Dick, have a try,' and I went to the old gentleman's side, trembling all the time, and Joe standing close to me in the dark, and went with him up the steep hill of the Adelphi. He had just passed an apple-stall there, Joe still following us, encouraging me all the time, while the old gentleman was engaged with the little dog. I took out a green 'kingsman' (handkerchief), next in value to a black silk handkerchief. (They are used a good deal as neckerchiefs by costermongers.) The gentleman did not perceive his loss. We immediately went to the arches and entered the van where Larry was, and Joe said to him, 'There is Dick's first trial, and you must give him a 'ray' for it,' i.e., 1*s*. 6*d*. After a deal of pressing we got 1*s*. for it.

"After that I gained confidence, and in the course of a few weeks I was considered the cleverest of the little band, never missing one boat coming in, and getting one or two handkerchiefs on each occasion. During the time we knew there were no boats coming we used to waste our money on sweets, and fruits, and went often in the evenings to the Victoria Theatre, and Bower Saloon, and other places. When we came out at twelve, or half-past twelve at night, we went to the arches again, and slept in the prison-van. This was the life I led till January, 1841.

"During that month several men came to us. I did not know, although I afterwards heard, they were brought by 'Larry' to watch me, as he had been speaking of my cleverness at the 'tail,' i.e., stealing from the tails of gentlemen's coats, and they used to make me presents. It seemed they were not satisfied altogether with me, for they did not tell me what they wanted, nor speak their mind to me. About the middle of the month I was seized by a gentleman, who caught me with his handkerchief in my hand. I was taken to Bow Street police station and got two months in Westminster Bridewell.

"I came out in March, and when outside the gate of Westminster Bridewell there was a cab waiting for me, and two of the men standing by who had often made me presents and spoken to me in the arches. They asked me if I would go with them, and took me into the cab. I was willing to go anywhere to better myself, and went with them to Flower-and-Dean Street, Brick Lane, Whitechapel. They took me to their own home. One of them had the first floor of a house there, the other had the second. Both were living with women, and I found out shortly afterwards that these men had lately had a boy, but he was transported about that time, though I did not know this then. They gave me plenty to eat, and one of the women, by name 'Emily,' washed and cleansed me, and I got new clothes to put on. For three days I was not asked to do anything, but in the meantime they had been talking to me of going with them, and having no more to do with the boys at the Adelphi, or with the 'tail,' but to work at picking ladies' pockets.

"I thought it strange at first, but found afterwards that it was more easy to work on a woman's pocket than upon a man's, for this reason: More persons work together, and the boy is well surrounded by companions older than himself, and is shielded from the eyes of the passers-by; and, besides, it pays better.

"It was on a Saturday, in company with three men, I set out on an excursion from Flower-and-Dean Street along Cheapside. They were young men, from nineteen to twenty-five years of age, dressed in fashionable style. I was clothed in the suit given me when I came out of prison, a beaver-hat, a little surtout-coat and trousers, both of black cloth, and a black silk necktie and collar, dressed as a gentleman's son. We went into a pastrycook's shop in St. Paul's Churchyard about half-past two in the afternoon, and had pastry there, and they were watching the ladies coming into the shop, till at last they followed one out, taking me with them.

"As this was my first essay in having anything to do in stealing from a woman, I believe they were nervous themselves, but they had well tutored me during the two or three days I had been out of prison. They had stood against me in the room while Emily walked to and fro, and I had practised on her pocket by taking out sometimes a lady's clasp purse, termed a 'portemonnaie,' and other articles out of her pocket, and thus I was not quite ignorant of what was expected of me. One walked in front of me, one on my right hand, and the other in the rear, and I had the lady on my left hand. I immediately 'fanned' her (felt her pocket) as she stopped to look in at a hosier's window, when I took her purse and gave it to one of them, and we immediately went to a house in Giltspur Street. We there examined what was in the purse. I think there was a sovereign, and about 17s.; I cannot speak positively how much. The purse was thrown away, as is the general rule, and we went down Newgate Street, into Cheapside, and there we soon got four more purses that afternoon, and went home by five o'clock p.m. I recollect how they praised me afterwards that night at home for my cleverness.

"I think we did not go out again till the Tuesday, and that and the following day we had a good pull. It amounted to about £19 each. They always take care to allow the boy to see what is in the purse, and to give him his proper share equal with the others, because he is their sole support. If they should lose him they would be unable to do anything till they got another. Out of my share, which was about £19, I bought a silver watch and a gold chain, and about this time I also bought an overcoat, and carried it on my left arm to cover my movements.

"A few weeks after this we went to Surrey Gardens, and I got two purses from ladies. In one of them were some French coins and a ring, that was afterwards advertised as either lost or stolen in the garden. We did very well that visit, and were thinking of going again, when I was caught in Fleet Street, and they had no means of getting me away, though they tried all they could to secure my escape. They could not do it without exposing themselves to too much suspicion. I was sentenced to three months' imprisonment in Bridge Street Bridewell, Blackfriars, termed by the thieves the Old Horse.

"This was shortly before Christmas, 1840. During my imprisonment I did not live on the prison diet, but was kept on good rations supplied to me through the kindness of my comrades out of doors bribing the turnkeys. I had tea of a morning, bread and butter, and often cold meat. Meat and all kinds of pastry was sent to me from a cook-shop outside, and I was allowed to sit up later than other prisoners. During the time I was in prison for these three months I learned to smoke, as cigars were introduced to me.

"When I came out we often used to attend the theatres, and I have often had as many as six or seven ladies' purses in the rear of the boxes during the time they were coming out. This was the time when the pantomimes were in their full attraction. It is easier to pick a female's pocket when she has several children with her to attract her attention than if she were there by herself.

"We went out once or twice a week, sometimes stopped in a whole week, and sallied out on Sunday. I often got purses coming down the steps at Spitalfields' Church. I believe I have done so hundreds of times. This church was near to us, and easily got at.

"We went to Madame Tussaud's, Baker Street, and were pretty lucky there. At this time we hired horses and a trap to go down to Epsom races, but did not take any of the women with us.

"I was generally employed working in the streets rather than at places of amusement, etc., and was in dread that my father or some of my friends might come and see me at some of these.

"When at the Epsom races, shortly after the termination of the race for the Derby, I was induced, much against my will, to turn my hand upon two ladies as they were stepping into a carriage, and was detected by the ladies. There was immediately an outcry, but I was got away by two of my comrades. The other threw himself in the way, and kept them back; was taken up on suspicion, committed for trial, and got four months' imprisonment.

"I kept with the other men, and we got another man in his place. When his time was expired they went down to meet him, and he did not go out for some time afterwards—for nearly a fortnight. After that we went out, and had different degrees of luck, and one of the men was seized with a decline, and died at Brompton in the hospital. Like the other stalls, he usually went well-dressed, and had a good appearance. His chief work was to guard me and get me out of difficulty when I was detected, as I was the support of the band.

"About this time, as nearly as I can recollect, when I was two months over thirteen years of age, I first kept a woman. We had apartments, a front and back room of our own. She was a tall, thin, genteel girl, about fifteen years of age, and very good-looking. I often ill-used her and beat her. She bore it patiently till I carried it too far, and at last she left me in the summer of 1844. During the time she was with me—which lasted for nine or ten months—I was very fortunate, and was never without £20 or £30 in my pocket, while she had the same in hers. I was dressed in fashionable style, and had a gold watch and gold guard.

"Meantime I had been busy with these men, as usual going to Cheapside, St. Paul's Churchyard, and Fleet Street. In the end of the year 1844 I was taken up for an attempt on a lady in St. Martin's Lane, near Ben Caunt's. The conviction was brought against me from the City, and I got six months in Tothill Fields Prison.

"This was my first real imprisonment of any length. At first I was a month in Tothill Fields, and afterwards three months in the City Bridewell, Blackfriars, where I had a good deal of indulgence, and did not feel the imprisonment so much. The silent system was strict, and being very wilful, I was often under punishment. It had such an effect on me that for the last six weeks of my imprisonment I was in the infirmary. The men came down to meet me when my punishment expired, and I again accompanied them to their house.

"During the time I had been in prison they had got another

boy, but they said they would willingly turn him away or give him to some other men; but I, being self-willed, said they might keep him. I had another reason for parting with them. When I went to prison I had property worth a good deal of money. On coming out I found they had sold it, and they never gave me value for it. They pretended it was laid out in my defence, which I knew was only a pretext.

"Before I was imprisoned my girl had parted from me, which was the beginning of my misfortunes.

"I would not go to work with them afterwards. I had a little money, and at a public-house I met with two men living down Gravel Lane, Ratcliffe Highway. I went down there, and commenced working with two of them on ladies' pockets, but in a different part of the town. We went to Whitechapel and the Commercial Road; but had not worked six weeks with them before I was taken up again, and was tried at Old Arbour Square, and got three months' imprisonment at Coldbath Fields. If I thought Tothill Fields was bad, I found the other worse.

"When I got out I had no one to meet me, and thought I would work by myself. It was about this time I commenced to steal gentlemen's watches.

"The first I took was from the fob of a countryman in Smithfield on a market day. It was a silver watch, which we called a 'Frying Pan'. It had not a guard, but an old chain and seals. It fetched me about 18s. I took off one of the seals which was gold, which brought me as much as the watch, if not more. I sold it to a man I was acquainted with in Field Lane, where I first lodged, after leaving the coffee-shop when I first came to London, and where the landlady gave me several nights' lodging gratuitously. I repaid her the small sum due her for her former kindness to me.

"I lodged there, and shortly after cohabited with another female. She was a big stout woman, ten years older than I; well-made, but coarse-featured. I did not live with her long—only three or four months. I was then only fifteen years of age. During that time I always worked by myself. Sometimes she would go out with me, but she was no help to me. I looked out for crowds at fairs, at fires, and on any occasion where there was a gathering of people, as at this time I generally confined myself to watches and pins from men.

"I was not so lucky then, and barely kept myself in respectability. My woman was very extravagant, and swallowed up all

I could make. I lived with her about four months, when I was taken up in Exmouth Street, Clerkenwell, and got four months' imprisonment in Coldbath Fields Prison.

"When my sentence was expired, she came to meet me at the gate of the prison, and we remained together only two days, when I heard reports that she had been unfaithful to me. I never charged her with it, but ran away from her.

"When I left her I went to live in Charles Street, Drury Lane. I stopped there working by myself for five or six months, and got acquainted with a young woman who has ever since been devoted to me. She is now thirty-three years of age, but looks a good deal older than she is, and is about middle height. We took a room and furnished it. I soon got acquainted with some of the swell-mob at the Seven Dials, and went working along with three of them upon the ladies' purses again. At this time I was a great deal luckier with them than I had been since I had left Tothill Fields Prison. I worked with them till April, 1847, visiting the chief places of public resort, such as the Surrey Gardens, Regent's Park, Zoological Gardens, Madame Tussaud's, the Coliseum, and other places. My other two comrades and I were arrested at the Coliseum for picking a lady's pocket. We were taken to Albany Street station-house, and the next day committed for trial at the sessions. I had twelve months' imprisonment for this offence, and the other two of four years' penal servitude, on account of previous convictions. I had only summary convictions, which were not produced at the trial.

"At this time summary convictions were not brought against a prisoner committed for trial.

"We were frequently watched by the police and detectives, who followed our track, and were often in the same places of amusement with us. We knew them as well as they knew us, and often eluded them. Their following us has often been the means of our doing nothing on many of these occasions, as we knew their eye was upon us.

"I came out of prison three or four days before the gathering of the Chartists on Kennington Common. My female friend met me as I came out.

"I went to this gathering on 10th April, 1848, along with three men. I took several ladies' purses there, amounting to £3 or £4, when we saw a gentleman place a pocketbook in the tail of his coat. Though I had done nothing at the tail for a long time, it was too great a temptation, and I immediately seized it. There was a bundle of bank-notes in it—7 ten-pound notes, 2 for twenty pounds, and 5 five-pound notes. We got from the fence or receiver £4 10s. for each of the £5, £8 10s. for the tens, and £18 for the £20 notes.

"The same afternoon I took a purse in Trafalgar Square with about eighteen sovereigns in it. I kept walking in company with the same men till the commencement of 1849, when I was taken ill and laid up with rheumatism. I lost the use of my legs in a great measure, and could not walk, and paid away my money to physicians. Before I got better, such articles as we had were disposed of, though my girl helped me as well as she could.

"In the early part of 1849, when I was not able to go out and do anything, Sally, who cohabited with me, went out along with another girl and commenced stealing in omnibuses. She was well-dressed and had a respectable appearance. I did not learn her to pick pockets, and was averse to it at first, as I did not wish to bring her into danger. I think she was trained by my pals. She was very clever, and supported me till I was able to go out again. I had to walk with a crutch for some time, but gradually got better and stronger. Some time after that I got into a row at the Seven Dials and was sent for a month to Westminster Prison for an assault.

"When I came out I was sorry to find that Sally was taken up and committed for trial for an omnibus robbery, and had got six months' imprisonment at Westminster. This was in 1850. I succeeded very well during the time she was in prison in picking ladies' pockets during the time of the Great Exhibition at Hyde Park.

"When she came out I had nearly £200 by me. I did not go out for some time, and soon made the money fly, for I was then a cribbage player and would stake as much as £2 or £3 on a game.

"In the end of the year 1851 I was pressed for the first time to have a hand at a crack in the City along with two other men. I was led through their representations to believe they were experienced burglars, but found afterwards, if they *were* experienced they were not very clever. Though they got a plan, they blundered in the execution of it in getting into the place, and went into the wrong room, so that they had to get through another wall, which caused us to be so late that it was gray in the morning before we got away; and we did not find so much as we expected.

"At the back of the premises we cut our way into the passage, and, according to the directions given to us in the plan that had been drawn, we had to go up to the second floor, and enter a door there. We found nothing in the room we had entered but neckties and collars, which would not have paid us for bringing them away. We then had to work our way through a back wall before we got into the apartment where the silks were stored. They cut through the brick wall very cleverly. We had all taken rum to steady our nerve before we went to the work.

"We had gone up the wrong staircase, which was the cause of our having to cut through the wall. There was only one man that slept in the house, and he was in a room on the basement. We at last, after much labour and delay, got into the right room, pressed the bolt back, and found we could get away by the other staircase. We got silks, handkerchiefs, and other drapery goods, and had about £18 each after disposing of them—which was about two-thirds of their value. We had a cab to carry away the things for us to the 'fence' who received them.

"We went to another burglary at Islington, and made an entrance into the house, but were disturbed, and ran away over several walls and gardens.

"We attempted a third burglary in the City. As usual we had a plan of it through a man that had been at work there, who put it up for us. This was a shop in which there were a great many Geneva watches. We got in at this time by the back window, and went upstairs. We were told that the master went away at 1 o'clock. On this occasion he had remained later than usual, looking over his business books. On seeing us he made an outcry and struggled with us. Assistance came immediately. Two policemen ran up to the house. In the scramble with the man in the house we tried to make for the door. The police could not get in, as the door was bolted. We were determined to make a rush out. I undid the chain and drew back the bolt. I got away, and had fled along two or three streets, when I was stunned by a man who carried a closed umbrella. Hearing the cry of 'Stop thief!' he drew out the umbrella, and I fell as I was running. I was thereupon taken back by one of the police, and found both of the others in custody. We were committed for trial next day, and sent to Newgate in the meantime for detention.

"My former convictions were not brought against me. My two companions had been previously at Newgate, and were sentenced the one to ten years' and the other to seven years' penal servitude, while I got eighteen months' imprisonment in Holloway Prison. I was the younger of the party, and had no convictions. I never engaged in a burglary after this. At this time I was twenty-two or twenty-three years of age.

"I came out of prison in 1853, and was unnerved for some time though my health was good. This was the effect of the solitary confinement.

"When I came out, I wrote home for the first time since I had been in London, and received a letter back stating that my father was dead after an illness of several years, and that I was to come home, adding that if I required money, they would send it me. Besides, there were several things they were to give me, according to my father's wishes.

"I went home, and had thoughts of stopping there. My mother was not in such good position as I expected, the property left by my grandfather having gone to a distant relative at my father's death. She was and is still in receipt of a weekly sum from the old Wesleyan fund for the benefit of the widows of ministers.

"I went home in the end of 1853, and had the full intention of stopping there, though I promised to Sally to be back in a few weeks. I soon got tired of country life, though my relations were very kind to me, and after remaining seven weeks at home, came back to London again about the commencement of 1854, and commenced working by myself at stealing watches and breast-pins. I did not work at ladies' pockets unless I had comrades beside me. I went and mingled in the crowds by myself.

"In the end of 1854 I got another six months' imprisonment at Hicks's Hall police court, and was sent to Coldbath Fields, and was told that if I ever come again before the criminal authorities, I would be transported.

"I came out in 1855, and have done very little since; acting occasionally as a stall to Sally in omnibuses, and generally carrying a portmanteau or something with me. I would generally sit in the omnibus on the opposite side to her, and endeavour to keep the lady, as well as I could, engaged in conversation, while she sat on her right hand. She got twelve months for this in 1855, and during the time she was in Westminster Prison I first commenced pattering in the streets. I did not again engage in thieving till the time of the illumination for the peace in 1856. In Hyde Park on this occasion I took a purse from a lady, containing nine sovereigns and some silver; and was living on this money when Sally was discharged at the expiry of her sentence.

"When she came out, I told her what I had been doing, and found she was much altered, and seemed to have a great disinclination to go out any more. She did not go for some time. I made a sufficient livelihood by pattering in the streets for nearly two years, when I got wet several times and was laid up with illness again. She then became acquainted with a woman who used to go on a different game, termed shoplifting. While the one kept the shopman engaged, the other would purloin a piece of silk, or other goods. At this time she took to drink. I found out after this she often got things, and sold them, before she came home, on purpose to get drink. News came to me one day that she had been taken up and committed for trial at Marylebone police court. I paid the counsel to plead her case, and she was acquitted.

"I then told her if she was not satisfied with what I was doing as patterer, that I would commence my former employment. So I did for some time during last year, till I had three separate remands at the House of Detention, Clerkenwell. The policeman got the stolen property, but was so much engrossed taking me he had lost sight of the prosecutor, who was never found, and I got acquitted.

"On this occasion I told Sally I would never engage in stealing again, and I have kept my word. I know if I had been tried at this time, and found guilty, I should have been transported.

"I have since then got my living by pattering in the streets. I earn my 2s. or 2s. 6d. in an hour, or an hour and a half in the evening, and can make a shift.

"For six or seven years, when engaged in picking pockets, I earned a good deal of money. Our house expenses many weeks would average from £4 to £5, living on the best fare, and besides, we went to theatres, and places of amusement, occasionally to the Cider Cellars and the Coal Hole.

"The London pickpockets are acquainted generally with each other, and help their comrades in difficulty. They frequently meet with many of the burglars. A great number of the women of pickpockets and burglars are shoplifters, as they require to support themselves when their men are in prison.

"A woman would be considered useless to a man if she could not get him the use of counsel, and keep him for a few days after he comes out, which she does by shoplifting, and picking pockets in omnibuses, the latter being termed 'Maltooling.'

"I have associated a good deal with the pickpockets over London, in different districts. You cannot easily calculate their weekly income, as it is so precarious, perhaps one day getting £20 or £30, and another day being totally unsuccessful. They are in general very superstitious, and if anything cross them they will do nothing. If they see a person they have formerly robbed they expect bad luck and will not attempt anything.

"They are very generous in helping each other when they get into difficulty or trouble but have no societies, as they could not be kept up. Many of them may be in prison five or six months of the year; some may get a long penal servitude, or transportation; or they may have the steel taken out of them, and give up this restless, criminal mode of life.

"They do not generally find stealing gentlemen's watches so profitable as picking ladies' pockets, for this reason, that the purse can be thrown away, some of the coins changed, and they may set to work again immediately; whereas, when they take a watch they must go immediately to the fence with it: it is not safe to keep it on their person. A good silver watch will now bring little more than 25s. or 30s., even if the watch has cost £6. A good gold watch will not fetch above £4. I have worked for two or three hours, and have got, perhaps, six different purses during that time; the purses I threw away, so that the robbery may not be traced. Suppose you take a watch; and you place it in your pocket, while you have also your own watch, if you happen to be detected, you are taken and searched, and there being a second watch found on you, the evidence is complete against you.

"The trousers-pockets are seldom picked, except in a crowd. It is almost impossible to do this in any other occasion, such as when walking in the street. A prostitute may occasionally do it, pattering with her fingers about a man's person when he is off his guard.

"I believe a large number of the thieves of London come from the provinces, and from the large towns, such as Leeds, Birmingham, Sheffield, Manchester, and Liverpool; from Birmingham especially, more than any other town in England. There are no foreigners pickpockets in London so far as I know. The cleverest of the native London thieves, in general, are the Irish cockneys.

"I never learned any business or trade, and never did a hard day's work in my life, and have to take to pattering for a livelihood. When men in my position take to an honest employment, they are sometimes pointed out by some of the police as having been formerly convicted thieves, and are often dismissed from service, and driven back into criminal courses.

"I am a sceptic in my religious opinions, which was a stumbling-block in the way of several missionaries, and other philanthropic men assisting me. I have read Paine, and Volney, and Holyoake, those infidel writers, and have also read the works of Bulwer, Dickens, and numbers of others. It gives a zest to us in our criminal life, that we do not know how long we may be at liberty to enjoy ourselves. This strengthens the attachment between pickpockets and their women, who, I believe, have a stronger liking to each other, in many cases, than married people."

HORSE AND DOG STEALERS

HORSE-STEALING

THESE robberies are not so extensive as they used to be in the metropolitan districts. They are generally confined to the rural districts, where horses are turned out to graze on marshes and in pasture-fields. Horses are stolen by a low unprincipled class of men, who travel the country dealing in them, who are termed "horse coupers," and sometimes by the wandering gipsies and tinkers. They journey from place to place, and observe where there is a good horse or pony, and loiter about the neighbourhood till they get an opportunity to steal it. This is generally done in the night time, and in most cases by one man.

After removing it from the park, they take it away by some by-road, or keep it shut up in a stable or outhouse till the "hue and cry" about the robbery has settled down. They then trim it up, and alter the appearance as much as possible, and take it to some market at a distance, and sell it—sometimes at an under price. This is their general mode of operation. Sometimes they proceed to London and dispose of it at Smithfield market. The party that steals it does not generally take it to the market, but leaves it in a quiet stable at some house by the way, till he meets with a low horse-dealer. The thief is often connected with horse-dealers, but may not himself be one.

Some Londoners are in the habit of stealing horses. These often frequent the Old Kent Road, and are dressed as grooms or stablemen. They are of various ages, varying from twenty to sixty years. The person who sells the horses gets part of the booty from the horse-stealer.

The mode of stealing by gipsies is somewhat similar. They pitch their tents on some waste ground by the roadside, or on the skirt of a wood, and frequently steal a horse when they get an opportunity. One will take it away who has been keeping unobserved within the tent, and the rest will remain encamped in the locality as if nothing had happened. They may remove it to a considerable distance, and get it into the covert of a wood, such as Epping Forest, or some secluded spot, and take the first opportunity to sell it.

Another class of persons travel about the country, dealing in small wares as Cheap Johns, who occasionally steal horses, or give information to abandoned characters who steal them.

These robberies of horses are generally committed in rural districts, and are seldom done in the metropolis, as horses are in general looked after, or locked up in stables. They are occasionally stolen in the markets in and around the metropolis, such as Smithfield and the new market at Islington.

Sometimes horses in carts, and cabs, and other vehicles are removed by thieves in the streets of the metropolis; but this is only done for a short time until they have rifled the goods. So soon as they have secured them, they leave the horse and vehicle, which come into the hands of the police and are restored to the owner.

The horses stolen are generally light and nimble, such as those used in phaetons and light conveyances, and not for heavy carts or drays.

DOG-STEALING

THESE robberies are generally committed by dog-fanciers and others who confine their attention to this class of felonies. They are persons of a low class, dressed variously, and are frequently followed by women. They steal fancy dogs ladies are fond of— spaniels, poodles, and terriers, sporting-dogs, such as setters and retrievers, and also Newfoundland dogs. These robberies are generally committed by men of various ages, but seldom by boys. Their mode of operation is this: In prowling over the metropolis, when they see a handsome dog with a lady or gentleman they follow it and see where the person resides. So soon as they have ascertained this they loiter about the house for days with a piece of liver prepared by a certain process, and soaked in some ingredient which dogs are uncommonly fond of. They are so partial to it they will follow the stranger some distance in preference to following their master. The thieves generally carry small pieces of this to entice the dog away with them, when they seize hold of it in a convenient place, and put it into a bag they carry with them.

Another method of decoying dogs is by having a bitch in heat. When any valuable dog follows it is picked up and taken home, when they wait for the reward offered by the owner to return it, generally from £1 to £5. The loss of the dog may be advertised in the *Times* or other newspapers, or by handbills circulated over the district, when some confederate of the thief will negotiate with the owner for the restoration of the dog. Information is sent if he will give a certain sum of money, such as £1, £2, or £5, the dog will be restored, if not it will be killed. This is done to excite sympathy.

Some dogs have been known to be stolen three or four times, and taken back to their owner by rewards. Sometimes when they steal dogs they fancy, they keep them and do not return them to the owner.

There is a class termed dog-receivers, or dog-fanciers, who undertake to return stolen dogs for a consideration. These parties are connected with the thieves, and are what is termed "in the ring," that is, in the ring of thieves. Dogs are frequently restored by agencies of this description. These parties receive dogs and let the owners have them back for a certain sum of money, while they receive part of the price shared with the thief.

Dog-stealing is very prevalent, particularly in the West End of the metropolis, and is rather a profitable class of felony. These thieves reside at the Seven Dials, in the neighbourhood of Belgravia, Chelsea, Knightsbridge, and low neighbourhoods, some of them men of mature years.

They frequently pick up dogs in the street when their owners are not near. But their general mode is to loiter about the houses and entice them away in the manner described. Sometimes they belong to the felon class, sometimes not. They are often connected with bird-fanciers, keepers of fighting-dogs, and persons who get up rat matches.

Some of those stolen are sent to Germany, where English dogs are sold at a high price.

HIGHWAY ROBBERS

THE highway robbers of the present day are a very different set from the bold reckless brigands who infested the metropolis and the highways in its vicinity in former times. There was a bold dash in the old highwayman, the Dick Turpins and Claud Du Vals of that day, not to be found in the thieves of our time, whether they lived in the rookeries of St. Giles's, Westminster, and the Borough, nestling securely amid dingy lanes and alleys, densely-clustered together, where it was unsafe for even a constable to enter; or whether they roamed at large on Blackheath and Hounslow Heath, or on Wimbledon Common, and Finchley Common, accosting the passing traveller, pistol in hand, with the stern command, "Stand and deliver."

The highwaymen of our day are either the sneaking thieves we have described, who adroitly slip their hands into your pockets, or low coarse ruffians who follow in the wake of prostitutes, or garotte drunken men in the midnight street, or strike them down by brutal violence with a life-preserver or bludgeon.

These felonies are generally committed in secluded spots and by-streets, or in the suburbs of the metropolis. Many robberies are committed on the highway by snatching with violence from the person. These are generally done in the dusk, and rarely during the day. When committed early in the evening, they are done in secluded places, intersected with lanes and alleys, where the thieves have a good opportunity to escape, such as in the Borough, Spitalfields, Shoreditch, Whitechapel, Drury Lane, Westminster, and similar localities. These are often done by one person, at other times by two or more in company, and generally by young men from nineteen years and upwards. The mode of effecting it is this. They see a person respectably dressed walking along the street, with a silver or gold chain, who appears to be off his guard. One of them as he passes by makes a snatch at it, and runs down one of the alleys or along one of the by-streets.

Sometimes the thief breaks the chain with a violent wrench. At other times the swivel, or ring, of the watch may give way, or a piece of the guard breaks off. The thief occasionally fails to get the watch. In these cases he can seldom be identified, because the party may not have had his eye on him, and may lose his presence of mind; and the thief may have vanished swiftly out of his sight.

Should the person to whom the watch belongs run after him, his companions often try to intercept him, and with this view throw themselves in his way. The thief is seldom caught at the time, unless he is pursued by some person passing by who has seen him commit the robbery, or who may have heard the cry "Stop thief."

These felonies are committed by men living in low neighbourhoods, who are generally known thieves; and are in most cases done during some disturbance in the street, or in a crowd, or upon a person the worse of liquor.

In September, 1859, Thomas Dalton, alias Thomas Davis, a stout-made man of about thirty years of age, and 5 feet 6 inches high, in company with another man, went to the regatta at Putney, near London, when Dalton snatched the watch of Mr. Friar, formerly the ballet-master at Vauxhall Gardens. Mr. Friar, being aware of the robbery, suddenly seized hold of both the men, when they wrestled with him. The other man got away, but he retained his hold of Dalton. On a policeman coming up Dalton dropped the watch. He was committed to the Surrey Sessions, tried on 15th September, 1859, and sentenced to ten years' penal servitude.

Dalton was one of five prisoners tried at the Central Criminal Court in December, 1847, for the murder of Mr. Bellchambers, at Westminster, having beaten in his brains with an iron bar in Tothill Street, Westminster, during the night. Dalton was then acquitted. Sales, one of the parties charged, was found guilty and hanged at Newgate.

They were seen in the company of the deceased in a publichouse in Orchard Street, Westminster, on the night of the murder, and had followed him out and robbed him of his money, watch, and seals. Dalton had been several times in custody, for being concerned with other persons in plate robberies; sneaking down into areas and opening the doors by means of skeleton keys, and carrying off the plate. One of the thieves went, dressed as a butcher, with an ox's tail, pretending the lady of the house had ordered it. While the servant went upstairs he put the plate into a basket he carried with him, and carried it away.

On the 23rd of March, 1850, he was in custody with three other notorious housebreakers for attempting to steal plate in

Woburn Square by skeleton keys along with four other thieves, when he was found guilty and got three months' imprisonment. One of them opened an area date about 10 o'clock in the morning, carrying a green-baize cloth containing three French rolls. Finding the servant in the kitchen, cleaning the plate, he told her he had brought the French rolls from the baker. The servant, who was an intelligent shrewd person, refused to go upstairs to her mistress. Meantime two detective officers, who had been on the look-out, arrested the four thieves and prevented the robbery.

On the 6th February, 1854, he was tried at Westminster, for snatching a watch from a gentleman in Parliament Street, while her Majesty was proceeding to open the Houses of Parliament. The gentleman, feeling the snatch at his watch, laid hold of Dalton, when he threw it down an area in front of the Treasury buildings.

As we have already said, Dalton was afterwards sentenced to transportation.

Another remarkable case of highway robbery took place several years ago by a man of the name of George Morris. He was above five feet nine inches high, stout-made, with dark whiskers, and of gentlemanly appearance. He snatched a watch from a man near the Surrey Theatre. Immediately on seizing hold of the watch he ran round St. George's Circus into the Waterloo Road, with the cry of "Stop thief!" ringing in his ears. In running down Waterloo Road he threw himself down intentionally into a heap of dirt in the street, when several people who were chasing him, and also a policeman, stumbled over him. He then got up as they lay on the ground and ran down a turning called Webber Row, down Spiller's Court, and got over a closet, then mounted the roof of some low cottages, and jumped off this into the garden at the other side belonging to lofty houses there under repair. Finding a crowd of people and the police close at his heels in the garden below, and being exceedingly nimble, he ran up the ladder like lightning, to the roof of the house. As the policemen were about to follow him he took hold of the ladder and threw it back, preventing all further chase. He disappeared from the top of this house and got to the roof of the Magdalen Institution, and would have made his escape but for the prompt exertions of the police. Some of them ran into a builder's yard and got several ladders and climbed up at different parts of the building and pursued him on the roof of the house—between the chapel and the governor's house. He stood at bay, and threatened to kill the first policeman who approached him, and kept them at defiance for half-an-hour.

Meantime several other policemen had mounted the back part of the chapel by means of a ladder, unperceived by Morris, while the others were keeping him in conversation. On seeing them approach he found all hope of escape was vain, and surrendered himself into the hands of the officers. He was tried at the Central Criminal Court, and sentenced to transportation for ten years.

Not long before he had assaulted a woman in the Westminster Road. There was a cry for the police, and he ran down Duke Street, Westminster Road. On turning the corner of the street he popped into a doorway. This was in the dusk of the evening. His pursuers ran past, thinking he had gone into one of the adjoining streets. As soon as they had passed by he was seen to come out and coolly walk back, as if nothing had occurred. A neighbour who had seen this gave him into the custody of the police about half-an-hour afterwards, and he was fined 40s. for assaulting the woman.

About this time a woman complained to a policeman at the Surrey Theatre that a tall, gentlemanly man had picked her pocket. The constable told her he had seen a well-known thief go into a neighbouring coffee-shop dressed in black. He took the woman over, and she immediately said that was not the man. She was not able to identify him, as he had turned his coat inside out. The coat he had on was black in the inside, and white on the exterior, and could be put on upon either side. He had in the meantime changed the coat, and the woman was thereby unable to recognise him. This enabled him on this occasion to escape the ends of justice.

Highway robberies are also effected by garotting. These are done in similar localities at dusk, frequently in foggy nights at certain seasons of the year, and seldom in the summer time. They are generally done in the by-streets, and in the winter time. A ruffian walks up and throws his arm round the neck of a person who has a watch, or whom he has noticed carrying money on his person. One man holds him tightly by the neck, and generally attacks from behind, or from the side. The garotter tries to get his arm under his chin, and presses it back, while with the other hand he holds his neck firmly behind. He does it so violently the man is almost strangled and is unable to cry out. He holds him in this position perhaps for a minute or two, while his companions, one or more, rifle his pockets of his watch and money.

Should the person struggle and resist he is pressed so severely by the neck that he may be driven insensible. When the robbery is effected they run off. In general they seize a man when off his guard, and it may be some time before he recovers his presence of mind. These are generally a different class of men from the persons who snatch the watch-chain. They have more of the bull-dog about them, and are generally strong men, and brutal in disposition. Many of them are inveterate thieves, returned convicts, ruffians hardened in crime. Their average age is from twenty-five and upwards, and they reside in low infamous neighbourhoods. Most of these depredations are committed in the East End of the metropolis, such as Whitechapel and its neighbourhood, or the dark slums in the Borough.

A remarkable case of garotting occurred in the metropolis in July, 1856. Two men went to a jeweller's shop in Mark Lane during the day, when the street was thronged with people. One of them was stout-made, about five feet six inches high, of dark complexion, and about forty-five years of age. The other, named James Hunter, alias Connell, was about five feet ten inches high, of robust frame, with dark whiskers, dressed in the first of fashion. One of the thieves kept watch outside while the other slipped in and laid hold, in the absence of the jeweller, of a lot of valuable jewellery. The shopman, who happened to be in the back parlour, ran into the shop and seized him. On seeing this his companion came in from the street to assist him, knocked the shopman down and gave him a severe wound on the head, when both hastily made their escape. One of them was taken when he had got a small distance off with some of the jewellery on his person, such as watches, rings, brooches, etc., but the other got away. This robbery was daringly done in the very middle of the day, near to the Corn Exchange, while in the heat of business. One of the robbers was taken and tried at the Central Criminal Court in July, 1856, and sentenced to ten years' transportation, having been previously convicted for felony.

From information received by the police, James Hunter alias Clifford alias Connell, the other person concerned in this robbery, was taken afterwards. A good-looking young apple-woman swore distinctly he was one of those parties. In running away he had thrown down her stand of apples, and also threw her down when she for a short time had seized hold of him.

He was tried at the Central Criminal Court in August, 1856, the following sessions, when the prisoner's counsel proved an alibi by calling his convicted confederate as a witness. His two sisters also swore he was in their house at Lambeth Walk on the day the robbery occurred, and had dinner and tea with his mother, who was an honest and respectable woman.

Other robberies are perpetrated by brutal violence with a life-preserver or bludgeon. It is usually done by one or more brutal men following a woman. The men are generally from thirty to forty years of age—some older—carrying a life-preserver or bludgeon. This is termed "swinging the stick", or the "bludgeon business." The woman walks forward, or loiters about, followed by the men, who are hanging in the rear. She walks as if she was a common prostitute, and is often about twenty-six or thirty years of age. She picks up a man in the street, possibly the worse of liquor; she enters into conversation, and decoys him to some quiet, secluded place, and may there allow him to take liberties with her person, but not to have carnal connection. Meantime she robs him of his watch, money, or other property, and at once makes off.

In some instances she is pursued by the person, who may have discovered his loss; when he is met by one of the men, who runs up, stops him, and inquires the direction to some part of London, or to some street, or will ask what he has been doing with his wife, and threaten to punish him for indecent conduct to her. During this delay the woman may get clear away. In some cases a quarrel arises, and the victim is not only plundered of his money, but severely injured by a life-preserver or bludgeon.

Cases of this kind occasionally occur in the East End and the suburbs of London. These women and men are generally old thieves and, when convicted, are often sentenced to transportation, being in most cases well known to the police.

Sometimes these robberies are committed by men without the connivance of women, as in a case which occurred in Drury Lane in August last, when a man was decoyed by several men from sympathy to accompany a drunken man to a public-house, and was violently robbed.

In the month of July, 1855, a woman stopped a man in the London Road, Southwark, one evening about twelve o'clock at night, and stole his watch. The party immediately detected the robbery, and laid hold of her. Upon this two men came up to her rescue, struck him in the face, and cut his cheek. They then gave him another severe blow on the head, and knocked him down senseless, while calling out for the police.

A policeman came up at this juncture and laid hold of Taylor, one of the men, and took him into custody with a life-preserver in his hand. Taylor was tried on 20th August, 1855, at the Central Criminal Court, and was sentenced to fourteen years' penal servitude.

Highway robberies by the pistol are seldom committed, though occasionally such instances do occur. These are seldom committed by professional thieves, as they generally manage to effect their object by picking pockets, and in the modes we have just described.

The old rookeries of thieves are no longer enveloped in mystery as formerly. They are now visited by our police inspectors and constables, and kept under strict surveillance.

A RAMBLE AMONG THE THIEVES' DENS IN THE BOROUGH

LEAVING the police-office at Stones End, along with a detective-officer, we went one afternoon to Gunn Street, a narrow by-street off the Borough Road, inhabited by costermongers, burglars, and pickpockets.

Here one of the most daring gangs of burglars and pickpockets in London met our eye, most of them in the dress of costermongers. A professional pickpocket, a well-attired young man, was seated on a costermonger's barrow. He was clothed in a black cloth coat, vest, and trousers, and shining silk hat, and was smoking a pipe, with two or three "pals" by his side. It was then about seven o'clock p.m., and as clear as mid-day. About forty young men, ranging from seventeen to thirty-five years of age, were engaged around a game of "pitch and toss," while others were lounging idle in the street.

We went forward through the crowd, and stood for some time alongside. At first they may have fancied we were come to arrest one or more of them, and were evidently prepared to give us a warm reception. On seeing us standing by smiling, they recovered their good-humour, and most of them continued to cluster together, but numbers sneaked off to their houses out of sight.

Here we saw a tall, robust man, with a dissipated and ruffianly look, smoking a long pipe, who had been an accomplice in an atrocious midnight murder.

He had narrowly escaped the gallows by turning Queen's evidence on his companions. He is a determined burglar. We could observe from the brutal, resolute, bull-dog look of the man that he was fit for any deed of heartless villainy when inflamed with strong drink.

Three burglars stood in the middle of the crowd, who soon after left it and entered a beershop in the street. One of them was dressed like a respectable mechanic. He was rather beneath the middle height, stout-made, with his nose injured and flattened, possibly done in some broil. Another was more brutal in appearance, and more degraded. The third burglar was not so resolute in character, and appeared to be an associate of the band.

Ten of the persons present had been previously convicted of robberies. The greater part, if not the whole of them, were thieves, or associates of thieves.

We next directed our way to the Mint, a well-known harbour of low characters, passing knots of thieves at the corners of the different streets as we proceeded along. Some were sneaks, and others pickpockets. In the neighbourhood of the Mint we found a number of children gambolling in the streets. One in particular arrested our attention, an interesting little girl of about five years of age, with a sallow complexion, but most engaging countenance, radiant with innocence and hope. Other sweet little girls were playing by her side, possibly the children of some of the abandoned men and women of the locality. How sad to think of these young innocents exposed to the contamination of bad companionships around them, and to the pernicious influence of the bad example of their parents!

We went into Evan's lodging-house, noted as a haunt for thieves. Passing through a group of young women who stood at the doorway, we went downstairs to an apartment below and saw about a dozen of young lads and girls seated around a table at a game of cards. One of these youths was a notorious pickpocket, though young in years, and had twice escaped out of Horsemonger Lane gaol. We were informed there was not a fourth of the persons present who usually frequent the house. After the first panic was over the young people resumed their game, some looking slyly at us, as if not altogether sure of our object. Others were lying extended on the benches along the side of the room. As we were looking on this curious scene the women in the flat above had followed us down and were peering from the staircase into the apartment to try and learn the object of our visit. As we left the house we took a glance over our shoulder and saw them standing at the door, following our movement.

We bent our steps to Kent Street and entered a beershop there. There were a number of thieves and "smashers" (utterers of base coin) hovering round the bar. The "smashers" were ordinary-looking men and women of the lower orders. We saw a party of thieves in the adjoining taproom, and seated ourselves for a short time among them. One of them was a dexterous swell-mobsman, who has been several times convicted and imprisoned. A dark-complexioned little man, about twenty-one years of age, an utterer of base coin, was lounging in the seat beside us. The swell-mobsman was evidently the leading man among them. He was a good-looking fair-haired youth, about twenty years of age, smart and decided in his movements, and with a good appearance, very unlike a criminal. He occasionally dresses in high style, in a superfine black suit, with white hat and crape, and occasionally drives out in fashionable vehicles.

We also visited Market Street, a narrow by-street off the Borough Road, a well-known rookery of prostitutes. A great number of simple, thoughtless young girls, from various parts of London and the country, leave their homes and settle down here and live on prostitution. Here we saw an organist performing in the street, surrounded by a dense crowd of young prostitutes, middle-aged women, and children of the lower class. Two young women, one with her face painted, and the other a slender girl about seventeen, with an old crownless straw bonnet on her head, and with the crown of it in one hand, and a stick in the other, were dancing in wild frolic to the strains of the organ, amid the merriment of the surrounding crowd, and to the evident amazement of the poor minstrel, while other rough-looking young dames were skipping gaily along the street.

In a brothel in this street an atrocious crime was perpetrated a few days ago by George Philips, a young miscreant, termed the Jew-boy, who resided there. A sailor, recently returned from

India, happened to enter this foul den. The inmates consisted of the Jew-boy's sister, a common prostitute, who cohabited with Richard Pitts, a well-known burglar, recently sentenced to transportation for ten years, another prostitute named Irish Julia, and this young villain, the Jew. After remaining for some time the sailor told them he was to leave their company. On hearing this, Philips's sister told her brother to stab him to the heart. He instantly took a knife from his pocket, opened it, and stabbed the sailor beneath the collar-bone. After committing this atrocious crime he coolly wiped the knife on the cuff of his guernsey, at the same time stating if the sailor had not got enough he would give him the other end of the knife. The sailor fell, apparently mortally wounded, and was removed to St. Thomas's Hospital.

His sister, on seeing what her brother had done by her order, desperately seized a bottle of laudanum in the room and drank off part of the contents, and still lies in a precarious state.

In this portion of Market Street we understand every house, from basement to attic, is occupied by prostitutes and thieves.

We entered an adjoining public-house, where three of these young women followed us to the bar, anxious to know the object of our visiting the district. They called for a pint of stout, which they drank off heartily, and stood loitering beside us to hear our conversation, so that they might have something to gossip about to their companions. The girl who frolicked in the street with the old bonnet was one of them, and had now laid this aside. She was fair-haired, and good-looking, but was very foolish and immodest in her movements. One of her companions was taller and more robust, but her conduct showed she was debased in her character, and lost to all sense of propriety. The other girl was tall and dark-eyed, and more quiet and calculating in her manner as she stood, in a light cotton dress, silently leaning against the door-post.

One evening in September, about eight o'clock, we took another ramble over the criminal district of the Borough.

As we went along Kent Street the lamps were lit, and the shops in the adjoining streets were illuminated with their flaring gas lights. On passing St. George's Church we saw a crowd collected around a drunken middle-aged Irishwoman. It was one of those motley scenes one often meets in the streets of London. Young people and middle-aged, old women and children were clustered together, some well-dressed, others in mechanic's dress begrimed with dust and sweat, and others hanging in rags and tatters. They were collected around this woman, who stood on the pavement, while the mass were gathered in the street, many of them looking on anxiously with eyes and mouth open, others grinning with delight, and some with sinister countenance, while she gesticulated wildly, yet in good humour, in a strong Irish accent, amid the applause of the auditory.

We could not hear the subject of her oration. On our coming up to her and remaining for a short time, curious to know the nature of the comedy, the woman went away, followed by part of the crowd, when she appeared to take her station again in the midst of them. We had no time to lose, and passed on.

On our proceeding farther into Kent Street, a good-looking girl, evidently belonging to the lower orders, stood in a doorway, with beaming smile, and beckoned us to enter. She had accosted us in like manner in the light of open day on our previous visit to Kent Street, while another young woman of her own age and size, apparently her sister, stood by her side. As on the former occasion we did not trust ourselves to these syren sisters, but again passed on, notwithstanding urgent solicitations to enter.

Farther along the street we saw a small group of men and boys—thieves and utterers of base coin. A young woman of about twenty-five years of age stood among them, who was a common prostitute and expert thief, although we could scarcely have known this from her heavy, stupid-looking countenance, which was bloated and dissipated. One of the group was a burglar. He was under the middle size, pockpitted, and had a callous, daring look about him. We had time to study the lines of his face. They soon divined our purpose, and skulked off in different directions, as we found the generality of such persons to do in the course of our visits. The men were of different ages, varying from seventeen to thirty, dressed similar to costermongers.

We bent our way to St. George's New Town, a by-street off Kent Street. On turning the corner from Kent Street, leading into St. George's New Town, we saw a cluster of men and women, varying in age from seventeen to forty, also dressed like those just described. Most of them were convicted thieves.

We then came back to Mint Street, leading out of High Street in the Borough to Southwark Bridge Road, which, as we have said, is very low and disreputable.

Leaving Mint Street and its dark, disreputable neighbourhood, we directed our way to Norfolk Street, a very narrow street, leading into Union Street in the Borough. This locality is much infested with pickpockets and also with "dragsmen," i.e., those persons who steal goods or luggage from carts and coaches. At one corner of this street we saw no less than seven or eight persons clustered together, several of them convicted thieves. They were dressed similar to those in the low neighbourhoods already described.

We then went into Little Surrey Street, Borough Road, where we entered a beershop. Here we found four men, from twenty-five to thirty-five years of age—expert burglars. One of them appeared to be a mechanic. He told us he was an engraver. This was the same burglar, with his nose flattened, we had seen on the previous occasion referred to. He was an intelligent, determined man, and acted as the head of the gang. The other two were the companions we had seen with him in Gunn Street. All of them were rather under the middle size. They were now better dressed than formerly, and apparently on the eve of setting out to commit some felony. They appeared trimmed up in working order. A prostitute, connected with them, with her eye blackened, stood by the bar. She was also well-attired, and ready to accompany them. Burglars of this class often have a woman to go before them, to carry their housebreaking tools, to the house they intend to enter, as they might be arrested on the way with the tools in their own possession. The woman was tolerably good-looking, and on setting out, was possibly getting primed with gin. The engraver has been convicted several times for picking pockets as well as for burglary. The other two are convicted burglars. There was a man of about forty years of age seated beside them in the beershop, who we learned was in a decline. The burglars are often liberal in supporting the invalids connected with them, and the latter lend a subordinate hand occasionally in their nefarious work, such as in assisting to dispose of the stolen property. One of their old "pals" died lately, and the burglars in the neighbourhood raised a subscription between them to defray his funeral expenses.

We proceeded to Market Street, Borough Road, where we had on the former occasion observed the scene of merriment with the organist and the young girls. But the street had now a very different appearance. Instead of the locality ringing with the light-hearted merriment and buffoonery of the young girls and groups of children, the dark pall of night was stretched over it. At every door as we passed we saw a female standing on the outlook for persons to enter their dens of prostitution and crime. They solicited us in whispers to enter, or tapped us gently on the shoulder, or seized us by the skirts of the coat. Some of them were young and good-looking, while others were old and bloated. We looked into several of the houses as we went along, and saw numbers of young prostitutes in their best attire, seated by the tables, or lolling on the seats. This part of Market Street is one of the lowest rookeries of prostitutes and thieves in London. Many a young girl has been ruined by entering these low broth-els. She may have been a servant out of a place, or she may have left her home in the metropolis, and betaken herself here to a life of infamy.

These prostitutes assist to maintain the burglars, pickpockets and other thieves when they are not successful in their lawless calling. Some of them are well-dressed and remarkably good-looking. They occasionally come home with men in cabs from the different theatres, and rob them in their dwellings, and turn them unceremoniously into the street, but do not strip them of their clothing. When their cash is done, they wish their company no longer.

In other low districts in the vicinity of Kent Street, prostitutes have been convicted for stealing the clothes of the unfortunates who have entered their dismal abodes.

Leaving Market Street and the alleys and slums of that locality behind us, we went along Newington Causeway, a far brighter and more salubrious scene. This is a wide business street, and one of the main streets on the Surrey side of the river, where, especially in the evenings, a good deal of shopping is carried on.

The south side of Newington Causeway, from Horsemonger Lane gaol to the Elephant and Castle, is crowded with shops, the street being lit up nearly as clear as day. There are several splendid gin-palaces in this locality, generally crowded with motley groups of people of various ranks and pursuits; and milliners' shops, with their windows gaily furnished with ladies' bonnets of every hue and style, and ribbons of every tint; and drapers' shops with cotton gown pieces, muslins, collars, and gloves of every form and colour. There are many boot- and shoe-shops, with assortments of fancy shoes as well as plain.

Upholsterers' shops,, with carpets and rugs of every pattern, and chemists, with their gay-coloured jars flaming like globes of red, blue, green and yellow fire. The street is filled with incessant tides of mechanics, tradesmen's wives, milliners, dressmakers, and others, going shopping or returning from their daily toil; and many respectable people take their evening's walk along this cheerful and bustling thoroughfare, which is a favourite place for promenading.

In walking along we noticed many young men and women in respectable attire. Here we saw some young, genteel milliners and dressmakers, and girls from other places of business, returning to their homes or lodgings, at the close of the day, and taking an occasional glance at the shop windows as they passed along. By their side we saw apparently some married women, out shopping with a new bonnet, or other article of dress, carefully wrapped up. In another part of the street we saw a shopman making love to a pretty girl, with clustering ringlets, who looked serenely upon him as he stood bareheaded outside the door of a drapery establishment.

Among the busy throng of people passing to and fro we observed two young women, pickpockets, dressed in brown cloaks, like milliners, and in fancy bonnets, passing quietly along. A person who did not know them personally could not have detected their criminal character. On following them a short way, they passed over to the other side of the street. From their features and from the similarity of their dress we could have guessed them to be sisters. They were apparently about twenty-five years of age.

As is generally the case with such persons, on being noticed they separated on the other side of the street to prevent our following their movements. One went off in one direction and the other in another; but meantime they had probably arranged to meet each other when out of the officer's sight.

The Borough is chiefly the locality of labouring people and small shopkeepers—the masses of the people—and has low neighbourhoods in many of the by-streets, infested by the dangerous classes. It contains specimens of almost all kinds of thieves, from the lowest to the most expert, though for the most part few of the swells reside here. Many of them prefer to live about the Kingsland Road.

They occasionally leave their own dwellings in other parts of the city, and come here, and live retired to be away from the surveillance of the police of their own district.

There are some expert "cracksmen" (burglars) here, dressed in fashionable style, who indulge in potations of brandy and champagne, and the best of liquors. In their appearance there is little or no trace of their criminal character. They have the look of sharp business men. They commit burglaries at country mansions, and sometimes at shops and warehouses, often extensive, and generally contrive to get safely away with their booty.

These crack burglars generally live in streets adjoining the New Kent Road and Newington Causeway, and groups of them are to be seen occasionally at the taverns beside the Elephant and Castle, where they regale themselves luxuriously on the choicest wines, and are lavish of their gold. From their superior manner and dress few could detect their real character. One might pass them daily in the street and not be able to recognise them.

HOUSEBREAKERS AND BURGLARS

THE expert burglar is generally very ingenious in his devices, and combines manual dexterity with courage. In his own sphere the burglar in manual adroitness equals the accomplished pick-pocket, while in personal daring he rivals our modern ruffians of the highway who perpetrate garotte robberies or plunder their victims with open violence.

Many of our London burglars have been trained from their boyhood. Some are the children of convicted thieves; some have for a time lived as sneaks, committing petty felonies when residing in low lodging-houses; others are the children of honest parents, mechanics and tradesmen, led into bad company and driven into criminal courses.

In treating of sneaks we alluded to the area-sneak, and lobby-sneak, watching a favourable opportunity and darting into the kitchen and pantry, and sometimes entering the apartments on the first floor and stealing the plate. We alluded to the lead-stealer finding his way to the house-top, and to the attic-thief adroitly slipping downstairs to the apartments below and carrying away valuables, jewellery, plate, and money. Here we see the points of transition, from the petty felon to the daring midnight robber plundering with violence.

We shall in the outset offer a few general remarks on the manner in which housebreaking and burglaries are effected in London, and then proceed to a more detailed account of the various modes pursued in the different districts.

Breaking into houses, shops and warehouses is accomplished in various ways, such as picking the locks with skeleton keys; inserting a thin instrument between the sashes and undoing the catch of the windows, which enables the thieves to lift up the under sash; getting over the walls at the back, and breaking open a door or window which is out of sight of the street, or other public place; lifting the cellar-flap or area-grating; getting into an empty house next door, or a few doors off, and passing from the roof to that of the house they intend to rob; entering by an attic-window, or trap-door, and if there are neither window nor door on the roof, taking off some of the tiles and entering the house. Sometimes the thieves will make an entry through a brick wall in an adjoining building, or climb the waterspout to get in at the window. These are the general modes of breaking into houses.

Sometimes when doors are fastened with a padlock outside and no other lock on the door, thieves will get a padlock as near like it as possible. They will then break off the proper lock, one of them will enter the house, and an accomplice will put on a lock as like it as possible to deceive the police, while one or more inside will meantime pack up the goods. Sometimes a well-dressed thief waylays a servant girl going out on errands in the evening, professes to fall in love with her, and gets into her confidence, till she perhaps admits him into the house when her master and mistress are out. Having confidence in him she shows him over the house, and informs him where the valuables are kept. If the house is well secured, so that there will be difficulty of breaking in by night, he manages to get an accomplice inside to secrete himself till the family has gone to bed, when he admits one or more of his companions into the house. They pack up all they can lay hold of, such as valuables and jewels. On such occasions there is generally one on the outlook outside, who follows the policeman unobserved, and gives the signal to the parties inside when it is safe to come out.

In warehouses one of the thieves frequently slips in at closing-time, when only a few servants are left behind, and are busy shutting up. He secretes himself behind goods in the warehouse, and when all have retired for the night, and the door locked, he opens it and lets in his companions to pack up the booty. Should it consist of heavy goods, they generally have a cart to take it away. They are sometimes afraid to engage a cabman unless they can get him to connive at the theft, and, besides, the number of the cab can be taken. They get the goods away in the following manner. If consisting of bulky articles, such as cloth, silks, etc., they fill large bags, similar to sacks, and get as much as they think the cart can conveniently hold, placed near the door. When the policeman has passed by on his round, the watch stationed outside gives the signal; the door is opened, the cart drives up, and four or five sacks are handed into it by two thieves in about a minute, when the vehicle retires. It is loaded and goes off sooner than a gentleman would take his carpet-bag and portmanteau into a cab when going to a railway station. The cart proceeds with the driver in one way, while the thieves walk off in a different direction. They close the outer door after them when they enter a shop or warehouse, most of which have spring locks. When the policeman comes round on his beat he finds the door shut, and there is nothing to excite his suspicion. The cart is never seen loitering at the door above a couple of minutes, and does not make its appearance on the spot till the robbery is about to be committed, when the signal is given.

Lighter goods, such as jewellery, or goods of less bulk, are generally taken away in carpet-bags in time to catch an early train, often about five or six o'clock, and the robbers being respectably-dressed, and in a neighbourhood where they are not known, pass on in most cases unmolested. Sometimes they pack up the goods in hampers, as if going off to some railway station. Where there is no one sleeping on the premises, and when they have come to learn where the party lives who keeps the keys, they watch him home at night after locking up, and set a watch on his house, that their confederates may not be disturbed when rifling the premises. If they are to remove the goods in the morning they do it about an hour before the warehouse is usually opened, so that neighbours are taken off their guard, supposing the premises are opened a little earlier than usual in consequence of being busy. Sometimes they stand and see the goods taken out, and pay no particular attention to it. In the event of the person who keeps the keys coming up sooner than usual, the man keeping watch hastens forward and gives the signal to his companions, if they have not left the warehouse.

It often happens when they have got an entry into a house, they have to break their way into the apartments in the interior to reach the desired booty, such as wrenching open an inner door with a small crowbar they term a jemmy, cutting a panel out of a door, or a partition, with a cutter similar to a centre-bit, which works with two or three knives; this is done very adroitly in a short space of time, and with very little noise. At other times, when on the floor above, they cut through one or more boards in the flooring, and frequently cut panes of glass in the windows with a knife or awl.

They get information as to the property in warehouses from porters and others unwittingly by leading them into conversation regarding the goods on the premises, the silks they have got, etc., and find out the part of the premises where they are to be found. Sometimes they go in to inspect them on the pretence of looking at some articles of merchandise.

It occasionally happens servants are in league with thieves, and give them information as to the hour when to come, and the easiest way to break in. Sometimes servants basely admit the thieves into the premises to steal, and give them impressions of the keys, which enables them to make other keys to enter the house. Thieves sometimes take a blank key without wards, cover it with wax, work it in the keyhole against the wards of the lock and by that means the impression is left in the wax. They then take it home and make a similar key. When looking into the lock they frequently strike a match on the doorway, and pretend to be lighting a pipe or cigar, which prevents passers by suspecting their object.

These are the general modes of housebreaking and burglary over the metropolis, but in order that we may have a more vivid and thorough conception of the subject, we shall give a more graphic detail of these felonies. We shall first advert to breaking into shops and warehouses, and then proceed to describe burglaries in various parts of the metropolis.

It frequently occurs that a thief enters a warehouse, or large shop, and secretes himself behind some goods, or in the cellar, or up the chimney. This could be done at any hour of the day, but is frequently managed when the servants or shopmen are out dining at mid-day, or towards evening, when the places of business are about to be closed. The thief may be respectably dressed, or not, according to the nature of the place of business. A person may call with some fictitious message, and keep one or more of the servants or shopmen in conversation while a confederate could meantime slip into the shop or warehouse, and if detected would seldom be suspected of being connected with this party. They sometimes hover for days in the neighbourhood of shops and warehouses they intend to plunder, and watch the most favourable opportunity to effect this object.

Towards evening when the servants are all gone, and the place of business closed, the rest of his companions come to the spot consisting of one or more men, a woman being occasionally employed. While they are aware that one of their gang is secreted on the premises, as a precaution they sometimes knock at the door or ring the bell to ascertain if the servants or shopmen are gone. Should they be lingering in the premises, arranging the goods, engaged with their business-books, accounts, or otherwise, they ask for Mr. So-and-so, or have some other fictitious message.

On the departure of the people belonging to the shop, the thief inside generally opens the door to his companions on the given signal, when they proceed to rifle the premises of Manchester goods, cottons, silks, shawls, satins, or otherwise, and to store them into large bags they bring with them, which they place beside the door, when filled, to be conveniently carried away. They wrench open the desks, money-drawers, and other lockfasts with a jemmy, chisel, or screw-driver, as well as any doors which may be locked, occasionally using the cutter and saw, or other tools, and pierce through brick and other partition walls with an auger or other instrument. In many cases the doors of the apartments in warehouses are left open so that the thief has free access to the property.

Meantime a man or woman is watching outside while the thieves are busy plundering within, keeping a special look-out for the policeman proceeding on his beat. They have many ingenious expedients to decoy him away, by conversation or otherwise. The policeman is generally from fifteen to twenty minutes in going round his beat, so that they have ample time to carry off the booty.

While the thieves are busy collecting their spoil, the door is shut with a spring lock, or fastened with a padlock by means of a key they may have made for the purpose, so that the policeman has no suspicion of what is passing within. The former frequently remain for several hours on the premises, while a person outside is keeping watch, waiting to hear their signal when they have got the booty packed and ready. Should the coast be clear outside, notice is conveyed to the cart or cab, loitering somewhere in the vicinity, or which drives up at a certain hour, when the door opens. The plunder is quickly handed into the vehicle, which drives smartly away. The door is then shut and the robbers walk off, possibly in a different direction to that in which the conveyance is gone.

Burglaries from jewellers' shops are frequently effected by means of skeleton keys, or otherwise, by one or more men. A woman often carries the tools to the shop, and keeps watch. So soon as a favourable opportunity occurs they unlock the door and enter the premises, while a man or woman watches outside, the woman perhaps walking along the street as though she were a common prostitute, or familiarly accosting the policeman or other persons she meets, and decoying them away from the shop.

In some cases, when she has not succeeded in getting the policeman away, she pretends to fall down in a fit, when he has possibly to take her to the nearest surgeon. Sometimes the woman feigns to be drunk, and is taken to the police station, which takes him off his beat. In the meanwhile the parties inside, with jemmy, chisel, saw, or other tools, and with silent lights and taper or dark lantern, break open the glass cases and boxes, and steal gold and silver watches, gold chains, brooches, pins, and other jewellery, which they deposit in a small carpet-bag, as well as rifle money from the desk.

Jewellers' shops are sometimes entered by the thief getting into an unoccupied house next door, or two or three houses off, and proceeding along the roofs to the attic or roof of the house to be robbed, and going in by the attic window, or removing a few of the slates. The thieves then go downstairs and cut their way through the door or partition, and effect an entry into the shop.

Most of the robberies in jewellers' shops have of late years been committed by means of false keys, or by cutting out a hole in the door or shutter with a cutter, which is done in a short space of time, and when the instrument is moistened it makes very little noise. This hole is covered with a piece of paper painted of the same colour as the door, and is pasted on, which prevents the police having any suspicion.

Sometimes jewellers' shops are entered by persons lodging in the floor above, or having access to it, and then cutting through the flooring and descending into the jeweller's shop by means of a rope-ladder they attach to the floor. At other times they are entered by cutting through the solid brick wall at the back of the shop.

Several years ago a very remarkable burglary took place at Mr. Acutt's large linen-drapery establishment in the Westminster Road. About four o'clock in the morning the policeman on duty heard a man give the signal at a shop door. The constable, believing thieves to be on the premises, sprung his rattle, roused up the inmates, and got the assistance of several other constables. When they entered the shop they found upwards of £30 worth of silks and satins, and other valuables packed up in bundles ready to be carried off. They found two thieves who had gained an entrance by getting over some closets, scaling a wall by means of the rain-spout, and walking along a high wall about nine inches thick. They then removed the skylight at the back, and let themselves down into the shop by a rope-ladder. By this means they got into the shop of Mr. Acutt.

On being scared by the police they jumped from one house to another, eight feet apart, over a height of about fifty feet, and there concealed themselves behind a stack of chimneys. Several policemen mounted to the roofs, but could not find them; and no one would venture to leap to the adjoining houses, whither the thieves had gone. An inspector of police ordered two men in plain clothes to be on the watch, believing they must be concealed somewhere on the housetops.

About eight o'clock in the morning a man of the name of Fitzgerald was out in a back court of an adjoining house washing himself, when the thieves came down by a spout, twenty feet long, communicating with the water cistern. On getting down one of them jumped on the back of Fitzgerald. He shouted out "murder and police," when two constables came up and took both of the thieves into custody.

On the trial it was said the prisoners' women had given several pounds to bribe this man, and he pretended he could not identify them, and they were acquitted. They have since been transported for other burglaries.

One of them was a man of thirty years of age, about five feet nine inches high, slim made, with a most daring countenance. The other was of middle stature, about twenty-six years of age, with pleasing appearance.

Another burglary took place in a silk warehouse in Cheapside in 1842. The burglars were admitted into an adjoining carpet warehouse by one of the warehousemen on a Saturday night, and broke through a brick-wall eight or nine inches thick, and made an entry into the silk warehouse. They did not steal any carpets, as they were too bulky. Goods were seen to be taken away by a cab on the Sunday afternoon. The padlock was meantime secure on the outdoor, so that the police had no suspicion.

The robbery was discovered on the Monday morning, when it was found from £1500 to £2000 had been carried off, and that a £100 bank note had also been taken from the desk of the carpet warehouse.

Soon after the foreman of the latter business establishment absconded, and has not since been heard of, and there is strong suspicion he had connived with the burglars.

We shall now treat of the burglaries in the metropolis, commencing with the lower, and proceeding to notice the higher burglars, termed the "cracksmen."

Burglaries in the working districts of the metropolis are effected in various ways—by one man mounting the shoulders of another and getting into a first-floor window, similar to acrobats, by climbing over walls leading to the rear of premises, cutting or breaking a pane of glass, and then unfastening the catch of the window with a sharp instrument, or by cutting a panel of a door with a sharp tool, such as an American "auger." Frequently they force the lock of the door with a jemmy. The lower class of burglars who have not proper tools sometimes use a screw-driver instead of a jemmy. In the forcing of the locks of drawers or boxes, in search of property, they use a small chisel with a fine edge, and occasionally an old knife.

There are frequently three persons employed in these burglaries—two to enter a house, and one to keep watch outside, to see that there is no person passing likely to detect. This man is generally termed a "crow." Sometimes a woman, called a "canary", carries the tools, and watches outside.

These low burglars carry off a booty of such small value that they are necessitated frequently to commit depredations. They steal male and female wearing apparel, and small articles of plate or jewellery, such as teaspoons or a watch.

They are from seventeen years of age and upwards, and reside in the Borough, Whitechapel, St. Giles, Shoreditch, and other low localities.

There is another kind of burglary committed by persons concealing themselves on the premises, which is often done in public-houses. The parties enter before the house is closed, by concealing themselves in the coal-cellar, skittle-ground, or other place where they are unobserved by those in charge of the house. These burglaries are done by low people, with whose previous mode of living the police are generally not acquainted. Very frequently they steal cigars, money in the till or on the shelves of the bar, left to give change to customers in the morning. There is another mode of entering public-houses, by the cellar flaps from the pavement in front of the house, or by going through the fanlight, and stealing property as before described, and returning the same way, sometimes letting themselves out by the front door, which has often a spring lock.

These burglaries are generally done at midnight, or between 1 and 5 o'clock.

There is a higher class of burglaries committed at fashionable residences over the metropolis, and at the mansions of the gentry and nobility, many of them in the West End districts.

The houses to be robbed are carefully watched for several weeks, sometimes for months, before the burglary is attempted. The thieves take great precautions in such cases. They glean information secretly as to the inmates of the house; where they sleep, and where valuable property is kept. Sometimes this is done by watching the lights over the house for successive nights. These burglaries are often "put up" by the persons who execute them. They frequently get some of their more engaging companions to court one of the servant girls, give her small presents, and gain her favour, with the ultimate object of gaining access to the house and plundering it. At other times, though more rarely, they endeavour to become acquainted with the male servants of the house—the butler, valet, coachman, or groom. Sometimes they try to learn from the servants through other parties becoming acquainted with them, if they cannot succeed themselves. At other times they gather information from tradesmen who are called to the house on jobbing work, such as painters, plumbers, glaziers, bell-hangers, tinsmiths, and others, some of whom live near the burglars in low neighbourhoods, or are frequently to be seen in the evenings in their company. We can point our finger at three of these base wretches. One of them lives in Whitefriars, Fleet Street, another in Tottenham Court Road, and a third in Newell Street, Wardour Street, Oxford Street. These three persons get up many of the burglaries in the West End and other parts of the metropolis, where they have work to do, when they find a suitable place. Some of them have put up burglaries for thirteen or fourteen years, and none of them have been detected, though suspected by the police. They never have a hand in the burglaries themselves, but secure a part of the booty. These "putters up" are from thirty to thirty-five years of age, and one of them has been convicted of a felony.

If the burglars cannot enter by the back of the premises, they go to the first-floor window in front, where there are no shutters. It matters not whether it be public or not; they will enter in a couple of minutes the premises by cutting the glass and undoing the catch.

The dwelling-houses in the West End have often been entered by the first-floor window; and servants have many times been wrongfully charged with these burglaries, and lost their places in consequence.

Burglars generally leave their haunts to plunder about twelve o'clock at midnight, often driving up in a cab to a short distance from the spot where the burglary is to be attempted; but they frequently do not enter the house till one or two in the morning. In general, they take some liquor, such as gin and brandy, to keep up their spirits, as they call it. The one who is to watch outside generally takes up his position first, and the others follow. This is arranged so that the persons who enter—generally two, sometimes three—should not be seen by the police or others near the house.

When the latter come up, and find their companion at his post, and see the coast clear, they instantly proceed to enter the house, in front, or behind, by the door or windows. Expert burglars go separate, to avoid suspicion.

On entering the house, they go about the work very cautiously and quietly, taking off their shoes, some walking in their stockings, and others with India-rubber overalls. If disturbed they very seldom leave their shoes or boots behind them.

Their chief object is to get plate, jewellery, cash, and other valuables. The drawing-room is usually on the first-floor in front; sometimes the whole of the first-floor is a drawing-room. They often find valuables in the drawing-room. They search parlour, kitchen, and pantry, and even open the servant's work-box for her small savings.

When they cannot get enough jewellery and plate they carry off wearing apparel. They often take money in the drawing-room from writing-desks and ladies' work-boxes. Experienced burglars do not spare time and trouble to look well for their plunder.

This is the general course adopted on entering a dwelling-house. In entering a shop, if they can find sufficient money to satisfy them, they do not carry off bulky property, but if there is no money in the desk or tills they rifle the goods, if they are of value.

In West End robberies there are often two good cracksmen, one to keep watch outside, while another is busy at his work of plunder within. The person outside has to be on the alert, as he has generally to keep watch over an experienced officer, and to let his companions know when it is safe for them to work or to come out.

When a catch is in the centre of the window it is opened with a knife. If there should be one on each side they will cut a pane of glass in less than fifteen seconds, and undo them. The burglars seldom think of carrying a diamond with them, but generally cut the glass with a knife, as the star-glazers do.

The shutters behind the window frame are often cut with what the burglars term a cutter. It cuts with two knives, with a centre-bit stock, and makes a hole sufficiently large to admit the burglar's arm.

When the shutters are opened there are often iron bars to guard the window. The burglars tie a piece of strong cord or rope about two of the bars, and insert a piece of wood about a foot in length between this rope, and twist the wood. The bar is thereby bent sufficient to allow them to enter, or it gives way in the socket. These bars are sometimes forced asunder by a small instrument called a jack, by which a worm worked by a small handle displaces them. The rope and stick are used when they have not a jack. The latter can be conveniently carried in the trousers pocket.

Woodwork, such as shutters, doors, and partitions, is often cut in late years with the cutter, instead of the jemmy, as the former is a more effective tool, and makes an opening more expeditiously. With this instrument a door or shutter can be pierced sufficiently large to admit the arm in a few minutes.

A brick wall requires more time. If there are no persons within hearing, an opening can be made sufficiently large for a man to pass through, in an hour. If there are people near the apartment, it requires to be more softly done, and frequently occupies two or three hours, even when done by an expert burglar. They generally pierce one brick with an auger, and displace it; after the first brick is out, they work with a jemmy, and take the mortar out, then pierce a brick on the other side of the wall.

Burglars cannot pick Chubb's patent locks. The best way to secure premises where no person sleeps is to have a good patent lock on the outer door, with an iron bar outside fastened by a patent Chubb lock. This acts with double safety. If they break it off on the outside, the policeman easily detects it when he comes round on his beat, which he is sure to do before they have got the other lock opened, and this prevents them getting in that way. If they break in from the roof, or from the back by cutting round the lock of an inside door, they do not get the outside door opened, and cannot get away any bulky goods. By this means the warehouse is more safe than if it was fastened any other way.

Common locks on doors are so easily picked by thieves that no warehouse ought to be left fastened in this way, unless there is a watchman over it.

Some cracksmen have what is called a petter-cutter, that is, a cutter for iron safes; an instrument made similar to a centre-bit, in which drills are fixed. They fasten this into the keyhole by a screw with a strong pressure outside. The turning part is so fixed that the drills cut a piece out over the keyhole sufficiently large to get to the wards of the lock. They then pull the bolt of the lock back and open the door.

Chubb's locks on iron safes are now made drill proof, so that they cannot be pierced.

Any person sleeping in a room, with valuable property in his possession, ought to have a chain on the door, like a street-door chain, as the common locks are so easily picked, and the masked thief, with dark lantern, can creep into the room without being heard. The rattling of the chain is sure to awaken the person sleeping.

Expert burglars are generally equipped with good tools. They have a jemmy, a cutter, a dozen of betties, better known as picklocks, a jack to remove iron bars, a dark lantern or a taper and some silent lights, and a life-preserver, and sometimes have a cord or rope with them, which can be easily converted into a rope ladder. A knife is often used in place of a chisel for opening locks, drawers, or desks. They often carry masks on their face, so that they might not be identified. The dark lantern is very small, with oil and cotton wick, and sometimes only shows a light about the size of a shilling, so that the reflection is not seen on the street without. Burglars often use the jemmy in place of picklocks. When they go out with their tools, they usually carry them wrapped up with list, so that they can throw them away without making a noise, should a policeman stop them, or attempt to arrest them. These are easily carried in the coat pocket, as they are not bulky. There are parties—sometimes old convicts—who lend tools out on hire.

When discovered by the inmates they are generally disposed to make their escape rather than to fight, and try to avoid violence unless hotly pursued. If driven to extremity, they are ready to use the life-preserver, jemmy, or other weapon.

Sometimes they carry a life-preserver of a peculiar style, consisting of a small ball attached to a piece of gut, that fastens round the wrist. With this instrument, easily carried in the palm of the hand, they can strike the persons who oppose them senselesss, and severely injure them.

In going up and down stairs, they often creep up not in the centre but the side of the stair, to avoid being heard, as it is apt to creak beneath the footstep, and they generally take off their shoes to move more stealthily along.

They often use the cutter to make an opening in the middle of the panel sufficiently large to admit the arm, to undo locks or bolts they cannot reach outside.

Sometimes when the key is inside, and the door locked, they open it with a small pair of plyers; others use a long piece of wire, with a hoop put through the keyhole to lay hold of the bowl of the key. When the hook is fastened in it, they can as easily undo the lock as if they turned the key from the inside. Some burglars prefer the wire, others use the plyers. They generally prefer the cutter to the centre-bit in removing the woodwork. It resembles the centre-bit, but takes a much larger piece out, and does so more speedily. The cutter costs from 15s. to £1. In the absence of a cutter, they sometimes work with a couple of gimlets and a knife, but this requires more time and makes more noise, though not sufficient to disturb the inmates of the house, if used expertly.

At the back of the house they enter through the kitchen window on the basement, or by the parlour window above it on the first floor, or by the window of the staircase alongside of the latter.

If experienced burglars, they listen at the doors of the apartments, and know by the breathing in general if the inmates are sound asleep. They sometimes begin their operations by going up to the highest floor, and work their way down, carrying off the plunder. After having finished what they call their work, they await the signal from the "watch" set outside. These signals are sometimes given by one or more coughs; some give a whistle, or sing a certain song, or tap on the door or shutter, or make a particular cry, understood between the parties.

Should the plunder be bulky, they will have a cart or a cab, or a costermonger's barrow, ready on a given signal to carry it away. They in general wait for the time when the police are changed, if the inmates are not getting up, sometimes coming out at the front door, but oftener at the back.

A remarkable case of burglary was committed in a dwelling-house in a fashionable square in the West End about twelve months ago, and was effected in this manner. One day a well-dressed young man passed by an area and took special notice of the cook, who happened to be looking out of the window. Another day the same young man in passing by accosted this servant, and made an appointment to meet her on a certain occasion to go out to walk. This correspondence lasted for a short time, when the young man was invited to tea at the house, to spend a social evening. He was accompanied by a "pal" of his, a young Frenchman, who courted the housemaid, while the other made love to the cook. During their visit to the house, the family being then absent, one of the young men pretended to be very unwell, and thought a walk in the garden at the back of the house would be beneficial to him, and was accompanied there by one of the servant girls.

Meanwhile the housemaid and her friend had adjourned to one of the upper rooms. It was proposed by the Frenchman that his lady-love should partake of some gin or brandy as refreshment, to which she consented. He went out for the purpose of purchasing it, while she went down stairs to the kitchen. On his going out he left the front-door open, by which one of his confederates, a third party, entered the house, and passed upstairs, broke open several lockfasts, and stole the whole of the plate.

The Frenchman, meanwhile, returned with the liquor, and went down stairs to the kitchen, where he made merry with his fair lady and her companions. When they were seated regaling themselves over this liquor the door-bell rang. One of the girls went to the door and found no person there. This was a signal agreed on between the thieves. One of the young men still pretending to feel unwell proposed to go home with his companion, promising to call on a future occasion, when they would be able to spend a more comfortable evening than they had done on account of his illness.

One of the servants on going upstairs after their departure, found the plate stolen. Information was given to the police, when these agreeable young men and their unknown friend were found to belong to a gang of most expert thieves. They were tried at

Westminster Sessions for this offence, and sentenced to three years' penal servitude.

About eighteen months ago, two desperate burglars attempted to enter a fashionable dwelling-house at Westbourne Park, Paddington, belonging to a merchant in the City. One of them was a tall, raw-boned, muscular man, of about twenty-five years of age, dressed in a blue frock coat, dark cord trousers, black vest and beaver hat. The other was a man of thirty years of age, short and stout, nearly similarly attired. The first had the appearance of a blacksmith, with a determined countenance; the other had a more pleasing aspect, yet resolute. They were armed with a long chisel and heavy crowbar.

They got over several walls, and came up along the back of this dwelling-house in the centre of these villas, situated on the edge of the Great Western Railway. On reaching the garden they went direct to the window of the dining-room on the ground floor.

As there had been several burglaries committed in the neighbourhood of those villas about this time, an experienced and able detective officer was sent out to watch.

While the detective, a tall, powerful, resolute man, was sitting alone in the dusk under a tree in an adjoining garden, and another criminal officer was stationed a short distance off, at about two o'clock in the morning the former officer heard the shutters crash in the windows of an adjoining house nearly in front of where he stood. The burglars had approached so softly he did not hear their footsteps, and was not aware of their presence till then. On hearing this noise he drew close to the house, and was seen by one of the thieves—the shortest one called Jack. The detective officer immediately sprung his rattle, rushed on this man and seized him. His companion on this ran from the end of the house and struck the officer across the back with a heavy crowbar. By a sudden movement of his body the latter partially avoided the force of the blow. Had it struck him on the head it would have killed him on the spot; and being a strong muscular man he knocked the shorter man down with a heavy walking-stick he had in his hand, and at the same time rushed on his taller companion, seized him by the throat, and endeavoured to wrench the iron bar from his grasp.

The other burglar had meantime made his escape into an adjoining garden, and was captured, after a desperate struggle, by the other criminal officer, who had come up.

During the scuffle between the officers and burglars the proprietor of the house, in a panic, threw up his bedroom window looking into the garden at the back of the house, and, without giving any call, fired off a pistol. He did this to alarm the neighbourhood, not being aware that the officers were so near him, and supposing that the burglars were in his house.

The other burglar was secured after a determined struggle, and both were with difficulty conveyed to the Marylebone police station by five strong officers. They were next day taken before the magistrates, and charged with attempting to enter this house, and with assaulting the officers in the execution of their duty. They were sentenced to three months each in Clerkenwell prison, with hard labour for the former offence, and with a similar punishment for the latter.

About two years ago a burglary was committed in Charles Street, Gloucester Terrace, Paddington, opposite the Cleveland Arms, by two men and a woman. One of the men was about forty-six years of age, an old desperate burglar, who had been twice transported, and was then on ticket-of-leave. Shortly before, he had been apprehended in St. George's burying-ground, at the rear of some houses in the Bayswater Road, with a screw-driver, jemmy, and dark lantern, when he was sentenced to three months' imprisonment as a rogue and vagabond.

He was a stout man, with very bushy whiskers, of a coarse appearance. The other was a young man about nineteen, dressed as a mechanic, of a cheerful countenance, with brown hair and moustache. The woman was about twenty-three years of age, short and stout, with an engaging appearance.

During the night, they had forced open an iron grating in front of a house in Charles Street, Paddington, and had let themselves down into the area. They bored three holes with a centre-bit in the door of the house, then cut the panel, and put their arm through, and undoing the fastening of the door, got into the kitchen. From this they went up to a door leading to the staircase, which was locked. They cut several holes with the centre-bit, and made an opening in this door in like manner. They then went upstairs to the first-floor, and stole a quantity of wearing apparel, and some jewellery, such as rings, studs, etc., and also a watch.

The inmates were sleeping at the top of the house, and had not been disturbed by these operations. The property rifled amounted to about £15.

One of the burglars left his hat behind him and a pair of old boots. The detective officer sent after them knew the hat to belong to this old-returned convict; went to Lisson Grove and arrested both the men, who happened to be together, and found part of the wearing apparel upon them. The remaining part of the property was traced as having been pledged by the woman, who was also apprehended. They were committed for trial for the burglary, and tried at the Old Bailey. The old man being an inveterate offender was sentenced to fifteen years' penal servitude; the others, who had been previously convicted, to four years'; and the girl to twelve months' imprisonment.

In the month of October, 1850, a burglary was committed by three men in the Regent's Park, which attracted considerable attention. One of them, named William Dyson, called the Galloway Doctor, was five feet six inches high, pockpitted, with pale face and red whiskers, and about thirty-two years of age; James Mahon, alias Holmsdale, five feet ten inches high, was robust in form, and aged thirty-four years; John Mitchell was five feet six inches high, stout made, with a pug nose, and aged forty years. They entered the house of Mr. Alford, an American merchant, in Regent's Park, at two o'clock in the morning. They climbed over a back wall into the garden, and got in through a back parlour window by pushing back the catch with a knife. They then forced the shutters open with a jemmy, got into the back-parlour where the butler was lying asleep, and unlocked the door to go through the house, as it was known that Mr. Alford was very wealthy. When they got on the staircase one of their feet slipped, which awoke the butler, who jumped up, and seized Dyson and Mahon, and wrestled with them, at the same time alarming the other inmates of the house. He was knocked down by a blow from a life-preserver, on which the burglars made their escape by jumping out of the back-parlour window again. The butler, on getting up, seized his fowling-piece, which lay loaded beside him, and told them as they were running away to stop, or he would fire upon them. He fired, and shot Mitchell in the back near the shoulder with goose shot, as he was getting over a back wall to make his escape.

The police, on hearing the report of the gun, came up and secured Holmsdale and Dyson in the garden, when they were taken to Marylebone police office.

Soon after an anonymous letter was sent to the police station of the M division stating there was a man in Surrey Street, Blackfriars Road, lying in bed in a certain house, who had been shot in the back when attempting a burglary in Regent's Park. He had on a woman's nightcap and nightgown, so that if any-one went into the room they would fancy him to be a female. Inspector Berry of the M division went to the above house, and found Mitchell in bed in female disguise. He was taken into custody, and made to dress in his own clothes. On examining them there were holes in his fustian frock-coat where the shot had passed through. He was taken to Marylebone police court and put alongside the other two prisoners, and identified as having been seen in the neighbourhood of the Regent's Park on the morning before the burglary was committed. He had been seen by the police to leave a notorious public-house frequented by burglars, at the Old Mint in the Borough. They were committed at the Central Criminal Court, tried on 25th November, 1850, convicted, and sentenced to be transported for life. Holmsdale having been previously transported for ten years, and Mitchell and Dyson also having been formerly convicted.

We took the particulars of the following burglary from the lips of a man who was a few years ago one of the most experienced and expert burglars in the metropolis, and give it as an instance of the ingenuity and daring of this class of London brigands:—

In the year 1850 a burglary was attempted to be committed at a furrier's at the corner of Regent Street near Oxford Street by three cracksmen. One of them, Henry Edgar, was about five feet seven inches high, of fair complexion, with large features brown hair, and gentlemanly appearance, dressed in elegant style, with jewellery, rings, and chain, and frilled shirt. A second party, Edward Edgar Blackwell, was the son of a respectable cutler in Soho, about five feet two inches high, of fair complexion, teeth out in front, with sullen look, also fashionably dressed, though in-ferior to the other. The third person was slim made, about five feet six inches high, dark complexion, with dark whiskers and genteel appearance, a gentle, but keen dark eye, and elegantly dressed.

They went to a public-house between ten and eleven o'clock, when the two former went back into a yard with the pretence of going to the water-closet. The publican did not miss them. The house was closed at twelve o'clock, and they were not discov-ered. The third party went out to give them their signal, but they, being impatient and accustomed to the work, thought they would try it themselves. They went up by a fire-escape, and got on to the parapet of the furrier's house, at the corner of Regent Street. Here they cut two panes of glass in a garret window, with a knife, at the same time removing the division between them. The servant going to bed in the dark, discovered the two men. Giving no alarm, she went down stairs to her master. The master came up, with two loaded pistols in his hands, presented them at the garret-window, telling them if they attempted to escape he would shoot them. Edward Edgar Blackwell was so frightened that he lost his presence of mind, and fell from the parapet into the yard, a height of three storeys, and was killed on the spot. Henry Edgar, being more courageous, made a desperate leap to the top of a house in Regent Street, and got through a trap-door, and made his way into a second floor front in Argyle Street, where people were sleeping, and alarmed them. To prevent their taking him, he leaped from a second floor window. Some people, passing-by, saw him jump from the window, and gave information to the police. He was, thereupon, arrested, and conveyed in a cab, with the dead body of his "pal," to Vine Street police station.

It was afterwards ascertained that his ankle was dislocated, and he was removed to Middlesex Hospital, where he was watched eight hours by successive policemen. His friends were allowed to see him, and by ingenious means one of them contrived to effect his escape. They conveyed him from the hospital in a cab to Green Street, Friars Street, Blackfriars Road; then removed him in a cab to the Commercial Road near Whitechapel. Soon after, his companions took a house for him in Corbett's Place, Spitalfields, when he was given into the hands of the police by a brother of one of his "pals," who went to Vine Street station, and lodged information. He was arrested before he could lay his hand on his pistols, committed for trial, and sentenced to penal servitude.

We give the following as an illustration of the ingenuity and perseverance of the cracksmen of the metropolis:—

A burglary was committed some years since, at a warehouse in the City, where the premises were securely fastened in front, and the servants were let out by a strong door at the back, secured by three strong locks. There was no one sleeping on the premises. The burglars had first to make keys to get through the outer door into the premises, and had then to get a key to a patent lock for an iron door into a private counting-house. They made another key for a very strong safe which, when opened, had a recess at the bottom enclosed with folding doors also secured by a patent lock. Before they got to the booty they had to make six keys of patent locks.

Not satisfied with this, they made a key for the patent lock of another iron door, leading to another portion of the premises where there was a second iron safe.

They were occupied four months getting the whole of these keys to fit, and had to watch favourable opportunities when the police were absent from that portion of their beat.

The thieves, during the night, carried off two iron boxes containing railway-shares, bills, and similar property to the extent of £13,000, besides other valuable articles.

Through the ingenuity of certain police-officers employed to trace the robbery, the whole of the script and documents were recovered while certain unprincipled Jews were negotiating to purchase them.

Some burglars, after they have secured valuable booty, do not attempt another burglary for a time. Others go out the very next night, and commit other depredations, as they are avaricious for money. Some of them lose it by keeping it loosely in the house, or placing it in the bank, when the women they cohabit with reap the benefit. These females often try to induce them to save money and place it in their names in the bank, so that if their paramour gets apprehended, they have the pleasure of spending his ill-gotten wealth.

Some cracksmen succeed occasionally in rifling large quantities of valuable property or money. In such instances they live luxuriously, and spend large sums on pleasure, women, wine, and gambling. Some of them keep their females in splendid style, and live in furnished apartments in quiet respectable streets. Others are afraid to keep women, as the latter are frequently the cause of their being brought to justice.

There are some old burglars at present keeping cabs, omnibuses, and public houses, whose wealth has been secured chiefly from plunder they have rifled from premises with their own hands, or received from burglars since they have abandoned their midnight work. They had the self-command to abandon their criminal courses after a time, while the most of the others have been more shortsighted. Some of these persons, though abounding in wealth, receive stolen goods, and are ready to open their houses at any hour of the night.

There are great numbers of expert cracksmen known to the police in different parts of the metropolis. Many of these reside on the Surrey side, about Waterloo Road and Kent Road, in the Borough, Hackney and Kingsland Roads, and other localities. Some of them have a fine appearance, and are fashionably dressed, and would not be known, except by persons personally acquainted with them.

A number of most expert cracksmen belonging to the felon class of Irish cockneys, have learned no trade, and have no fixed occupation. Others come to their ranks who have been carpenters and smiths, brass-finishers, shoemakers, mechanics, and even tailors. Sometimes fast young men have taken to this desperate mode of life. Some pickpockets, daring in disposition, or driven to extremity, have become burglars. In a short time they learn to use their tools with great expertness; great numbers have been trained by a few leading burglars; some are as young as sixteen or seventeen years; others as old as forty or forty-five—incorrigible old convicts.

Tools are secretly made for them in London, Sheffield, Manchester, Birmingham, and other places. Some burglars keep a set of fine tools of considerable value. Others have indifferent instruments, and are not so expert.

They find very convenient agents in some of the cab-drivers of the metropolis, who for a piece of money are very ready to assist in conveying them at night to the neighbourhood of the houses where they perpetrate their burglaries, and in carrying off the stolen property, and some of the employers of these cab-drivers are as willing to receive it at an underprice.

They have no difficulty in finding unprincipled people to open their houses to receive the stolen property temporarily or otherwise. There are many houses of well-known receivers; then there are hundreds of low public-houses, beer-shops, coffee-shops, brothels, and other places of bad character, where they can leave it for a few hours, or for days, placing one of their gang in the house for a time, until they have arranged with the receivers to purchase it. There are certain well-known beer-shops and public-houses where the burglars meet with the receivers. They meet them in beer-shops in the purlieus of Whitechapel, and in the quieter public-houses and splendid gin-palaces of the West End.

There are a number of French burglars in London, who are as ingenious, daring and expert as the English. There are also some Germans and a few Italians, but who are not considered so clever.

Few of the cracksmen in the metropolis are married—though some are. They often live with prostitutes, or with servants, and other females they have seduced. Some have children whom they send to school but many of them have none. They frequently train up some of their boys to enter the fanlights or windows, and to assist them in their midnight villainies.

While most of the burglars are city-trained, a number come from Liverpool, Manchester, Birmingham, Sheffield, and Bristol. These occasionally work with the London thieves, and the London thieves go occasionally to the provinces to work with them. This is done in the event of their being well known to the police.

For example, a gang of Liverpool thieves might know a house there where valuable property could be conveniently reached. Their being in the neighbourhood might excite suspicion. Under these circumstances they sometimes send to thieves they are acquainted with in London, who proceed thither and plunder the house. Sometimes, in similar circumstances, the London burglars get persons from the provinces to commit robberies in the metropolis—both parties sharing in the booty. In a place where they are not known, they do it themselves.

The burglars in our day are not in general such desperate men as those in former times. They are better known to the police than formerly, and are kept under more strict surveillance. Many of the cracksmen have been repeatedly subjected to prison disci-pline, and have their spirits in a great measure subdued. The crime of our country is not so bold and open as in the days of the redoubt-able men whose dark deeds are recorded in the Newgate Calendar. It has assumed more subtle forms, instead of bold swagger and defiance—and has more of the secret, restless, and deceitful character of our great arch-enemy.

NARRATIVE OF A BURGLAR

THE following narrative was given us by an expert burglar and returned convict we met one evening in the West End of the metropolis. For a considerable number of years he had been engaged in a long series of burglaries connected with several gangs of thieves, and had been so singularly cunning and adroit in his movements he had never been caught in the act of plunder; but was at last betrayed into the hands of the police by one of his confederates, who had quarrelled with him while indulging rather freely in liquor. He was often employed as a putter up of burglaries in various parts of the metropolis, and was generally an outsider on the watch while some of his pals were rifling the house. We visited him at his house in one of the gloomiest lanes in a very low neighbourhood, inhabited chiefly by thieves and prostitutes, and took down from his lips the following recital. In the first part of his autobiography he was very frank and candid, but as he proceeded became more slow and calculating in his disclosures. We hinted to him he was "timid." "No," he replied. "I am not timid, but I am cautious, which you need not be surprised at." He was then seated by the fire beside his paramour, a very clever woman, whose history is perhaps as wild and romantic as his own. He is a slim-made man, beneath the middle size, with a keen, dark, intelligent eye, and about thirty-six years of age. He is good-looking, and very smart in his movements, and was in the attire of a well-dressed mechanic.

"I was born in the city of London in the year 1825. My father was foreman to a coach and harness-maker in Oxford Street. My mother, before her marriage, was a milliner. They had eleven children, and I was the youngest but two. I had six brothers and four sisters. My father had a good salary coming in to support his family, and we lived in comfort and respectability up to his death. He died when I was only about eight years old. My mother was left with eleven children, with very scanty means. Having to support so large a family she soon after became reduced in circumstances. My eldest brother was subject to fits, and died at the age of twenty-four. He occupied my father's place while he lived. My second brother went to work at the same shop, but got into idle and dissipated habits, and was thrown out of employment. He afterwards got a situation in a lacemaker's shop, and had to leave for misconduct. He then went to a druggist's, and had to leave for the same cause. After this he got a situation as potman to a public-house, which completed his ruin. He took every opportunity to lead his younger brothers astray instead of setting us a good example.

"My brother next to him in age did not follow his bad courses, but I was not so fortunate. I went to school at Mr. Low's, Harp Alley, Farringdon Street, but I did not stay there long. At nine years of age I was sent out to work, to help to support myself. I went to work at cotton-winding, and only got 3s. a week. I sometimes worked all night, and had 9d. for it, in addition to my 3s., and often gained 3s. a week besides the six days' wages. I was very happy then to think I could earn so much money, being so young. At this time I was only nine years of age. My brother tried to tempt me to pilfer from my master, but he failed then. I afterwards got a better situation at a trunkmaker's in the City. There my mistress and young master took a liking to me. I was earning 7s. a week, and was only ten years of age. At this time my brother succeeded in tempting me to rob my employers after I had been two months in their service. I carried off wearing apparel and silver plate to the value of several pounds, which my brother disposed of, while he only gave me a few halfpence. I was suspected to be the thief, and was discharged in consequence. I got another situation in a bookbinder's shop, and was not eleven years old then. My brother did not succeed for two or three months to get me to plunder my master, although he often tried to prevail on me to do so. My master had no plate to lose.

"I used to take out boards of books; one night my brother met me coming from the binder's with a truck loaded with books, stopped me, and pretended to be very kind by giving me money to go and buy a pie at a pie-shop. When I came out I found the books were gone and the truck empty. My brother was standing at the door waiting me, but he had companions who meantime emptied the truck of the whole of the contents. I told him he must know who had taken them, but he told me he did not. He desired me to say to my master that a strange man had sent me to get a pie for him and one for myself, and when I came back the books and the man had both disappeared. He told me if I did not say this I would get myself into trouble and him too. I went and told my master the tale my brother had told me. He sent for a policeman, and tried to frighten me to tell the truth. I would not alter from what I had told him, though he tried very hard to get me to do so. He kept me till Saturday night and discharged me, but endeavoured in the meanwhile to get me to unfold the truth, so I was thrown out of employment again.

"I then went to work at the blacking trade, and had a kinder master than ever. My wages were 7s. a week. I then made up my mind that my brother should not tempt me to steal another time. I was in this situation a year and nine months before my brother succeeded in inducing me to commit another robbery. My master was very kind and generous to me, increased my wages from 7*s.* to 16*s.* a week as I was becoming of more service to him.

"We made the blacking with sugar-candy and other ingredients. I was the only lad introduced into the apartment where the blacking was made and the sugar-candy was kept. My brother tempted me to bring him a small quantity of sugar-candy at first. I did so, and he threatened to let my mother know if I did not fetch more. At first I took home 7 lbs of candy, and at last would carry off a larger quantity. I used to get a trifle of money from my brother for this. Being strongly attached to him, up to this time he had great influence over me.

"One day, after bringing him a quantity of sugar-candy, I watched him to see where he sold it. He went into a shop in the City where the person retailed sweets. After he came out of the shop I went in and asked the man in the shop if he would buy some from me, as I was the brother of the young man who had just called in, and had got him the sugar-candy. He told me he would buy as much as I liked to bring.

"I used to bring large quantities to him, generally in the evening, and carried it in a bag. The sugar-candy I should have mixed in the blacking I laid aside till I had an opportunity of carrying it to the receiver. My master continued to be very fond of me, and had strong confidence in me until I got a young lad into the shop beside me, who knew what I had been doing, and informed him of my conduct. He wanted to get me discharged, as he thought he would get my situation, which he did. He told my master I was plundering him; but my master would not believe him until he pointed out a low coffee-house where I used to go, which was frequented by bad characters. My master came into this den of infamy one evening when I was there, and persuaded me to come away with him, which I did. He told me he would forget all I was guilty of, if I would keep better company and behave myself properly in future. I conducted myself better for about a week, but I had got inveigled into bad company through my brother. These lads waited about my employer's premises for me at meal-times and at night. At last they prevailed on me again to go to the same coffee-house. The young lad I had got into the shop beside me soon found means to acquaint my master. He came to see me in the coffee-house again; but I had been prevailed on to drink that evening, and was the worse of intoxicating liquor, although I was not fourteen years of age. My master tried all manner of kind means to persuade me to leave that house, but I would not do so, and insulted him for his kindness.

"On the following morning he paid a visit to my mother's house while I was at breakfast. My mother and he tried to persuade me to go back and finish my week's work, but I was too proud, and would not go back. He then paid my mother my fortnight's wages, and said if I would attend church twice each week he would again take me back into his service. I never attended any church at all, for I had then got into bad habits, and cared no more about work.

"I lived at home with my mother for a short time, and she was very kind to me, and gave me great indulgence. She wished me to remain at home with her to assist in her business as a greengrocer, and used to allow me from 1s. to 1s. 3d. of pocket-money a day. My old companions still followed me about, and prevailed on me to go to the Victoria Theatre. On one of these occasions I was much struck with the play of Oliver Twist. I also saw Jack Sheppard performed there, and was much impressed with it.

"Soon after this I left my mother's house, and took lodgings at the coffee-house, where my master found me, and engaged in an open criminal career. About this time ladies generally carried reticules on their arm. My companions were in the habit of following them and cutting the strings, and carrying them off. They sometimes contained a purse with money and other property. I occasionally engaged in these robberies for about three months. Sometimes I succeeded in getting a considerable sum of money; at other times only a few shillings.

"I was afterwards prevailed on to join another gang of thieves, expert shoplifters. They generally confined themselves to the stationers' shops, and carried off silver pencil-cases, silver and gold mounted scent-bottles, and other articles, and I was engaged for a month at this.

"Being well-dressed, I would go into a shop and price an article of jewellery, or such like valuable, and after getting it in my hand would dart out of the shop with it. I carried on this system occasionally, and was never apprehended, and became very venturesome in robbery.

"I was then about sixteen years of age. A young man came from sea of the name of Philip Scott, who had in former years been a playmate of mine. He requested me to go to one of the theatres with him, when Jack Sheppard was again performed.

We were both remarkably pleased with the play, and soon after determined to try our hand at housebreaking.

"He knew of a place in the City where some plate could be got at. We went out one night with a screw-driver and a knife to plunder it. I assisted him in getting over a wall at the back of the house. He entered from a back-window by pushing the catch back with a knife. He had not been in above three quarters of an hour when he handed me a silver pot and cream-jug from the wall. I conveyed these to the coffee-shop in which we lodged, when we afterwards disposed of them. The young man was well acquainted with this house as his father was often employed jobbing about it.

"After this I cohabited with a female, but my 'pal' did not, although we lived in the same house.

"Soon after we committed another burglary in the south-side of the metropolis, by entering the kitchen window of a private house at the back. I watched while my comrade entered the house. He cut a pane of glass out, and drew the catch back. After gathering what plate he could find lying about, he went up-stairs and got some more plate. We sold this to a receiver in Clerkenwell for about £9 18s. From this house we also carried off some wearing apparel. Each of us took three shirts, two coats and an umbrella.

"Some time after this we made up our minds to try another burglary in the city. We secreted ourselves in a brewer's yard beside the house we intended to plunder, about eight o'clock in the evening, before it was shut up. We cut a panel out of a shutter in the dining-room window on the first floor, but were disturbed when attempting this robbery. I ran off and got away. My companion was not so fortunate; he was captured, and got several months' imprisonment.

"A week after I joined two other burglars. We resolved to attempt a burglary in a certain shop in the East End of the metropolis. There happened to be a dog in the shop. As usual I kept watch outside, while the other two entered from the first-floor window, which had no shutters. So soon as they got in the dog barked. They cut the dog's throat with a knife, and began to plunder the shop of pencil cases, scent-bottles, postage-stamps, etc., and went up-stairs, and carried off pieces of plate. The inmates of the house slept in the upper part of the house. The property when brought to the receiver sold for about £42.

"Another burglary was committed by us at a haberdasher's shop in the West End. While I kept watch, the other two climbed to the top of a warehouse at the back of the shop, wrenched open the window on the roof, and having tied a rope to an iron bar, they lowered themselves down, broke open the desks and till, and got a considerable sum of money, nearly all in silver. They then went to the first-floor drawing-room window over the shop. and entered. The door of this room being locked, they cut out a panel, put their arm through and forced back the lock. They found only a small quantity of plate along with a handsome gold watch and chain. The few articles of plate sold for 38s., and the watch and chain for £7 15s.

"The thieves entered about one o'clock at midnight, and went out about a quarter past five in the morning.

"These are the only jobs I did with these two men, until my comrade came out of prison, when we commenced again. We committed burglaries in different parts of London, at silk-mercers, stationers' shops, and dwelling-houses—some of considerable value; in others the booty was small.

"In these burglaries numbers of other parties were engaged with us—some of them belonging to the Borough, others to St. Giles's, Golden Lane, St. Luke's, and other localities.

"In 1850 I took a part in a burglary in a shop in the south-side of the metropolis along with two other parties. One went inside, and the others were on the watch without. We got access to the shop by the back-yard of a neighbouring public-house, which is usually effected in this way. One person goes to the bar, and gets into conversation with the barmaid, while one or more of their 'pals' takes a favourable opportunity of slipping back into the yard or court behind the house. This is often done about a quarter of an hour, or half an hour, before the house is shut up. The party who kept the barmaid in conversation, would go to the back of the house, and assist the other burglar who was to enter the house in getting over the wall. So soon as this is effected, his other 'pal' comes out again. If the wall can be easily climbed, the party who enters lurks concealed in the water-closet, or some of the out-houses, till the time of effecting the burglary.

"The house intended to be entered is sometimes five or six houses away from this public-house, and sometimes the next house to it.

"When all is ready, the outside man gives the signal. The signal given from the front, such as a cough or otherwise, can be heard by his confederate behind the house. On hearing it the latter begins his work. In this instance the burglar entered the premises by cutting open the shutters of a window in the first floor to the back. He then cut a pane of glass and removed the catch, and went down stairs into the shop, and took from a desk about £60 in money, with several valuable snuff-boxes and other articles. He had to wait till the morning before he could get out. The police seemed to have a suspicion that all was not right, but he got out of the shop about the time when the police were changed.

"I was connected with another burglary, committed in the same year in the West End in a linendraper's shop. It was entered from a public-house in the same manner as in the one described. The same person was engaged inside, while the others were stationed outside. The signal to begin work was given about one o'clock. He had first to remove an iron bar at the first floor landing window to the back, which he did with his jack. (The bars had been seen in the day-time, and we bought this instrument to remove them.) He removed the bar in ten minutes, cut a pane of glass, and removed the two catches. By this means he effected an entry into the house, and to his surprise found the drawing-room was left unlocked. He proceeded there, and got nearly a whole service of plate. After he had gathered the plate up, he made his way towards the shop, cutting through the door which intercepted him. He went to the desk and found £72 in silver money, and £12 in gold. He also packed up half a dozen of new shirts and half a dozen of silk handkerchiefs.

"He was ready to come out of the house, but a coffee-stall being opposite, and the policeman taking his coffee there, the outside man could not give him the signal for some time. To the great surprise of the burglar in the shop, he heard the servant coming down stairs, when he opened the door, and rushed suddenly out, while the policeman was on the kerb near by. He bade the policeman good morning as he passed along with two large bundles in his hands.

"He had not gone fifty yards round the corner of the street, before the servant appeared at the door and asked the policeman as to the person who had just come out. Along with another two constables he gave chase to the burglar, but, being an active, athletic man, he effected his escape.

"I was engaged with two others in another burglary in the West End soon afterwards. Three persons were engaged in it: one to enter, and other two 'pals' to keep watch. We got access to the house by a mews, and got on the top of a wall, when I gave the end of a rope to my companion to hold by while he slid down on the other side. The house was entered at the kitchen window by removing two narrow bars with the jack, and sliding back the catch. There was no booty to be found in the kitchen. On going up-stairs our 'pal' got several pieces of plate, and other articles. On coming down into the shop, he got a quantity of receipt-stamps with a few postage-stamps.

"The putter up of this robbery was a connection of the people of the house.

"I was connected with another burglary in the south-side of the metropolis. A man who frequented a public-house there put up a burglary in a stationer's shop. Two persons were engaged in it, and got access to the premises to be plundered from the public-house. He then climbed several walls, and got access to the shop by a fanlight from behind. Here we found a large sum of money in gold and silver, which had been deposited in a bureau, some plate, and other articles. His 'pal' went to him at half past three, and gave him the signal. He came out soon after, and had only gone a short distance off when he heard a call for the police, and the rattle of the policeman was sprung.

"After a desperate struggle with two constables, he was arrested and taken to the station, with the stolen property in his possession. He was tried and found guilty of committing the burglary, and for assaulting the constables by cutting and wounding them, and was sentenced to fourteen years' transportation, having been four times previously convicted.

"I have been engaged in many depredations from 1840 to 1851, many of which were 'put up' by myself.

"In the year 1851 I was transported several years for burglary. I returned home on a ticket of leave in 1854, and was sent back in the following year for harbouring an escaped convict. I returned home in 1858, at the expiry of my sentence, and since that time have abandoned my former criminal life."

NARRATIVE OF ANOTHER BURGLAR

ONE evening as we had occasion to be in a narrow dark by-street in St. Giles's, we were accosted by a burglar—a returned convict whom we had met on a former occasion in the course of our rambles. We had repeatedly heard of this person as one of the most daring thieves in the metropolis, and were on the look-out for him at the very time when he fortunately crossed our path. He is a fair-complexioned man, of thirty-two years of age, about 5 feet 2 inches in height, slim made, with a keen gray eye. He was dressed in dark trousers, brown vest, and a gray frock coat buttoned up to the chin, and a cap drawn over his eyes. We hesitated at first as to whether this little man was capable of executing such venturesome feats; when he led us along the dark street to an adjoining back court, took off his shoes and stockings, and ran up a waterspout to the top of a lofty house, and slid down again with surprising agility. Before we parted that evening, he was recommended to us by another burglar, a returned convict, and by another most intelligent young man, whom we are sorry to say has been a convicted criminal. He afterwards paid us a visit, when we were furnished with the following recital:—

"I was born in the parish of St. Giles's in the Fields, in the year 1828. My father was a soldier in the British service; after his discharge he lived for some time in the neighbourhood of St. Giles's. He was an Irishman from the county of Limerick. My mother belonged to Cork. My eldest sister was married to a plasterer in London; my second sister has been sentenced to four years, and another sister to five years' transportation, both for stealing watches on different occasions. I have another sister, who lately came out of prison after eighteen months' imprisonment, and is now living an honest life.

"I was never sent by my parents to school, but have learned to read a little by my own exertions; I have no knowledge of writing and arithmetic. I was sent out to get my living at ten years of age by selling oranges in the streets in a basket, and was very soon led into bad company. I sometimes played at pitch and toss, which trained me to gamble, and I often lost my money by this means.

"I often remained out all night, and slept in the dark arches of the Adelphi on straw along with some other boys—one of them was a pickpocket who learned me to steal. It was not long before I was apprehended and committed at the Middlesex Assizes, and received six months' imprisonment.

"At this time I learned to swim, and was remarkably expert at it: when the tide was out I often used to swim across the

Thames for sport. I continued to pick pockets occasionally for two years and was at one time remanded for a week on a criminal charge and afterwards discharged. I used to take ladies' purses by myself, and stole handkerchiefs, snuff-boxes, and pocketbooks from the tails of gentlemen's coats.

"I left my home on the expiry of my six months' imprisonment for stealing a pocket-book. My parents would gladly have taken me back, but I would not go. At this time I associated with a number of juvenile thieves. I had a good suit of clothes, which had been purchased before I went to prison, and having a respectable appearance I took to shop-lifting. I worked at this about seven months, when I was arrested for stealing a coat at a shop in the Borough Road, and was sentenced to three months in Brixton Prison.

"When I got out of prison I went to St. Giles's and cohabited with a prostitute. I was then about seventeen years of age. She was a fair girl, about five feet three inches in height, inclined to be stout—a very handsome girl, about seventeen years of age. Her people lived in Tottenham Court Road, and were very respectable. She had been led astray before I met her, through the bad influence of another girl, and was a common prostitute. She was very kind-hearted. She was not long with me when I engaged with other two persons in a housebreaking in the West End of the metropolis. On the basement of the house we intended to plunder was a counting-house, while the upper floors were occupied by the family as a dwelling-house. Our chief object was to get to the counting-house, which could be entered from the back. Our mode of entering was this: At one o'clock in the morning, one of the party was set to watch in the street, to give us the signal when no one was near—a young man was on the watch, while I and another climbed up by a waterspout to the roof of the counting-house. There was no other way of getting in but by cutting the lead off the house and making an opening sufficient for us to pass through.

"The signal was given to enter the house, but at this time the policeman saw our shadow on the roof and sprung his rattle. The party who was keeping watch and my 'pal' on the roof both got away, but I hurt myself in getting down from the house-top to the street. I was apprehended and lodged in prison, and was tried at Middlesex Assizes and sentenced to nine months' imprisonment.

"So soon as the time was expired, I met with another gang of burglars, more expert than the former. At this time I lived at Shoreditch, in the East End of the metropolis. Four of us were associated together, averaging from twenty-two to twenty-three years of age. We engaged in a burglary in the City. It was hard to do. I was one of those selected to enter the shop; we had to climb over several walls before we reached the premises we intended to plunder. We cut through a panel of the back door. On finding my way into the shop I opened the door to my companions. We packed up some silks and other goods, and remained there very comfortable till the change of the policeman in the morning, when a cart was drawn up to the door, and the outside man gave us the signal. We drew the bolts and brought out the bags containing the booty, put them into the cart, and closed the door after us. We drove off to our lodgings, and sent for a person to purchase the goods. We got a considerable sum by this burglary, which was divided among us. I was then about twenty-two years of age. Our money was soon expended in going to theatres and in gambling, and besides we lived very expensively on the best viands, with wines and other liquors.

"We perpetrated another burglary in the West End. Three of us were engaged in it; one was stationed to watch, while I and another pal had to go in. We entered an empty house by skeleton-keys, and got into the next house; we lifted the trap off and got under the roof, and found an undertrap was fastened inside. We knew we could do nothing without the assistance of an umbrella. My comrade went down to our pal on the watch, and told him to buy an umbrella from some passer-by, the night being damp and rainy. We purchased one from a man in the vicinity for 2s.; my comrade brought it up to me under the roof. Having cut away several lathes, I made an opening with my knife in the plaster, and inserted the closed umbrella through it, and opened it with a jerk, to contain the falling wood and plaster. I broke some of the lathes off, and tore away some of the mortar, which fell in the umbrella. We effected an entry into the house from the roof. On going over the apartments we did not find what we expected; after all our trouble we only got £35, some trinkets, and one piece of plate.

"Burglars become more expert at their work by experience. Many of them are connected with some of the first mechanics in the metropolis. Wherever a patent lock can be found they frequently get a key to fit it. In this way even Chubbs and Bramahs can be opened, as burglars endeavour to get keys of this description of locks. They sometimes give £5 for the impression of a single key, and make one of the same description, which serves for the same size of such locks on other occasions. An experienced burglar thereby has more facilities to open locks — even those which are patented.

"I was connected with another two pals in burglary in a dwelling-house at the West End. It was arranged that I should enter the house. I was lifted to the top of a wall about sixteen feet high, at the back of the premises, and had to come down by the ivy which grew on the garden wall; I had to get across another wall. The ivy was very thick, so that I had to cut part of it away to allow me to get over. I entered the house by the window without difficulty, having removed the catch in the middle with my knife. On a dressing-table in one of the bedrooms I found a gold watch, ring and chain, with £3 15s. in money, and a brace of double-barrelled pistols, which I secured. In the drawing-room I found some dessert-spoons, a punch-ladle and other pieces of silver plate — I looked to them to see they had the proper mark of silver; I found them to be silver, and folded them up carefully and put them into my pocket. On looking into some concealed drawers in a cabinet I found a will and other papers, which I knew were of no use to me; I put them back in their place and did not destroy any of them. I also found several articles of jewellery, and a few Irish one-pound notes. I put them all carefully in my pocket and came to the front door. The signal was given that the cab was ready; I went out, drew the door close after me, and went away with the booty.

"I entered about half-past eleven o'clock at night, and came out at half-past two o'clock. I saw a servant-girl sleeping in the back kitchen, and two young ladies in a back-parlour. I did not go up to the top floors, but heard them snoring. They awoke and spoke two or three times, which made me be careful.

"I went along the passage very softly, in case I should have awakened the two young ladies in the back-parlour as well as the servant in the kitchen. All was so quiet that the least sound in the world would have disturbed them.

"I opened the door gently, and came out when the signal was given by my comrades. It was a cold, wet morning, which was favourable to us, as no one was about the street to see us, and the policeman was possibly, as on similar occasions, standing in some corner smoking his pipe. I jumped into the cab along with my two pals, and went to Westminster. The booty amounted to a considerable sum, which was divided among us. We spent the next three or four weeks very merrily along with our girls. On this occasion we gave the cabman two sovereigns for his trouble, whether the burglary came off or not, and plenty of drink.

"A short time after, a person came up to me with whom I had associated, and played cards over some liquor in the West End. He was a young man out of employment. He thus accosted me, 'Jim, how are you getting on?' I answered, 'Pretty well.' He asked me if I had any job on hand. I said I had not. I inquired if he had anything for me to do. He said he would give me a turn at the house of an old mistress of his. He told me the dressing-case with jewels lay in a back room on a table, but cautioned me to be very careful the butler did not see me, as he was often going up and down stairs. Two of us resolved to plunder the house. My companion was on the outside to watch, while I had to enter the house.

"I got in with a skeleton-key while they were at supper, and got up the stairs without any one observing me. On going to the back room I was disturbed by a young lady coming up stairs. I ran up to the second floor above to hide myself, and found a bed in the apartment. I concealed myself underneath the bed, when the lady and her servant came into the room with a light. They closed the door and pulled the curtains down, when the lady began to undress in presence of the servant. The servant began to wash her face and neck. The lady was a beautiful young creature. While lying under the bed I distinctly saw the maid put perfume on the lady's under linen. She then began to dress and decorate herself, and told the servant she was going out to her supper. She said she would not be home till two or three o'clock in the morning, and did not wish the servant to remain up for her, but to leave the lamp burning. As soon as she and the waiting-maid had left the room, I got out of my hiding-place, and on looking around saw but a small booty, consisting of a small locket and gold chain; a gold pencil-case, and silver thimble. As I was returning down stairs with them in my pocket to get to the first floor back, I got possession of a case of jewels, which I thought of great value. I returned to the hall, and came out about twelve o'clock without any signal from my comrade.

"On taking the jewels to a person who received such plunder, he told us they were of small value, and were not brilliants and emeralds as we fancied. They were set in pure gold of the best quality, and only brought us £22.

"To look at them we fancied they would have been worth a much higher sum, and were sadly disappointed.

"Soon after we resolved on another burglary in the West End. One kept watch without while two of us entered the house by a grating underneath the shop window, and descended into the kitchen by a rope. We got a signal to work. The first thing we did was to lift up the kitchen window. When we got in we pulled the kitchen window down, drew down the blind, and lighted our taper. We looked round and saw nothing worth removing. We went to the staircase to get into the shop. As we were wrenching open a chest of drawers, a big cat which happened to be in the room was afraid of us. We got pieces of meat out of the safe and threw them to the cat. The animal was so excited that it jumped up on the mantelpiece and broke a number of ornaments. This disturbed an old gentleman in the first-floor front. He called out to his servant, 'John, there is somebody in the house.' We had no means of getting the door open, and had to go out by the window. The old gentleman came down stairs in his nightgown with a brace of pistols, just as we were going out of the window. He fired, but missed us. I jumped so hastily that I hurt my bowels, and was conveyed by my companions in a cab to Westminster, and lay there for six weeks in an enfeebled condition. My money was spent, and as my young woman could not get any, my companions said you had better have a meeting of our 'pals'. A friendly meeting was held, and they collected about £8 to assist me.

"When I recovered, to my great loss my companion was taken on account of a job he had been attempting in Regent's Park. He was committed to the Old Bailey, tried, and transported for life. He was a good pal of mine, and for a time I supported his wife and children. On another occasion, I and another comrade met a potman at the West End. He asked us for something to drink, as he said he was out of work. We did so, and also gave him something to eat. We entered into conversation with him. He told us about a house he lately served in, and said there could be a couple of hundreds got there or more before the brewer's bill was paid. We found out when the brewer's bill was to be paid. We asked the man where this money was kept. He told us that we would find it in the second-floor back.

"We made arrangements as to the night when we would go. Three of us went out as usual. We found the lady of the house and her daughter serving at the bar. We had to pass the bar to go upstairs. There was a row got up in the tap-room with my companions. While the landlady ran in to see what was the matter, and the daughter ran out for the policeman, I slipped upstairs and got into the room. The policeman knew one of my companions when he came in, and at once suspected there was some design. He asked if there had been any more besides these two. The landlady said there was another. I was coming down stairs with the cash-box when I heard this conversation. The constable asked leave to search the house. I ran with the cash-box up the staircase, and looked in the back room to see if there was any place to get away, but there was none. I took the cash-box up to the front garret, and was trying to break it open, but in the confusion I could not.

"I fled out of the garret window and got on the roof to hide from the policeman. My footsteps were observed on the carpet and on the gutters as I went out and slipped in the mud on the roof. I intended to throw the cash-box to my companions, but they gave me the signal to get away. I had just time to take my boots off when another constable came out of the garret window of the other house. I had no other alternative but to get along the roof where they could not follow me, and besides I was much nimbler than they. I went to the end of the row of houses, and did not go down the garret window near me. Seeing a waterspout leading to a stable-yard, I slipt down it, and climbed up another spout to the roof of the stable. I lay there for five hours till the police changed.

"I managed to get down and went into the stable-yard, when the stable-man cried out, 'Hollo! here he is.' I saw there was no alternative but to fight for it. I had a jemmy in my pocket. He laid hold of me, when I struck him on the face with it, and he fell to the ground. I fled to the door, and came out into the main street, returned into Piccadilly, and passed through the Park gates. On coming home to Westminster I found one of my comrades had not come home. We sent to the police-station, and learned he was there. We sent him some provisions, and he gave us notice in a piece of paper concealed in some bread that I should keep out of the way as the police were after me, which would aggravate his case.

"I then went to live at Whitechapel. Meantime some clever detectives were on my track, from information they received from the girls we used to cohabit with. We heard of this from a quarter some would not suspect. He told us to keep out of the way, and that he would let us know should he get any further information. At last my companion was committed for trial, tried, and sentenced to seven years' transportation. I did not join in any other burglary for some time after this, as the police were vigilantly looking for me. I kept myself concealed in the house of a cigar-maker in Whitechapel.

"Another pal and I went one evening to a public-house in Whitechapel. My pal was a tall, athletic young fellow, of about nineteen years, handsomely dressed, with gold ring and pin, intelligent and daring. We had gone in to have a glass of rum-and-water, when we saw a sergeant belonging to a regiment of the line sitting in front of the bar. He asked us if we would have anything to drink. We said we would. He called for three glasses of brandy-and-water, and asked my companion if he would take a cigar. He did so. The sergeant said he was a fine young man, and would make an excellent soldier. On this he pulled out a purse of money and looked at the time on his gold watch. My comrade looked to me and gave me a signal, at the same time saying to the soldier, 'Sergeant, I'll 'list'. He took the shilling offered him, and pretended to give him his name and address, giving a false alias, so that he should not be able to trace him.

"He called for half-a-pint of rum-and-water, and put down the shilling he received from the sergeant. We took him into the bagatelle-room, and tried to get him to play with us, as we had a number of counterfeit sovereigns and forged cheques about us. He would not play except for a pint of half-and-half. On this he left us, and went in the direction of the barracks in Hyde Park. My comrade said to me, 'We shall not leave him till we have plundered him.' I was then the worse for liquor. We followed him. When he reached the Park gates I whispered to my companion that I would garotte him if he would assist me. He said he would. On this I sprung at his neck. Being a stronger man than I, he struggled violently. I still kept hold of him until he became senseless. My companion took his watch, his pocket-book, papers, and money, consisting of some pieces of gold, and a £5 note. We sold the gold watch and chain for £8.

"Along with my pal, I went into a skittle-ground in the City to have a game at skittles by ourselves, when two skittle-sharps who knew us well quarrelled with us about the game. My companion and I made a bet with them, which we lost, chiefly owing to my fault, which irritated him. He said, 'Never mind; there is more money in the world, and we will have it ere long, or they shall have us.' One of the skittle-sharps said to us insultingly, 'Go and thieve for more, and we will play you.' On this we got angry at them. My pal took up his life-preserver, and struck the skittle-sharp on the head.

"A policeman was sent for to apprehend him. I put the life-preserver in the fire as the door was shut on us, and we could not get away. On the policeman coming in my pal was to be given in charge by the landlord and landlady of the house. The skittle-sharp who had been struck rose up bleeding, and said to the landlord and landlady, 'What do you know of the affair? Let us settle the matter between ourselves.' The policeman declined to interfere. We took brandy-and-water with the skittle-sharps, and parted in the most friendly terms.

"One day we happened to see a gentleman draw a pocket-book out of his coat-pocket, and relieve a poor crossing sweeper with a piece of silver. He returned it into his pocket. I said to my pal, 'Here is a piece of money for us.' I followed after him and came up to him about Regent's Park, put my hand into his coat-pocket, seized the pocket-book, and passed it to my comrade. An old woman who kept an apple-stall had seen me; and when my back was turned went up and told the gentleman. The latter followed us until he saw a policeman, while I was not aware of it; being eager to know the contents of the pocket-book I handed to my comrade, he being at the time in distress. We went into a public-house to see the contents, and called for a glass of brandy-and-water. We found there were three £10 notes and a £5 note, and two sovereigns, with some silver. The policeman meantime came in and seized my hand, and at the same time took the pocket-book from me before I had time to prevent him.

"The gentleman laid hold of my companion, but was struck to the ground by the latter. He then assisted to rescue me from the policeman. By the assistance of the potman and a few men in the taproom, they overpowered me, but my comrade got away. I was taken to the police court and committed for trial, and was afterwards tried and sentenced to seven years' transportation.

"On one occasion, after my return from transportation, I and a companion of mine met a young woman we were well acquainted with who belonged to our own class of Irish cockneys. She was then a servant in a family next door to a surgeon. She asked us how we were getting on, and treated us to brandy. We asked her if we could rifle her mistress's house, when she said she was very kind to her, and she would not permit us to hurt a hair of her head or to take away a farthing of her property. She told us there was a surgeon who lived next door—a young man who was out at all hours of the night, and sometimes all night. She informed us there was nobody in the house but an old servant who slept upstairs in a garret.

"The door opened by a latch-key, and when the surgeon was out the gas was generally kept rather low in the hall. We watched him go out one evening at eleven o'clock, applied a key to the door, and entered the house. The young woman promised to give us the signal when the surgeon came in. We had not been long in when heard the signal given. I got under the sofa in his surgical room; the gas used to burn there all night while he was out. My companion was behind a chest of drawers which stood at a small distance from the wall. As the surgeon came in I saw him take his hat off, when he sat down on the sofa above me.

"As he was taking his boots off, he bent down and saw one of my feet under the sofa. He laid hold of it, and dragged me from under the sofa. He was a strong man, and kneeled on my back with my face turned to the floor. I gave a signal to my companion behind him, who struck him a violent blow on the back, not to hurt him, but to stun him, which felled him to the floor. I jumped up and ran out of the door with my companion. He ran after us and followed us through the street while I ran in my stockings. Our female friend, the servant, had the presence of mind and courage to run into the house and get my boots. She carried them into the house of her employer, and then looked out and gave the alarm of 'Thieves!' We got a booty of £43.

"One night I went to an Irish penny ball in St. Giles's, and had a dance with a young Irish girl of about nineteen years of age. This was the first time she saw me. I was a good dancer, and she was much pleased with me. She was a beautiful and handsome girl—a costermonger, and a good dancer. We went out and had some intoxicating liquor, which she had not been used to. She wished me to make her a present of a white silk handkerchief, with the shamrock, rose, and thistle on it, and a harp in the middle, which I could not refuse her. She gave me in exchange a green handkerchief from her neck. We corresponded after this for some time. She did not know then that I was a burglar and thief. She asked me my occupation, and I told her I was a pianoforte maker. One night I asked her to come out with me to go to a penny Irish ball. I kept her out late, and seduced her. She did not go back to her friends any more, but cohabited with me.

"One night after this we went to a public singing-room, and I got jealous by her taking notice of another young man. I did not speak to her that night about it. Next morning I told her it was better that she should go home to her friends, as I would not live with her any more.

"She cried over it, and afterwards went home. Her friends got her a situation in the West End as a servant, but she was pregnant at the time with a child to me. She was not long in service before her young master fell in love with her, and kept her in fashionable style, which he has continued to do ever since. She now lives in elegant apartments in the West End, and her boy, my son, is getting a college education. I do not take any notice of them now.

"One night on my return from transportation I met two old associates. They asked me how I was, and told me they were glad to see me. They inquired how I was getting on. I told them I was not getting along very well. They asked me if I was associated with anyone. I told them I was not, and was willing to go out with them to a bit of work. These men were burglars, and wished me to join them in plundering a shop in the metropolis. I told them I did not mind going with them. They arranged I should enter the shop along with another 'pal,' and the other was to keep watch. On the night appointed for the work we met an old watchman, and asked him what o'clock it was. One of our party pretended to be drunk, and said he would treat him to two or three glasses of rum. Meantime I and my companion entered the house by getting over a back wall and entering a window there by starring the glass and pulling the catch back. When we got in we did not require to break open any lockfast. We packed up apparel of the value of £60. We remained in the shop till six o'clock, when the change of officers took place. The door was then unbolted—a cab was drawn up to the shop. I shut the door and went off in one direction on foot, while one 'pal' went off in a cab, and the other to the receiver at Whitechapel.

"I have been engaged in about eighteen burglaries besides other depredations, some of them in fashionable shops and dwelling-houses in the West End. Some of them have been effected by skeleton keys, others by climbing waterspouts, at which I am considered to be extraordinary nimble, and others by obtaining an entry through the doors or windows. I have been imprisoned seven times in London and elsewhere, and have been twice transported. Altogether I have been in prison for about fourteen years.

"My first wife died broken-hearted the second time I was transported. Since I came home this last time I have lived an honest industrious life with my second wife and family."

FELONIES ON THE RIVER THAMES

THERE are a great number of robberies of various descriptions committed on the Thames by different parties. These depredations differ in value, from the little ragged mudlark stealing a piece of rope or a few handfuls of coals from a barge, to the lighterman carrying off bales of silk several hundred pounds in value. When we look to the long lines of shipping along each side of the river, and the crowds of barges and steamers that daily ply along its bosom, and the dense shipping in its docks, laden with untold wealth, we are surprised at the comparatively small aggregate amount of these felonies.

THE MUDLARKS

THEY generally consist of boys and girls, varying in age from eight to fourteen or fifteen; with some persons of more advanced years. For the most part they are ragged, and in a very filthy state, and are a peculiar class, confined to the river. The parents of many of them are coalwhippers—Irish cockneys—employed getting coals out of the ships, and their mothers frequently sell fruit in the street. Their practice is to get between the barges, and one of them lifting the other up will knock lumps of coal into the mud, which they pick up afterwards; or if a barge is ladened with iron, one will get into it and throw iron out to the other, and watch an opportunity to carry away the plunder in bags to the nearest marine-storeshop.

They sell the coals among the lowest class of people for a few halfpence. The police make numerous detections of these offences. Some of the mudlarks receive a short term of imprisonment, from three weeks to a month, and others two months with three years in a reformatory. Some of them are old women of the lowest grade, from fifty to sixty, who occasionally wade in the mud up to the knees. One of them may be seen beside the Thames Police-office, Wapping, picking up coals in the bed of the river, who appears to be about sixty-five years of age. She is a robust woman, dressed in an old cotton gown, with an old straw bonnet tied round with a handkerchief, and wanders about without shoes and stockings. This person has never been in custody. She may often be seen walking through the streets in the neighbourhood with a bag of coals on her head.

In the neighbourhood of Blackfriars Bridge clusters of mudlarks of various ages may be seen from ten to fifty years, young girls and old women, as well as boys.

They are mostly at work along the coal wharves where the barges are lying aground, such as Shadwell and Wapping, along Bankside, Borough; above Waterloo Bridge, and from the Temple down to St. Paul's Wharf. Some of them pay visits to the City Gasworks, and steal coke and coal from their barges, where the police have made many detections.

As soon as the tide is out they make their appearance, and remain till it comes in. Many of them commence their career with stealing rope or coals from the barges, then proceed to take copper from the vessels, and afterwards go down into the cabins and commit piracy.

These mudlarks are generally strong and healthy, though their clothes are in rags. Their fathers are robust men. By going too often to the public-house they keep their families in destitution, and the mothers of the poor children are glad to get a few pence in whatever way they can.

SWEEPING BOYS

THIS class of boys sail about the river in very old boats, and go on board empty craft with the pretext of sweeping them. They enter barges of all descriptions, laden with coffee, sugar, rice, and other goods, and steal anything they can lay their hands on, often abstracting headfasts, ropes, chains, &c. In some instances they cut the bags and steal the contents, and dispose of the booty to marine-store dealers. They are generally very ragged and wretched in appearance, and if pursued take to the water like a rat, splashing through the mud, and may be seen doing so chased by the police. In general they are expert swimmers. Their ages range from twelve to sixteen. They are dressed similar to the other ragged boys over the metropolis. The fathers of most of them are coalwhippers, but many of them are orphans. They are strong, healthy boys, and some of them sleep in empty barges, others in low lodging-houses at 3*d.* a night. Some live in empty houses, and many of them have not had a shirt on for six months, and their rags are covered with vermin.

In the summer many sleep in open barges, and often in the winter, when they cover themselves with old mats, sacks, or tarpaulins. Their bodies are inured to this inclement life. They never go to church, and few of them have been to school.

Two little boys of this class, the one nine and the other eleven years of age, lived for six months on board an old useless barge at Bermondsey, and for other five months in an old uninhabited house, and had not a clean shirt on during all that time. At night they covered themselves with old mats and sacks, their clothes being in a wretched state. Seeing them in this neglected condition, an inspector of police took them into custody and brought them before a magistrate, with the view to get them provided for. The magistrate sent them to the workhouse for shelter.

These boys are of the same class with the mudlarks before referred to, but are generally a few years older.

SELLERS OF SMALL WARES

FELONIES are occasionally committed by boys who go on board vessels with baskets containing combs, knives, laces, &c., giving them in exchange for pieces of rope, sometimes getting fat and bones from the cooks. In many instances the owners are robbed by the crew giving away ropes belonging to the ship for such wares. These parties occasionally pilfer any small article they see lying about the ship, sometimes carrying off watches when they have an opportunity. They generally try to get on board foreign vessels about to sail, so that when robberies are committed the parties do not remain to prosecute them, and the thieves are consequently discharged.

They are generally from fourteen to eighteen years of age, and many of them reside with their parents in Rosemary Lane and other low neighbourhoods about the East End.

This is a peculiar class of boys who confine their attention to the ships, barges, and coasting vessels, and do not commit felonies in other parts of the metropolis.

LABOURERS ON BOARD SHIP, ETC.

THESE men are employed to discharge cargoes on board steam vessels arriving from the coast, and also foreign vessels. They are frequently detected pilfering by the police and secreting about their clothes small quantities of tallow, coffee, sugar, meat, and other portable goods. These parties abstract articles from the hold, but do not go down into cabins. They have ample opportunity of breaking open some of the boxes and packages and of extracting part of the contents. As they have no facility to get large quantities on shore, they confine themselves to petty pilfering. Most of their booty is kept for their own consumption, unless they succeed in carrying off a large quantity, which rarely occurs. In these cases they dispose of it at a chandler's shop.

DREDGEMEN OR FISHERMEN

THESE are men who are in the habit of coming out early in the morning, as the tide may suit, for the purpose of dredging from the bed of the river coals which are occasionally spilled in weighing when being transferred into the barges. If these parties are not successful in getting coals there, they invariably go alongside of a loaded barge and carry off coals and throw a quantity of mud over them, to make it appear as if they had got them from the bed of the river. The police have made numerous detections. Some have been imprisoned, and others have been transported. The same class of men go alongside of vessels and steal the copper funnels and ropes, and go to the nearest landing place to sell them to marine-store dealers, who are always in readiness to receive anything brought to them. The doors are readily opened to them, early and late.

To deceive the police these unprincipled dealers have carts calling every morning at their shops to take away the metals and other goods they may have bought during the previous day and night.

SMUGGLING

NUMEROUS articles of contraband goods are smuggled by seamen on their arrival from foreign ports, such as tobacco, liquors, shawls, handkerchiefs, &c.

Several years ago an officer in the Thames police was on duty at five in the morning. While rowing by the Tower he saw in the dusk two chimney sweeps in a boat leaving a steam vessel, having with them two bags of soot. He boarded the boat along with two officers, and asked them if they had anything in their possession liable to Custom-house duty. They answered they had not. Upon searching the bags of soot he found several packages of foreign manufactured tobacco, weighing 48 lbs. The parties were arrested and taken to the police station, and were fined £100 each, or six months' imprisonment. Not being able to pay they were imprisoned.

These two sweeps had no doubt carried on this illegal traffic for some time, being employed on the arrival of the boats to clean the funnels and the flues of the boilers.

Some time ago a sailor came ashore late at night at the Shadwell Dock, who had just arrived from America. According to the usual custom he was searched, when several pounds of tobacco were found concealed about his person. He was tried at the police court, and sentenced to pay a small fine.

In July, 1858, about midnight, a police constable was passing East Lane, Bermondsey, when he saw a bag at the top of a street containing something rather bulky, which aroused his suspicions. On proceeding farther he saw a man carrying another bag up the street from a boat in the river. He got the assistance of another constable, and apprehended the man carrying the bag, and also the waterman that conveyed it ashore. The two bags were found to contain 220 lbs. of Cavendish tobacco. Both persons were detained in the Thames police station, and taken before a magistrate at Southwark police court. Prosecution was ordered by the Board of Customs, and both were fined £100 each, and in default sentenced to six months' imprisonment. Being unable to pay the fine, they suffered imprisonment.

In February, 1860, information was given to an inspector of the Thames police of a smuggling traffic which was being carried on in the Shadwell Basin, London Docks, from an American vessel named the *Amazon*. The steward was in the practice of carrying the tobacco about a certain hour in the morning from the vessel through a private gate at the Shadwell Basin. Vigilant watch was kept over this gate by the inspector, with the assistance of a constable. About eight o'clock in the morning he saw a man coming up who answered the description given him. He followed

him into a tobacconist's shop in King David Lane, Shadwell.
The officer on going in saw a carpet bag handed over the counter.
He seized it, and brought the man with him to the police station.
A communication was then made to the Board of Customs, who
sent an officer to the Thames Police Station. On making search
on board the ship, they found about two cwts. of tobacco. The
man was tried, and sentenced to pay a fine of £100, or suffer
six months' imprisonment.

FELONIES BY LIGHTERMEN

NUMEROUS depredations are perpetrated by lightermen, employed
to navigate barges by the owners of various steam-vessels in the
river or in the docks, and are intrusted with valuable cargoes, the
value varying from £10 to £20,000. They have been assisted in
these robberies by persons little suspected by the public, but
well-known to the police.

They have got cargoes from vessels in the wharves, or docks,
to convey for trans-shipment and delivery along different parts
of the river, and manage on their way to abstract part of the
cargo they are in charge of. Sometimes these robberies are effected
on the way, sometimes when they are waiting outside the dock
for the tide to go in. When they have not such articles on board
their own barges, they remove cargoes from other craft while the
crew may be on shore at supper, or otherwise. Sometimes they
carry away articles about their person, such as tobacco, brandy,
wine, opium, tea, etc.

They occasionally steal an empty barge, and go alongside of
another barge as if they were legally employed to put the cargo
into another craft, and turn the barge into some convenient
place, where they may have a cart or van in readiness to remove
the property. Sometimes they have a cab for this purpose. Two
days often elapse before the police get information of these
robberies.

In one instance a barge was taken up Bow Creek, with about
twenty bundles of whalebone and twenty bags of saltpetre,
which were conveyed away in a van to the city. The police traced
the booty to a marine store-dealer. The value of the property
was £400. Two well-known thieves were tried for the robbery,
but were acquitted.

In April, 1858, Thomas Turnbull and Charles Turnbull, brothers, both lightermen and notorious river thieves, were charged with a robbery from two barges at Wapping. Two lightermen were in charge of two barges laden, the one with lac dye and the other with cases of wire, near to the entrance of the London Docks. These men having gone on shore for refreshment, the two thieves rowed an empty barge alongside the two barges, and took one chest of lac dye from one of them and a case of wire card from the other, in value about £25. They took the barge with the stolen property over to Rotherhithe, and landed at the Elephant Stairs, where it was conveyed away in a cart. The property was never recovered, but the police, after making great exertions, got sufficient evidence to convict the parties, who were sentenced to eighteen months each at the Central Criminal Court.

These unprincipled lightermen could get a good livelihood by honest labour, varying from 30s. to £2 a week; but they are dissipated and idle in their habits, and resort to thieving. They often spend their time in dancing and concert-rooms, and are to be seen at the Mahogany Bar at Close Square and Paddy's Goose, Ratcliffe Highway. They generally cohabit with prostitutes. They are a different class of men from the tier-rangers, or river pirates, who also live with prostitutes. The lightermen's women are generally smart and well-dressed, and do not belong to the lowest order as those of the tier-rangers do. The ages of this class of thieves generally range from twenty to thirty years.

THE RIVER PIRATES

THIS class of robberies is committed among the shipping in both sides of the river, from London Bridge to Greenhithe, but is most prevalent from London Bridge to the entrance of the West India Dock. The depredations are committed in the docks as well as on the river, but not so much in the former, as they are better protected. Robberies in the docks are generally done in the daytime. In the river, the chief object the thieves have in view is to enter the vessel at midnight, as they know that when vessels arrive the seamen are often fatigued and worn out, and they get a favourable opportunity of getting on board and stealing. They steal from all classes of vessels, but chiefly from brigs and barges. They take any boat from the shore and go on board the vessels, as if they were seamen, being dressed as watermen and seamen. When they get on board they go to the cabin or forecastle. Their chief object is to secure wearing apparel and money. Watches are often to be found hanging up in the cabin, and clothes are also to be found there. In the forecastle the clothes are generally contained in a bag hanging up by the side or bow of the ship. After they have effected their purpose they row ashore and turn the boat adrift.

There is another mode of stealing they adopt. They get on board the ships as if they belonged to some of them, and represent they belong to a certain ship in a line of vessels commonly called a "tier." They proceed to the forecastle, where if they find no one moving about, they go down and plunder. If they are seen by any of the crew they pretend they belong to some other ship, and ask if this ship is named so and so. They then say they cannot get on board their own ship, and wish the crew to allow them to remain for the night.

In many instances the stolen property is found on their person, such as coats, vests, trousers, boots, etc., and their own clothes are left behind. They are generally from eighteen to thirty years of age, and are powerful athletic men.

These robberies are greatly on the decrease, owing to the vigilance of the police.

Several years ago there was a cry of police between twelve midnight and two o'clock on board a vessel lying in Union Pier, Wapping. The crew of a police galley proceeded to the spot, and ascertained that two thieves had been on board a vessel there, and had concealed themselves somewhere in it, or in the barges alongside. After searching some time they discovered a notorious river thief in one of the barges. He was a stout-made man, about five feet nine inches in height, and twenty-two years of age. A desperate struggle ensued between him and the police. He struck the inspector with a heavy iron bar on the back a very severe blow, which rendered him henceforth unfit for active duty. The pirate resisted with great desperation, and defied the police for some time.

At last they drew their cutlasses, and succeeded in taking him. He was brought to the police station, convicted, and sentenced to three months' imprisonment. He was afterwards indicted for the assault on the inspector, and sentenced to fifteen months' hard labour. Since that time he has been transported twice for similar offences.

A few years since several river pirates were suspected of being on board a vessel at Bermondsey, where they had stolen a silver watch from the cabin. One of the gang was detected by the crew of the vessel and detained. The crew shouted out for the police, when three of their pals drew up to the side of the vessel in a small boat, representing themselves to be policemen, with numbers chalked on their coats. The captain of the vessel gave the man into their custody, and handed over the watch to one of them. Next morning the captain went to the police-station to see if the party was there. It was then the police heard of the robbery, when it was found the supposed officers and the thief were a party of river pirates who had infested the river for a long time. As the ship was just setting sail the case was dropped.

Some time ago three constables went on duty at midnight in consequence of a number of midnight robberies having been committed all over the river, especially at Deptford, from the ships lying there. They went out in a private boat in plain clothes. On getting to Deptford they proceeded up the creek. After remaining there in the dusk about an hour they heard a loud knocking, and suspected that some one was taking the copper from the bottom of a vessel lying there.

The constables drew up to the vessel with their boat, and found two men with a quantity of copper in a boat, with chisels and a chopper they had been using. They arrested them, and were coming out of the creek with the two boats when they discovered two other notorious river thieves climbing down the chains of a vessel lying alongside the wharf. They had been down in the forecastle, and having disturbed the crew were making their escape when the officers saw them.

The officers thereupon made for the vessel, and succeeded in apprehending them, and took them into their boat after a desperate resistance.

The first two were convicted and sentenced, one to three months and the other to six months' imprisonment, and the latter were sentenced to three months each in Maidstone gaol.

The Commissioners of Police rewarded the constables with a gratuity for their vigilance and gallant conduct.

Many of these tier-rangers or river pirates have a ruffianly appearance, and generally live with prostitutes, on both sides of the river, at St. George's, Bluegate Fields, the Borough, and Bermondsey.

They confine themselves to robberies on the river, and are frequently transported by the time they are thirty years of age. Occasionally a returned convict comes back for a time, when he generally resumes his former villainies, and is again sent abroad.

These tier-rangers in most cases have sprung from the ranks of the mudlarks, and step by step have advanced further in crime, until they have become callous brutal ruffians, living as brigands on the sides of the river.

NARRATIVE OF A MUDLARK

THE following narrative was given us by a mudlark we found on a float on the river Thames at Millwall, to the eastward of Ratcliffe Highway. He was then engaged, while the tide was in, gathering chips of wood in an old basket. We went to the riverside along with his younger brother, a boy of about eleven years of age, we saw loitering in the vicinity. On our calling to him, he got the use of a boat lying near, and came toward us with alacrity. He was an Irish lad of about thirteen years of age, strong and healthy in appearance, with Irish features and accent. He was dressed in a brown fustian coat and vest, dirty greasy canvas trousers roughly-patched, striped shirt with the collar folded down, and a cap with a peak.

"I was born in the county of Kerry in Ireland in the year 1847, and am now about thirteen years of age. My father was a ploughman, and then lived on a farm in the service of a farmer, but now works at loading ships in the London Docks. I have three brothers and one sister. Two of my brothers are older than I. One of them is about sixteen, and the other about eighteen years of age. My eldest brother is a seaman on board a screwship, now on a voyage to Hamburg; and the other is a seaman now on his way to Naples. My youngest brother you saw beside me at the river side. My sister is only five years of age, and was born in London. The rest of the family were all born in Ireland. Our family came to London about seven years ago, since which time my father has worked at the London Docks. He is a strong-bodied man of about thirty-four years of age. I was sent to school along with my elder brothers for about three years, and learned reading, writing, and arithmetic. I was able to read tolerably well, but was not so proficient in writing and arithmetic. One of my brothers has been about three years, and the other about five years at sea.

"About two years ago I left school, and commenced to work as a mudlark on the river, in the neighbourhood of Millwall, picking up pieces of coal and iron, and copper, and bits of canvas on the bed of the river, or of wood floating on the surface. I commenced this work with a little boy of the name of Fitzgerald. When the bargemen heave coals to be carried from their barge to the shore, pieces drop into the water among the mud, which we afterwards pick up. Sometimes we wade in the mud to the ankle, at other times to the knee. Sometimes pieces of coal do not sink, but remain on the surface of the mud; at other times we seek for them with our hands and feet.

"Sometimes we get as many coals about one barge as sell for 6d. On other occasions we work for days and only get perhaps as much as sells for 6d. The most I ever gathered in one day, or saw any of my companions gather, was about a shilling's worth. We generally have a bag or a basket to put the articles we gather into. I have sometimes got so much at one time that it filled my basket twice, before the tide went back. I sell the coals to the poor people in the neighbourhood, such as in Mary Street and Charles Street, and return again and fill my bag or basket and take them home or sell them to the neighbours. I generally manage to get as many a day as sell for 8d.

"In addition to this, I often gather a basket of wood on the banks of the river, consisting of small pieces chipped off planks to build the ships or barges, which are carried down with the current and driven ashore. Sometimes I gather four or five baskets of these in a day. When I get a small quantity they are always taken home to my mother. When successful in finding several basketfuls, I generally sell part of them and take the rest home. These chips or stray pieces of wood are often lying on the shore or among the mud, or about the floating logs; and at other times I seize pieces of wood floating down the river a small distance off; I take a boat lying near and row out to the spot and pick them up. In this way I sometimes get pretty large beams of timber. On an average I get 4d. or 6d. a day by finding and selling pieces of wood; some days only making 2d., and at other times 3d. We sell the wood to the same persons who buy the coals.

"We often find among the mud, in the bed of the river, pieces

of iron; such as rivets out of ships, and what is termed washers and other articles cast away or dropped in the iron-yards in building ships and barges. We get these in the neighbourhood of Limehouse, where they build boats and vessels. I generally get some pieces of iron every day, which sells at ¼d. a pound, and often make 1d. or 2d. a day, sometimes 3d., at other times only a farthing. We sell these to the different marine-store dealers in the locality.

"We occasionally get copper outside Young's dock. Sometimes it is new and at other times it is old. It is cut from the side of the ship when it is being repaired, and falls down into the mud. When the pieces are large they are generally picked up by the workmen; when small they do not put themselves to the trouble of picking them up. The mudlarks wade into the bed of the river and gather up these and sell them to the marine store dealer. The old copper sells at 1½d. a pound, the new copper at a higher price. I only get copper occasionally, though I go every day to seek for it.

"Pieces of rope are occasionally dropped or thrown overboard from the ships or barges and are found embedded in the mud. We do not find much of this, but sometimes get small pieces. Rope is sold to the marine store dealers at ½d. a pound. We also get pieces of canvas, which sells at ½d. a pound. I have on some occasions got as much as three pounds.

"We also pick up pieces of fat along the river-side. Sometimes we get four or five pounds and sell it at ¾d. a pound at the marine stores; these are thrown overboard by the cooks in the ships, and after floating on the river are driven on shore.

"I generally rise in the morning at six o'clock, and go down to the river-side with my youngest brother you saw beside me at the barges. When the tide is out we pick up pieces of coal, iron, copper, rope and canvas. When the tide is in we pick up chips of wood. We go upon logs, such as those you saw me upon with my basket, and gather them there.

"In the winter time we do not work so many hours as in the summer; yet in winter we generally are more successful than in the long days of summer. A good number of boys wade in summer who do not come in winter on account of the cold. There are generally thirteen or fourteen mudlarks about Limehouse in the summer, and about six boys steadily there in the winter, who are strong and hardy, and well able to endure the cold.

"The old men do not make so much as the boys because they

are not so active; they often do not make more than 6*d*. a day, while we make 1*s*. or 1*s*. 6*d*.

"Some of the mudlarks are orphan boys and have no home. In the summer time they often sleep in the barges or in sheds or stables or cow-houses, with their clothes on. Some of them have not a shirt, others have a tattered shirt which is never washed, as they have no father nor mother, nor friend to care for them. Some of these orphan lads have good warm clothing; others are ragged and dirty, and covered with vermin.

"The mudlarks generally have a pound of bread to breakfast, and a pint of beer when they can afford it. They do not go to coffee-shops, not being allowed to go in, as they are apt to steal the men's 'grub.' They often have no dinner, but when they are able they have a pound of bread and 1*d*. worth of cheese. I never saw any of them take supper.

"The boys who are out all night lie down to sleep when it is dark, and rise as early as daylight. Sometimes they buy an article of dress, a jacket, cap, or pair of trousers from a dolly or rag-shop. They get a pair of trousers for 3*d*. or 4*d*., an old jacket for 2*d*., and an old cap for ½*d*. or 1*d*. When they have money they take a bed in a low lodging-house for 2*d*. or 3*d*. a night.

"We are often chased by the Thames police and the watermen, as the mudlarks are generally known to be thieves. I take what I can get as well as the rest when I get an opportunity.

"We often go on board of coal barges and knock or throw pieces of coal over into the mud, and afterwards come and take them away. We also carry off pieces of rope, or iron, or anything we can lay our hands on and easily carry off. We often take a boat and row on board of empty barges and steal small articles, such as pieces of canvas or iron, and go down into the cabins of the barges for this purpose, and are frequently driven off by the police and bargemen. The Thames police often come upon us and carry off our bags and baskets with the contents.

"The mudlarks are generally good swimmers. When a barge-man gets hold of them in his barge on the river, he often throws them into the river, when they swim ashore and then take off their wet clothes and dry them. They are often seized by the police in boats, in the middle of the river, and thrown overboard, when they swim to the shore. I have been chased twice by a police galley.

"On one occasion I was swimming a considerable way out in

the river when I saw two or three barges near me, and no one in them. I leaped on board of one and went down into the cabin, when some of the Thames police in a galley rowed up to me. I ran down naked beneath the deck of the barge and closed the hatches, and fastened the staple with a piece of iron lying near, so that they could not get in to take me. They tried to open the hatch, but could not do it. After remaining for half-an-hour I heard the boat move off. On leaving the barge they rowed ashore to get my clothes, but a person on shore took them away, so that they could not find them. After I saw them proceed a considerable distance up the river I swam ashore and got my clothes again.

"One day, about three o'clock in the afternoon, as I was at Young's Dock, I saw a large piece of copper drop down the side of a vessel which was being repaired. On the same evening, as a ship was coming out of the docks, I stripped off my clothes and dived down several feet, seized the sheet of copper and carried it away, swimming by the side of the vessel. As it was dark, I was not observed by the crew nor by any of the men who opened the gates of the dock. I fetched it to the shore, and sold it that night to a marine-store dealer.

"I have been in the habit of stealing pieces of rope, lumps of coal, and other articles for the last two years; but my parents do not know of this. I have never been tried before the police court for any felony.

"It is my intention to go to sea, as my brothers have done, so soon as I can find a captain to take me on board his ship. I would like this much better than to be a coal-heaver on the river."

RECEIVERS OF STOLEN PROPERTY

WHEN we look to the number of common thieves prowling over the metropolis—the thousands living daily on beggary, prostitution, and crime—we naturally expect to find extensive machineries for the receiving of stolen property. These receivers are to be found in different grades of society, from the keeper of the miserable low lodging-houses and dolly shops in Petticoat Lane, Rosemary Lane, and Spitalfields, in the East End, and Dudley Street and Drury Lane in the West End of the metropolis, to the pawnbroker in Cheapside, the Strand, and Fleet Street, and the opulent Jews of Houndsditch and its vicinity, whose coffers are said to be overflowing with gold.

DOLLY SHOPS

As we walk along Dudley Street, near the Seven Dials,—the Petticoat Lane of the West End,—a curious scene presents itself to our notice. There we do not find a colony of Jews, as in the East End, but a colony of Irish shopkeepers, with a few cockneys and Jews intermingled among them. Dudley Street is a noted mart for old clothes, consisting principally of male and female apparel, and second-hand boots and shoes.

We pass by several shops without sign-boards—which by the way is a characteristic of this strange by-street—where boots and shoes, in general sadly worn, are exposed on shelves under the window, or carefully ranged in rows on the pavement before the shop. We find a middle-aged or elderly Irishman with his leathern apron, or a young Irish girl brushing shoes at the door, in Irish accent inviting customers to enter their shop.

We also observe old clothes stores, where male apparel is suspended on wooden rods before the door, and trousers, vests, and coats of different descriptions, piled on chairs in front of the shop. or exposed in the dirty unwashed windows, while the shopmen loiter before the door, hailing the customers as they pass by.

Alongside of these we see what is more strictly called dolly or leaving shops—the fertile hot-beds of crime. The dolly shop is often termed an unlicensed pawn-shop. Around the doorway, in some cases of ordinary size, in others more spacious, we see a great assortment of articles, chiefly of female dress, suspended on the wall—petticoats, skirts, stays, gowns, shawls, and bonnets of all patterns and sizes, the gowns being mostly of dirty cotton, spotted and striped; also children's petticoats of different kinds, shirt-fronts, collars, handkerchiefs, and neckerchiefs exposed in the window. As we look into these suspicious-looking shops we see large piles of female apparel, with articles of men's dress heaped around the walls, or deposited in bundles and paper packages on shelves around the shop, with strings of clothes hung across the apartment to dry, or offered for sale. We find in some of the back-rooms, stores of shabby old clothes, and one or more women of various ages loitering about.

In the evening these dolly shops are dimly lighted, and look still more gloomy and forbidding than during the day.

Many of these people buy other articles besides clothes. They are in the habit of receiving articles left with them, and charge 2*d*. or 3*d*. a shilling on the articles, if redeemed in a week. If not redeemed for a week, or other specified time, they sell the articles, and dispose of them, having given the party a miserably small sum, perhaps only a sixth or eighth part of their value. These shops are frequented by common thieves, and by poor dissipated creatures living in the dark slums and alleys in the vicinity, or residing in low lodging-houses. The persons who keep them often conceal the articles deposited with them from the knowledge of the police, and get punished as receivers of stolen property. Numbers of such cases occur over the metropolis in low neighbourhoods. For this reason the keepers of these shops are often compelled to remove to other localities.

The articles they receive, such as old male and female wearing apparel, are also resetted by keepers of low coffee-houses and lodging-houses, and are occasionally bought by chandlers, low hairdressers, and others.

They also receive workmen's tools of an inferior quality, and cheap articles of household furniture, books, etc., from poor dissipated people, beggars, and thieves; many of which would be rejected by the licensed pawnbrokers.

They are frequently visited by the wives and daughters of the poorest labouring people, and others, who deposit wearing apparel, or bed-linen, with them for a small piece of money when they are in want of food, or when they wish to get some intoxicating liquor, in which many of them indulge too freely. They are also haunted by the lowest prostitutes on like errands. The keepers of dolly shops give more indulgence to their regular customers than they do to strangers. They charge a less sum from them, and keep their articles longer before disposing of them.

It frequently occurs that these low traders are very unscrupulous, and sell the property deposited with them when they can make a small piece of money thereby.

There is a pretty extensive traffic carried on in the numerous dolly shops scattered over the metropolis, as we may find from the extensive stores heaped up in their apartments, in many cases in such dense piles as almost to exclude the light of day, and from the groups of wretched creatures who frequent them— particularly in the evenings.

The principal trade in old clothes is in the East End of the metropolis—in Rosemary Lane, Petticoat Lane, and the dark by-streets and alleys in the neighbourhood, but chiefly at the Old Clothes Exchange, where huge bales are sold in small quantities to crowds of traders, and sent off to various parts of Scotland, England, and Ireland, and exported abroad. The average weekly trade has been estimated at about £1,500.

PAWNBROKERS, ETC.

A GREAT amount of valuable stolen property passes into the hands of pawnbrokers and private receivers. The pawnbrokers often give only a third or fourth of the value of the article deposited with them, which lies secure in their hands for twelve months.

A good many of them deal honestly in their way, and are termed respectable dealers; but some of them deal in an illegal manner, and are punished as receivers. Many of those who are reputed as the most respectable pawnbrokers, receive stolen plate, jewellery, watches, etc.

When plate is stolen, it is sometimes carried away on the night of the robbery in a cab, or other conveyance, to the house of the burglars. Some thieves take it to a low beershop, where they lodge for the night; others to coffee-shops; others to persons living in private houses, pretending possibly to be bootmakers, watch-makers, copper-plate printers, tailors, marine-store dealers, etc. Such parties are private receivers well-known to the burglars. The doors of their houses are opened at any time of the night.

Burglars frequently let them know previously when they are going to work, and what they expect to get, and the crucible or silver pot is kept ready on a slow fire to receive the silver plate, sometimes marked with the crest of the owner. Within a quarter of an hour a large quantity is melted down. The burglar does not stay to see the plate melted, but makes his bargain, gets his money, and goes away.

These private receivers have generally an ounce and a quarter for their ounce of silver, and the thief is obliged to submit after he has gone into the house. The former are understood in many cases to keep quantities of silver on hand before they sell it to some of the refiners, or other dealers, who give them a higher price for it, generally 4*s*. 10*d*. per ounce. The burglar himself obtains only from 3*s*. 6*d*. to 4*s*. an ounce.

The receivers we refer to—well-known to the cracksmen of the metropolis—live at White Hart Yard, Catherine Street, Strand; Vinegar Yard, Catherine Street, Strand; Russell Street, Covent Garden; Gravel Lane; Union Street; Friars Street; Blackfriars' Road; Oakley Street; Westminster Road; Eagle Street, Holborn; King Street, Seven Dials; Wardour Street, Oxford Street; Tottenham Place, Tottenham Court Road; Upper Afton Place, Newport Market; George's Street, Hampstead Road; Clarendon Street, Somers Town; Philip's Buildings, Somers Town; New North Place and Judd Street, Gray's Inn Road; Red Lion Street, Clerkenwell; Wilderness Row, Clerkenwell; Golden Lane; Banner Street; Banner Row; Long Alley; Tim Street; Middlesex Street, Whitechapel; Brick Lane, Whitechapel; Halfmoon Passage, Union Street, Spitalfields; Whitechapel Road; Commercial Road; Rosemary Lane, and other localities.

These persons receive plate, silk, satins, and other valuable booty.

There are also several refiners in different parts of the metropolis who generally have silver pots or crucibles on the fire ready to melt whatever plate may be taken in. Some of them are German Jews, others are English people.

These furnaces are generally in a small workshop or parlour at the back of the shop. These receivers profess to sell jewellery, lace, and other articles, which are exposed in the shop windows. They are licensed to buy gold and silver, and offer to give fair value for precious stones.

The jewellery stolen is taken to these same fences and sold at less than a third of its value. The names are then erased, and the articles are taken to pieces, and sold to different jewellers over the metropolis. Stolen bank-notes and jewellery are often sent abroad by these fences to avoid detection.

The following prices are generally received from the fences for stolen bank-notes: —

> For a £5 bank-note, from £4 to £4 10s.
> „ £10 „ „ £8 15s. to £9.
> „ £20 „ about £16 10s.
> „ £50 „ „ £35.

As the notes rise in value they give a smaller proportionate sum for them, as they may have more trouble in getting them exchanged.

Silks and satins, and such like goods, are often conveyed to the fence in a cab on the night or morning the robbery is effected; the dealer generally gets previous notice, and expects to receive them.

In addition to the watch set at the house where the robbery is to be committed, there is often a watch stationed near the house of the receiver to look after the movements of the policeman in his locality. One of the burglars goes in the cab direct from the shop or warehouse where the robbery has been committed to the house of the receiver, and possibly at a short distance from the house gets a quiet signal from the watch as to whether it is safe to approach. If not, he can make a detour with the cab, and come back a little afterwards when the coast is clear. The burglar and the cabman remove the bags of goods into the house of the receiver, when the vehicle drives off. The driver of the cab is generally paid according to the value of the booty.

Sometimes these goods are taken to a coffee-house, where the people are acquainted with the burglars, and where one of the burglars remains till the booty is sold and removed, or otherwise disposed of. The fence, who has got notice of the plunder from some of the thieves, often comes and takes it away himself. The keeper of the coffee-house is well paid for his trouble.

Silks and satins are generally sold to the fence at 1s. a yard, whatever the quality of the fabric. Silk handkerchiefs of excellent quality are sold at 1s. each; good broadcloth from 4s. to 5s. a yard, possibly worth from £1 1s. to £1 5s.; neckties, sold in the shops from 1s. 6d. to 2s. each, are given away for 4d. to 6d. each; kid-gloves, worth from 2s. to 3s. 6d., are sold at 6d. a pair; and women's boots, worth from 6s. 6d. to 10s. 6d., are given for 2s.

Silks and satins of the value of £4,500, have been sold for £515, the chief proportion of the spoil thus coming into the hands of the unprincipled receiver.

Numerous cases of receiving stolen property are tried at our police-courts and sessions, as well as at the Old Bailey. We shall only adduce one illustration.

Some time ago a bale of goods was stolen from a passage in a warehouse in the City. The case was put in the hands of the police. They were a peculiar class of goods. Information was given to persons in that line of business. A few weeks after it was ascertained that the stolen property had been offered for sale by a person who produced a sample. They were ultimately traced to a place in the City, not far distant from where they had been stolen. They were seized by two officers of police. The man who was selling them was an agent, and had no hand in the robbery. He would not give up the name of the person who had sent them to him. He was taken into custody, and he and the goods were sent to the police station.

Seeing the dilemma in which he was placed, this man, when in custody, stated that he had received the goods from a well-known Jewish dealer, who was thereupon arrested. On searching his premises the officers found a great part of the booty of twelve burglaries, and of three other robberies, one of them being a quantity of jewellery of great value, the whole of the property amounting to from £2,000 to £3,000.

He was tried, convicted, and sentenced to fourteen years' transportation.

From the statistics of the metropolitan police we find the number of houses of bad character, which may be used to receive stolen property, to be as follows:—

163 houses of receivers of stolen goods.
255 public-houses.
103 beer-shops.

The resort of thieves and prostitutes.

154 coffee-shops.
101 other suspected houses.
1,706 brothels and houses of ill-fame.
361 tramps' lodging-houses.

2,843

THE BONE-GRUBBER

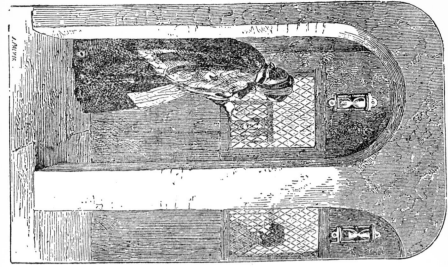

Compartment on the side for Visitors

FRIENDS VISITING PRISONERS

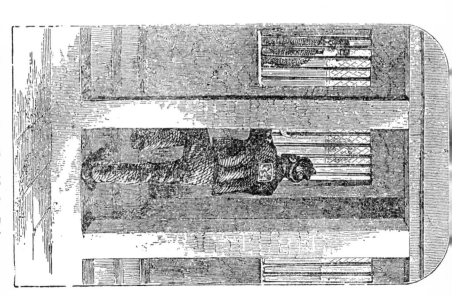

Compartment on the side for Prisoners

NARRATIVE OF A RETURNED CONVICT

WE give the following brief autobiography of a person who has recently returned from one of our penal settlements, having been transported for life. In character he is very different from the generality of our London thieves, having hot African blood in his veins and being a man of passionate, unbridled character. He was formerly a daring highway robber. He was introduced to us accidentally in Drury Lane by a Bow Street police officer, who occasionally acts as a detective. On this occasion the latter displayed very little tact and discretion, which made it exceedingly difficult for us to get from him even the following brief tale:—

"I was born in a tent at Southampton, on the skirts of a forest, among the gipsies, my father and mother being of that stock of people. We had generally about seven or eight tents in our encampment, and were frequently in the forest between Surrey and Southampton. The chief of our gang, termed the gipsy king, had great influence among us. He was then a very old, silver-headed man, and had a great number of children. I learned when a boy to play the violin, and was tolerably expert at it. I went to the public-houses and other dwellings in the neighbourhood, with three or four other gipsy boys, who played the triangle and drum, as some of the Italian minstrels do. We went during the day and often in the evening. At other times we had amusement beside the tents, jumping, running, and single-stick, and begged from the people passing by in the vehicles or on foot.

"During the day some of the men of our tribe went about the district, and looked out over the fields for horses which would suit them, and came during the night and stole them away. They never carried away horses from the stables. They generally got their booty along the by-roads, and took them to the fairs in the neighbourhood and sold them, usually for about £10 or £12. The horses they stole were generally light and nimble, such as might be useful to themselves. They disfigured them by putting a false mark on them, and by clipping their mane and tail. When a horse is in good order they keep it for a time till it becomes more thin and lank, to make it look older. They let the horse generally go loose on the side of a road at a distance from their encampment, till they have an opportunity to sell it; and it is generally placed alongside one or two other horses, so that it is not so much observed. The same person who steals it frequently takes it to the fair to be sold.

"The gipsies are not so much addicted to stealing from farms as is generally supposed. They are assisted in gaining a livelihood by their wives and other women going over the district telling fortunes. Some of them take to hawking for a livelihood. This is done by boys and girls, as well as old men and women. They sell baskets, brushes, brooms, and other articles.

"I spent my early years wandering among the gipsies till I was thirteen years of age, and was generally employed going about the country with my violin, along with some of my brothers.

"My father died when I was about six years of age. A lady in Southampton, of the Methodist connexion, took an interest in my brothers and me, and we settled there with our mother, and afterwards learned coach-making. I lived with my mother in Southampton for five or six years. My brothers were well-behaved, industrious boys, but I was wild and disobedient.

"The first depredation I committed was when thirteen years old. I robbed my mother of a box of old-fashioned coins and other articles, and went to Canterbury, where I got into company with prostitutes and thieves. The little money I had was soon spent.

"After this I broke the window of a pawnbroker's shop as a cart was passing by, put my hand through the broken pane of glass, and carried off a bowl of gold and silver coins, and ran off with them and made my way to Chatham.

"Some time after this I was, one day at noon, in the highway between Chatham and Woolwich, when I saw a carriage come up. The postillion was driving the horses smartly along. A gentleman and lady were inside, and the butler and a female servant were on the seat behind. I leaped on the back of the conveyance as it was driving past, and took away the portmanteau with the butler's clothes, and carried it off to the adjoining woods. I sold them to a Jew at Southampton for £3 or £4.

"Shortly after I came up to London, and became acquainted with a gang of young thieves in Ratcliffe Highway. I lived in a coffee-house there for about eighteen months. The boys gained their livelihood picking gentlemen's pockets, at which I soon became expert. After this I joined a gang of men, and picked ladies' pockets, and resided for some time at Whitechapel.

"Several years after I engaged with some other men in highway robbery. I recollect on one occasion we learned that a person was in the habit of going to one of the City banks once a week for a large sum of money—possibly to pay his workmen. He was generally in the habit of calling at other places in town on business, and carried the money with him in a blue serge bag. We followed him from the bank to several places where he made calls, until he came to a quiet by-street near London Bridge. It was a dark wintry night, and very stormy. I rushed upon him and garotted him, while one of my companions plundered him of his bag. He was a stout old man, dressed like a farmer. I was then about twenty-two years of age.

"At this time I went to music and dancing saloons, and played on my violin.

"Soon after I went to a fair at Maidstone with several thieves, all young men like myself. One of us saw a farmer in the market, a robust middle-aged man, take out his purse with a large sum of money. We followed him from the market. I went a little in advance of my companions for a distance of sixteen miles, till we came to a lonely cross turning surrounded with woods. The night happened to be dark. I went up to him and seized him by the leg, and pulled him violently off his horse, and my companions came up to assist me. While he lay on the ground we rifled his pockets of a purse containing about £500 and some silver money. He did not make very much resistance and we did not injure him. We came back to London and shared the booty among us.

"About the time of the great gathering of the Chartists on Kennington Common, in 1848, I broke into a pawnbroker's shop in the metropolis and stole jewellery to the amount of £2,000, consisting of watches, rings, etc., and also carried off some money. I sold the jewels to a Jewish receiver for about £500. I was arrested some time after, and tried for this offence, and sentenced to transportation for life.

"I returned from one of the penal settlements about a year ago, and have since led an honest life."

COINING

THIS class of felonies is as prevalent as ever in the metropolis, and is carried on in many of the low neighbourhoods.

It is generally effected in this way. Take a shilling, or other sterling coin, scour it well with soap and water; dry it, and then grease it with suet or tallow; partly wipe this off, but not wholly. Take some plaster of Paris, and make a collar either of paper or tin. Pour the plaster of Paris on the piece of coin in the collar or band round it. Leave it until it sets or hardens, when the impression will be made. You turn it up and the piece sticks in the mould. Turn the reverse side, and you take a similar impression from it; then you have the mould complete. You put the pieces of mould together, and then pare it. You make a channel in order to pour the metal into it in a state of fusion, having the neck of the channel as small as possible. The smaller the channel the less the imperfection in the "knerling."

You make claws to the mould, so that it will stick together while you pour the metal into it. But before doing so, you must properly dry it. If you pour the hot metal into it when damp, it will fly in pieces. This is the general process by which counterfeit coin is made. When you have your coin cast, there is a "gat," or piece of refuse metal, sticks to it. You pare this off with a pair of scissors or a knife—generally a pair of scissors—then you file the edges of the coin to perfect the "knerling."

The coin is then considered finished, except the coating. At this time it is of a bluish colour, and not in a state fit for circulation, as the colour would excite suspicion.

You get a galvanic battery with nitric acid and sulphuric acid, a mixture of each diluted in water to a certain strength. You then get some cyanide and attach a copper wire to a screw of the battery. Immerse that in the cyanide of silver when the process of electro-plating commences.

The coin has to pass through another process. Get a little lampblack and oil, and make it into a sort of composition, "slumming" the coin with it. This takes the bright colour away and makes it fit for circulation. Then wrap the coins up separately in paper so as to prevent them rubbing. When coiners are going to circulate them, they take them up and rub each piece separately. The counterfeit coin will then have the greatest resemblance to genuine coin, if well-manufactured.

While this is the general mode by which it is made, a skilful artificer, or keen-eyed detective, can trace the workmanship of different makers.

Counterfeit coin is manufactured by various classes of people —costermongers, mechanics, tailors, and others—and is generally confined to the lower classes of various ages. Girls of thirteen years of age sometimes assist in making it.

It is made in Westminster, Clerkenwell, the Borough, Lambeth, Drury Lane, the Seven Dials, Lisson Grove, and other low neighbourhoods of the metropolis, at all hours of the day and night.

There are generally two persons engaged in making it—sometimes four. In nine cases out of ten, men and women are employed in it together. The man generally holds the mould with an iron clamp, that is an iron hook doubled in the shape of plyers or tongues, to prevent the heat from burning their hands. The women, generally pour the metal into it. One person could make the coin alone, but this would be too tedious. While engaged in this work they fasten the doors of their room or dwelling, and have generally a person on the look-out they term a "crow," in case the officers of justice should make their appearance, and detect them in the act.

The officers make a simultaneous rush into the house after having forced open the door with a blow from a sledge-hammer, so as to detect the parties in the very act of coining. On such occasions the men endeavour to destroy the mould, while the women throw the counterfeit coin into the fire, or into the melted metal, which effectually injures it. This is done to prevent the officers getting these articles into their possession as evidence against them.

The coiners frequently throw the hot metal at the officers, or the acids they use in their coining processes, or they attempt to strike them with a chair or stool, or other weapon that comes in their way. In most cases they resist until they are overpowered and secured.

Counterfeit coin is generally made of Britannia metal spoons and other ingredients, and very seldom of pewter pots, though formerly this was the case.

. Sometimes four impressions are cast from each mould at the same instant; in other cases two or three. If too near each other the powerful heat of the metal in casting half-crowns or crowns would make the moulds fly. Hence there must be spaces between each impression. Smaller coins, such as sixpences or shillings, can be placed nearer to each other in the mould. On each occasion when they cast the coin they blow the dust off the mould to keep it perfectly clear, so as not to injure in the slightest degree the impression. When the latter is imperfect a new mould must be made. The coiner can use the same mould again in less than a minute to make other counterfeit coins.

Sometimes a quart basinful is made on a single occasion; at other times a very small quantity only.

The coiners have agents at different public-houses to dispose of their counterfeit coin, and some of them stand in the street to sell it. Sometimes it is sold to their private agents in their own dwellings, or sent out to parties who purchase it from them. The latter parties generally pay 1*d.* for a shilling's worth. Then these agents sell it to the utterers for 2*d.* a shilling, 3*d.* for two shillings, 3½*d.* for a half-crown, and 4*d.* a crown. Some coiners charge 5*d.* for five shillings' worth.

The detection of counterfeit coin in the metropolis is under the able management of Mr. Brennan, a skilful and experienced public officer, who keeps a keen surveillance over this department of crime.

In 1855 Mr. Brennan, along with Inspector Bryant of G Division, and other officers, went to the neighbourhood of Kent Street for the purpose of apprehending a person of the name of Green, better known by the cognomen of "Charcoal." The street door was open, and the officers proceeded to the top floor up a winding staircase. The house consisted of three floors. On passing upstairs they were met by three men on the top landing, very robust, their ages averaging from twenty-four to thirty-six. One of them, named Brown, was a noted Devonshire wrestler, and a powerful-bodied man.

These men attempted to force their way down. Mr. Brennan manfully resisted and tried to keep them up, and force them back into the room. Brown leaped over him while struggling with the other two. On Mr. Brennan's son and Inspector Bryant coming up to his assistance, the other two men were arrested and secured in the yard.

A third man came out of the room and was passing by Mr. Brennan, and in doing so hit him on the head with a saucepan, and forced him against the staircase window. His son came up to his assistance, when he struck this new assailant on the arm with a crowbar, and partially disabled him. At this time the frame of the staircase window gave way and he fell into the court.

One of the men in the house jumped from the window of the staircase on the roof of a shed, and fell right through it, and was followed by Constable Neville, of the G Division, who jumped after him and secured him. The former was a man of about five feet eight inches high, powerfully built. Other two men were beaten back into the room and secured, along with two women. Five out of a party of seven men were arrested, and the other two effected their escape. The officers only expected to see one man and a woman in this house.

After they succeeded in forcing the two men back into the room, the man named "Charcoal" struggled desperately, and used every effort to smash the mould. They found sufficient fragments of it as evidence against them that they had been making half-crowns, shillings, and sixpences, besides a large quantity of counterfeit coin.

The officers were obliged to remain in the house and yard until they sent to the police station for additional assistance. The prisoners were tried at the Old Bailey and sentenced to various terms of imprisonment, from six months to fourteen years. The Recorder from the bench recommended to Mr. Brennan a compensation of £10 for the manly and efficient part he had acted on this trying occasion.

In 1845 Mr. Brennan received information that a man who resided at Bath Place, Old Street Road, was making counterfeit coin. This house consisted of two rooms, the one above the other. Mr. Brennan went there, accompanied by Sergeant Cole of the G Division, leaving a police-constable at the end of the court. He broke open the door with a sledge-hammer, and attempted to run upstairs, and was met at the door by the coiner, who tried to rush back into the room, when the former seized him by a leathern apron he had on. In the struggle both he and Mr. Brennan were hurled down to the bottom of the staircase, a distance of eleven steps. The officer was severely injured on the back of the head, and the coiner's knee struck against his belly, yet this brave officer, though severely injured, kept hold of the coiner.

At this time Cole was struggling with the coiner's wife and daughter, while their bull-dog seized him by the leg of his trousers. The dog kept hold of him for about twenty-five minutes. Latterly the three parties were secured.

Meanwhile the constable whom he had left at the end of the court heard the disturbance, and entered and assisted in securing the prisoners.

The woman was tall and masculine in appearance, and the girl was thirteen years of age.

On securing this desperate coiner Mr. Brennan proceeded upstairs and found four galvanic batteries in full play, and about five hundred pieces of counterfeit coin in various stages of manufacture—crowns, half-crowns, shillings and sixpences. The prisoner was committed to Newgate for trial. His wife was acquitted, she having acted under his direction. He was sentenced to fifteen years' transportation. The girl was sentenced to two years' imprisonment for the exceedingly active part she had taken in the affair.

Mr. Brennan on this occasion was severely injured in his gallant struggle.

Several years ago Mr. Brennan went to apprehend a man of the name of Morris near Westminster. The street door of the house, which consisted of three stories, was shut, but was suddenly burst open by the blow of a sledge-hammer. On running up to the top floor he found his hat struck against something, and found there was a flap let down over the "well" of the staircase, which was dreadfully armed with iron spikes of about three or four inches long, and about the same distance apart, and it seemed utterly impossible to force it up.

The man meantime effected his escape through the roof, and ran along the roofs and jumped a depth of twenty-five feet on the roof of a shed, and was much injured. He was carried away by his friends to Birmingham, and kept in a hospital till he recovered. He then left London for two years.

Afterwards he made his appearance in the neighbourhood of Kent Street in the Borough, where Mr. Brennan went to apprehend him, assisted by several other officers. He paid him a visit at seven o'clock on a winter's evening. The coiner was sitting in the middle of the floor making half-crowns. One of the windows of the house was open. On hearing the officers approach he jumped clean out of the window on the back of an officer who was stationed there to watch—the height of one storey. Mr. Brennan followed him as he ran off without his coat along some adjoining streets, and caught sight of him passing through a back door that led into some gardens. Here he fled into a house, the floor of which went down a step. There was a bed in the room with three children in it. Mr. Brennan missed his footing and fell across the bed, and narrowly escaped injuring one of the children by the fall. The father and mother of the children were standing at the fire. The man stepped forward to the officer and was about to use violence when Mr. Brennan told him who he was and his errand, which quieted him.

Meantime Mr. Brennan tripped up the coiner as he was endeavouring to escape, and threw him on the floor, secured him and put him into a cab, where a low mob, which had meantime gathered in this disreputable neighbourhood, tried to rescue the coiner from the hands of the officers. They threw brickbats, stones and other missiles to rescue the prisoner.

While the officers were conveying him to the police-station this coiner, while handcuffed, endeavoured to throw himself in a fit of frantic passion beneath the wheels of a waggon to destroy himself, but was prevented by the officers. When in Horsemonger Gaol he refused for a time to take any food.

He was tried at the Old Bailey, and sentenced to thirty years' transportation for coining and assaulting the officers in the execution of their duty.

FORGERS

FORGERY is the fraudulent making or altering a written instrument, to the detriment of another person. To constitute a forgery it is not necessary that the whole instrument should be fictitious. Making an insertion, alteration, or erasure, on any material part of a genuine document, by which any of the lieges may be defrauded; the insertion of a false signature to a true instrument, or a real signature to a false one, or the altering of the date of a bill after acceptance, are all forgeries. There are different classes of these. For example, there are forgeries of bank notes, of cheques, of acceptances, wills, and other documents.

Bank Notes

THERE are many forgeries of Bank of England notes, executed principally at Birmingham. In the engraving and general appearance the counterfeit so closely resembles the genuine note that an inexperienced eye might be easily deceived. The best way to detect them is carefully to look to the water-mark embossed in the paper, which is not like a genuine note. When the back of the former is carefully inspected, the water-mark will be found to be indented, or pressed into the paper. The paper of a forged note is generally of a darker colour than a good one. To take persons off their guard, forgers frequently make the notes very dirty, so as to give them the appearance of a much-worn good note. They are frequently uttered by pretended horse-dealers, in fairs and markets, and at hotels and public-houses by persons who pretend to be travellers, and who order goods from trades-people in the provincial towns and pay them with forged notes. This is often done before banking hours on the Monday, when they might be detected, but by this time the person who may have offered them has left the town. This is the common way of putting them off in London and the other towns in England. Sometimes they utter them by sending a woman, dressed as a servant, to a public-house or to a tradesman for some article, and in this manner get them exchanged—perhaps giving the address of her master as residing in the vicinity, which is sure to be false. Tradesmen are frequently taken off their guard by this means, and give an article, often of small value, with the change in return for a note. They sometimes do not discover it to be false till several days afterwards, when it is taken to the bank and detected there.

An experienced banking clerk or a keen-eyed detective, ac-customed to inspect such notes, know them at once. It sometimes happens they are so well executed that they pass through provin-cial banks, and are not detected till they come to the Bank of England.

They generally consist of £5 or £10 notes, and are given to agents who sell them to the utterer, and the makers are not known to them. Knowingly to have in our possession a forged bank note, without a lawful excuse, the proof of which lies on the party charged, or to have forging instruments in our possession, is a criminal offence.

There are also forged notes of provincial banks, but these are not so numerous as those of the Bank of England. The provincial banks have generally colours and engine-turned engraving on their notes. Some have a portion of the note pink, green, or other colours, more difficult and expensive to forge than the Bank of England note, which is on plain paper with an elaborate water-mark.

Numerous cases occur before the criminal courts, where utterers of forged notes are convicted and punished.

A case of this kind was tried at Guildhall, in October, 1861. A marine-store dealer in Lower Whitecross Street was charged with feloniously uttering two forged Bank of England notes for £5 and £10, with the intent to defraud Mr. Crouch, the proprietor of the "Queen's Head" tavern, in Whitecross Street. The store-dealer had waited on him to get them exchanged. Mr. Crouch paid them to his distiller, who took them to the Bank of England, when they were sent back, detected as forgeries.

The prisoner was committed to Newgate.

Many forged notes of the Bank of England are now in circulation. They may be detected by wetting them, when the watermark disappears. The vignette is often clumsily engraved. In other respects the forgery is cleverly executed.

Cheques

A CHEQUE is a draft or order on a banker, by a person who has money in the bank, directing the banker to pay the sum named therein to the bearer or the person named in the cheque, which must be signed by the drawer. Cheques are generally payable to the bearer, but sometimes made payable to the person who is named therein. The place of issue must be named, and the cheque must bear the date of issue. A *crossed* cheque has the name of a banker written across the face of it, and must be paid through that banker. If presented by any other person it is not paid without rigid inquiry. The word banker includes any person, corporation, or Joint-Stock Company, acting as bankers.

The form of the cheque is seldom forged; it is generally the signature. Sometimes the body of the cheque that contains the genuine signature is forged. For instance, in a cheque for eight pounds the letter "y" may be added to the word "eight," which makes it "eighty"; and a cypher appended to the figure "8", making it "80", to correspond with the writing. The forms of cheques are frequently obtained by means of a forged order, such as A knowing B to have an account at a bank, A writes a letter to the banker purporting to come from B, asking for a cheque-book, which the banker frequently sends on the faith of the letter being genuine. Sometimes cheque-books are stolen by burglars and other thieves who enter business premises. By some device they get the signature of a person who has money in that bank, and forge it to the stolen cheques. It has been known for forgers who wanted to obtain money from a bank, to go to a solicitor whom they knew kept a bank account. One of them would instruct the solicitor to enter an action against one of his confederates for a pretended debt. After proceedings had been instituted the party would pay the amount claimed to the solicitor; and his companion, who had given instructions in reference to the action, then goes and gets a cheque for the amount, and by that means obtains the genuine signature, and is enabled to insert a facsimile of it in forged cheques. By this means he obtains money from the bank. Cases of this kind very frequently occur.

Sometimes forgeries are done by clerks and others who have an opportunity of getting the signature of their employer. They forge his name, or alter the body of the cheque. In many commercial houses the body of the cheque is filled up by the confidential clerk and taken to the head of the firm, who signs it. These forgeries are sometimes for a small sum, at other times for a large amount.

Several cases of uttering forged cheques were lately tried before the police-courts.

A respectable-looking young woman, who described herself as a domestic servant, was brought before the Lord Mayor, charged with uttering a cheque for £5 18*s*., purporting to be signed by Mr. W. P. Bennett, with intent to defraud a banking firm in London. She had recently been on a visit to London and had been lent a small sum of money by another servant in town, along with some dresses, amounting to 10*s*. 6*d*.

On the 30th October the latter young woman received a letter from the prisoner enclosing a forged cheque, and at the same time stating that a young man with whom she had been keeping company had died, and had given her this cheque to get cashed. If the servant could not get away to get the cheque cashed, the prisoner wished her to lend her what she was able, to go to the young man's funeral. On presenting the cheque at the banker's the forgery was discovered.

It appeared from the evidence that the prisoner had been lodging in the same house with Mr. Bennett, whose signature she forged.

A young man of respectable appearance residing in the neighbourhood of Fleet Street, was tried at Guildhall lately, charged with uttering a cheque for £6, well knowing the same to be a forgery. He had gone to the landlord of a public-house in Essex Street, Bouverie Street, and asked him to cash it. It was drawn by Josiah Evans in favour of C. B. Bennett, Esq., and indorsed by the latter. The cheque was on Sir Benjamin Hayward, Bart., and Co., of Manchester. When presented at the bank it was returned with a note stating that no such person had an account there, and they did not know any of the names. The criminal was then arrested, and committed for trial.

Forged Acceptance

A BILL of exchange is a mercantile contract written on a slip of paper, whereby one person requests another to pay money on his account to a third person at the time therein specified. The person who draws the bill is termed the drawer, the party to whom it is addressed before acceptance is called the drawee—afterwards the acceptor. The party for whom it is drawn is termed the payee, who indorses the bill, and is then styled the indorser, and the party to whom he transfers it is called the indorsee. The person in possession of the bill is termed the holder.

An acceptance is an engagement to pay the bill, the person writing the word accepted across the bill with his name under it. This may be *absolute* or *qualified*. An *absolute* acceptance is an engagement to pay the bill according to its request. A *qualified* acceptance undertakes to do it conditionally.

Bills are either inland or foreign. The inland bill is on one piece of paper; foreign bills generally consist of three parts called a "set"; so that should the bearer lose one, he may receive payment for the other. Each part contains a condition that it shall be paid provided the others are unpaid. These bills require to have a stamp of proper value to make them valid.

Forgeries of bills seldom consist of the whole bill, but either the acceptor's signature, or that of the drawer, or the indorser. Sometimes the contents of the bill is altered to make it payable earlier.

These forgeries are not so numerous, and are frequently done by parties who get the bills in a surreptitious way. It often happens that one party draws the bill in another name, forging the acceptance, and passes it to a third party who is innocent of the forgery. If the person who forged the acceptance pays the money to the bank where the bill is payable when it is due, the forgery is not detected. When he is not able to pay in the money it is discovered. It happens in this way: A, B and C are commercial men, A stands well in the commercial world; B draws a bill in his name, and without his knowledge. The name of A being good, the bill passes to C without any suspicion. If B can meet it at the time it is due, A does not know that his name has been used.

If the bill is not paid at the proper time, C takes it to A, and thus discovers the forgery.

Forged Wills

A WILL is a written document in which the testator disposes of his property after his death. It is not necessary that it should be written on stamped paper, as no stamp duty is required till the death of the testator, when the will is proved in court in the district where he resided. The essentials are that it should be legible, and so intelligible, that the testator's intention can be clearly understood.

If the will is not signed by the testator, it must be signed by some other person by his direction, and in his presence; two or more witnesses being present who must attest that the will was signed, and the signature acknowledged by the testator in their presence.

No will is valid unless signed at the foot of the page, or at the end by the testator, or by some other person in his presence, and by his direction. Marriage revokes a will previously made.

A codicil is a supplement, or addition to the will, altering some part, or making an addition. It may be written on the same document, or on another paper, and folded up with the original instrument. There can only be one will, yet there may be a number of codicils attached to it, and the last is equally binding as the first, if they are not contradictory.

Forgeries of wills are generally done by relations, who get a fictitious will prepared in their favour contrary to the genuine will. On the death of the supposed testator, the forged will is put forth as the genuine one, and the other is destroyed.

All parties expecting property on the death of a relative or friend, and finding none, should be careful to have the signatures of the witnesses examined, to test whether they are genuine; and also the signature of the testator.

Every will can be seen at the district court, where they are proved, on the payment of a shilling. Such an examination is the only likely method of detecting the forgery.

There are several other classes of forgery in addition to those already noticed, such as forging certificates of character, and bills of lading.

A case of the latter kind was recently tried at Guildhall. A merchant, near the Haymarket, and an artist also in the West End, were arraigned with having feloniously forged and altered certain bills of lading; one of these represented ten casks of alkali amounting to the value of £84, and another, twenty-six casks of alkali worth £140, with the intention of defrauding certain merchants in London. All the bills of lading were with one exception to a certain extent genuine, that is, were filled up in the first instance. But after being signed by the wharfinger, they were altered by the introduction of words and figures, to represent a larger quantity of goods than had been shipped. The prisoners were committed for trial.

CHEATS

EMBEZZLERS

THIS is the crime of a servant appropriating to his own use the money or goods received by him on account of his master, and is perpetrated in the metropolis by persons both in inferior and superior positions.

Were a party to advance money or goods to an acquaintance or friend, for which the latter did not give a proper return, the case would be different, and require to be sued for in a civil action.

Embezzlement is often committed by journeymen bakers entrusted by their employers with quantities of bread to distribute to customers in different parts of the metropolis, by brewer's draymen delivering malt liquors, by carmen and others engaged in their various errands. A case of this kind occurred recently. A carman in the service of a coal merchant in the West End was charged with embezzling £6 1s. 6d. He had been in the habit of going out with coals to customers, and was empowered to receive the money, but had gone into a public-house on his return, got intoxicated, and lost the whole of his cash. He was tried at Westminster Police Court, and sentenced to pay a fine of £10 with costs. This crime is frequent among this class. The chief inducements which lead to it are the habits of drinking, prevalent among them, gambling in beershops, attending music-saloons, such as the Mogul, Drury Lane, and Paddy's Goose, Ratcliffe Highway, and attending running matches. Their pay is not sufficient to enable them to indulge in those habits, and this leads them to commit the crime of embezzlement.

Persons in trade frequently send out their shopmen to receive orders, and obtain payment for goods supplied to families at their residence, and are occasionally entrusted with goods on stalls. In June, 1861, a respectable-looking young man was placed at the bar of the Southwark Police Court, charged with having embezzled £39, the property of a bookselling firm in the Strand. He had been entrusted with a stall where he sold books and newspapers, and was called to account for the receipts daily. One day he neglected to send £8, the receipts of the previous Saturday, and for other seven days he had given no proper count and reckoning. He admitted the neglect, and confessed he had appropriated the money. He was paid at the rate of £1 10*s.* a month, which with commission amounted to about £6 or £7.

A clerk and salesman in the service of a draper in Camberwell was charged with embezzling various sums of money belonging to this employer. It was his duty each night to account for the goods he disposed of, and the money he received. One morning he went out with a quantity of goods, and did not return at the proper time, when his employer found him in a beer-shop in the Blackfriars Road. On asking him what had become of the goods, he replied he had left them at a public-house in the Borough, which was untrue. In the account-book found upon him it was ascertained that he had received several sums of money he had not accounted for.

A robbery by a young man of this class was very ingeniously detected a few weeks ago, and brought before the Marlborough Street Police Court.

A shopman to a cheesemonger in Oxford Street was charged with stealing money from the till. He had been in his employer's service for ten months, and served at the counter along with three other shopmen. The cheesemonger having found a considerable deficiency in his receipts suspected his honesty, especially as he was in the habit of attending places of amusement, and indulging in other extravagances he knew were beyond his means. He marked three half-crowns and put them in the till to which the young man had access. Soon after he saw the latter put in his hand and take out a piece of money. He made an excuse to send the shopman out for a moment, and on examining the till, missed one of the marked pieces of money. He thereupon gave information to the police, and again placed money in the till similarly marked, leaving a police-officer on the watch. The shopman was again detected, he was then arrested, and taken to the police-station.

Many young men of this class are wretchedly paid by their employers and have barely enough to maintain them and keep them in decent clothing. Many of them spend their money foolishly on extravagant dress, or associating with girls, attending music-saloons, such as Weston's, in Holborn; the Pavilion, near the Haymarket; Canterbury Hall; the Philharmonic, Islington; and others. Some frequent the Grecian Theatre, City Road, and other gay resorts, and are led into crime. In one season eighteen girls were known to have been seduced by fast young men, and to become prostitutes through attending music-saloons in the neighbourhood of Tottenham Court Road.

Embezzlements are occasionally committed by females of various classes. Some of them, by fraudulent representations, obtain goods from various tradesmen, consisting of candles, soap, sugar, as on account of their customers. Some women of a higher class, such as dressmakers, and others, are entrusted with merinos, silks, satins, and other drapery goods which they embezzle.

A young married woman was lately tried at Guildhall on a charge of disposing of a quantity of silk entrusted to her. It appeared from the evidence of the salesman of the silk manufacturer, that this female applied to him for work, at the same time producing a written recommendation purporting to come from a person known by the firm. Materials to the value of £5 15s. were given her to be wrought up into an article of dress. On applying for it at the proper time, he found she had sold the materials, and had left her lodging. While the work was supposed to be in progress, the firm had also given her £2 13s. on partial payment. She pleaded poverty as the cause of her embezzling the goods.

Parties connected with public societies occasionally embezzle the money committed to their charge. The secretary of a friendly society in the East End was brought before the Thames Police Court, charged with embezzling various sums of money he had received on account of the society. The secretary of another friendly society on the Surrey side, was lately charged at Southwark Police Court with embezzling upwards of £100. This society has branches in all parts of the kingdom, but the central office is in the metropolis. The secretary had been in their service for upwards of two years, at a fixed salary. It was his duty to receive contributions from the country, and town members; and to account for the same to the treasurer. He recently absconded, when large defalcations were discovered amounting to upwards of £100.

A considerable number of embezzlements are committed by commercial travellers, and by clerks in lawyers' offices, banks, commercial firms, and government offices. Some of them of great and serious amounts.

Tradesmen and others in the middle class, and some respectable labouring men, and mechanics, place their sons in counting-houses, or other establishments superior to their own position; these foolishly try to maintain the appearance of their fellow-clerks who have ampler pecuniary means. This often leads to embezzling the property of the employer or firm.

Crimes of this class are occasionally committed by lawyers' clerks, who are in many cases wretchedly paid, as well as by some who have handsome salaries. Numerous embezzlements are also perpetrated in commercial firms, by their servants; some of them to the value of many thousand pounds.

A commercial traveller was lately brought up at the Mansion House, charged with embezzlement. It appears he travelled for a firm in the City, and had been above ten years in their service at a salary of £1 1s. per day. It was his duty to take orders and collect accounts as they became due. Some days he received from the customers certain sums and afterwards paid a less amount to the firm, keeping the rest of the money in his hands, which he appropriated. Another day he received a sum of money he never accounted for. He was committed for trial.

An embezzlement was committed by a cashier to a commercial firm in the City. It appeared from the evidence, he had been in the service of his employers for ten years, and kept the petty cash-book; with an account of all sums paid. He had to account for the amounts given him as petty cash, and for disbursements whenever he should be called.

From the extravagant style in which he was living, which reached the ear of the firm, their suspicions were aroused, and one of them asked him to bring his books into the counting-house, and render the customary account of the petty cash. His employer discovered the balance of some of the pages did not correspond with the balance brought forward, and asked the cashier to account for it, when he acknowledged that he had appropriated the difference to his own use.

Several items were then pointed out, ranging over a number of months, in which he had plundered his employers of several hundred pounds. This was effected in a very simple way; by carrying the balance of the cash in hand to the top of next page £100 less than it was on the preceding page, and by calling the disbursements when his employers checked the accounts, £100 more than they really were.

The books of commercial firms are frequently falsified in other modes, to effect embezzlements.

These defalcations often arise from fast life, extravagant habits, and gambling. Many fashionable clerks in lawyers' offices, banks, and Government offices, frequent the Oxford and Alhambra music halls, the West End theatres, concerts, and operas. They attend the Holborn Assembly Room and the Argyle Rooms, and are frequently to be seen at masked balls, and at Cremorne Gardens during the season. They occasionally indulge in midnight carousals in the Turkish divans and supper-rooms. Some Government clerks have high salaries, and keep a mistress in fashionable style, with brougham and coachman, and footman; others maintain their family in a state their salary is unable to support, all of which lead step by step to embezzlement and ruin.

MAGSMEN, OR SHARPERS

This is a peculiar class of unprincipled men, who play tricks with cards, skittles, &c., &c., and lay wagers with the view of cheating those strangers who may have the misfortune to be in their company.

Their mode of operation is this: There are generally three of them in a gang—seldom or never less. They go out together, but do not walk beside each other when they are at work. One may be on one side of the street, and the other two arm-in-arm on the other. They generally dress well, and in various styles; some are attired as gentlemen, others as country farmers. In one gang, a sharper dressed as a coachman in livery, and in another they have a confederate attired as a parson, and wearing green spectacles.

Many of them start early in the morning from the bottom of Holborn Hill, and branch off in different directions in search of dupes. They frequent Fleet Street, Oxford Street, Strand, Regent Street, Shoreditch, Whitechapel, Commercial Road, the vicinity of the railway stations, and the docks. They are generally to be seen wandering about the streets till four o'clock in the afternoon, unless they have succeeded in picking up a stranger likely to be a victim. They visit the British Museum, St. Paul's, Westminster Abbey, and the Crystal Palace, &c., and on market days attend the fairs.

The person who walks the street in front of the gang is generally the most engaging and social; the other two keep in sight, and watch his movements. As the former proceeds along he keenly observes the persons passing. If he sees a countryman or foreigner pass who appears to have money, or a person loitering by a shop-window, he steps up to him and probably enters into conversation regarding some object in sight.

For instance, in passing Somerset House in the Strand, he will go up to him and ask what noble building that is, hinting at the same time that he is a stranger in London. Having entered into conversation, the first object he has in view is to learn from the person the locality to which he belongs. The sharp informs him he has some relation there, or knows some person in the town or district. (Many of the magsmen have travelled a good deal, and are acquainted with many localities, some of them speak several foreign languages.) He may then represent that he has a good deal of property, and is going back to this village to give so much money to the poor. It sometimes occurs in the course of conversation he proposes to give the stranger a sum of money to distribute among the poor of his district, as he is specially interested in them, and may at the same time produce his pocket-book, with a bundle of flash notes. This may occur in walking along the street. He will then propose to enter a beer-shop, or gin-palace to have a glass of ale or wine. They go in accordingly. When standing at the bar, or seated in the parlour, one of his confederates enters, and calls for a glass of liquor.

This party appears to be a total stranger to his companion. He soon enters as it were casually into conversation, and they possibly speak of their bodily strength. A bet is made that one of them cannot throw a weight as many yards as the other. They make a wager, and the stranger is asked to go with them as referee, to decide the bet. They may call a cab, and adjourn to some well-known skittle-alley. On going there they find another confederate, who also pretends to be unacquainted with the others. One of the two who made the wager as to throwing the weight may pace the skittle-ground to find its dimensions, and pretend it is not long enough.

They will then possibly propose to have a game at skittles, and will bet with each other that they will throw down the pins in so many throws.

The sharp who introduced the stranger, and assumes to be his friend, always is allowed to win, perhaps from 5*s*. to 10*s*., or more, as the case may be. He plays well, and the other is not so good. Up to this time the intended victim has no hand in the game. Another bet is made, and the stranger is possibly induced to join in it with his agreeable companion, and it is generally arranged that he wins the first time.

He is persuaded to net for a higher amount by himself, and not in partnership, which he loses, and continues to do so every time till he has lost all he possessed.

He is invariably called out to the bar by the man who introduced him to the house, when they have a glass together, and in the meantime the others escape.

The sharp will say to the victim after staying there a short time, "I believe these men not to be honest; I'll go and see where they have gone, and try and get your money back." He goes out with the pretence of looking after them, and walks off. The victim proceeds in search of them, and finds they have decamped, leaving him penniless.

They have a very ingenious mode of finding out if the person they accost has money in his pocket. This is done after he is introduced into the public-house when getting a glass of ale. The second confederate comes in invariably. The two magsmen begin to converse as to the money they have with them. One pretends he has so much money, which the other will dispute. They possibly appear to get very angry, and one of them makes a bet that he can produce more money than any in the company. They then take out their cash, and induce the stranger to do so, to find which of them has got the highest amount. They thus learn how much money he has in his possession.

When they find he has a sufficient sum, they adjourn to a house they are accustomed to use for the purpose of paying the sum lost by the wager. It generally happens the stranger has most, and wins the bet.

On arriving at this house they wish a stamped receipt for the cash. Being a stranger he is asked as a security to leave something as a deposit till he returns. At the same time this sharp takes out a bag of money containing medals instead of sovereigns, or a pocket-book with flash notes.

He soon comes back with a receipt stamp, but a dispute invariably arises whether it will do. He suggests that someone else should go and get one. The stranger is urged to go for one. In the same manner he leaves money on the table as a security that he will return.

He may not know where to get the receipt stamp, and one of them proposes to accompany him. They walk along some distance together, when this man will say, "I don't much like these two men you have left your money with; do you know them?" He will then advise him to go back, and see if his cash is all right. On his return he finds them both gone, and his money has also disappeared.

We shall now notice several of the tricks they practise to delude their victims.

The Card Tricks

THESE are not often practised in London but generally at race-courses and country fairs, or where any pastime is going on. Only three cards are used. There is one picture card along with two others. They play with them generally on the ground or on their knee. There are always several persons in a gang at this game. One works the cards shuffling them together, and then deals them on the ground. They bet two to one no one will find the picture card (the Knave, King, or Queen). One of the confederates makes a bet that he can find it, and throws down a sovereign or half sovereign, as the case may be.

He picks up one of the cards, which will be the picture card, or the one they propose to find. The sharp dealing the cards bets that no one will find the same card again. Some simpleton in the crowd will possibly bet from £1 to £10 that he can find it. He picks up a card, which is not the picture card and cannot be, as it has been secretly removed from the pack, and another card has been substituted in its place.

Skittles

THEY generally depend on the ability of one of their gang when engaged in this game, so that he shall be able to take the advantage when wanted. When they bet and find their opponent is expert, he is expected to be able to beat him. In every gang there is generally one superior player. He may pretend to play indifferently for a time, but has generally superior skill, and wins the bet.

Thimble and Pea

IT is done in this way. There are three thimbles and a pea. These are generally worked by a man dressed as a countryman, with a smock-frock, at country fairs, racecourses, and other places without the metropolitan police district. They commence by working the pea from one thimble to another, similar to the card trick, and bet in the same way until some person in the company—not a confederate—will bet that he can find the pea. He lifts up one of the thimbles and ascertains that it is not there. Meantime the pea has been removed. It is secreted under the thumb nail of the sharp, and is not under either of the thimbles.

The Lock

WHILE the sharps are seated in a convenient house with their dupe, a man, a confederate of theirs, may come in, dressed as a hawker, offering various articles for sale. He will produce a lock which can be easily opened by a key in their presence. He throws the lock down on the table and bets anyone in the room they cannot open it. One of his companions will make a bet that he can open it. He takes it up, opens it easily, and wins the wager.

He will show the stranger how it is opened; after which, by a swift movement of his hand, he substitutes another similar lock in its place which cannot be opened. The former is induced possibly to bet that he is able to open it.

The lock is handed to him; he thinks it is the same and tries to open it, but does not succeed, and loses his wager.

There are various other tricks somewhat of a similar character, on which they lay wagers and plunder their dupes. They have a considerable number of moves with cards, and are ever inventing new dodges or "pulls" as they term them.

They chiefly confine themselves on most occasions to the tricks we have noticed. Sometimes, however, they play at whist, cribbage, roulette, loo, and other card games, and manage to get the advantage in many ways. One of them will look at the card of his opponent when playing, and will telegraph to some of the others by various signs and motions, understood among themselves, but unintelligible to a stranger.

The same sharpers who walk the streets of London attend country fairs and racecourses, in different dress and appearance, as if they had no connexion with each other.

If often happens one of them is arrested for these offences and is remanded. Before the expiry of the time his confederates generally manage to see the dupe, and restore his property on the condition he shall keep out of the way and allow the case to drop. The female who cohabits with him, or possibly his wife, may call on him for this purpose, and give him part or the whole of his money.

Their ages average from twenty to sixty years. Many of them are married and have families; others cohabit with well-dressed women—pickpockets and shoplifters.

Some are in better condition than others. They are occasionally shabbily dressed and in needy condition; at other times in most respectable attire—some appear as men of fashion.

They are generally very heartless in plundering their dupes. Not content with stripping him of the money he may have on his person—sometimes a large sum—they try to get the cash he has deposited in the bank, and strip him of his watch and chain, leaving him without a shilling in his pocket.

There is no formal association between the several gangs, yet from their movements there appears to be an understanding between them. For example, if a certain gang has plundered a victim in Oxford Street, it will likely remove to another district for a time, and another party of magsmen will take their place.

Magsmen are of various grades. Some are broken-down trades-men, others have been brokers and publicans and french-polishers, while part of their number are convicted felons. Numbers of them are betting-men and attend races; indeed, most of them are connected with this disreputable class. Many of them reside in the neighbourhood of Waterloo Road and King's Cross, and in quiet streets over the metropolis.

They are frequently brought before the police-courts, charged with conspiracy with intent to defraud; but the matter is in general secretly arranged with the prosecutor, and the case is allowed to drop.

Sometimes when the sharps cannot manage to defraud the strangers they meet with, they snatch their money from them with violence.

In the beginning of November, 1861, two sharps were brought before the Croydon police-court, charged with being concerned, with others not in custody, in stealing £116, the property of a baker, residing in the country.

As the prosecutor, a young man, was going along a country road he met one of the sharps and a man not in custody. At this time there were four men on the road playing cards. He remained for a few minutes looking at them. The man who was the companion of the sharp asked him to accompany him to a railway hotel, and ordered a glass of ale for himself.

A man not in custody then asked a sharp to lend him some money, saying he would get him good security: upon which the latter offered to lend him the sum of £50 at five per cent. interest. On the stranger being represented to this person as a friend, he offered to lend him as large a sum of money as he could produce himself, to show that he was a respectable and substantial person. The sharp then told the baker to go home and get £100 and he would lend him that sum. He did so, one of the sharps accompanying him nearly all the way to his house. The dupe returned with a £10 note. They told him it was not enough, and wished him to leave it in their hands and to bring £100. He went out leaving the £10 on the table as security for his coming back with more money.

He returned with £100 in bank notes and gold and counted it out on the table. The sharp pretended then to be willing to lend £100 at five per cent., but added that he must have a stamped receipt. The dupe left his money on the table covered with his handkerchief, and went out to get a stamp, and on his return found the sharps and his money had disappeared.

A few days after, the victim happening to be in London, saw one of them in the street, and gave him into custody.

A few weeks ago three skittle-sharps, well-dressed men, were brought before the Southwark police court, charged with robbing a country waiter of £40 in Bank of England notes. It appeared from the evidence, that the prosecutor met a man in High Street, Southwark, on an afternoon, who offered to show him the way to the Borough Road. They entered a public-house on the way, when the other prisoners came in. One of them pulled out a number of notes, and said he had just come into possession of a fortune. It was suggested, in the course of conversation, they should go to another house to throw a weight, and the prosecutor was to go and see they had fair play.

They accordingly went to another house, but instead of throwing the weight, skittles were introduced, and they played several games. The prosecutor lost a sovereign, which was all the money he had with him. One of the sharps bet £20 that the waiter could not produce £60 within three hours. He accepted the bet and went with two of them to Blackheath, and returned to the public-house with the money, amounting to £40 in bank notes and £20 in gold. They went to the skittle-ground, when one of them snatched the notes out of his hand, and they all decamped.

They were apprehended that night by Mr. Jones, detective at Tower Street station.

The statistic of this class of crime will be given when we come to treat of swindlers.

SWINDLERS

SWINDLING is carried on very extensively in the metropolis in different classes of society, from the young man who strolls into a coffee-house in Shoreditch or Bishopsgate, and decamps without paying his night's lodging, to the fashionable rogue who attends the brilliant assemblies in the West End. It occurs in private life and in the commercial world in different departments of business. Large quantities of goods are sent from the provinces to parties in London, who give orders and are entirely unknown to those who send them, and fictitious references are given, or references to confederates in town connected with them.

We select a few illustrations of various modes of swindling which prevail over the metropolis.

A young man calls at a coffee-house, or hotel, or a private lodging, and represents that he is the son of a gentleman in good position, or that he is in possession of certain property, left him by his friends, or that he has a situation in the neighbourhood, and after a few days or weeks decamps without paying his bill, perhaps leaving behind him an empty carpet bag, or a trunk, containing a few articles of no value.

An ingenious case of swindling occurred in the City some time since. A fashionably attired young man occupied a small office in White Lion Court, Cornhill, London. It contained no furniture, except two chairs and a desk. He obtained a number of bracelets from different jewellers, and quantities of goods from different tradesmen to a considerable amount, under false pretences. He was apprehended and tried before the police court, and sentenced to twelve months' imprisonment with hard labour.

At the time of his arrest he had obtained possession of a handsome residence at Abbey Wood, Kent, which was evidently intended as a place of reference, where no doubt he purposed to carry on a profitable system of swindling.

Swindlers have many ingenious modes of obtaining goods, sometimes to a very considerable amount, from credulous tradesmen, who are too often ready to be duped by their unprincipled devices. For example, some of them of respectable or fashionable appearance may pretend they are about to be married, and wish to have their house furnished. They give their name and address, and to avoid suspicion may even arrange particulars as to the manner in which the money is to be paid. A case of this kind occurred in Grove Terrace, where a furniture-dealer was requested to call on a swindler by a person who pretended to be his servant, and received directions to send him various articles of furniture. The goods were accordingly sent to the house. On a subsequent day the servant called on him at his premises, with a well-dressed young lady, whom she introduced as the intended wife of her employer, and said they had called to select some more goods. They selected a variety of articles, and desired they should be added to the account. One day the tradesman called for payment, and was told the gentleman was then out of town, but would call on him as soon as he returned. Soon after he made another call at the house, which he found closed up, and that he had been heartlessly duped. The value of the goods amounted to £58 18*s*. 4*d*.

Swindling is occasionally carried on in the West End in a bold and brilliant style by persons of fashionable appearance and elegant address. A lady-like person who assumed the name of Mrs. Gordon, and sometimes Mrs. Major Gordon, and who represented her husband to be in India, succeeded in obtaining goods from different tradesmen and mercantile establishments at the West End to a great amount, and gave references to a respectable firm as her agents. Possessing a lady-like appearance and address, she easily succeeded in obtaining a furnished residence at St. John's Wood, and applied to a livery stablekeeper for the loan of a brougham, hired a coachman, and got a suit of livery for him, and appeared in West End assemblies as a lady of fashion. After staying about a fortnight at St. John's Wood she left suddenly, without settling with any of her creditors. She addressed a letter to each of them, requesting that their account should be sent to her agents, and payment would be made as soon as Captain Gordon's affairs were settled. She expressed regret that she had been called away so abruptly on urgent business.

She was usually accompanied by a little girl, about eleven

years of age, her daughter, and by an elderly woman, who attended to domestic duties.

She was afterwards convicted at Marylebone police court, under the name of Mrs. Helen Murray, charged with obtaining large quantities of goods from West End tradesmen by fraudulent means.

A considerable traffic in commercial swindling in various forms is carried on in London. Sometimes fraudulently under the name of another well-known firm; at other times under the name of a fictitious firm.

A case of this kind was tried at the Liverpool assizes, which illustrates the fraudulent system we refer to. Charles Howard and John Owen were indicted for obtaining goods on false pretences. In other counts of their indictment they were charged with having conspired with another man named Bonar Russell—not in custody—with obtaining goods under false pretences. The prosecutor Thomas Parkenson Luthwaite, a currier at Barton in Westmoreland, received an order by letter from John Howard and Co., of Droylesden, near Manchester, desiring him to send them a certain quantity of leather, and reference was given as to their respectability. The prosecutor sent the leather and a letter by post containing the invoice. The leather duly arrived at Droylesden; but the police having received information gave notice to the railway officials to detain it, until they got further knowledge concerning them. Howard and Russell went to the station, but were told they could not get the leather, as there was no such firm as Howard and Co. at Droylesden. Howard replied that there was—that he lived there. It was subsequently arranged that the goods should be delivered, on the party producing a formal order. On the next day Owen came with a horse and cart to Droylesden station, and asked for the goods, at the same time producing his order.

They were delivered to him, when he put them in his cart and drove off. Two officers of police in plain clothes accosted him, and asked for a ride in his cart which he refused. The officers followed him, and found he did not go to Droylesden, but to a house at Hulme near Manchester, as he had been directed. This house was searched, and Howard and Russell were arrested. Howard having been admitted to bail, did not appear at the trial.

On farther inquiries it was found there was no such firm as John Howard and Co. at Droylesden, but that Howard and

Russell had taken a house there which was not furnished, and where they went occasionally to receive letters addressed to Howard and Co., Droylesden. Owen was acquitted; Howard was guilty of conspiracy with intent to defraud.

A number of cases occur where swindlers attempt to cheat different societies in various ways. Two men were tried at the police court a few days ago for unlawfully attempting to cheat and defraud a loan society to obtain £5. The prisoners formed part of a gang of swindlers, who operated in this way:—Some of them took a house for the purpose of giving references to others, who applied to loan societies for an advance of money, and produced false receipts for rent and taxes. They had carried on this system for years, and many of them had been convicted. Some of the gang formerly had an office in Holborn, where they defrauded young men in search of situations by getting them to leave a sum of money as security. They were tried and convicted on this charge.

There is another heartless system of base swindling perpetrated by a class of cheats, who pretend to assist parties in getting situations, and hold flaming inducements through advertisement in the newspapers to working men, servants, clerks, teachers, clergymen, and others; and contrive to get a large income by duping the public.

A swindler contrived to obtain sums of 5s. each in postage stamps or post-office orders, from a large number of people, under pretence of obtaining situations for them as farm bailiffs. An adver-tisement was inserted in the newspaper, and in reply to the several applicants, a letter was returned, stating that although the appli-cant was among the leading competitors another party had secured the place. At the same time another attempt was made to inveigle the dupe, under the pretence of paying another fee of 5s., with the hope of obtaining a similar situation in prospect. The swindler intimated that the only interest he had in the matter was the agent's fee, charged alike to the employer and the employed, and generally paid in advance. He desired that letters addressed to him should be directed to 42, Sydney Street, Chorl-ton-upon-Medlock. He had an empty house there, taken for the purpose, with the convenience of a letter-box in the door into which the postman dropped letters twice a day. A woman came immediately after each post and took them away.

On arresting the woman, the officers found in her basket 87

letters, 44 of them containing 5s. in postage stamps, or a post-office order payable to the swindler himself. Nearly all the others were letters from persons at a distance from a post office, who were unable to remit the 5s., but promised to send the money when they got an opportunity.

On a subsequent day, 120 letters were taken out of the letter-box, most of them containing a remittance. This system had been in operation for a month. One day 190 letters were delivered by one post. It was estimated that no fewer than 3,000 letters had come in during the month, most of them enclosing 5s.; and it is supposed the swindler has received about £700, a handsome return for the price of a few advertisements in newspapers, a few lithographed circulars, a few postage-stamps, and a quarter of a year's rent of an empty house.

Another case of a similar kind occurred at the Maidstone assizes. Henry Moreton, aged 43, a tall gentlemanly man, and a young woman aged 19 years, were indicted for conspiring to obtain goods and money by false pretences. The name given by the male prisoner was known to be an assumed one. It was stated that he was well connected and formerly in a good position in society.

At the trial, a witness deposed that an advertisement had appeared in a Cornish newspaper, addressed to Cornish miners, stating they could be sent out to Australia by an English gold-mining company, and would be paid £20 of wages per month, to commence on their arrival at the mines. The advertisement also stated that if 1s. or twelve postage stamps were sent to Mr. Henry Moreton, Chatham, a copy of the stamped agreement and full particulars as to the company, would be given.

The prisoner was arrested, and 41 letters found in his posses-sion, addressed to "Mr. H. Moreton, Chatham": 25 of the letters contained twelve postage stamps each and some of them had 1s. inside. It was ascertained the female cohabited with him. It appeared that he had pawned 482 stamps on the 14th Febru-ary, for £1 15s., 289 on the 21st, for £1, and 744 on another day.

Eighty-two letters came in one day, chiefly from Ireland and Cornwall.

On searching a box in his room they found a large quantity of Irish and Cornish newspapers, many of them containing the advertisement referred to.

He was found guilty, and was sentenced to hard labour for fifteen months. The young woman was acquitted.

The judge, in passing sentence, observed that the prisoner had been convicted of swindling poor people, and his being respectably connected aggravated the case.

We give the following illustration of an English swindler's adventures on the continent.

A married couple were tried at Pau, on a charge of swindling. The husband represented himself to be the son of a colonel in the English army and of a Neapolitan princess. His wife pretended to be the daughter of an English general. They said they were allied to the families of the Dukes of Norfolk, Leinster, and Devonshire. They came in a post-chaise to the Hotel de France, accompanied by several servants, lived in the style of persons of the highest rank, and ran up a bill of 6,000 francs. As the landlord declined to give credit for more, they took a chateau, which they got fitted up in a costly way. They paid 2,500 francs for rent, and were largely in debt to the butcher, tailor, grocer, and others. The lady affected to be very pious, and gave 895 francs to the abbé for masses.

An English lady who came from Brussels to give evidence, stated that her husband had paid 50,000 francs to release them from a debtors' prison at Cologne, as he believed them to be what they represented. It was shown at the trial that they had received letters from Lord Grey, the King of Holland, and other distinguished personages. They were convicted of swindling and condemned to one year's imprisonment, or to pay a fine of 200 francs.

On hearing the sentence the woman uttered a piercing cry and fainted in her husband's arms, but soon recovered. They were then removed to prison.

The assumption of a variety of names, some of them of a high-resounding and pretentious character, is resorted to by swindlers giving orders for goods by letter from a distance—an address is also assumed of a nature well calculated to deceive; as an instance, we may mention that an individual has for a long period of time fared sumptuously upon the plunder obtained by his fraudulent transactions, of whose aliases and pseudo residences the following are but a few:—

Creighton Beauchamp Harper; the Russets, near Edenbridge.
Beauchamp Harper; Albion House, Rye.
Charles Creighton Beauchamp Harper; ditto.

Neanberrie Harper, M.N.I.; The Broadlands, Winchelsea.
Beauchamp Harper: Halden House, Lewes.
R. E. Beresford: The Oaklands, Chelmsford.

The majority of these residences existed only in the imagination of this indefatigable cosmopolite. In some cases, he had christened a paltry tenement let at the rent of a few shillings per week "House"; a small cottage in Albion Place, Rye, being magnified into "Albion House". When an address is assumed having no existence, his plan is to request the postmaster of the district to send letters, &c., to his real address—generally some little distance off—a similar notice also being given at the nearest railway station. The goods ordered are generally of such a nature as to lull suspicion, viz., a gun, as "I am going to a friend's grounds to shoot and I want one immediately"; "a silver cornet"; "two umbrellas, one for me and one for Mrs. Harper"; "a fashionable bonnet with extra strings, young looking, for Mrs. Harper"; "white lace frock for Miss Harper, immediately"; "a violet-coloured velvet bonnet for my sister", &c., &c., ad infinitum.

A person, pretending to be a German baron, some time ago ordered and received goods to a large amount from merchants in Glasgow. It was ascertained he was a swindler. He was a man of about forty years of age, 5 feet 8 inches high, and was accompanied by a lady about twenty-five years of age. They were both well-educated people, and could speak the English language fluently.

A fellow, assuming the name of the Rev. Mr. Williams, pursued a romantic and adventurous career of swindling in differen positions in society, and was an adept in deception. On ont occasion, by means of forged credentials, he obtained an appointe ment as curate in Northamptonshire, where he conducted himself for some time with a most sanctimonious air. Several marriages were celebrated by him, which were apparently satisfactorily performed. He obtained many articles of jewellery from firms in London, who were deceived by his appearance and position. He wrote several modes of handwriting, and had a plausible manner of insinuating himself into the good graces of his victims.

He died a very tragical death. Having been arrested for swindling he was taken to Northampton. On his arrival at the railway station there, he threw himself across the rails and was crushed to death by the train.

There is a mode of extracting money from the unwary, practised by a gang of swindlers by means of mock auctions. They dispose of watches, never intended to keep time, and other spurious articles, and have confederates, or decoys, who pretend to bid for the goods at the auctions, and sometimes buy them at an under price; but they are by arrangement returned soon after, and again offered for sale.

BEGGARS AND CHEATS

BEGGING-LETTER WRITERS

FOREMOST among beggars, by right of pretention to blighted prospects and correct penmanship, stands the Begging-Letter Writer. He is the connecting link between mendicity and the observance of external respectability. He affects white cravats, soft hands, and filbert nails. He oils his hair, cleans his boots, and wears a portentous stick-up collar. The light of other days of gentility and comfort casts a halo of "deportment" over his well-brushed, white-seamed coat, his carefully darned blackcloth gloves, and pudgy gaiters. He invariably carries an umbrella, and wears a hat with an enormous brim. His once raven hair is turning grey, and his well-shaved whiskerless cheeks are blue as with gunpowder tattoo. He uses the plainest and most respectable of cotton pocket-handkerchiefs, and keeps his references as to character in the most irreproachable of shabby leather pocketbooks. His mouth is heavy, his underlip thick, sensual, and lowering, and his general expression of pious resignation contradicted by restless, bloodshot eyes, that flash from side to side, quick to perceive the approach of a compassionate looking clergyman, a female devotee, or a keen-scented member of the Society for the Suppression of Mendicity.

Among the many varieties of mendacious beggars, there is none so detestable as this hypocritical scoundrel, who, with an ostentatiously-submissive air, and false pretence of faded fortunes, tells his plausible tale of undeserved suffering, and extracts from the hearts and pockets of the superficially goodhearted their sympathy and coin. His calling is a special one, and requires study, perseverance, and some personal advantages. The begging-letter writer must write a good hand, speak grammatically, and have that shrewd perception of character peculiar to fortune-tellers, horoscopists, cheap-jacks, and pedlars. He "must read and write, and cast accounts"; have an intuitive knowledge of the "nobility and landed gentry"; be a keen physiognomist, and an adept at imitation of handwritings, old documents, quaint ancient orthography, and the like. He must possess an artistic eye for costume, an unfaltering courage, and have tears and hysterics at immediate command.

His great stock-in-trade is his register. There he carefully notes down the names, addresses, and mental peculiarities of his victims, and the character and pretence under which he robbed them of their bounty. It would not do to tell the same person the same story twice, as once happened to an unusually audacious member of the fraternity, who had obtained money from an old lady for the purpose of burying his wife, for whose loss he, of course, expressed the deepest grief. Confident in the old lady's kindness of heart and weakness of memory, three months after his bereavement he again posted himself before the lady's door, and gave vent to violent emotion.

"Dear me!" thought the old lady, "there's that poor man who lost his wife some time ago." She opened the window, and, bidding the vagabond draw nearer, asked him what trouble he was in at present.

After repeated questioning the fellow gurgled out. "That the wife of his bosom, the mother of his children, had left him for that bourne from which no traveller returns, and that owing to a series of unprecedented and unexpected misfortunes he had not sufficient money to defray the funeral expenses, and —"

"Oh, nonsense!" interrupted the old lady. "You lost your wife a quarter of a year ago. You couldn't lose her twice; and as to marrying again, and losing again in that short time, it is quite impossible!"

I subjoin some extracts from a Register kept by a begging-letter writer, and who was detected and punished: —

Cheltenham. May 14, 1852.

Rev. John Furby.—Springwood Villa. Low Church.—Fond of architecture—Dugdale's Monastica—Son of architect—Lost his life in the "Charon," U.S. packet—£2 and suit of clothes—Got reference.

Mrs. Branxholme—Clematis Cottage—Widow—Through Rev. Furby, £3 and prayer-book.

Gloucester. May 30.

Mrs. Captain Daniels.———Street.—Widow—Son drowned off Cape, as purser of same ship, "The Thetis"—£5 and old sea-chest. N.B.: Vamosed next day—Captain returned from London—Gaff blown in county paper. Mem.: Not to visit neighbourhood for four years.

Lincoln. June 19.

Andrew Taggart.———Street.—Gentleman—Great abolitionist of slave trade—As tradesman from U.S., who had lost his custom by aiding slope of fugitive female slave—By name Naomi Brown—£5. N.B.: To work him again, for he is good. Grantham. July 1.

Charles James Campion.—Westby House.—Gentleman—Literary —Writes plays and novels—As distant relative of George Frederick Cooke, and burnt out bookseller—£2 2s. N.B.: Gave me some of his own books to read—Such trash—Cadger in one—No more like cadger than I'm like Bobby Peel—Went to him again on 5th—Told him I thought it wonderful, and the best thing out since Vicar of Wakefield—Gave me £1 more—Very good man—To be seen to for the future. Huntingdon. July 15.

Mrs. Siddick.———Street.—Widow—Cranky—Baptist—As member of persuasion from persecution of worldly-minded relatives —£10—Gave her address in London—Good for a £5 every year—Recognized inspector—Leave to-night.

There are, of course, many varieties of the begging-letter writer; but although each and all of them have the same pretentions to former respectability, their mode of levying contributions is entirely different. There are but few who possess the versatility of their great master—Bampfylde Moore Carew; and it is usual for every member of the fraternity to chalk out for himself a particular "line" of imposition—a course of conduct that renders him perfect in the part he plays, makes his references and certificates continually available, and prevents him from "jostling" or coming into collision with others of his calling who might be "on the same lay as himself, and spoil his game!" Among the many specimens, one of the most prominent is the

Decayed Gentleman

THE conversation of this class of mendicant is of former greatness, of acquaintance among the nobility and gentry of a particular county—always a distant one from the scene of operations—of hunting, races, balls, meets, appointments to the magistracy, lord-lieutenants, contested elections, and marriages in high life. The knowledge of the things of which he talks so fluently is gleaned from files of old county newspapers. When at fault, or to use his own phrase "pounded", a ready wit, a deprecating shrug, and a few words, such as, "Perhaps I'm mistaken—I used to visit a good deal there, and was introduced to so many who have forgotten me now—my memory is failing, like everything else"—extricate him from his difficulty and increase his capital of past prosperity and present poverty. The decayed gentleman is also a great authority on wines—by right of a famous sample—his father "laid down" in eighteen eleven, "the comet year, you know," and is not a little severe upon his past extravagance. He relishes the retrospection of the heavy losses he endured at Newmarket, Doncaster, and Epsom in "forty-two and three," and is pathetic on the subject of the death of William Scott. The cause of his ruin he attributes usually to a suit in the Court of Chancery, or the "fatal and calamitous Encumbered Irish Estates Bill." He is a florid impostor and has a jaunty sonorous way of using his lean, threadbare, silk pocket-handkerchief, that carries conviction even to the most sceptical.

It is not uncommon to find among these degraded mendicants one who has really been a gentleman, as far as birth and education go, but whose excesses and extravagances have reduced him to mendicity. Such cases are the most hopeless. Unmindful of decent pride, and that true gentility that rises superior to circumstance, and finds no soil upon the money earned by labour, the lying, drunken, sodden wretch considers work "beneath him"; upon the shifting quicksands of his own vices rears an edifice of vagabond vanity, and persuades himself that, by forfeiting his manhood, he vindicates his right to the character of gentleman.

The letters written by this class of beggar generally run as follows. My readers will, of course, understand that the names and places mentioned are the only portions of the epistles that are fictitious.

"Three Mermaids Inn, Pond Lane.

April—, 18.

"Sir, or Madam,

"Although I have not the honour to be personally acquainted with you, I have had the advantage of a introduction to a member of your family, Major Sherbrook, when with his regiment at Malta; and my present disadvantageous circumstances emboldens me to write to you, for the claims of affliction upon the heart of the compassionate are among the holiest of those kindred ties that bind man to his fellow-being.

"My father was a large landed proprietor at Peddlethorpe, ———shire. I, his only son, had every advantage that birth and fortune could give me claim to. From an informality in the wording of my father's will, the dishonesty of an attorney, and the rapacity of some of my poor late father's relatives, the property was, at his death, thrown into Chancery, and for the last four years I have been reduced to—comparatively speaking—starvation.

"With the few relics of my former prosperity I have long since parted. My valued books, and, I am ashamed to own, my clothes, are gone. I am now in the last stage of destitution, and, I regret to say, in debt to the worthy landlord of the tavern from which I write this, to the amount of eight and sixpence. My object in coming to this part of the country was to see an old friend, whom I had hoped would have assisted me. We were on the same form together at Rugby—Mr. Joseph Thurwood of Copesthorpe. Alas! I find that he died three months ago.

"I most respectfully beg of you to grant me some trifling assistance. As in my days of prosperity I trust my heart was never deaf to the voice of entreaty, nor my purse closed to the wants of the necessitous; so, dear sir, or madam, I hope that my request will not be considered by you as impertinent or intrusive.

"I have the honour to enclose you some testimonials as to my character and former station in society; and trusting that the Almighty Being may never visit you with that affliction which it has been his all-wise purpose to heap on me, I am

"Your most humble and
"Obliged servant,
"Frederick Maurice Stanhope,
"Formerly of Stanhope House,———shire."

The Broken-Down Tradesman

THE broken-down tradesman is a sort of retail dealer in the same description of article as the decayed gentleman. The unexpected breaking of fourteen of the most respectable banking-houses in New York, or the loss of the cargoes of two vessels in the late autumnal gales, or the suspension of payment of Haul, Strong, and Chates, "joined and combined together with the present commercial crisis, has been the means of bringing him down to his present deplorable situation," as his letter runs. His references are mostly from churchwardens, bankers, and dissenting clergymen, and he carries about a fictitious set of books—day-book, ledger, and petty-cash book, containing entries of debts of large amounts, and a dazzling display of the neatest and most immaculate of commercial cyphering. His conversation, like his correspondence, is a queer jumble of arithmetic and scripture. He has a wife whose appearance is in itself a small income. She folds the hardest-working-looking set of hands across the cleanest of aprons, and curtseys with the humility of a pew-opener. The clothes of the worthy couple are shabby, but their persons and linen are rigorously clean. Their cheeks shine with yellow soap, as if they were rasped and bees-waxed every morning. The male impostor, when fleecing a victim, has the habit of washing his hands "with invisible soap and imperceptible water," as though he were waiting a customer. The wedded pair—and, generally, they are really married—are of congenial dispositions and domestic turn of mind, and get drunk, and fight each other, or go half-price to the play according to their humour. It is usually jealousy that betrays them. The husband is unfaithful, and the wife "peaches"; through her agency the police are put upon the track, and the broken-down tradesman is committed. In prison he professes extreme penitence, and has a turn for scriptural quotation, that stands him in good stead.

On his release he takes to itinerant preaching, or political lecturing. What becomes of him after those last resources it is difficult to determine. The chances are that he again writes begging letters, but "on a different lay."

The Distressed Scholar

THE distressed scholar is another variety of the same species, a connecting-link between the self-glorification of the decayed gentleman and the humility of the broken-down tradesman. He is generally in want of money to pay his railway-fare, or coach-hire, to the north of England, where he has a situation as usher to an academy—or he cannot seek for a situation for want of "those clothes which sad necessity has compelled him to part with for temporary convenience." His letters, written in the best small hand, with the finest of upstrokes and fattest of down-strokes, are after this fashion:

"Star Temperance Coffee House,
"Gravel Walk.

"Sir, or Madam,

"I have the honour to lay my case before you, humbly entreating your kind consideration.

"I am a tutor, and was educated at St. ———'s College, Cambridge. My last situation was with the Rev. Mr. Cross, Laburnum House, near Dorking. I profess English, Latin, Greek, mathematics, and the higher branches of arithmetic, and am well read in general literature, ancient and modern. 'Rudem esse omnino in nostris poetis est inertissimae signitae signum.'

"I am at present under engagement to superintend the scholastic establishment of Mr. Tighthand of the classical and commercial academy, ———, Cumberland, but have not the means of defraying the expenses of my journey, nor of appearing with becoming decency before my new employer and my pupils.

"My wardrobe is all pledged for an amount incommensurate with its value, and I humbly and respectfully lay my case before you, and implore you for assistance, or even a temporary accommodation.

"I am aware that impostors, armed with specious stories, often impose on the kind-hearted and credulous. 'Nervi atque artus est sapientiae—non temere credere.' I have therefore the honour to forward you the enclosed testimonials from my former employer and others as to my character and capacity.

"That you may never be placed in such circumstances as to compel you to indite such an epistle as the one I am at present penning is my most fervent wish. Rely upon it, generous sir—or madam—that, should you afford me the means of gaining an honourable competence, you shall never have to repent your timely benevolence. If, however, I should be unsuccessful in my present application, I must endeavour to console myself with the words of the great poet. 'Aetas ipsa solatium omnibus affert,' or with the diviner precept: 'And this too shall pass away.'

"I have, sir—or madam—the honour to be
"Your humble and obedient servant,
"Horace Humm."

A gracefully flourished swan, with the date in German text on his left wing, terminates the letter.

The Kaggs Family

THIS case of cleverly organised swindling fell beneath the writer's personal observation.

In a paved court, dignified with the name of a market, leading into one of the principal thoroughfares of London, dwelt a family whom, from fear of an action for libel which, should they ever read these lines, they would assuredly bring, I will call Kaggs. Mr. Kaggs, the head of the family, had commenced life in the service of a nobleman. He was a tall, portly man, with a short nose, broad truculent mouth, and a light, moist eye. His personal advantages and general conduct obtained him promotion, and raised him from the servants' hall to the pantry. When he was thirty years of age: he was butler in the family of a country gentleman, whose youngest daughter fell in love, ran away with, and—married him. The angry father closed his doors against them, and steeled his heart to the pathetic appeals addressed to him by every post. Mr. Kaggs, unable to obtain a character from his last place, found himself shut out from his former occupation. His wife gave promise of making an increase to the numbers of the family, and to use Mr. Kaggs's own pantry vernacular, "he was flyblown and frost-bitten every joint of him."

It was then that he first conceived the idea of making his wife's birth and parentage a source of present income and provision for old age. She was an excellent penwoman, and for some months had had great practice in the composition of begging letters to her father. Mr. Kaggs's appearance being martial and imposing, he collected what information he could find upon the subject, and passed himself off for a young Englishman of good family, who had been an officer in the Spanish army, and served "under Evans!" Mrs. Kaggs's knowledge of the county families stood them in good stead, and they begged themselves through England, Scotland, and Wales, and lived in a sort of vulgar luxury, at no cost but invention, falsehood, and a ream or so of paper.

It was some few years ago that I first made their acquaintance. Mrs. Kaggs had bloomed into a fine elderly lady, and Mr. Kaggs's nose and stomach had widened to that appearance of fatherly responsibility and parochial importance that was most to be desired. The wife sunk to the husband's level, and had brought up her children to tread in the same path. Their family, though not numerous, was a blessing to them, for each child, some way or another, contrived to bring in money. It was their parents' pride that they had given their offspring a liberal education. As soon as they were of an age capable of receiving instruction, they were placed at a respectable boarding school, and, although they only stayed in it one half-year, they went to another establishment for the next half-year, and so managed to pick up a good miscellaneous education, and at the same time save their parents the cost of board and lodging.

James Julian Kaggs, the eldest and only son, was in Australia "doing well," as his mamma would often say—though in what particular business or profession was a subject on which she preserved a discreet silence. As I never saw the young man in question, I am unable to furnish any information respecting him.

Catherine Kaggs, the eldest daughter, was an ugly and vulgar girl, on whom a genteel education and her mother's example of elegance and refinement had been thrown away. Kitty was a sort of Cinderella in the family, and being possessed of neither tact nor manner to levy contributions on the charitable, was sentenced to an out-door employment, for which she was well fitted. She sold flowers in the thoroughfare, near the market.

The second daughter, Betsey, was the pride of her father and mother, and the mainstay of the family. Tall, thin, and elegant, interesting rather than pretty, her pale face and subdued manners, her long eyelashes, soft voice, and fine hands, were the very requisites for the personation of beggared gentility and dilapidated aristocracy. Mrs. Kaggs often said, "That poor Kitty was her father's girl, a Kaggs all over—but that Bessie was a Thorncliffe (her own maiden name) and a lady every inch!"

The other children were a boy and girl of five and three years old, who called Mrs. Kaggs "Mamma," but who appeared much too young to belong to that lady in any relation but that of grandchildren. Kitty, the flower girl, was passionately fond of them, and "Bessie" patronised them in her meek, maidenly way, and called them her dear brother and sister.

In the height of the season Miss Bessie Kaggs, attired in shabby black silk, dark shawl, and plain bonnet, would sally forth to the most aristocratic and fashionable squares, attended by her father in a white neck-cloth, carrying in one hand a small and fragile basket, and in the other a heavy and respectable umbrella.

Arrived at the mansion of the intended victim, Miss Bessie would give a pretentious knock, and relieve her father of the burthen of the fragile basket. As the door opened, she would desire her parent, who was supposed to be a faithful retainer, to wait, and Mr. Kaggs would touch his hat respectfully and retire to the corner of the square, and watch the placards in the public-house in the next street.

"Is Lady —— within?" Miss Betsey would inquire of the servant.

If the porter replied that his lady was out, or could not receive visitors, except by appointment, Miss Betsey would boldly demand pen, ink, and paper, and sit down and write, in a delicate, lady's hand, to the following effect:—

"Miss Thirlbrook presents her compliments to the Countess of ——, and most respectfully requests the honour of enrolling the Countess's name among the list of ladies who are kindly aiding her in disposing of a few necessaries for the toilette.

"Miss Thirlbrook is reduced to this extreme measure from the sad requirements of her infirm father, formerly an officer in his majesty's —d Regiment, who, from a position of comfort and affluence, is now compelled to seek aid from the charitable, and to rely on the feeble exertions of his daughter: a confirmed cripple and valetudinarian, he has no other resources.

"The well-known charity of the Countess of —— has induced Miss Thirlbrook to make this intrusion on her time. Miss T. will do herself the honour of waiting upon her ladyship on Thursday, when she earnestly entreats the favour of an interview, or an inspection of the few articles she has to dispose of.

"Monday."

This carefully concocted letter—so different from the usual appeals—containing no references to other persons as to character or antecedents, generally had its effect, and in a few days Betsey would find herself tête-à-tête with the Countess——.

On entering the room she would make a profound curtsey, and, after thanking her ladyship for the honour, would open the fragile basket, which contained a few bottles of scent, some fancy soaps, ornamental envelopes, and perforated notepapers.

"Sit down, Miss Thirlbrook," the Countess would open the conversation. "I see the articles. Your note, I think, mentioned something of your being in less fortunate ——"

Miss Betsey would lower her eyelashes and bend her head—

not too deferentially, but as if bowing to circumstances for her father—her dear father's sake—for this was implied by her admirably concealed histrionic capability.

The lady would then suggest that she had a great many claims upon her consideration, and would delicately inquire into the pedigree and circumstances of Lieutenant Thirlbrook, formerly of his Majesty's —d Regiment.

Miss Betsey's replies were neither too ready nor too glib. She suffered herself to be drawn out, but did not advance a statement, and so established in her patroness's mind the idea that she had to deal with a very superior person. The sum of the story of this interesting scion of a fallen house was, that her father was an old Peninsular officer—as would be seen by a reference to the Army List (Miss Betsey had found the name in an old list); that he had left the service during the peace in 1814; and that a ruinous law-suit, arising from railway speculations, and an absconding agent, had reduced them to—to—to their present position—and that six years ago, an old wound—received at Barossa—had broken out, and laid her father helpless on a sick bed. "I know that these articles," Betsey would conclude, pointing to the fancy soaps and stationery, "are not such perhaps as your ladyship is accustomed to; but if you would kindly aid me by purchasing some of them —if ever so few—you would materially assist us; and I hope that —that we should not prove—either undeserving or ungrateful."

When, as sometimes happened, ladies paid a visit to Lieut. Thirlbrook, everything was prepared for their reception with a dramatic regard for propriety. The garret was made as clean and as uncomfortable as possible. Mr. Kaggs was put to bed, and the purpled pinkness of his complexion toned down with violet powder and cosmetics. A white handkerchief, with the Thirlbrook crest in a corner, was carelessly dropped upon the coverlid. A few physic bottles, an old United Service paper, and a ponderous Bible lay upon a ricketty round table beside him. Mrs. Kaggs was propped up with pillows in an arm-chair near the fireplace and desired to look rheumatic and resigned. Kitty was sent out of the way; and the two children were dressed up in shabby black, and promised plums if they would keep quiet. Miss Betsey herself, in grey stuff and an apron, meek, mild and matronly beyond her years, glided about softly, like a Sister of Mercy connected with the family.

My readers must understand that Mr. Kaggs was the sole tenant

of the house he lived in, though he pretended that he only occupied
the garrets as a lodger.

During the stay of the fashionable Samaritans, Lieut. Thirlbrook—who had received a wound in his leg at Barossa, under
the Duke—would say but little, but now and then his mouth
would twitch as with suppressed pain. The visitors were generally
much moved at the distressing scene. The gallant veteran—the
helpless old lady—the sad and silent children—and the ministering
angel of a daughter, were an impressive spectacle. The ladies
would promise to exert themselves among their friends, and do
all in their power to relieve them.

"Miss Thirlbrook," they would ask, as Miss Betsey attended
them to the street-door, "those dear little children are not your
brother and sister, are they?"

Betsey would suppress a sigh, and say, "They are the son and
daughter of my poor brother, who was a surgeon in the Navy
—they are orphans. My brother died on the Gold Coast, and his
poor wife soon followed him. She was delicate, and could not bear
up against the shock. The poor things have only us to look to,
and we do for them what lies in our power."

This last stroke was a climax. "She never mentioned them
before!" thought the ladies. "What delicacy! What high feeling!
These are not common beggars, who make an exaggerated statement of their griefs."

"Miss Thirlbrook, I am sure you will pardon me for making
the offer; but those dear children upstairs do not look strong.
I hope you will not be offended by my offering to send them a
luncheon now and then—a few delicacies—nourishing things—to
do them good."

Miss Betsey would curtsey, lower her eyelids, and say, softly,
"They are not strong."

"I'll send my servant as soon as I get home. Pray use this trifle
for the present," (the lady would take out her purse,) "and good
morning, Miss Thirlbrook. I must shake hands with you. I consider myself fortunate in having made your acquaintance."

Betsey's eyes would fill with tears, and as she held the door
open, the expression of her face would plainly say: "Not only
for myself, oh dear and charitable ladies, but for my father—my
poor father—who was wounded, at Barossa, in the leg—do I
thank you from the depths of a profoundly grateful heart."

When the basket arrived, Miss Betsey would sit down with

her worthy parents and enjoy whatever poultry or meat had not been touched; but anything that had been cut, anything "second-hand," that dainty and haughty young lady would instruct her sister Kitty to give to the poor beggars.

This system of swindling could not, of course, last many years, and when the west end of London became too hot to hold them, the indefatigable Kaggses put an advertisement into the Times and Morning Post, addressed to the charitable and humane, saying that "a poor, but respectable family required a small sum to enable them to make up the amount of their passage to Australia, and that they could give the highest references as to character."

The old certificates were hawked about, and for more than two years they drove a roaring trade in money, outfits, and neces-saries for a voyage. Mr Kaggs, too, made a fortunate hit. He purchased an old piano, and raffled it at five shillings a head. Each of his own family took a chance. At the first raffle Miss Betsey won it, at the second, Miss Kitty, on the third, Mr. Kaggs, on the fourth, his faithful partner, and on the fifth and last time, a particular friend of Miss Kitty's, a young lady in the green-grocery line. This invaluable piece of furniture was eventually disposed of by private contract to a dealer in Barret's Court, Oxford Street, and, a few days after, the Kaggs family really sailed for Melbourne, and I have never since heard of them.

Among the begging-letter fraternity there are not a few persons who affect to be literary men. They have at one time or another been able to publish a pamphlet, a poem, or a song—generally a patriotic one, and copies of these works—they always call them "works"—they constantly carry about with them to be ready for any customer who may turn up. I have known a notable member of this class of beggars for some years. He was introduced to me as a literary man by an innocent friend who really believed in his talent. He greeted me as a brother craftsman, and immediately took from his breast-pocket of his threadbare surtout a copy of one of his works. "Allow me," he said, "to present you with my latest work; it is dedicated, you will perceive, to the Right Honour-able the Earl of Derby—here is a letter from his lordship compli-menting me in the most handsome terms;" and before I could look into the book, the author produced from a well-worn black pocket-book a dirty letter distinguished by a large red seal. Sure enough it was a genuine letter beginning "The Earl of Derby presents his compliments," and going on to acknowledge the

receipt of a copy of Mr. Driver's work. Mr. Driver—I will call
my author by that name—produced a great many other letters,
all from persons of distinction, and the polite terms in which
they were expressed astonished me not a little. I soon, however,
discovered the key to all this condescension. The work was a political one, glorifying the Conservative party, and abounding with
all sorts of old-fashioned Tory sentiments. The letters Mr. Driver
showed me were of course all from Tories. The "work" was quite
a curiosity. It was called a political novel. It had for its motto,
"Pro Rege, Lege, Aris et Focis," and the dedication to the Right
Honourable the Earl of Derby was displayed over a whole page
in epitaph fashion. At the close of our interview Mr. Driver
pointed out to me that the price of the work was two shillings.
Understanding the hint, I gave him that amount, when he called
for pen and ink, and wrote on the fly leaf of the work, "To——
——, Esq. with the sincere regards of the author.—J. Fitzharding
Driver." On looking over the book—it was a mere paper-covered
pamphlet of some hundred pages—I found that the story was not
completed. I mentioned this to Mr. Driver the next time I met
him, and he explained that he meant to go to press—that was a
favourite expression of his—to go to press with the second volume
shortly. Ten years, however, have elapsed since then, and Mr.
Driver has not yet gone to press with his second volume. The last
time I met him he offered me the original volume as his "last new
work," which he presumed I had never seen. He also informed
me that he was about to publish a patriotic song in honour of the
Queen. Would I subscribe for a copy—only three-and-sixpence—
and he would leave it for me? Mr. Driver had forgotten that I had
subscribed for this very song eight years previously. He showed
me the selfsame MS. of the new national anthem, which I had
perused so long ago. The paper had become as soft and limp and
dingy as a Scotch one-pound note, but it had been worth a good
many one-pound notes to Mr. Fitzharding Driver. Mr. Driver
has lived upon this as yet unpublished song, and that unfinished
political novel, for ten years and more. I have seen him often
enough to know exactly his *modus operandi*. Though practically
a beggar, Mr. Driver is no great rogue. Were you to dress him
well, he might pass for a nobleman. As it is, in his shabby genteel
clothes he looks a broken-down swell. And so in fact he is. In his
young days he had plenty of money, and went the pace among
the young bloods of Bond Street. Mr. Driver's young days were

the days of the Regent. He drove a dashing phaeton-and-four then, and lounged and gambled, and lived the life of a man about town. He tells you all that with great pride, and also how he came to grief, though this part of the story is not so clear. There is no doubt that he had considerable acquaintance among great people in his prosperous days. He lives now upon his works, and the public-house parlours of the purlieus of the West End serve him as publishing houses. He is a great political disputant, and his company is not unwelcome in those quarters. He enters, takes his seat, drinks his glass, joins in the conversation, and, as he says himself, shows that he is a man of parts. In this way he makes friends among the tradesmen who visit these resorts. They soon find out that he is poor, and an author, and moved both to pity and admiration, each member of the company purchases a copy of that unfinished political novel, or subscribes for that new patriotic song, which I expect will yet be in the womb of the press when the crack of doom comes. I think Mr. Driver has pretty well used up all the quiet parlours of W. district by this time. Not long ago I had a letter from him enclosing a prospectus of a new work to be entitled "Whiggery, or the Decline of England," and soliciting a subscription to enable him to go to press with the first edition. I have no doubt that every conservative member of both houses of Parliament has had a copy of that prospectus. Mr. Fitzharding Driver will call at their houses for an answer, and some entirely out of easy charity, and others from a party feeling of delight at the prospect of the Whigs being abused in a book even by this poor beggar, will send him down half-crowns, and enable the poor wretch to eat and drink for a few months longer. On more than one occasion while I have known him, Mr. Driver has been on the point of "being well off again," to use his own expression. His behaviour under the prospect was characteristic of the man, his antecedents, and his mode of life. He touched up his seedy clothes, had some cotton-velvet facing put to his thread-bare surtout, revived his hat, mounted a pair of shabby patent-leather boots, provided himself with a penny cane, adorned with an old silk tassel, and appeared each day with a flower in his button-hole. In addition to these he had sewn into the breast of his surtout a bit of parti-coloured ribbon to look like a decoration. In this guise he came up to me at the Crystal Palace one day, and appeared to be in great glee. His ogling and mysterious manner puzzled me. Judge of my astonishment when this hoary, old, tottering, toothless beggar informed me, with many self-satisfied chuckles, that a rich widow, "a fine dashing woman, sir," had fallen in love with him and was going to marry him. The marriage did not come off, the pile is worn away from the velvet facings, the patent-leather boots have become mere shapeless flaps of leather, the old broad-brimmed hat is past the power of reviver, and the Bond Street buck of the days of the Regent now wanders from public-house to public-house selling lucifer matches. He still however carries with him a copy of his "work," the limp and worn MS. of his anthem, and the prospectus of "Whiggery, or the Decline of England." These and the letters from distinguished personages stand him in better stead than the lucifer-matches, when he lights upon persons of congenial sympathies.

Advertising Begging-Letter Writers

AMONG many begging-letter writers who appealed to sentiment the most notorious and successful was a man of the name of Thomas Stone, alias Stanley, alias Newton. He had been in early life transported for forgery, and afterwards tried for perjury; and when his ordinary methods of raising money had been detected and exposed, he resorted to the ingenious expedient of sending an advertisement to the "Times," of which the following is a copy:—

"To the Charitable and Affluent.

"At the eleventh hour a young and most unfortunate lady is driven by great distress to solicit from those charitable and humane persons who ever derive pleasure from benevolent acts, some little *pecuniary assistance*. The advertiser's condition is almost hopeless, being, alas! friendless, and reduced to the last extremity. The smallest aid would be most thankfully acknowledged, and the fullest explanation given. Direct Miss T. C. M., Post-office, Great Randolph St., Camden New Town."

This touching appeal was read by a philanthropic gentleman who sent the advertiser £5, and afterwards £1 more, to which he received a reply in the following words:—

"Sir,—I again offer my gratitude for your charitable kindness. I am quite unable to speak the promptings of my heart for your great goodness to me, an entire stranger, but you may believe me, sir, I am very sincerely thankful. You will, I am sure, be happy to hear I have paid the few trifling demands upon me,

and also obtained sufficient of my wearing apparel to make a
decent appearance; but it has swallowed up the whole of your
generous bounty, or I should this day have moved to the
Hampstead Road, where a far more comfortable lodging has
been offered me, and where, sir, if you would condescend to call,
I would cheerfully and with pleasure relate my circumstances
in connexion with my past history, and I do hope you might
consider me worthy of your further notice. But it is my earnest
desire to support myself and my dearest child by my own industry. As I mentioned before, I have youth and health, and
have received a good education, but alas! I fear I shall have a
great difficulty in obtaining employment such as I desire, for
I have fallen! I am a mother, and my dear poor boy is the child
of sin. But I was deceived—cruelly deceived by a base and heartless villain. A licence was purchased for our marriage; I believed all; my heart knew no guile; the deceptions of the world
I had scarcely ever heard of; but too soon I found myself destroyed and lost, the best affections of my heart trampled
upon, and myself infamous and disgraced. But I did not continue
to live in sin. Oh, no! I despised and loathed the villain who so
deceived me. Neither have I received, nor would I, one shilling
from him. I think I stated in my first letter I am the daughter of
a deceased merchant; such is the case; and had I some friends
to interest themselves for me, I do think it would be found I am
entitled to some property; however, it would be first necessary to
explain personally every circumstance, and to you, sir, I would
unreservedly explain all. And oh! I do earnestly hope you would,
after hearing my sad tale, think there was some little palliation
of my guilt.

"In answer to the advertisement I had inserted, I received
many offers of assistance, but they contained overtures of such
nature that I could not allow myself to reply to any of them.
You, sir, have been my best friend, and may God bless you for
your sympathy and kindness. I am very desirous to remove,
but cannot do so without a little money in my pocket. Your
charity has enabled me to provide all I required, and paid that
which I owed, which has been a great relief to my mind. I hope
and trust that you will not think me covetous or encroaching
upon your goodness, in asking you to assist me with a small sum
further, for the purpose named. Should you, however, decline to
do so, believe me, I should be equally grateful; and it is most

painful and repugnant to my feelings to ask, but I know not to whom else to apply. Entreating your early reply, however it may result, and with every good wish, and the sincerest and warmest acknowledgments of my heart, believe, sir, always your most thankful and humble servant.

"Frances Thorpe.

"Please direct T. C. M., Post-office, Crown Street, Gray's Inn Road."

With the same sort of tale, varying the signature to Fanny Lyons, Mary Whitmore, and Fanny Hamilton, etc., Mr. Stone continued to victimise the public, until the Society for the Supression of Mendicity laid him by the heels. He was committed for trial at Cerkenwell Sessions, and sentenced to transportation for seven years.

I must content myself with these few specimens of the begging-letter impostors; it would be impossible to describe every variety. Sometimes they are printers, whose premises have been destroyed by fire; at others, young women who have been ruined by noble-men and are anxious to retrieve themselves; or widows of naval officers who have perished in action or by sickness. There was a long run upon "aged clergymen, whose sands of life were fast running out" but the fraud became so common that it was soon "blown."

The greatest blow that was ever struck at this species of im-position was the establishment of the Begging-Letter Depart-ment by the Society for the Suppression of Mendicity. In the very first case they investigated they found the writer—who had penned a most touching letter to a well-known nobleman—crouching in a fireless garret in one of the worst and lowest neigh-bourhoods of London. This man was discovered to be the owner and occupier of a handsomely furnished house in another part of the town, where his wife and family lived in luxury. The follow-ing is a specimen of a most artful begging letter from America.

"Ellicot's Mills, Howard Co., Maryland,
United States.

June 6, 1859.

"My dearest Friend,

"Why—why have you not written, and sent me the usual remittances? Your silence has caused me the greatest uneasiness. Poor dear Frederick is dying and we are in the extremest want.

The period to hear from you has past some time, and no letter. It is very strange! What can it mean?

"In a short time your poor suffering son will be at rest. I shall then trouble you no more; but—oh! I beseech you, do not permit your poor son to die in want. I have expended my last shilling to procure him those little necessaries he must and shall have. Little did I think when, long, long years ago, I deserted all, that you might be free and happy, that you would fail me in this terrible hour of affliction—but you have not—I know you have not. You must have sent, and the letter miscarried. Your poor dying son sends his fondest love. Poor dear fellow!—he has never known a father's care; still, from a child, he has prayed for, revered, and loved you—he is now going to his Father in heaven, and, when he is gone my widowed heart will break. When I look back upon the long past, although broken-hearted and crushed to the earth, yet I cannot tutor my heart to regret it, for I dearly loved you. Yes, and proved it, dearest friend, by forsaking and fleeing with my poor fatherless boy to this strange and distant land, that you might be free and happy with those so worthy of you; and, believe me when I say that your happiness has been my constant prayer. In consequence of poor dear Frederick's sickness we are in the greatest distress and want. I have been compelled to forego all exertion, and attend solely upon him; therefore, do, I pray you, send me, without an instant's delay, a £10 note. I must have it, or I shall go mad. Your poor suffering boy must not die in misery and want. Send the money by return mail, and send a Bank of England note, for I am now miles away from where I could get a draught cashed. I came here for the benefit of poor dear Frederick, but I fear it has done him no good. We are now among strangers, and in the most abject distress, and unless you send soon, your afflicted unoffending boy will starve to death. I can no longer bear up against poverty, sickness, and your unkindness; but you must have sent; your good, kind heart would not permit you to let us die in want. God bless you, and keep you and yours. May you be supremely happy! Bless you! In mercy send soon, for we are in extremest want.

"Remaining faithfully,

"Your dearest friend,

"Kate Stanley.

"Pay the postage of your letter to me, or I shall not be able to obtain it, for I am selling everything to live."

The above affecting letter was received by the widow of a London merchant six months after his death. The affair was investigated and proved to be an imposture. The moral character of Mr. — — had been irreproachable. American begging letter writers read the obituaries in English newspapers and ply their trade, while the loss of the bereaved relatives of the man whose memory they malign is recent.

Ashamed Beggars

By the above title I mean those tall, lanthorn-jawed men, in seedy well-brushed clothes who, with a ticket on their breasts, on which a short but piteous tale is written in the most respectable of large-hand, and with a few boxes of lucifer matches in their hands, make no appeal by word of mouth, but invoke the charity of passers-by by meek glances and imploring looks—fellows who, having no talent for "patter," are gifted with great powers of facial pathos, and make expression of feature stand in lieu of vocal supplication. For some years I have watched a specimen of this class, who has a regular "beat" at the West End of London. He is a tall man, with thin legs and arms, and a slightly-protuberant stomach. His "costume" (I use the word advisedly, for he is really a great actor of pantomime) consists of an old black dress coat, carefully buttoned, but left sufficiently open at the top to show a spotlessly white shirt, and at the bottom, to exhibit an old grey waistcoat; and a snowy apron, which he wears after the fashion of a Freemason, forgetting that real tradesmen are never seen in their aprons except behind the counter. A pair of tight, dark, shabby trousers, black gaiters without an absent button, and heavy shoes of the severest thickness, cover his nether man. Round his neck is a red worsted comforter which, neatly tied at the throat, descends straight and formally beneath his coat, and exhibits two fringed ends, which fall, in agreeable contrast of colour, over the before-mentioned apron. I never remember seeing a beggar of this class without an apron and a worsted comforter—they would appear to be his stock-in-trade, a necessary portion of his outfit; the white apron to relieve the sombre hue of his habiliments, and show up their well-brushed shabbiness; the scarlet comforter to contrast with the cadaverous complexion which he owes to art or nature. In winter the comforter also serves as an advertisement that his great-coat is gone.

The man I am describing wears a "pad" round his neck, on which is written:—

Kind Friends and Christian Brethren!
I was once a
Respectable Tradesman,
doing a Good Business;
till Misfortune reduced me to
this Pass!
Be kind enough to Buy
Some of the Articles I offer,
and you will confer a
Real Charity!

In his hands, on which he wears scrupulously-darned mittens, he carries a box or two of matches, or a few quires of notepaper or envelopes, and half-a dozen small sticks of sealing-wax. He is also furnished with a shabby genteel looking boy of about nine years old, who wears a Shakespearian collar, and the regulation worsted comforter, the ends of which nearly trail upon the ground. The poor child, whose features do not in the least resemble the man's, and who, too young to be his son, is too old, to be his grandson, keeps his little hands in his large pockets, and tries to look as unhappy and half-starved as he can.

But the face of the beggar is a marvellous exhibition! His acting is admirable! Christian resignation and its consequent fortitude are written on his brow. His eyes roll imploringly, but no sound escapes him. The expression of his features almost pronounces, "Christian friend, purchase my humble wares, for *I scorn to beg.* I am starving, but tortures shall not wring the humiliating secret from my lips." He exercises a singular fascination over old ladies, who slide coppers into his hand quickly, as if afraid that they shall hurt his feelings. He pockets the money, heaves a sigh, and darts an abashed and grateful look at them that makes them feel how keenly he appreciates their delicacy. When the snow is on the ground he now and then introduces a little shiver, and with a well-worn pocket-handkerchief stifles a cough that, he intimates by a despairing dropping of his eyelids, is slowly killing him.

The Swell Beggar

A singular variety of this sort of mendicant used to be seen some years ago in the streets of Cambridge. He had been a gentleman of property, and had studied at one of the colleges. Race-courses, billiard-tables, and general gambling had reduced him to beggary; but he was too proud to ask alms. As the "Ashamed Beggar" fortifies himself with a "pad", this swell-beggar armed himself with a broom. He swept a crossing. His clothes—he always wore evening dress——were miserably ragged and shabby; his hat was a broken Gibus, but he managed to have good and fashionable boots; and his shirt collar, and wrist bands were changed every day. A white cambric handkerchief peeped from his coat tail pocket, and a gold eye-glass dangled from his neck. His hands were lady like; his nails well kept; and it was impossible to look at him without a mingled feeling of pity and amusement.

His plan of operations was to station himself at his crossing at the time the ladies of Cambridge were out shopping. His antics were curiously funny. Dangling his broom between his forefinger and thumb, as if it were a light umbrella or riding whip, he would arrive at his stand, and look up at the sky to see what sort of weather might be expected. Then, tucking the broom beneath his arm he would take off his gloves, fold them together and put them into his coat pockets, sweep his crossing carefully, and when he had finished, look at it with admiration. When ladies crossed, he would remove his broken hat and smile with great benignity, displaying at the same time a fine set of teeth. On wet days his attentions to the fair sex knew no bounds. He would run before them and wipe away every little puddle in their path. On receiving a gratuity, which was generally in silver, he would remove his hat and bow gracefully and gratefully. When gentlemen walked over his crossing he would stop them and, holding his hat in the true mendicant fashion, request the loan of a shilling. With many he was a regular pensioner. When a mechanic or poor looking person offered him a copper, he would take it, and smile his thanks with a patronising air, but he never took off his hat to less than sixpence. He was a jovial and boastful beggar, and had a habit of jerking at his stand up collar, and pulling at his imperial coxcombically. When he considered his day's work over, he would put on his gloves and, dangling his broom in his careless elegant way, trip home to his lodging. He never used a broom but one day, and gave the old ones to his landlady. The undergraduates were kind to him, and encouraged his follies; but the college dons looked coldly on him, and when they passed him he would assume an expression of impertinent indifference as if he cut them. I never heard what became of him. When I last saw him he looked between forty and fifty years of age.

Clean Family Beggar

CLEAN Family Beggars are those who beg or sing in the streets, in numbers varying from four to seven. I need only particularise one "gang" or "party," as their appearance and method of begging will do as a sample of all others.

Beggars of this class group themselves artistically. A broken-down looking man, in the last stage of seediness, walks hand-in-hand with a palefaced, interesting little girl. His wife trudges on his other side, a baby in one arm; a child just able to walk steadies itself by the hand that is disengaged; two or three other children cling about the skirts of her gown, one occasionally detaching himself or herself—as a kind of rear or advanced guard from the main body—to cut off stragglers and pounce upon falling halfpence, or look piteously into the face of a passer by. The clothes of the whole troop are in that state when seediness is dropping into rags; but their hands and faces are perfectly clean—their skins literally shine—perhaps from the effect of a plentiful use of soap, which they do not wash off before drying themselves with a towel. The complexions of the smaller children, in particular, glitter like sandpaper, and their eyes are half closed, and their noses corrugated, as with constant and compulsory ablution. The baby is a wonderful specimen of washing and get-ting-up of ornamental linen. Altogether, the Clean Family Beggars form a most attractive picture for quiet and respectable streets, and "pose" themselves for the admiration of the thrifty matrons, who are their best supporters.

Sometimes the children of the Clean Family Beggars sing— sometimes the father "patters." This morning a group passed my window, who both sang and "pattered." The mother was absent, and the two eldest girls knitted and crochetted as they walked along. The burthen of the song which the children shrieked out in thin treble, was,

"And the wild flowers are springing on the plain."

The rest of the words were undistinguishable. When the little ones had finished, the man, who evidently prided himself upon his powers of eloquence, began, in a loud, authoritative, oratorical tone:—

"My dear friends,—It is with great pain, and affliction, and trouble, that I present myself and my poo—oor family before you, in this wretched situation, at the present moment; but what can I do? Work I cannot obtain, and my little family ask me for bread! Yes, my dear friends—my little family ask me for bread! Oh, my dear friends, conceive what your feelin's would be if, like me, at the present moment, your poo-oor dear children asked for bread, and you had it not to give them! What then could you do? God send, my dear friends, that no individual, no father of a family, nor mother, nor other individual, with children, will ever, or ever may be drove to do what—or, I should say, that which I am now a doing of, at the present moment. If any one in this street, or in the next, or in any of the streets in this affluent neighbourhood, had found theirselves in the situation in which I was placed this morning, it would be hard to say what they could, or would have done; and I assure you, my dear friends—yes, I assure you, from my heart, that it is very possible that many might have been drove to have done, or do worse, than what I am a doing of, for the sake of my poo—oor family, at the present moment, if they had been drove, by suffering, as I and my poo—oor wife have been the morning of this very day. My wife, my kind friends, is now unfortunately ill through unmerited starvation, and is ill a-bed, from which, at the present moment, she cannot rise. Want we have known together, my dear friends, and so has our poo-oor family, and baby, only eight months old. God send, my dear friends, that none of you, and none of your dear babes, and families, that no individual, which now is listening to my deep distress, at the present moment, may ever know the sufferin's to which we have been reduced, is my fervent prayer! All I want to obtain is a meal's victuals for my poo—oor family!"

(Here the man caught my eye, and immediately shifted his ground.)

"You will ask me, my dear friends," he continued in an argumentative manner, "you will ask me how and why it is and what is the reason which I cannot obtain work? Alas! my dear friends, it is unfortunately so at the present moment. I am a silk-weaver in Bethnal Green, by trade, and the noo International Treaty with France, which Mr. Cobden—" (here he kept his eye on me, as if the political reason were intended for my especial behoof) "—Which Mr. Cobden, my dear friends, was depooted to go to the French emperor, Louis Napoleon, to agree upon, betwixt this country and France, which the French manufacturers sends goods into this country, without paying no dooty, and undersells the native manufacturers, though, my dear friends, our workmanship is as good, and English silk as genuine as French, I do assure you. Leastways, there is no difference, except in pattern, and, through the neglect of them as ought to look after it better, that is, to see we had the best designs; for design is the only thing—I mean designs and pattern—in which they can outdo us; and also, my dear friends, ladies as go to shops will ask for foreign goods—it is more to their taste than English, at the present moment; and so it is, that many poo—oor families at Bethnal Green and Spitalfields—and Coventry likewise, is redooced to the situation which I myself—that is, to ask your charity—am a doing of—at the present moment."

I gave a little girl a penny, and the man, still fixing me with his eye, continued—

"You will ask me, my dear friends, p'r'aps, how it is that I do not apply to the parish? why not to get relief for myself, my de—ar wife, and little family? My kind friends, you do not know the state in which things is with the poor weavers of Bethnal Green, and, at the present moment, Spitalfields likewise. It comes of the want of knowledge of the real state of this rich and 'appy country, its material prosperity and resources, which you, at this end of the town, can form no idea of. There is now sixteen or seventeen thousand people out of work. Yes, my dear friends, in about two parishes there is sixteen or seventeen thousand individuals—I mean, of course, counting their poo—oor families and all, which at the present moment cannot obtain bread. Oh, my dear friends, how grateful ought you to be to God that you and your dear families are not out of work, and can obtain a meal's victuals, and are not like the sufferin' weavers of Bethnal Green—and Spitalfields, and Coventry likewise, through the loss of trade; for, my dear friends, if you were like me, forced to what I am doing now at the present moment, etc., etc., etc."

NAVAL AND MILITARY BEGGARS

NAVAL and Military Beggars are most frequently met with in towns situated at some distance from a seaport or a garrison. As they are distinct specimens of the same tribe, they must be separately classified. The more familiar nuisance is the

Turnpike Sailor

THIS sort of vagabond has two lays, the "merchant" lay and the "R'yal Navy" lay. He adopts either one or the other, according to the exigencies of his wardrobe, his locality, or the person he is addressing. He is generally the offspring of some inhabitant of the most notorious haunts of a seaport town, and has seldom been at sea, or when he has, has run away after the first voyage. His slang of seamanship has been picked up at the lowest public-houses in the filthiest slums that offer diversion to the genuine sailor.

When on the "merchant lay" his attire consists of a pair of tattered trousers, an old guernsey-shirt, and a torn straw-hat. One of his principal points of "costume" is his bare feet. His black silk handkerchief is knotted jauntily round his throat after the most approved models at the heads of penny ballads, and the outsides of songs. He wears small gold earrings, and has short curly hair in the highest and most offensive state of glossy greasiness. His hands and arms are carefully tattooed—a foul anchor, or a long-haired mermaid sitting on her tail and making her toilette, being the favourite cartoons. In his gait he endeavours to counterfeit the roll of a true seaman, but his hard feet, knock-knees, and imperceptibly acquired turnpike-trot betray him. His face bears the stamp of diabolically low cunning, and it is impossible to look at him without an association with a police-court. His complexion is coarse and tallowy, and has none of the manly bronze that exposure to the weather, and watching the horizon, give to the real tar.

I was once walking with a gentleman who had spent the earlier portion of his life at sea, when a turnpike sailor shuffled on before us. We had just been conversing on nautical affairs, and I said to him—

"Now, there is a brother sailor in distress; of course, you will give him something?"

"*He* a sailor!" said my friend, with great disgust. "Did you see him spit?"

The fellow had that moment expectorated.

I answered that I had.

"He spit to wind'ard!" said my friend.

"What of that?" said I.

"A regular landsman's trick," observed my friend. "A real sailor never spits to wind'ard. *Why, he couldn't.*"

We soon passed the fellow, who pulled at a curl upon his forehead, and began in a gruff voice, intended to convey the idea of hardships, storms, shipwrecks, battles, and privations.

"God — bless — your — 'onors — give — a — copper — to — a — poor — sailor — as — hasn't — spliced — the — main — jaw — since — the — day — 'fore — yesterday — at — eight — bells — God — love — yer — 'onors — do! — I — 'aven't — tasted — sin' — the — day — 'fore — yesterday — so — drop — a — cop — poor — seaman — do."

My friend turned round and looked the beggar full in the face.

"What ship?" he asked quickly.

The fellow answered glibly.

"What captain?" pursued my friend.

The fellow again replied boldly, though his eyes wandered uneasily.

"What cargo?" asked my inexorable companion.

The beggar was not at fault, but answered correctly.

The name of the port, the reason of his discharge, and other questions were asked and answered; but the man was evidently beginning to be embarrassed. My friend pulled out his purse as if to give him something.

"What are you doing here?" continued the indefatigable inquirer. "Did you leave the coast for the purpose of trying to find a ship *here?*" (We were in Leicester.)

The man stammered and pulled at his useful forelock to get time to collect his thoughts and invent a good lie.

"He had a friend in them parts as he thought could help him."

"How long since you were up in the Baltic?"

"Year—and—a—arf,—yer—'onor."

"Do you know Kiel?"

"Yes,—yer—'onor."

"D'ye know the 'British Flag' on the quay there?"

"Yes,—yer—'onor."

"Been there often?"

"Yes,—yer—'onor."

"Does Nick Johnson still keep it?"

"Yes,—yer—'onor."

"Then," said my friend, after giving vent to a strong opinion as to the beggar's veracity, "I'd advise you to be off quickly for there's a policeman, and if I get within hail of him I shall tell him you're an impostor. There's no such house on the quay. Get out, you scoundrel!"

The fellow shuffled off, looking curses, but not daring to express them.

On the "R'yal Navy" lay, the turnpike sailor assumes different habiliments, and altogether a smarter trim. He wears coarse blue trousers symmetrically cut about the hips, and baggy over the foot. A "jumper," or loose shirt of the same material, a tarpaulin hat, with the name of a vessel in letters of faded gold, is stuck on the back of his neck, and he has a piece of whipcord, or "lanyard" round his waist, to which is suspended a jack-knife, which if of but little service in fighting the battles of his country, has stood him in good stead in silencing the cackling of any stray poultry that crossed his road, or in frightening into liberality the female tenant of a solitary cottage. This "patter," or "blob," is of Plymouth, Portsmouth, Cawsen' Bay, Hamoaze—ships paid off, prize-money, the bo'sen and the first le'etnant. He is always an able-bodied, never an ordinary seaman, and cannot get a ship "becos orders is at the Hadmiralty as no more isn't to be put into commission." Like the fictitious merchant-sailor he calls every landsman "your honour," in accordance with the conventional rule observed by the jack tars in nautical dramas. He exhibits a stale plug of tobacco, and replaces it in his jaw with ostentatious gusto. His chief victims are imaginative boys fresh from "Robinson Crusoe," and "Tales of the Ocean," and old ladies who have relatives at sea. For many months after a naval battle he is in full force, and in inland towns tells highly-spiced narratives of the adventures of his own ship and its gallant crew in action. He is profuse in references to "the cap'en," and interlards his account with, "and the cap'en turns round, and he says to me, he says—" He feels the pulse of his listener's credulity through their eyes, and throws the hatchet with the enthusiasm of an artist. "When we boarded 'em," I heard one of these vagabonds say—"oh, when we boarded 'em!" but it is beyond the power

BOYS EXERCISING AT TOTHILL FIELDS PRISON

INTERIOR OF DRURY LANE THEATRE

of my feeble pen to relate the deeds of the turnpike true blue, and his ship and its gallant, gallant crew, when they boarded 'em. I let him run out his yarn, and then said, "I saw the account of the action in the papers, but they said nothing of boarding. As I read it, the enemy were in too shallow water to render that manoeuvre possible; but that till they struck their flag, and the boats went out to take possession, the vessels were more than half a mile apart."

This would have posed an ordinary humbug, but the able-bodied liar immediately, and with great apparent disgust, said, "The papers! the noo—o—o—spapers! d——n the noo—o—o—s-papers. You don't believe what they says, surely. Look how they sarved out old Charley Napier. Why, sir, *I was there, and I ought to know.*"

At times the turnpike sailor roars out a song in praise of British valour by sea; but of late this "lay" has been unfrequent. At others he borrows an interesting-looking little girl, and tying his arm up in a sling, adds his wounds and a motherless infant to his other claims upon the public sympathy. After a heavy gale and the loss of several vessels, he appears with a fresh tale and a new suit of carefully chosen rags. When all these resources fail him he is compelled to turn merchant, or "duffer," and invests a small capital in a few hundred of the worst, and a dozen or two of the very best, cigars. If he be possessed of no capital he steals them. He allows his whiskers to grow round his face, and lubricates them in the same liberal manner as his shining hair. He buys a pea-coat, smart waistcoat, and voluminous trousers, discards his black neckerchief for a scarlet one, the ends of which run through a massive ring. He wears a large pair of braces over his waistcoat, and assumes a half-foreign air, as of a mariner just returned from distant climes. He accosts you in the streets mysteriously, and asks you if you want "a few good cigars?" He tells you they are smuggled, that he "run" them himself, and that the "Custom-'us horficers" are after him. I need hardly inform my reader that the cigar he offers as a sample is excellent, and that, should he be weak enough to pur-chase a few boxes, he will not find them "according to sample." Not unfrequently the cigar "duffer" lures his victim to some low tavern to receive his goods, where in lieu of tobacco, shawls, and laces, he finds a number of cut-throat-looking confederates, who plunder and illtreat him.

It must not be forgotten that at times a begging sailor may be met, who has really been a seaman, and who is a proper object of benevolence. When it is so, he is invariably a man past middle age, and offers for sale or exhibition a model of a man-of-war or a few toy yachts. He has but little to say for himself, and is too glad for the gift of a pair of landsmen's trousers to trouble himself about their anti-nautical cut. In fact, the real seaman does not care for costume, and is as frequently seen in an old shooting-coat as a torn jacket; but despite his habiliments, the true salt oozes out in the broad hands that dangle heavily from the wrists, as if wanting to grip a rope or a handspike; in the tender feet accustomed to the smooth planks of the decks and in the settled, far-off look of the weather-beaten head, with its fixed expression of the aristocracy of subordination.

In conclusion, a real sailor is seldom or never seen inland, where he can have no chance of employment, and is removed from the sight of the sea, docks, shipmates, and all things dear and familiar to him. He carries his papers about him in a small tin box, addresses those who speak to him as "sir" and "marm," and never as "your honour" or "my lady"; is rather taciturn than talkative, and rarely brags of what he has seen, or done, or seen done. In these and all other respects he is the exact opposite of the turnpike sailor.

Street Campaigners

SOLDIER beggars may be divided into three classes: those who really have been soldiers and are reduced to mendicancy, those who have been ejected from the army for misconduct, and those with whom the military dress and bearing are pure assumptions.

The difference between these varieties is so distinct as to be easily detected. The first, or soldier proper, has all the evidence of drill and barrack life about him; the eye that always "fronts" the person he addresses; the spare habit, high cheekbones, regulation whisker, stiff chin, and deeply-marked line from ear to ear. He carries his papers about him, and when he has been wounded or seen service, is modest and retiring as to his share of glory. He can give little information as to the incidents of an engagement, except as regards the deeds of his own company, and in conversation speaks more of the personal qualities of his officers and comrades than of their feats of valour. Try him which way you will he never will confess that he has killed a man.

He compensates himself for his silence on the subject of fighting by excessive grumbling as to the provisions, quarters, &c., to which he has been forced to submit in the course of his career. He generally has a wife marching by his side—a tall strapping woman, who looks as if a long course of washing at the barracks had made her half a soldier. Ragged though he be, there is a certain smartness about the soldier proper, observable in the polish of his boots, the cock of his cap, and the disposition of the leather strap under his lower lip. He invariably carries a stick, and when a soldier passes him, casts on him an odd sort of look, half envying, half pitying, as if he said, "Though you are better fed than I, you are not so free!"

The soldier proper has various occupations. He does not pass all his time in begging; he will hold a horse, clean knives and boots, sit as a model to an artist, and occasionally take a turn at the wash-tub. Begging he abhors, and is only driven to it as a last resource.

If my readers would inquire why a man so ready to work should not be able to obtain employment, he will receive the answer that universally applies to all questions of hardship among the humbler classes—the vice of the discharged soldier is intemperance.

The second sort of soldier-beggar is one of the most dangerous and violent of mendicants. Untamable even by regimental discipline, insubordinate by nature, he has been thrust out from the army to prey upon society. He begs but seldom, and is dangerous to meet with after dark upon a lonely road, or in a sequestered lane. Indeed, though he has every right to be classed among those who will not work, he is not thoroughly a beggar, but will be met with again, and receive fuller justice at our hands, in the, to him, more congenial catalogue of thieves.

The third sort of street campaigner is a perfect impostor who, being endowed, either by accident or art, with a broken limb or damaged feature, puts on an old military coat, as he would assume the dress of a frozen-out gardener, distressed dockyard labourer, burnt-out tradesman, or scalded mechanic. He is imitative, and in his time plays many parts. He "gets up" his costume with the same attention to detail as the turnpike sailor. In crowded busy streets he "stands pad," that is, with a written statement of his hard case slung round his neck, like a label round a decanter. His bearing is most military; he keeps his neck straight, his chin in, and his thumbs to the outside seams of his trousers; he is stiff as an embalmed preparation, for which, but for motion of his eyes, you might mistake him. In quiet streets and in the country he discards his "pad" and begs "on the blob", that is, he "patters" to the passers-by, and invites their sympathy by words of mouth. He is an ingenious and fertile liar, and seizes occasions such as the late war in the Crimea and the mutiny in India as good distant grounds on which to build his fictions.

I was walking in a high-road, when I was accosted by a fellow dressed in an old military tunic, a forage-cap like a charity boy's, and tattered trousers, who limped along barefoot by the aid of a stick. His right sleeve was empty, and tied up to a button-hole at his breast, à la Nelson.

"Please your honour," he began, in a doleful exhausted voice, "bestow your charity on a poor soldier which lost his right arm at the glorious battle of Inkermann."

I looked at him, and after considerable experience in this kind of imposition, could at once detect that he was "acting".

"To what regiment did you belong?" I asked.

"The Thirty—, sir."

I looked at his button and read Thirty—

"I haven't tasted bit o' food, sir, since yesterday at half-past four, and then a lady give me cruster bread," he continued.

"The Thirty—!" I repeated. "I knew the Thirty—. Let me see—who was the colonel?"

The man gave me a name, with which I suppose he was provided.

"How long were you in the Thirty—?" I inquired.

"Five year, sir."

"I had a schoolfellow in that regiment, Captain Thorpe, a tall man with red whiskers—did you know him?"

"There was a captain, sir, with large red whiskers, and I think his name was Thorpe; but he wasn't captain of my company, so I didn't know for certain," replied the man, after an affected hesitation.

"The Thirty— was one of the first of our regiments that landed, I think?" I remarked.

"Yes, your honour, it were."

"You impudent impostor!" I said; "the Thirty— did not go out till the spring of '53. How dare you tell me you belonged to it?"

The fellow blanched for a moment, but rallied and said, "I didn't like to contradict your honour for fear you should be angry and wouldn't give me nothing."

"That's very polite of you," I said, "but still I have a great mind to give you into custody. Stay; tell me who and what you are, and I will give you a shilling and let you go."

He looked up and down the road, measured me with his eye, abandoned the idea of resistance, and replied:

"Well, your honour, if you won't be too hard on a poor man which finds it hard to get a crust anyhow or way, I don't mind telling you I never was a soldier." I give his narrative as he related it to me.

"I don't know who my parents ever was. The fust thing as I remember was the river side (the Thames), and running in low tide to find things. I used to beg, hold hosses, and sleep under dry arches. I don't remember how I got any clothes. I never had a pair of shoes or stockings till I was almost a man. I fancy I am now nearly forty years of age.

"An old woman as kept a rag and iron shop by the water-side give me a lodging once for two years. We used to call her 'Nanny'; but she turned me out when she caught me taking some old nails and a brass cock out of her shop; I was hungry when I done it, for the old gal gi' me no grub, nothing but the bare floor for a bed.

"I have been a beggar all my life, and begged in all sorts o' ways and all sorts o' lays. I don't mean to say that if I see anything laying about handy that I don't mouch it (i.e., steal it). Once a gentleman took me into his house as his servant. He was a very kind man; I had a good place, swell clothes, and beef and beer as much as I liked; but I couldn't stand the life, and I run away.

"The loss o' my arm, sir, was the best thing as ever happen'd to me; I turn out with it on all sorts o' lays, and it's as good as a pension. I lost it poaching; my mate's gun went off by accident, and the shot went into my arm. I neglected it, and at last was obliged to go to a orspital and have it off. The surgeon as ampitated it said that a little longer and it would ha' mortified.

"The Crimea's been a good dodge to a many, but it's getting stale; all dodges are getting stale; square coves (i.e., honest folks) are so wide awake."

"Don't you think you would have found it more profitable,

had you taken to labour or some honester calling than your present one?" I asked.

"Well, sir, p'raps I might," he replied; "but going on the square is so dreadfully confining."

FOREIGN BEGGARS

THESE beggars appeal to the sympathies as "strangers"—in a foreign land, away from friends and kindred, unable to make their wants known, or to seek work, from ignorance of the language.

In exposing the shams and swindles that are set to catch the unwary, I have no wish to check the current of real benevolence. Cases of distress exist, which it is a pleasure and a duty to relieve. I only expose the "dodges" of the beggar by profession—the beggar by trade—the beggar who lives by begging, and nothing else, except, as in most cases, where he makes the two ends of idleness and self-indulgence meet—by thieving.

Foreign beggars are generally so mixed up with political events, that in treating of them, it is more than usually difficult to detect imposition from misfortune. Many high-hearted patriots have been driven to this country by tyrants and their tools, but it will not do to mistake every vagabond refugee for a noble exile, or to accept as a fact that a man who cannot live in his own country, is necessarily persecuted and unfortunate, and has a claim to be helped to live in this.

The neighbourhood of Leicester Square is, to the foreign political exile, the foreign political spy, the foreign fraudulent tradesman, the foreign escaped thief, and the foreign convict who has served his time, what, in the middle-ages, sanctuary was to the murderer. In this modern Alsatia—happily for us, guarded by native policemen and detectives of every nation in the world—plots are hatched, fulminating powder prepared, detonating-balls manufactured, and infernal machines invented, which wielded by the hands of men whose opinions are so far beyond the age in which they live, that their native land has cast them out for ever, are destined to overthrow despotic government, restore the liberty of the subject, and, in a wholesale sort of way, regenerate the rights of man.

Political spies are the monied class among these philanthropic desperadoes. The political regenerators, unless furnished with means from some special fund, are the most miserable and abject. Mr. Thackeray has observed that whenever an Irishman is in difficulties he always finds another Irishman worse off than himself, who talks over creditors, borrows money, runs errands, and makes himself generally useful to this incarcerated fellow-countryman. This observation will apply equally to foreigners.

There is a timid sort of refugee, who, lacking the courage to arrive at political eminence or cash, by means of steel, or poison, is a hanger-on of his bolder and less scrupulous compatriot. This man, when deserted by his patron, is forced to beg. The statement that he makes as to his reasons for leaving the dear native land that the majority of foreigners are so ready to sing songs in praise of, and to quit, must be, of course, received with caution.

The French Beggar

MY reader has most likely, in a quiet street, met a shabby little man, who stares about him in a confused manner, as if he had lost his way. As soon as he sees a decently-dressed person he shuffles up to him, and taking off a "casquette" with considerably more brim than body, makes a slight bow, and says in a plaintive voice, "Parlez français, m'sieu?"

If you stop and, in an unguarded moment, answer "Oui," the beggar takes from his breast-pocket a greasy leather book, from which he extracts a piece of carefully folded paper, which he hands you with a pathetic shrug.

The paper, when opened, contains a small slip, on which is written in a light, foreign hand—

"You are requested to direct the bearer to the place to which he desires to go, as he cannot speak English!"

The beggar then, with a profusion of bows, points to the larger paper.

"Mais, m'sieu, ayez la bonté de lire. C'est Anglais."

The larger paper contains a statement in French and English, that the bearer Jean Baptiste Dupont is a native of Troyes, Champagne, and a fan-maker by trade; that paralysis in the hand has deprived him of the power of working; that he came to England to find a daughter, who had married an Englishman and was dwelling in Westminster, but that when he arrived he found they had departed for Australia; that he is fifty-two years of age, and is a deserving object of compassion, having no means of returning to Troyes, being an entire stranger to England, and having no acquaintances or friends to assist him.

This statement is without any signature, but no sooner have you read it than the beggar, who would seem to have a blind credence in the efficacy of documents, draws from his pocket-book a certificate of birth, a register of marriage, a passport, and a permission to embark, which, being all in a state of crumpled greasiness, and printed and written in French, so startles and confounds the reader, that he drops something into the man's hand and passes on.

I have often been stopped by this sort of beggar. In the last case I met with I held a long talk with the man—of course, in his own language, for he will seldom or never be betrayed into admitting that he has any knowledge of English.

"Parlez français, m'sieu?"

"Yes, I do," I answered. "What do you want?"

"Deign, monsieur, to have the bounty to read this paper which I have the honour to present to monsieur."

"Oh, never mind the papers!" I said, shortly. "Can't you speak English?"

"Alas, monsieur, no!"

"Speak French, then!"

My quick speaking rather confused the fellow, who said that he was without bread, and without asylum; that he was a tourneur and ebeniste (turner, worker in ebony and ivory, and cabinet-maker in general) by trade, that he was a stranger, and wished to raise sufficient money to enable him to return to France.

"Why did you come over to England?" I asked.

"I came to work in London," he said, after pretending not to understand my question the first time.

"Where?" I inquired.

At first I understood him to answer Sheffield, but I at last made out that he meant Smithfield.

"What was your master's name?"

"I do not comprehend, monsieur—if monsieur will deign to read—"

"You comprehend me perfectly well; don't pretend that you don't—that is only shuffling (tracasserie)."

"The name of my master was Johnson."

"Why did you leave him?" I inquired.

"He is dead, monsieur."

"Why did you not return to France at his death?" was my next question.

"Monsieur, I tried to obtain work in England," said the beggar.

"How long did you work for Mr. Johnson?"

"There was a long time, monsieur, that—"

"How long?" I repeated. "How many years?"

"Since two years."

"And did you live in London two years, and all that time learn to speak no English?"

"Ah, monsieur, you embarrass me. If monsieur will not deign to aid me, it must be that I seek elsewhere—"

"But tell me how it was you learnt no English," I persisted.

"Ah, monsieur, my comrades in the shop were all French."

"And you want to get back to France?"

"Ah, monsieur, it is the hope of my life."

"Come to me to-morrow morning at eleven o'clock—there is my address." I gave him the envelope of a letter. "I am well acquainted with the French Consul at London Bridge, and at my intercession I am sure that he will get you a free passage to Calais; if not, and I find he considers your story true, I will send you at my own expense. Good night!"

Of course the man did not call in the morning, and I saw no more of him.

Destitute Poles

IT is now many years since the people of this country evinced a strong sympathy for Polish refugees. Their gallant struggle, compulsory exile, and utter national and domestic ruin raised them warm friends in England; and committees for the relief of destitute Poles, balls for the benefit of destitute Poles, and subscriptions for the relief of the destitute Poles were got up in every market-town. Shelter and sustenance were afforded to many gentlemen of undoubted integrity, who found themselves penniless in a strange land, and the aristocracy feted and caressed the best-born and most gallant. To be a Pole, and in distress, was almost a sufficient introduction, and there were few English families who did not entertain as friend or visitor one of these unfortunate and suffering patriots.

So excellent an opportunity for that class of foreign swindlers which haunt roulette-tables, and are the pest of second-rate hotels abroad, was of course made use of. Crowds of adventurers, "got up" in furs, and cloaks, and playhouse dresses, with padded breasts and long moustachios, flocked to England, and assuming the title of count, and giving out that their patrimony had been sequestered by the Emperor of Russia, easily obtained a hearing and a footing in many English families, whose heads would not have received one of their own countrymen except with the usual credentials.

John Bull's partiality for foreigners is one of his well-known weaknesses; and valets, cooks, and couriers in their masters' clothes, and sometimes with the titles of that master whom they had seen shot down in battle, found themselves objects of national sympathy and attention. Their success among the fair sex was extraordinary; and many penniless adventurers, with no accomplishments beyond card-sharping, and a foreign hotel waiter's smattering of continental languages, allied themselves to families of wealth and respectability. All, of course, were not so fortunate; and after some persons had been victimised, a few inquiries made, and the real refugee gentlemen and soldiers had indignantly repudiated any knowledge of the swindlers or their pretensions, the pseudo-Polish exiles were compelled to return to their former occupations. The least able and least fortunate were forced to beg, and adopted exactly the same tactics as the French beggar, except that instead of certificates of birth, and passports, he exhibited false military documents, and told lying tales of regimental services, Russian prisons, and miraculous escapes.

The "destitute Pole" is seldom met with now, and would hardly have demanded a notice if I had not thought it right to show how soon the unsuccessful cheat or swindler drops down into the beggar, and to what a height the "Polish fever" raged some thirty years ago. It would be injustice to a noble nation if I did not inform my reader that but few of the false claimants to British sympathy were Poles at all. They were Russians, Frenchmen, Hungarians, Austrians, Prussians, and Germans of all sorts.

The career of one fellow will serve to show with what little ingenuity the credulous can be imposed on. His real name is lost among his numerous aliases, neither do I know whether he commenced life as a soldier, or as a valet; but I think it probable that he had combined those occupations and been regimental servant to an officer. He came to London in the year 1833 under the name of Count Stanislas Soltiewski, of Ostralenka; possessed of a handsome person and invulnerable audacity, he was soon received into decent society, and in 1837 married a lady of some fortune, squandered her money, and deserted her. He then changed his name to Levieczin, and travelled from town to town, giving political lectures at townhalls, assembly-rooms, and theatres. In 1842 he called himself Doctor Telecki, said he was a native of Smolensk, and set up a practice in Manchester, where he contracted a large amount of debts. From Manchester he eloped with one of his patients, a young lady to whom he was married in 1845, in Dublin, in which place he again endeavoured to practise as a physician. He soon involved himself in difficulties, and quitted Dublin, taking with him funds which had been entrusted to him as treasurer of a charitable institution. He left his second wife, and formed a connexion with another woman, travelled about, giving scientific lectures, and sometimes doing feats of legerdemain. He again married a widow lady who had some four or five hundred pounds, which he spent, after which he deserted her. He then became the scourge and terror of hotelkeepers, and went from tavern to tavern living on every luxury, and, when asked for money, decamping, and leaving behind him nothing but portmanteaux filled with straw and bricks. He returned to England and obtained a situation in a respectable academy as a teacher of French and the guitar. Here he called himself Count Hohenbreitenstein-Boitzenburg.

Under this name he seduced a young lady, whom he persuaded he could not marry on account of her being a Protestant, and of his being a Count of the Holy Roman Empire in the pontifical degree. By threatening exposure he extracted a large sum of money from her friends, with which he returned to London, where he lived for some time by begging letters, and obtaining money on various false pretences. His first wife discovered him, and he was charged with bigamy, but owing to some technical informality was not convicted. He then enlisted in the 87th regiment, from which he shortly after deserted. He became the associate of thieves and the prostitutes who live in the neighbourhood of Waterloo Road. After being several times imprisoned for petty thefts he at length earned a miserable living by conjuring in low public-houses, where he announced himself as the celebrated Polish professor of legerdemain, Count Makvicz.

He died in August, 1852, and oddly enough, in a garret in Poland Street, Oxford Street.

Of modern Polish swindlers and beggars, the most renowned is Adolphus Czapolinski. This "shabby genteel man of military appearance"—I quote the daily papers—"has been several times incarcerated, has again offended, and been again imprisoned. His fraudulent practices were first discovered in 1860." The following is from the "Times", of June the 5th of that year:—

"Bow Street.—A military-looking man, who said his name was Lorenzo Noodt, and that he had served as captain in one or our foreign legions during the Crimean war, was brought before Mr. Henry on a charge of attempting to obtain money by false and fraudulent pretences from the Countess of Waldegrave."

Mr. George Granville Harcourt (the husband of Lady Waldegrave), deposed:

"I saw the prisoner to-day at my house in Carlton Gardens, where he called by my request in reference to a letter which Lady Waldegrave had received from him. It was a letter soliciting charitable contributions, and enclosing three papers. The first purported to be a note from Lady Stafford, enclosing a post-office order for £3. I know her ladyship's handwriting, and this is like it, but I cannot say whether it is genuine. The second is apparently a note from Colonel Macdonald, sending him a post-office order for £4 on the part of the Duke of Cambridge. The third is a note purporting to be written by the secretary of the Duke d'Aumale. This note states that the duke approves this person's departure for Italy, and desires his secretary to send him £5. We were persuaded that it could not be genuine, in the first place, as we have the honour of being intimate with the Duke d'Aumale. We perfectly well knew that he would not say to this individual, or to anyone else, that he approved his departure for Italy; in the second place, there are mistakes in the French which render it impossible that the duke's secretary should have written it; in the third place, the name is not that of the secretary, though resembling it. Under all the circumstances, I took an opportunity of asking both the secretary and the Duke d'Aumale whether they had any knowledge of this communication, and they stated that they knew nothing of it. The duke said that it was very disagreeable to him that he should be supposed to be interfering to forward the departure of persons to Italy, which would produce an impression that he was meddling in the affairs of that country.

I wrote to the prisoner to call on me, in order to receive back his papers. At first another man called, but on his addressing me in French I said, 'You are an Italian, not a German. I want to see the captain himself.' To-day the prisoner called. I showed the papers, and asked him if they were the letters he had received, and if he had received the money referred to in those letters. To both questions he replied in the affirmative. The officer Horsford, with whom I had communicated in the meanwhile, was in the next room. I called him in, and he went up to Captain Noodt, telling him he was his prisoner. He asked why? Horsford replied, for attempting to obtain money by means of a forged letter. He then begged me not to ruin him, and said that the letter was not written by him."

The prisoner's letter to Lady Waldegrave was then read as follows:—

"Milady Countess,—I am foreigner, but have the rank of captain by my service under English colours in the Crimean war, being appointed by her Majesty's brevet. I have struggled very hard, after having been discharged from the service, but, happily, I have been temporarily assisted by some persons of distinction, and the Duke of Cambridge. To-day, milady Countess, I have in object to ameliorate or better my condition, going to accept service in Italian lawful army, where by the danger I may obtain advancement. Being poor, I am obliged to solicit of my noble patrons towards my journey. The Duc d'Aumale, the Marchioness of Stafford, &c., kindly granted me their contributions. Knowing your ladyship's connexion with those noble persons, I take the liberty of soliciting your ladyship's kind contribution to raise any funds for my outfit and journey. In 'appui' of my statements I enclose my captain's commission and letters, and, in recommending myself to your ladyship's consideration, I present my homage, and remain,

"Your humble servant

"CAPTAIN L. B. NOODT."

The letter of the pretended secretary was as follows:—

"Monsieur le Capitaine,—Son altesse Monseigneur le Duc d'Aumale approuve votre départ pour l'Italie, et pour vous aider dans la dépense de votre voyage m'a chargé de vous transmettre £5, ci inclus, que vous m'obligerez de m'en accuser la réception.

"Agréez, monsieur le capitaine, l'assurance de ma consideration distinguée.

"Votre humble serviteur,

"CHS. COULEUVRIER, Sec."

The prisoner, who appeared much agitated, acknowledged the dishonesty of his conduct, but appealed to the pity of Mr. Harcourt, saying that he had suffered great hardships, and had been driven to this act by want. It was sad that an officer bearing the Queen's commission should be so humiliated. The letter was not written by himself, but by a Frenchman who led him into it.

Mr. Henry said he had brought the humiliation on himself. He must be well aware that the crime of forgery was punished as severely in his own country as here. The prisoner should have the opportunity of producing the writer of the letter, or of designating him to the police. On the recommendation to mercy of Mr. Harcourt, he was only sentenced to one month's imprisonment.

On July 9th he was brought up to Marlborough Street by Horsford, the officer of the Mendicity Society, charged with obtaining by false and fraudulent pretences the sum of £3 from Lady Stafford. Since his imprisonment it had been discovered that his real name was Adolphus Czapolinski, and that he was a Pole. The real Captain Noodt was in a distant part of the kingdom, and Czapolinski had obtained surreptitious possession of his commission, and assumed his name. The indefatigable Mr. Horsford had placed himself in communication with the secretary of the Polish Association, who had known the prisoner (Czapolinski) for twenty-five years. It would seem that in early life he had been engaged under various foreign powers, and in 1835 he came to this country and earned a scanty maintenance as a teacher of languages; that he was addicted to drinking, begging, and thieving, and upon one occasion, when usher in a school, he robbed the pupils of their clothes, and even fleeced them of their trifling pocket-money. While in the House of Detention he had written to Captain Wood, the secretary of the Mendicity Society, offering to turn approver. The letter in question ran thus:—

"Sir,—Permit me to make you a request, which is, not to press your prosecution against me, and I most solemnly promise you that for this favour all my endeavours will be to render you every assistance for all the information you should require. I was very wrong to not speak to you when I was at your office, but really I was not guilty of this charge because the letter containing the post-office order was delivered to Captain Noodt. I was only the messenger from Lady Stafford.

"Look, Captain Wood, I know much, and no one can be so able to render you the assistance and information of all the foreigners than me. Neither any of your officers could find the way; but if you charge me to undertake to find I will, on only one condition—that you will stop the prosecution. The six weeks of detention were quite sufficient punishment to me for the first time; and let it be understood that for your condescension to stop the prosecution all my services shall be at your orders, whenever you shall require, without any remuneration. My offers will be very advantageous to you under every respect. Send any of your clerks to speak with me to make my covenant with you, and you will be better convinced of my good intentions to be serviceable to you.—I am, &c.,

"A. CZAPOLINSKI."

He was sentenced to three months' imprisonment and hard labour.

Czapolinski is one of the most extraordinary of the beggars of the present day. He raises money both by personal application and by letter. He has been known to make from £20 to £60 per day. He is a great gambler, and has been seen to lose—and to pay—upwards of £100 at a gambling house in the neighbourhood of Leicester Square in the course of a single night and morning.

Hindoo Beggars

ARE those spare, snake-eyed Asiatics who walk the streets, coolly dressed in Manchester cottons, or chintz of a pattern commonly used for bed-furniture, to which the resemblance is carried out by the dark, polished colour of the thin limbs which it envelopes. They very often affect to be converts to the Christian religion, and give away tracts; with the intention of entrapping the sympathy of elderly ladies. They assert that they have been high-caste Brahmins, but as untruth, even when not acting professionally, is habitual to them, there is not the slightest dependence to be placed on what they say. Sometimes, in the winter, they "do shallow," that is, stand on the kerb-stone of the pavement, in their thin, ragged clothes, and shiver as with cold and hunger, or crouch against a wall and whine like a whipped animal; at others they turn out with a small, barrel-shaped drum, on which they make a monotonous noise with their fingers, to which music they sing and dance. Or they will "stand pad with a fakement," i.e. wear a placard upon their breasts, that describes them as natives of Madagascar, in distress, converts to Christianity, anxious to get to a seaport where they can work their passage back. This is a favourite artifice with Lascars—or they will sell lucifers, or sweep a crossing, or do anything where their picturesque appearance, of which they are proud and conscious, can be effectively displayed. They are as cunning as they look, and can detect a sympathetic face among a crowd. They never beg of soldiers, or sailors, to whom they always give a wide berth as they pass them in the streets.

From the extraordinary mendacity of this race of beggars —a mendacity that never falters, hesitates, or stumbles, but flows on in an unbroken stream of falsehood—it is difficult to obtain any reliable information respecting them. I have, however, many reasons for believing that the following statement, which was made to me by a dirty and distressed Indian, is moderately true. The man spoke English like a cockney of the lowest order. I shall not attempt to describe the peculiar accent or construction which he occasionally gave to it.

"My name is Joaleeka. I do not know where I was born. I never knew my father. I remember my mother very well. From the first of my remembrance I was at Dumdum, where I was servant to a European officer—a great man—a prince—who had more than a hundred servants beside me. When he went away to fight, I followed among others—I was with the baggage. I never fought myself, but I have heard the men (Sepoys) say that the prince, or general, or colonel, liked nothing so well as fighting, except tiger hunting. He was a wonderful man, and his soldiers liked him very much. I travelled over a great part of India with Europeans. I went up country as far as Secunderabad, and learned to speak English very well—so well that, when I was quite a young man, I was often employed as interpreter, for I caught up different Indian languages quickly. At last I got to interpret so well that I was recommended to————, a great native prince who was coming over to England. I was not his interpreter, but interpreter to his servants. We came to London. We stopped in an hotel in Vere Street, Oxford Street. We stayed here some time. Then my chief went over to Paris, but he did not take all his servants with him. I stopped at the hotel to interpret for those who remained. It was during this time that I formed a connexion with a white woman. She was a servant in the hotel. I broke my caste, and from that moment I knew that it would not do for me to go back to India. The girl fell in the family way and was sent out of the house. My fellow servants knew of it and as many of them hated me, I knew that they would tell my master on his return. I also knew that by the English laws in England I was a free man, and that my master could not take me back against my will. If I had gone back, I should have been put to death for breaking my caste. When my master returned from France, he sent for me. He told me that he had heard of my breaking my caste, and of the girl, but that he should take no notice of it; that I was to return to Calcutta with him, where he would get me employment with some European officer; that I need not fear, as he would order his servants to keep silent on the subject. I salaamed and thanked him, and said I was his servant for ever; but at the same time I knew that he would break his word, and that when he had me in his power, he would put me to death. He was a very severe man about caste. I attended to all my duties as before and all believed that I was going back to India—but the very morning that my master started for the coast, I ran away. I changed my clothes at the house of a girl I knew—not the same one as I had known at the hotel, but another. This one lived at Seven Dials. I stopped indoors for many days, till this girl, who could read newspapers, told me that my master had sailed away. I felt very glad, for though I knew my master could not force me to go back with him, yet I was afraid for all that, for he knew the King and Queen and had been invited by the Lord Mayor to the City. I liked England better than India, and English women have been very kind to me. I think English women are the handsomest in the world. The girl in whose house I hid, showed me how to beg. She persuaded me to turn Christian, because she thought that it would do me good—so I turned Christian. I do not know what it means, but I am a Christian, and have been for many years. I married that girl for some time. I have been married several times. I do not mean to say that I have ever been to church as

rich folks do; but I have been married without that. Sometimes
I do well, and sometimes badly. I often get a pound or two by
interpreting. I am not at all afraid of meeting any Indian who
knew me, for if they said anything I did not like, I should call out
'Police!' I know the law better than I did. Everything is free in
England. You can do what you like, if you can pay, or are not
found out. I do not like policemen. After the mutiny in 1857 I did
very badly. No one would look at a poor Indian then—much less
give to him. I knew that the English would put it down soon,
because I know what those rascals over there are like. I am living
now in Charles Street, Drury Lane. I have been married to my
present wife six years. We have three children and one dead.
My eldest is now in the hospital with a bad arm. I swept a crossing
for two years; that was just before the mutiny. All that knew me
used to chaff me about it, and call me Johnny Sepoy. My present
wife is Irish, and fought two women about it. They were taken to
Bow Street by a policeman, but the judge would not hear them.
My wife is a very good wife to me, but she gets drunk too often.
If it were not for that, I should like her better. I ran away from
her once, but she came after me with all the children. Sometimes
I make twelve shillings a week. I could make much more by
interpreting, but I do not like to go among the nasty natives of
my country. I believe I am more than fifty years of age."

Negro Beggars

THE negro beggar so nearly resembles the Hindoo that what
I have said of one, I could almost say of the other. There are,
however, these points of difference. The negro mendicant, who
is usually an American negro, never studies the picturesque in
his attire. He relies on the abject misery and down trodden
despair of his appearance, and generally represents himself as
a fugitive slave—with this exception, his methods of levying
contributions are precisely the same as his lighter skinned
brother's.

Some years ago it was a common thing to see a negro with
tracts in his hand, and a placard upon his breast, upon which was
a wood-cut of a black man, kneeling, his wrists heavily chained,
his arms held high in supplication, and round the picture, forming
a sort of proscenium or frame, the words: "Am I not a man and
a brother?" At the time that the suppression of the slave trade

created so much excitement, this was so excellent a "dodge" that many white beggars, fortunate enough to possess a flattish or turned-up nose, dyed themselves black and "stood pad" as real Africans. The imposture, however, was soon detected and punished.

There are but few negro beggars to be seen now. It is only common fairness to say that negroes seldom, if ever, shirk work. Their only trouble is to obtain it. Those who have seen the many negroes employed in Liverpool, will know that they are hard-working, patient, and, too often, underpaid. A negro will sweep a crossing, run errands, black boots, clean knives and forks, or dig, for a crust and a few pence. The few impostors among them are to be found among those who go about giving lectures on the horrors of slavery, and singing variations on the "escapes" in that famous book "Uncle Tom's Cabin." Negro servants are seldom read of in police reports, and are generally found to give satisfaction to their employers. In the east end of London negro-beggars are to be met with, but they are seldom beggars by profession. Whenever they are out of work they have no scruples, but go into the streets, take off their hats, and beg directly.

I was accosted by one in Whitechapel, from whom I obtained the following statement:—

"My father was a slave, so was my mother. I have heard my father say so. I have heard them tell how they got away, but I forget all about it. It was before I was born. I am the eldest son. I had only one brother. Three years after his birth my mother died. My father was a shoe-black in New York. He very often had not enough to eat. My brother got a place as a servant, but I went out in the streets to do what I could. About the same time that my father, who was an old man, died, my brother lost his place. We agreed to come to England together. My brother had been living with some Britishers, and he had heard them say that over here niggers were as good as whites; and thad the whites did not look down on them and ill-treat them, as they do in New York. We went about and got odd jobs on the quay, and at last we hid ourselves in the hold of a vessel, bound for Liverpool. I do not know how long we were hid, but I remember we were terribly frightened lest we should be found out before the ship got under weigh. At last hunger forced us out, and we rapped at the hatches; at first we were not heard, but when we shouted out, they opened the hatches, and took us on deck. They flogged us

very severely, and treated us shamefully all the voyage. When
we got to Liverpool, we begged and got odd jobs. At last we got
engaged in a travelling circus, where we were servants, and used to
ride about with the band in beautiful dresses, but the grooms
treated us so cruelly that we were forced to run away from that.
I forget the name of the place that we were performing at, but
it was not a day's walk from London. We begged about for some
time. At last, my brother—his name is Aaron—got to clean the
knives and forks at a slap-bang (an eating-house) in the city.
He was very fortunate, and used to save some bits for me. He
never takes any notice of me now. He is doing very well. He lives
with a great gentleman in Harewood Square, and has a coat with
silver buttons, and a gold-laced hat. He is very proud, and I do
not think would speak to me if he saw me. I don't know how
I live, or how much I get a week. I do porter's work mostly, but
I do anything I can get. I beg more than half the year. I have
no regular lodging. I sleep where I can. When I am in luck, I have
a bed. It costs me threepence. At some places they don't care to
take a man of colour in. I sometimes get work in Newgate Market,
carrying meat, but not often. Ladies give me halfpence oftener
than men. The butchers call me 'Othello,' and ask me why I killed
my wife. I have tried to get aboard a ship, but they won't have
me. I don't know how old I am, but I know that when we got
to London, it was the time the Great Exhibition was about. I can
lift almost any weight when I have had a bit of something to eat.
I don't care for beer. I like rum best. I have often got drunk,
but never when I paid for it myself."

DISASTER BEGGARS

THIS class of street beggars includes shipwrecked mariners, blown-
up miners, burnt-out tradesmen, and lucifer droppers. The majority of them are impostors, as is the case with all beggars who
pursue begging pertinaciously and systematically. There are no
doubt genuine cases to be met with, but they are very few, and
they rarely obtrude themselves. Of the shipwrecked mariners
I have already given examples under the head of Naval and
Military Beggars. Another class of them, to which I have not
referred, is familiar to the London public in connection with
rudely executed paintings representing either a shipwreck, or

more commonly the destruction of a boat by a whale in the North Seas. This painting they spread upon the pavement, fixing it at the corners, if the day be windy, with stones. There are generally two men in attendance, and in most cases one of the two has lost an arm or a leg. Occasionally both of them have the advantage of being deprived of either one or two limbs. Their misfortune so far is not to be questioned. A man who has lost both arms, or even one, is scarcely in a position to earn his living by labour, and is therefore a fit object for charity. It is found, however, that in most instances the stories of their misfortunes printed underneath their pictures are simply inventions, and very often the pretended sailor has never been to sea at all. In one case which I specially investigated, the man had been a bricklayer, and had broken both his arms by falling from a scaffold. He received some little compensation at the time, but when that was spent he went into the streets to beg, carrying a paper on his breast describing the cause of his misfortune. His first efforts were not successful. His appearance (dressed as he was in workman's clothes) was not sufficiently picturesque to attract attention, and his story was of too ordinary a kind to excite much interest. He had a very hard life of it for some length of time; for, in addition to the drawback arising from the uninteresting nature of his case, he had had no experience in the art of begging, and his takings were barely sufficient to procure bread. From this point I will let him tell his own story:—

A Shipwrecked Mariner

"I HAD only taken a penny all day, and I had had no breakfast, and I spent the penny in a loaf. I was three nights behind for my lodging, and I knew the door would be shut in my face if I did not take home sixpence. I thought I would go to the work'ouse, and perhaps I might get a supper and a lodging for that night. I was in Tottenham Court Road by the chapel, and it was past ten o'clock. The people were thinning away, and there seemed no chance of anything. So says I to myself I'll start down the New Road to the work'ouse. I knew there was a work'ouse down that way, for I worked at a 'ouse, next it once, and I used to think the old paupers looked comfortable like. It came across me all at once, that I one time said to one of my mates, as we was sitting on the scaffold, smoking our pipes, and looking over the work'ouse wall, 'Jem, them old chaps there seems to do it pretty tidy; they have their soup and bread, and a bed to lie on, and their bit o' baccy, and they comes out o' a arternoon and basks in the sun, and has their chat, and don' seem to do no work to hurt 'em.' And Jem he says, 'It's a great hinstitooshin, Enery,' says he, for you see Jem was a bit of a scollard, and could talk just like a book. 'I don't know about a hinstitooshin, Jem,' says I, 'but what I does know is that a man might do wuss nor go in there and have his grub and his baccy regular, without nought to stress him, like them old chaps.' Somehow or other that 'ere conversation came across me, and off I started to the work'ouse. When I came to the gate I saw a lot of poor women and children sitting on the pavement round it. They couldn't have been hungrier than me, but they were awful ragged, and their case looked wuss. I didn't like to go in among them, and I watched a while a little way off. One woman kep on ringing the bell for a long time, and nobody came, and then she got desperate, and kep a-pulling and tinging like she was mad, and at last a fat man came out and swore at her and drove them all away. I didn't think there was much chance for me if they druv away women and kids, and such as them, but I thought I would try as I was a cripple, and had lost both my arms. So I stepped across the road, and was just agoing to try and pull the bell with my two poor stumps when someone tapped me on the shoulder. 'What are you agoing to do?' says he. 'I was agoing to try and ring the work'ouse bell,' says I. 'What for?' says he. 'To ask to be took in,' says I. And then the sailor man look at me in a steady kind of way, and says, 'Want to get into the work'ouse, and you got ne'er an arm? You're a infant,' says he. 'If you had only lost one on 'em now, I could forgive you, but—' 'But surely,' says I, 'it's a greater misfortune to lose two nor one; half a loaf's better nor no bread, they say.' 'You're a infant,' says he again. 'One off ain't no good; both on 'em's the thing. Have you a mind to earn a honest living?' says he, quite sharp. 'I have,' says I; 'anything for a honest crust.' 'Then,' says he, 'come along o' me.' So I went with the sailor man to his lodging in Whitechapel, and a very tidy place it was, and we had beef-steaks and half a gallon o' beer, and a pipe, and then he told me what he wanted me to do. I was to dress like him in a sailor's jacket and trousers and a straw 'at, and stand o' one side of a picture of a shipwreck, wile he stood on the t'other. And I consented and he learned me some sailors' patter, and at the end of the week he got me the togs, and then I went out with him. We

did only middlin' the first day, but after a bit the coppers tumbled
in like winkin'. It was so affectin' to see two mariners without
ne'er an arm between them, and we had crowds round us. At the
end of the week we shared two pound and seven shillings, which
was more nor a pound than my mate ever did by his self. He
always said it was pilin' the hagony to have two without ne'er
an arm. My mate used to say to me, 'Enery, if your stumps had
only been a trifle shorter, we might ha' made a fortune by this
time; but you waggle them, you see, and that frightens the old
ladies.' I did well when Trafalgar Jack was alive. That was my
mate, sir; but he died of the cholera, and I joined another pal who
had a wooden leg; but he was rough to the kids, and got us both
into trouble. How do I mean rough to the kids? Why, you see,
the kids used to swarm round us to look at the picture just like
flies round a sugar-cask, and that crabbed the business. My mate
got savage with them sometimes, and clouted their heads, and
one day the mother o' one o' the brats came up a-screaming awful
and give Timber Bill, as we called him, into custody, and he was
committed for a rogue and vagabond. Timber Bill went into the
nigger line afterwards and did well. You may have seen him, sir.
He plays the tambourine, and dances, and the folks laugh at his
wooden leg, and the coppers come in in style. Yes, I'm still in the
line, but it's a bad business now."

Blown-up Miners

THESE are simply a variety of the large class of beggars who get
their living in the streets, chiefly by frequenting public-houses
and whining a tale of distress. The impostors among them—and
they are by far the greater number—do not keep up the character
of Blown-up miners all the year round, but time the assumption
to suit some disaster which may give colour to their tale. After
a serious coal-mine accident "blown-up miners" swarm in such
numbers all over the town that one might suppose the whole of the
coal-hands of the north had been blown south by one explosion.
The blown-up miner has the general appearance of a navvy; he
wears moleskin trousers turned up nearly to the knees, a pair
of heavy-laced boots, a sleeved waistcoat, and commonly a shapeless felt hat of the wide-awake fashion. He wears his striped shirt
open at the neck, showing a weather-browned and brawny chest.
The state of his hands and the colour of his skin show that he has

been accustomed to hard work, but his healthy look and fresh colour give the lie direct to his statement that he has spent nearly the whole of his life in working in the dark many hundred feet beneath the surface of the earth. Many of them do not pretend that they have been injured by the explosion of the mine, but only that they have been thrown out of work. These are mostly excavators and bricklayers' labourers, who are out of employ in consequence of a stoppage of the works on which they have been engaged, or more often, as I have proved by inquiry, in consequence of their own misconduct in getting drunk and absenting themselves from their labour. These impostors are easily detected. If you cross-question them as to the truth of their stories, and refer to names and places which they ought to be acquainted with if their representations were genuine, they become insolent and move away from you. There are others, however, who are more artful, and whose tales are borne out by every external appearance, and also by a complete knowledge of the places whence they pretend to have come. These men, though sturdy and horny-fisted, have a haggard, pallid look, which seems to accord well with the occupation of the miner. They can converse about mining operations, they describe minutely the incidents of the accident by which they suffered, and they have the names of coal-owners and gangsmen ever ready on their tongues. In addition to this they bare some part of their bodies—the leg or the arm—and show you what looks like a huge scald or burn. These are rank impostors, denizens of Wentworth Street and Brick Lane, and who were never nearer to Yorkshire than Mile End gate in their lives. Having met with one or two specimens of 'real' distressed miners, I can speak with great certainty of the characteristics which mark out the impostor. For many years past there has always been an abundance of work for miners and navigators; indeed the labour of the latter has often been at a premium; cases of distress arise among them only from two causes—ill-health and bodily disaster. If they are in health and found begging it is invariably during a long journey from one part of the country to another. The look and manner of these miners forbids the idea of their being systematic mendicants or impostors. They want something to help them on the road, and they will be as grateful for a hunk of bread and cheese as for money. If you cross-question these men they never show an uncomfortable sense of being under examination, but answer you frankly as if you were merely holding a friendly conversation with them. Miners are very charitable to each other, and they think it no shame to seek aid of their betters when they really need it. Of the device called the "scaldrum dodge," by which beggars of this class produce artificial sores, I shall have to treat by-and-bye.

Burnt-out Tradesmen

WITH many begging impostors the assumption of the "burnt-out tradesman" is simply a change of character to suit circumstances; with others it is a fixed and settled role. The burnt-out tradesman does not beg in the streets by day; he comes out at night, and his favourite haunts are the private bars of public-houses frequented by good company. In the day-time he begs by a petition, which he leaves at the houses of charitable persons with an intimation that he will call again in an hour. In the evening he is made up for his part. He lurks about a public-house until he sees a goodly company assembled in the private bar, and then, when the "gents," as he calls them, appear to be getting happy and comfortable, he suddenly appears among them, and moves them by the striking contrast which his personal appearance and condition offers to theirs. Like many others of his class he has studied human nature to some purpose, and he knows at a glance the natures with which he has to deal. Noisy and thoughtless young men, like clerks and shopmen, he avoids. They are generally too much occupied with themselves to think of him or his misfortunes; and having had no experience of a responsible position, the case of a reduced tradesman does not come home to them. A quiet and sedate company of middle-aged tradesmen best suits his purpose. They know the difficulties and dangers of trade, and maybe there are some of them who are conscious that ruin is impending over themselves. To feeling men of this class it is a terrible shock to see a man, who has once been well-to-do like themselves, reduced to getting a living by begging. The burnt-out tradesman's appearance gives peculiar force to his appeal. He is dressed in a suit of black, greasy and threadbare, which looks like the last shreds of the dress suit which he wore on high days and holidays, when he was thriving and prosperous. His black satin stock, too, is evidently a relic of better days. His hat is almost napless; but it is well brushed—indicating care and neatness on the part of its owner. His shoes are mere shapeless envelopes of leather, but the uppers are carefully polished, and the strings neatly tied. When the burnt-out tradesman enters a bar he allows his appearance to have its due effect before he opens his mouth, or makes any other demonstration whatever. In this he seems to imitate the practice of the favourite comedian, who calculates upon being able to bespeak the favour of his audience by merely showing his face. The beggar, after remaining motionless for a moment, to allow the company fully to contemplate his miserable appearance, suddenly and unexpectedly advances one of his hands, which until now has been concealed behind his coat, and exposes to view a box of matches. Nothing can surpass the artistic skill of this mute appeal. The respectable look, and the poor, worn clothes, first of all—the patient, broken-hearted glance accompanied by a gentle sigh—and then the box of matches! What need of a word spoken? Can you not read the whole history? Once a prosperous tradesman, the head of a family, surrounded by many friends. Now, through misfortune, cast out of house and home, deserted by his friends, and reduced to wander the streets and sell matches to get his children bread. Reduced to sell paltry matches! he who was in a large way once, and kept clerks to register his wholesale transactions! It is seldom that this artist requires to speak. No words will move men who can resist so powerful an appeal. When he does speak he does not require to say more than—"I am an unfortunate tradesman, who lost everything I possessed in the world by a disastrous fire—" Here the halfpence interrupt his story, and he has no need to utter another word, except to mutter his humble thanks.

There are a great many beggars of this class, and they nearly all pursue the same method. They are most successful among tradesmen of the middle class, and among the poor working people. One of them told me that the wives of working men were, according to his experience, the most tender-hearted in London. "The upper classes, the swells, ain't no good," he said; "they subscribe to the Mendicity Society, and they thinks every beggar an impostor. The half-and-half swells, shopmen and the likes, ain't got no hearts, and they ain't got no money, and what's the good. Tradesmen that ain't over well off have a fellow feeling; but the workmen's wives out a-marketing of a Saturday night are no trouble. They always carries coppers—change out of sixpence or a something—in their hands, and when I goes in where they are a havin' their daffies—that's drops of gin, sir—they looks at me, and says, 'Poor man!' and drops the coppers, whatever it is, into my hand, and p'raps asks me to have a half-pint o' beer besides. They're good souls, the workmen's wives."

There is a well-known beggar of this class who dresses in a most unexceptionable manner. His black clothes are new and glossy, his hat and boots are good, and to heighten the effect he wears a spotless white choker. He is known at the West End by the name of the 'Bishop of London." His aspect is decidedly clerical. He has a fat face, a double chin, his hat turns up extensively at the brim, and, as I have said, he wears a white neck-cloth. When he enters a bar the company imagine that he is about to order a bottle of champagne at least; but when he looks round and produces the inevitable box of matches, the first impression gives way either to compassion or extreme wonder. So far as my experience serves me, this dodge is not so successful as the one I have just described. A person with the most ordinary reasoning powers must know that a man who possesses clothes like those need not be in want of bread; but if the power of reasoning were universally allotted to mankind, there would be a poor chance for the professional beggar. There never was a time or place in which there were not to be found men anxious to avoid labour, and yet to live in ease and enjoyment, and there never was a time in which other men were not, from their sympathy, their fears, or their superstition, ready to assist the necessitous, or those who appeared to be so, and liable to be imposed upon or intimidated, according as the beggar is crafty or bold.

As a rule the burnt-out tradesmen whom I have described are impostors, who make more by begging than many of those who relieve them earn by hard and honest labour. The petitions which they leave at houses are very cleverly drawn out. They are generally the composition of the professional screevers, whose practices I shall have to describe by-and-by. They have a circumstantial account of the fire by which the applicant "lost his all," and sometimes furnish an inventory of the goods that were destroyed. They are attested by the names of clergymen, churchwardens, and other responsible persons, whose signatures are imitated with consummate art in every variety of ink. Some specimens of these petitions and begging letters will be found under the head of "Dependants of Beggars."

Lucifer Droppers

THE lucifer droppers are impostors to a man—to a boy—to a girl. Men seldom, if ever, practise this "dodge." It is children's work; and the artful way in which boys and girls of tender years pursue it, shows how systematically the seeds of mendicancy and crime are implanted in the hearts of the young Arab tribes of London. The artfulness of this device is of the most diabolical kind; for it trades not alone upon deception, but upon exciting sympathy with the guilty at the expense of the innocent. A boy or a girl takes up a position on the pavement of a busy street, such as Cheapside or the Strand. He, or she—it is generally a girl —carries a box or two of lucifer matches, which she offers for sale. In passing to and fro she artfully contrives to get in the way of some gentleman who is hurrying along. He knocks against her and upsets the matches which fall in the mud. The girl immediately begins to cry and howl. The bystanders, who are ignorant of the trick, exclaim in indignation against the gentleman who has caused a poor girl such serious loss, and the result is that either the gentleman, to escape being hooted, or the ignorant passers-by, n false compassion, give the girl money. White peppermint lozenges are more often used than lucifers. It looks a hopeless case, indeed, when a trayful of white lozenges fall in the mud.

Bodily Afflicted Beggars

BEGGARS who excite charity by exhibiting sores and bodily deformities are not so commonly to be met with in London as they were some years ago. The officers of the Mendicity Society have cleared the streets of nearly all the impostors, and the few who remain are blind men and cripples. Many of the blind men are under the protection of the Society, which furnishes them with books printed in raised type which they decipher by the touch. Others provide their own books and are allowed to sit on door steps or in the recesses of the bridges without molestation from the police. It has been found on inquiry that these afflicted persons are really what they appear to be—poor, helpless, blind creatures, who are totally incapacitated from earning a living, and whom it would be heartless cruelty to drive into the workhouse, where no provision is made for their peculiar wants.

The bodily afflicted beggars of London exhibit seven varieties.

1. Those having real or pretended sores, vulgarly known as the "Scaldrum Dodge." 2. Having swollen legs. 3. Being crippled, deformed, maimed, or paralysed. 4. Being blind. 5. Being subject to fits. 6. Being in a decline. 7. "Shallow Coves," or those who exhibit themselves in the streets, half-clad, especially in cold weather.

First, then, as to those having real or pretended sores. As I have said, there are few beggars of this class left. When the officers of the Mendicity Society first directed their attention to the suppression of this form of mendicancy, it was found that the great majority of those who exhibit sores were unmitigated impostors. In nearly all the cases investigated the sores did not proceed from natural causes, but were either wilfully produced or simulated. A few had lacerated their flesh in reality; but the majority had resorted to the less painful operation known as the "Scaldrum Dodge". This consists in covering a portion of the leg or arm with soap to the thickness of a plaister, and then saturating the whole with vinegar. The vinegar causes the soap to blister and assume a festering appearance, and thus the passer-by is led to believe that the beggar is suffering from a real sore. So well does this simple device simulate a sore that the deception is not to be detected even by close inspection. The "Scaldrum Dodge" is a trick of very recent introduction among the London beggars. It is a concomitant of the advance of science and the progress of the art of adulteration. It came in with penny postage, daguerreotypes, and other modern innovations of a like description. In less scientific periods within the present century it was wholly unknown; and sores were produced by burns and lacerations which the mendicants inflicted upon themselves with a ruthless hand. An old man who has been a beggar all his life, informed me that he had known a man prick the flesh of his leg all over, in order to produce blood and give the appearance of an ulcerous disease. He is now upwards of seventy years of age. At my solicitation he made the following statement without any apparent reserve.

Seventy Years A Beggar

"I HAVE been a beggar ever since I was that high—ever since I could walk. No, I was not born a cripple. I was thirty years of age before I broke my leg. That was an accident. A horse and cart drove over me in Westminster. Well; yes, I was drunk. I was

able-bodied enough before that. I was turned out to beg by my
mother. My father, I've heard, was a soldier; he went to Egypt,
or some foreign part, and never came back. I never was learnt
any trade but begging, and I couldn't turn my hand to nothing
else. I might have been learnt the shoemaking; but what was the
use? Begging was a better trade then; it isn't now though. There
was fine times when the French war was on. I lived in Westminster
then. A man as they called Copenhagen Jack, took a fancy to me,
and made me his valet. I waited upon, fetched his drink, and so
forth. Copenhagen Jack was a captain; no, not in the army, nor
in the navy neither. He was the captain of the Pye Street beggars.
There was nigh two hundred of them lived in two large houses,
and Jack directed them. Jack's word was law, I assure you. The
boys—Jack called them his boys, but there was old men among
them, and old women too—used to come up before the captain
every morning before starting out for the day, to get their orders.
The captain divided out the districts for them, and each man
took his beat according to his directions. It was share and share
alike, with an extra for the captain. There was all manner of
"lays," yes, cripples and darkies. We called them as did the blind
dodge, darkies—and "shakers" them as had fits—and shipwrecked mariners, and—the scaldrum dodge, no; that's new;
but I know what you mean. They did the real thing then—scrape
the skin off their feet with a bit of glass until the blood came.
Those were fine times for beggars. I've known many of 'em bring
in as much as thirty shillings a day, some twenty, some fifteen.
If a man brought home no more than five or six shillings, the
captain would enter him, make a note of him, and change his
beat. Yes, we lived well. I've known fifty sit down to a splendid
supper, geese and turkeys, and all that, and keep it up until
daylight, with songs and toasts. No, I didn't beg then; but I did
before, and I did after. I begged after, when the captain came to
misfortune. He went a walking one day in his best clothes, and
got pressed, and never came back, and there was a mutiny among
them in Pye Street, and I nearly got murdered. You see, they
were jealous of me, because the captain petted me. I used to dress
in top-boots and a red coat when I waited on the captain. It was
his fancy. Romancing? I don't know what you mean. Telling lies,
oh! It's true, by ——. There's nothing like it nowadays. The new
police and this b—— Mendicity Society has spoilt it all. Well,
they skinned me; took off my fine coat and boots, and sent me

out on the orphan lay in tatters. I sat and cried all day on the door steps, for I was really miserable now my friend was gone, and I got lots of halfpence, and silver too, and when I took home the swag they danced round me and swore that they would elect me captain if I went on like that; but there was a new captain made, and when they had their fun out, he came and took the money away, and kicked me under the table. I ran away the next day, and went to a house in St. Giles's, where I was better treated. There was no captain there; the landlord managed the house, and nobody was master but him. There was nigh a hundred beggars in that house, and some two or three hundred more in the houses next it. The houses are not standing now. They were taken down when New Oxford Street was built; they stood on the north side. Yes; we lived well in St. Giles's—as well as we did in Westminster. I have earned 8, 10, 15, ay, 30 shillings a day, and more nor that sometimes. I can't earn one shilling now. The folks don't give as they did. They think everybody an imposture now. And then the police won't let you alone. No; I told you before, I never was anything else but a beggar. How could I? It was the trade I was brought up to. A man must follow his trade. No doubt I shall die a beggar, and the parish will bury me."

Having Swollen Legs

BEGGARS who lie on the pavement and expose swollen legs are very rarely to be met with now. The imposture has been entirely suppressed by the police and the officers of the Mendicity Society. This is one of the shallowest of all the many "dodges" of the London beggars. On reflection any one, however slightly acquaint-ed with the various forms of disease, must know that a mere swelling cannot be a normal or chronic condition of the human body. A swelling might last a few days, or a week; but a swelling of several years' standing is only to be referred to the continued application of a poisonous ointment or to the binding of the limb with ligatures, so as to confine the blood and puff the skin.

Cripples

VARIOUS kinds of cripples are still to be found, begging in the streets of London. As a rule the police do not interfere with them, unless they know them to be impostors. A certain number of well-known cripples have acquired a sort of prescriptive right to be where they please. The public will be familiar with the personal appearance of many of them. There is the tall man on crutches, with his foot in a sling, who sells stay laces; the poor wretch without hands, who crouches on the pavement and writes with the stumps of his arms; the crab-like man without legs, who sits strapped to a board, and walks upon his hands; the legless man who propels himself in a little carriage, constructed on the velocipede principle; the idiotic-looking youth who "stands pad with a fakement" shaking in every limb as if he were under the influence of galvanism. These mendicants are not considered to be imports, and are allowed to pursue begging as a regular calling. I cannot think, however, that the police exercise a wise discretion in permitting some of the more hideous of these beggars to infest the streets. Instances are on record of nervous females having been seriously frightened, and even injured, by seeing men without legs or arms crawling at their feet. A case is within my own knowledge, where the sight of a man without legs or arms had such an effect upon a lady in the family way that her child was born in all respects the very counterpart of the object that alarmed her. It had neither legs nor arms. This occurrence took place at Brighton about eleven years ago. I have frequently seen ladies start and shudder when the crab-like man I have referred to has suddenly appeared, hopping along at their feet. I am surprised that there is no home or institution for cripples of this class. They are certainly deserving of sympathy and aid; for they are utterly incapacitated from any kind of labour. Impostors are constantly starting up among this class of beggars; but they do not remain long undetected. A man was lately found begging, who pretended that he had lost his right arm. The deception at the first glance was perfect. His right sleeve hung loose at his side, and there appeared to be nothing left of his arm but a short stump. On being examined at the police office his arm was found strapped to his side, and the stump turned out to be a stuffing of bran. Another man simulated a broken leg by doubling up that limb and strapping his foot and ankle to his thigh. Paralysis is frequently simulated with success until the actor is brought before the police surgeon, when the cheat is immediately detected.

A Blind Beggar

A BLIND beggar, led by a dog, whom I accosted in the street, made the following voluntary statement. I should mention that he seemed very willing to answer my questions, and while he was talking kept continually feeling my clothes with his finger and thumb. The object of this, I fancy, must have been to discover whether I was what persons of his class call a "gentleman" or a poor man. Whether he had any thoughts of my being an officer I cannot say.

"I am sixty years of age; you wouldn't think it, perhaps, but I am. No, I was not born blind; I lost my sight in the smallpox, five and twenty years ago. I have been begging on the streets eighteen years. Yes, my dog knows the way home. How did I teach him that? Why, when I had him first, the cabmen and busmen took him out to Camden Town, and Westminster, and other places, and then let him go. He soon learnt to find his way home. No, he is not the dog I had originally; that one died; he was five and twenty years old when he died. Yes, that was a very old age for a dog. I had this one about five years ago. Don't get as much as I used to do? No, no, my friend. I make about a shilling a day, never—scarcely never—more, sometimes less—a good deal less; but some folks are very kind to me. I live at Poole's Place, Mount Pleasant. There are a good many engineers about there, and their wives are very kind to me; they have always a halfpenny for me when I go that way. I have my beats. I don't often come down this way (Gower Street), only once a month. I always keep on this side of Tottenham Court Road; I never go over the road; my dog knows that. I am going down there," (pointing); "that's Chenies Street. Oh, I know where I am; next turning to the right is Alfred Street, the next to the left is Francis Street, and when I get to the end of that the dog will stop; but I know as well as him. Yes, he's a good dog, but never the dog I used to have; he used always to stop when there was anybody near, and pull when there was nobody. He was what I call a steady dog, this one is young and foolish like; he stops sometimes dead, and I goes on talking, thinking there is a lady or gentleman near; but it's only other dogs that he's stopping to have a word with. No, no, no, sir." This he said when I dropped some more coppers into his hat, having previously given him a penny. "I don't want that. I think I know your voice, sir; I'm

sure I've heard it before. No! ah, then I'm mistaken." Here again
he felt my coat and waistcoat with an inquiring touch; apparently
satisfied, he continued, "I'll tell you, sir, what I wouldn't tell to
everyone; I've as nice a little place at Mount Pleasant as you
would desire to see. You wouldn't think I was obliged to beg
if you saw it. Why, sir, I beg many times when I've as much
as sixteen shillings in my pocket; leastwise not in my pocket, but
at home. Why, you see, sir, there's the winter months coming
on, and I lays by what I can against the wet days, when I can't
go out. There's no harm in that, sir. Well, now, sir, I'll tell you
there's a man up there in Sussex Street that I know, and he said
to me just now, as I was passing the public house, 'Come in, John,
and have a drop of something.' 'No, thank ye,' says I, 'I don't
want drink; if you want to give me anything give me the money.'
'No,' says he, 'I won't do that, but if you come in and have something to drink I'll give you sixpence.' Well, sir. I wouldn't go.
It wouldn't do, you know, for the likes of me, a blind man getting
his living by begging, to be seen in a public-house; the people
wouldn't know, sir, whether it was my money that was paying
for it or not. I never go into a public-house; I has my drop at
home. Oh, yes, I am tired—tired of it; but I'll tell you, sir, I think
I'll get out of it soon. Do you know how that is, sir? Well, I think
I shall get on to Day and Martin's Charity in October; I'm promised votes, and I'm in hopes this time. God bless you, sir."

There was for many years in the city a blind man with a dog,
who was discovered to be a rank impostor. The boys found it
out long before the police did. They used to try and take the
money out of the little basket that the dog carried in his mouth,
but they never succeeded. The moment a boy approached the
basket the blind man ran at him with his stick, which proved,
of course, that the fellow could see. Some of my readers may
recollect seeing in the papers an account of a respectable young
girl who ran away from her home and took up with this blind
man. She cohabited with him, in fact, and it was found that
they lived in extravagance and luxury on the blind beggar's
daily takings.

Beggars Subject To Fits

BEGGARS subject to fits are impostors, I may say, wholly without
exception. Some of them are the associates and agents of thieves,
and fall down in the street in assumed fits in order to collect a

crowd and afford a favourable opportunity to the pickpockets, with whom they are in league. The simulation of fits is no mean branch of the beggar's art of deception. The various symptoms—the agitation of the muscles, the turning up of the whites of the eyes, the pallor of the face and the rigidity of the mouth and jaw—are imitated to a nicety; and these symptoms are sometimes accompanied by copious frothing at the mouth. I asked Mr. Horsford, of the Mendicity Society, how this was done, and received the laconic answer—"Soap." And this brought to my memory that I had once seen an actor charge his mouth with a small piece of soap to give due *vraisemblance* to the last scene of *Sir Giles Overreach*. I was shown an old woman who was in the habit of falling down in assumed fits simply to get brandy. She looked very aged and poor, and I was told she generally had her fits when some well-dressed gentleman was passing with a lady on his arm. She generally chose the scene of her performance close to the door of a public-house, into which some compassionate person might conveniently carry her. She was never heard to speak in her fits except to groan and mutter "brandy", when that remedy did not appear to suggest itself to those who came to her aid. An officer said to me, "I have known that old woman have so many fits in the course of the day that she has been found lying in the gutter dead drunk from the effect of repeated restoratives. She has been apprehended and punished over and over again, but she returns to the old dodge the minute she gets out. She is on the parish; but she gets money as well as brandy by her shamming."

I have heard that there are persons who purposely fall into the Serpentine in order to be taken to the receiving-house of the Humane Society, and recovered with brandy. One man repeated the trick so often that at last the Society's men refused to go to his aid. It is needless to say that he soon found his way out of the water unaided, when he saw that his dodge was detected.

Being In A Decline

No form of poverty and misfortune is better calculated to move the hearts of the compassionate than this. You see crouching in a corner, a pale-faced, wan young man, apparently in the very last stage of consumption. His eyes are sunk in his head, his jaw drops, and you can almost see his bones through his pallid skin.

He appears too exhausted to speak; he coughs at intervals, and places his hand on his chest as if in extreme pain. After a fit of coughing he pants pitifully, and bows his head feebly as if he were about to die on the spot. It will be noticed, however, as a peculiarity distinguishing nearly all these beggars, that the sufferers wear a white cloth bound round their heads overtopped by a black cap. It is this white cloth, coupled with a few slight artistic touches of colour to the face, that produces the interesting look of decline. Any person who is thin and of sallow complexion may produce the same effect by putting on a white night-cap, and applying a little pink colour round the eyes. It is the simple rule observed by comedians, when they make up for a sick man or a ghost. These beggars are all impostors; and they are now so well-known to the police that they never venture to take up a fixed position during the day, but pursue their nefarious calling at night at public-houses and other resorts when they can readily make themselves scarce should an officer happen to spy them out.

"Shallow Coves"

THIS is the slang name given to beggars who exhibit themselves in the streets half clad, especially in cold weather. There are a great many of these beggars in London, and they are enabled to ply their trade upon the sympathies of the public with very little check owing to the fact that they mostly frequent quiet streets, and make a point of moving on whenever they see a policeman approaching. A notorious "shallow cove," who frequents the neighbourhood of the Strand and St. Martin's Lane, must be well-known to many of my readers. His practice is to stand at the windows of bakers and confectioners, and gaze with an eager famished look at the bread and other eatables. His almost naked state, his hollow, glaring eye, like that of a famished dog, his long thin cheek, his matted hair, his repeated shrugs of uneasiness as if he were suffering from cold or vermin, present such a spectacle of wretchedness as the imagination could never conceive. He has no shirt, as you can see by his open breast; his coat is a thing of mere shreds; his trousers, torn away in picturesque jags at the knees, are his only other covering, except a dirty sodden-looking round-crowned brown felt hat, which he slouches over his forehead in a manner which greatly heightens his aspect of misery. I was completely taken in when I first saw this man greedily glaring in at a baker's window in St. Martin's Lane. I gave him twopence to procure a loaf, and waited to see him buy it, anxious to have the satisfaction of seeing him appease such extreme hunger as I had never—I thought—witnessed before. He did not enter the shop with the alacrity I expected. He seemed to hesitate, and presently I could see that he was casting stealthy glances at me. I remained where I was, watching him; and at last when he saw I was determined to wait, he entered the shop. I saw him speak to the woman at the counter and point at something; but he made no purchase, and came out without the bread, which I thought he would have devoured like a wolf, when he obtained the money to procure it. Seeing me still watching him, he moved away rapidly. I entered the shop, and asked if he had bought anything. "Not he, he don't want any bread," said the mistress of the shop. "I wish the police would lock him up, or drive him away from here, for he's a regular nuisance. He pretends to be hungry, and then when people give him anything, he comes in here and asks if I can sell him any bits. He knows I won't, and he don't want' em. He is a regular old soldier, he is, sir."

I received confirmation of this account from Mr. Horsford, who said that the fellow had been sent to prison at least thirty times. The moment he gets out he resorts to his old practices. On one occasion, when he was taken, he had thirteen shillings in his pocket—in coppers, sixpences and threepenny and fourpenny bits. Soft-hearted old ladies who frequent the pastry-cooks are his chief victims.

"Shallow coves" have recently taken to Sunday begging. They go round the quiet streets in pairs, and sing psalm tunes during church hours. They walk barefooted, without hats, and expose their breasts to show that they have no under clothing.

The "shallow cove" is a very pitiable sight in winter, standing half-naked, with his bare feet on the cold stones. But give him a suit of clothes and shoes and stockings, and the next day he will be as naked and as wretched-looking as he is to-day. Nakedness and shivers are his stock in trade.

Famished Beggars

THE famished beggars, that is, those who "make up" to look as if they were starving, pursue an infinite variety of dodges. The most common of all is to stand in some prominent place with a placard on the breast, bearing an inscription to the effect that the beggar is "starving," or that he has "a large family entirely dependent upon him." The appeal is sometimes made more forcible by its brevity, and the card bears the single word, "Destitute." In every case where the beggar endeavours to convey starvation by his looks and dress it may be relied upon that he is an impostor, a lazy fellow, who prefers begging to work, because it requires less exertion and brings him more money. There are some, however—blind men and old persons—who "stand pad," that is to say, beg by exhibition of a written or printed paper, who are not impostors; they are really poor persons who are incapacitated from work, and who beg from day to day to earn a living. But these beggars do not get up an appearance of being starved, and indeed some of them look very fat and comfortable.

The beggars who chalk on the pavement "I am starving," in a round scholastic hand, are not of this class. It does not require much reflection to discern the true character of such mendicants. As I have frequently had occasion to observe, the man who begs day after day, and counts his gains at the rate of from twelve to twenty shillings a week, cannot be starving. You pass one of these beggars in the morning, and you hear the coppers chinking on the pavement as they are thrown to him by the thoughtless or the credulous; you pass him again in the evening, and there is still the inscription "I am starving". This beggar adds hypocrisy to his other vices. By his writing on the pavement he would give you to understand that he is too much ashamed to beg by word of mouth. As he crouches beside his inscription he hides his head. The writing, too, is a false pretence. "I am starving" is written in so good a hand that you are led to believe that the wretch before you has had a good education, that he has seen better days, and is now the victim of misfortune, perhaps wholly undeserved. It should be known, however, that many of these beggars cannot write at all; they could not write another sentence except "I am starving" if it were to save their lives. There are persons who teach the art of writing certain sentences to beggars, but their pupils learn to trace the letters mechanically. This is the case with the persons who draw in coloured chalk on the pavement. They can draw a mackerel, a broken plate, a head of Christ, and a certain stereotyped sea-view with a setting sun, but they cannot draw anything else, and these they trace upon a principle utterly unknown to art. There is one beggar of this class who frequents the King's Cross end of the New Road, who writes his specimens backwards, and who cannot do it any other way. He covers a large flag-stone with "copies" in various hands, and they are all executed in the true "copper-plate" style. They are all, however, written backwards.

The distinction made by the magistrates and the police between those who draw coloured views and those who merely write "I am starving" in white chalk, exhibits a nicety of discrimination which is not a little amusing. When the officers of the Mendicity Society first began to enforce their powers with rigour (in consequence of the alarming increase of mendicancy) they arrested these flag-stone artists with others. The magistrates, however, showed an unwillingness to commit them, and at length it was laid down as a rule that these men should not be molested unless they obstructed a thoroughfare or created a disturbance. This decision was grounded upon the consideration that these street artists did some actual work for the money they received from the public; they drew a picture and exhibited it, and might therefore be fairly regarded as pursuing an art. So the chalkers of mackerel were placed in the category of privileged street exhibitors. The "I am starving" dodge, however, has been almost entirely suppressed by the persevering activity of Mr. Horsford and his brother officers of the Mendicity Society.

One of the latest devices of famished beggars which has come under my notice I shall denominate

The Choking Dodge

A WRETCHED-LOOKING man, in a state of semi-nudity, having the appearance of being half-starved and exhausted, either from want of food or from having walked a long way, sat down one day on the doorstep of the house opposite mine. I was struck by his wretched and forlorn appearance, and particularly by his downcast looks. It seemed as if misery had not only worn him to the bone, but had crushed all his humanity out of him. He was more like a feeble beast, dying of exhaustion and grovelling in the dust, than a man. Presently he took out a crust of dry bread and attempted to eat it. It was easy to see that it was a hard crust, as hard as stone, and dirty, as if it had lain for some days in the street. The wretch gnawed at it as a starved dog gnaws at a bone.

The crust was not only hard, but the beggar's jaws seemed to want the power of mastication. It seemed as if he had hungered so long that food was now too late. At length he managed to bite off a piece; but now another phase of his feebleness was manifested—he could not swallow it. He tried to get it down, and it stuck in his throat. You have seen a dog with a bone in his throat, jerking his head up and down in his effort to swallow: that was the action of this poor wretch on the door-step. I could not but be moved by this spectacle, and I opened the window and called to the man. He took no heed of me. I called again. Still no heed; misery had blunted all his faculties. He seemed to desire nothing but to sit there and choke. I went over to him and, tapping him on the shoulder, gave him twopence, and told him to go to the public-house and get some beer to wash down his hard meal. He rose slowly, gave me a look of thanks, and went away in the direction of the tavern. He walked more briskly than I could have conceived possible in his case, and something prompted me to watch him. I stood at my door looking after him, and when he got near the public-house he turned round. I knew at once that he was looking to see if I were watching him. The next minute he turned aside as if to enter the public-house. The entrance stood back from the frontage of the street, and I could not tell, from where I stood, whether he had gone into the house or not. I crossed to the other side, where I could see him without being noticed. He had not entered the house, but was standing by the door. When he had stood there for a few minutes he peeped out cautiously and looked down the street towards the place where he had left me. Being apparently satisfied that all was right, he emerged from the recess and walked on. I was now determined to watch him further. I had not long to wait for conclusive evidence of the imposture which I now more than suspected. The man walked slowly along until he saw some persons at a first-floor window, when he immediately sat down on a door-step opposite and repeated the elaborate performance with the hard crust which I have already described. This I saw him do four times before he left the street, in each case getting money. It is needless to say that this fellow was a rank impostor. One of his class was apprehended some time ago—it might have been this very man—and no less than seven shillings were found upon him. These men frequent quiet by-streets, and never, or rarely, beg in the busy thoroughfares. I will give another case, which I shall call.

The Offal-Eater

THE most notable instance of this variety of the famished beggars which has come under my notice is that of a little old man who frequents the neighbourhood of Russell Square. I have known him now for two years, and I have seen him repeat his performance at least a score of times. The man has the appearance of a cutler. He wears a very old and worn, but not ragged, velveteen coat with large side-pockets, a pair of sailor's blue trousers a good deal patched, a very, very bad pair of shoes, and a chimney-pot hat, which seems to have braved the wind and rain for many years, been consigned to a dust-bin, and then recovered for wear. He is below the average height, and appears to be about seventy years of age. This little old man makes his appearance in my street about eleven o'clock in the forenoon. He walks down the pavement listlessly, rubbing his hands and looking about him on every side in a vacant bewildered manner, as if all the world were strange to him, and he had no home, no friend, and no purpose on the face of the earth. Every now and then he stops and turns his face towards the street, moving himself uneasily in his clothes, as if he were troubled with vermin. All this time he is munching and mumbling some food in a manner suggestive of a total want of teeth. As he pauses he looks about as if in search of something. Presently you see him pick up a small piece of bread which has been thrown out to the sparrows. He wipes it upon his velveteen coat and begins to eat it. It is a long process. He will stand opposite your window for full ten minutes mumbling that small piece of bread, but he never looks up to inspire compassion or charity he trusts to his pitiful mumblings to produce the desired effect, and he is not disappointed. Coppers are flung to him from every window, and he picks them up slowly and listlessly, as if he did not expect such aid, and scarcely knew how to apply it. I have given him money several times, but that does not prevent him from returning again and again to stand opposite my window and mumble crusts picked out of the mud in the streets. One day I gave him a lump of good bread, but in an hour after I found him in an adjacent street exciting charity in the usual way. This convinced me that he was an artful systematic beggar, and this impression was fully confirmed on my following him into a low beer-shop in St. Giles's and finding him comfortably seated with his feet up in a chair, smoking a long pipe, and discussing a pot of ale. He knew me in a moment, dropped his feet from the chair, and tried to hide his pipe. Since that occasion he has never come my way.

PETTY TRADING BEGGARS

THIS is perhaps the most numerous class of beggars in London. Their trading in such articles as lucifers, boot-laces, cabbage-nets, tapes, cottons, shirt-buttons, and the like, is in most cases a mere "blind" to evade the law applying to mendicants and vagrants. There are very few of the street vendors of such petty articles as lucifers and shirt-buttons who can make a living from the profits of their trade. Indeed, they do not calculate upon doing so. The box of matches, or the little deal box of cottons, is used simply as a passport to the resorts of the charitable. The police are obliged to respect the trader, though they know very well that under the disguise of the itinerant merchant there lurks a beggar.

Beggars of this class use their trade to excite compassion and obtain a gift rather than to effect a sale. A poor half-clad wretch stands by the kerb exposing for sale a single box of matches, the price being "only a halfpenny." A charitable person passes by and drops a halfpenny or a penny into the poor man's hand, and disdains to take the matches. In this way a single box will be sufficient for a whole evening's trading, unless some person should insist upon an actual "transaction," when the beggar is obliged to procure another box at the nearest oilman's. There are very few articles upon which an actual profit is made by legitimate sale. Porcelain shirt-buttons, a favourite commodity of the petty trading beggars, would not yield the price of a single meal unless the seller could dispose of at least twenty dozen in a day. Cottons, stay-laces, and the like, can now be obtained so cheaply at the shops that no one thinks of buying these articles in the streets unless it be in a charitable mood. Almost the only commodities in which a legitimate trade is carried on by the petty traders of the streets are flowers, songs, knives, combs, braces, purses, portmonnaies. The sellers of knives, combs, etc., are to a certain extent legitimate traders, and do not calculate upon charity. They are cheats, perhaps, but not beggars. The vendors of flowers and songs, though they really make an effort to sell their goods, and often realise a tolerable profit, are nevertheless beggars, and trust to increase their earnings by obtaining money without giving an equivalent. A great many children are sent out by their parents to sell flowers during the summer and autumn. They find their best market in the bars of public-houses, and especially those frequented by prostitutes. If none else give prostitutes a good character, the very poor do. "I don't know what we should do but for them," said an old beggar-woman to me one day. "They are good-hearted souls—always kind to the poor. I hope God will forgive them." I have had many examples of this sympathy for misfortune and poverty on the part of the fallen women of the streets. A fellow feeling no doubt makes them wondrous kind. They know what it is to be cast off, and spurned, and despised; they know, too, what it is to starve, and, like the beggars, they are subject to the stern "move on" of the policeman.

The relations which subsist between the prostitutes and the beggars reveal some curious traits. Beggars will enter a public-house because they see some women at the bar who will assist their suit. They offer their little wares to some gentlemen at the bar, and the women will say, "Give the poor devil something," or "Buy bouquets for us," or if the commodity should be laces or buttons, they say, "Don't take the poor old woman's things; give her the money." And the gentlemen, just to show off, and appear liberal, do as they are told. Possibly, but for the pleading of their gay companions, they would have answered the appeal with a curse and gruff command to begone. I once saw an old woman kiss a bedizened prostitute's hand in real gratitude for a service of this kind. I don't know that I ever witnessed anything more touching in my life. The woman, who a few minutes before had been flaunting about the bar in the reckless manner peculiar to her class, was quite moved by the old beggar's act, and I saw a tear mount in her eye and slowly trickle down her painted cheek, making a white channel through the rouge as it fell. But in a moment she dashed it away, and the next was flaunting and singing as before. Prostitutes are afraid to remain long under the influence of good thoughts. They recall their days of innocence, and overpower them with an intolerable sadnesss—a sadness which springs of remorse. The gay women assume airs of patronage towards the beggars, and as such are looked up to; but a beggar-woman, however poor, and however miserable, if she is conscious of being virtuous, is always sensible of her superiority in that respect. She is thankful for the kindness of the "gay lady," and extols her goodness of heart; but she pities while she admires, and mutters as a last word, "May God forgive her." Thus does one touch of nature make all the world akin, and thus does virtue survive all the buffets of evil fortune to raise even a beggar to the level of the most worthy, and be a treasure dearer and brighter than all the pleasures of the world.

The sellers of flowers and songs are chiefly boys and young girls. They buy their flowers in Covent Garden, when the refuse of the market is cleared out, and make them up into small bouquets, which they sell for a penny. When the flower season is over they sell songs—those familiar productions of Ryle, Catnach and company, which, it is said, the great Lord Macaulay was wont to collect and treasure up as collateral evidences of history. Some of the boys who pursue this traffic are masters of all the trades that appertain to begging. I have traced one boy, by the identifying mark of a most villainous squint, through a career of ten years. When I first saw him he was a mere child of about four years of age. His mother sent him with a ragged little girl (his sister) into public-house bars to beg. Their diminutive size attracted attention and excited charity. By-and-by, possibly in consequence of the interference of the police, they carried pennyworths of flowers with them, at other times matches, and at others halfpenny sheets of songs. After this the boy and girl appeared dressed in sailor's costume (both as boys) and sung duets. I remember that one of the duets, which had a spoken part, was not very decent; the poor children evidently did not understand what they said; but the thoughtless people at the bar laughed and gave them money. By-and-by the boy became too big for this kind of work, and I next met him selling fuzees. After the lapse of about a year he started in the shoe-black line. His station was at the end of Endell Street, near the baths; but as he did not belong to one of the regularly organised brigades, he was hunted about by the police, and could not make a living. On the death of the crossing-sweeper at the corner he succeeded to that functionary's broom, and in his new capacity was regarded by the police as a useful member of society. The last time I saw him he was in possession of a costermonger's barrow, selling mackerel. He had grown a big, strong fellow, but I had no difficulty in identifying the little squinting child who begged and

sold flowers and songs in public-house bars, with the strong
loud-lunged vendor of mackerel. I suppose this young beggar
may be said to have pursued an honourable career, and raised
himself in the world. Many who have such an introduction to
life finish their course in a penal settlement.

There are not a few who assume the appearance of petty
traders for the purpose of committing thefts, such as picking
a gentleman's pocket when he is intoxicated, and slinking into
parlours to steal bagatelle balls. Police spies occasionally disguise
themselves as petty traders. There is a well-known man who goes
about with a bag of nuts, betting that he will tell within two how
many you take up in your hand. This man is said to be a police
spy. I have not been able to ascertain whether this is true or not;
but I am satisfied that the man does not get his living by his
nut trick. In the day-time he appears without his nuts, dressed
in a suit of black, and looking certainly not unlike a policeman
in mufti.

Among the petty trading beggars there are a good many
idiots and half-witted creatures, who obtain a living—and a very
good one, too—by dancing in a grotesque and idiotic manner
on the pavement to amuse children. Some of them are not such
idiots as they appear, but assume a half-witted appearance to
give oddness to their performance, and excite compassion for
their misfortune. The street boys are the avengers of this imposition
upon society.

The idiot performer has a sad life of it when the boys gather
about him. They pull his clothes, knock off his hat, and pelt him
with lime and mud. But this persecution sometimes redounds
to his advantage; for when the grown-up folks see him treated
thus, they pity him the more. These beggars always take care
to carry something to offer for sale. Halfpenny songs are most
commonly the merchandise.

The little half-witted Italian man who used to go about grind-
ing an organ that "had no inside to it," as the boys said, was
a beggar of this class, and I really think he traded on his constant
persecution by the *gamins*. Music, of course, he made none, for
there was only one string left in this battered organ; but he always
acted so as to convey the idea that the boys had destroyed his
instrument. He would turn away at the handle in a desperate
way, as if he were determined to spare no effort to please his
patrons; but nothing ever came of it but a feeble tink-a-tink at

long intervals. If his organ could at any time have been spoiled, certainly the boys might have done it; for their great delight was to put stones in it, and batter in its deal back with sticks. I am informed that this man had a good deal more of the rogue than of the fool in his composition. A gentleman offered to have his organ repaired for him, but he declined; and at length when the one remaining string gave way he would only have that one mended. It was his "dodge" to grind the air, and appear to be unconscious that he was not discoursing most eloquent music.

Tract-selling in the streets is a line peculiar to the Hindoos. I find that the tracts are given to them by religious people, and that they are bought by religious people, who are not unfrequently the very same persons who provided the tracts. Very few petty trading beggars take to tract-selling from their own inspiration; for in good sooth it does not pay, except when conducted on the principle I have just indicated. Some find it convenient to exhibit tracts simply to evade the law applying to beggars and vagrants, but they do not use them if they can procure a more popular article. In these remarks it is very far from my intention to speak of "religious people" with any disrespect. I merely use the expression "religious people" to denote those who employ themselves actively and constantly in disseminating religious publications among the people. Their motives and their efforts are most praiseworthy, and my only regret is that their labours are not rewarded by a larger measure of success.

An Author's Wife

IN the course of my inquiry into the habits, condition, and mode of life of the petty trading beggars of London, I met with a young woman who alleged that the publications she sold were the production of her husband. I encountered her at the bar of a tavern, where I was occupied in looking out for "specimens" of the class of beggars which I am now describing. She entered the bar modestly and with seeming diffidence. She had some printed sheets in her hand. I asked her what they were. She handed me a sheet. It was entitled the *Pretty Girls of London*. It was only a portion of the work, and on the last page was printed "to be continued." "Do you bring this out in numbers?"

I asked. "Yes, sir," she replied, "it is written by my husband, and he is continuing it from time to time." "Are you then his publisher?" I inquired. "Yes, sir, my husband is ill a-bed, and I am obliged to go out and sell his work for him." I looked through the sheet, and I saw that it was not a very decent work. "Have you ever read this?" I enquired. "Oh yes, sir, and I think it's very clever; don't you think so, sir?" It certainly was written with some little ability, and I said so; but I objected to its morality. Upon which she replied, "But it's what takes, sir." She sold several copies while I was present, at twopence each; but one or two gave her fourpence and sixpence. As she was leaving I made further inquiries about her husband. She said he was an author by profession, and had seen better days. He was very ill, and unable to work. I asked her to give me his address as I might be of some assistance to him. This request seemed to perplex her; and at length she said, she was afraid her husband would not like to see me; he was very proud. I have since ascertained that this author's pretty little wife is a dangerous impostor. She lives, or did live at the time I met her, at the back of Clare Market, with a man (not her husband) who was well-known to the police as a notorious begging-letter writer. He was not the author of anything but those artful appeals, with forged signatures, of which I have given specimens under the heading of "Screevers." I was also assured by an officer that the pretended author's wife had on one occasion been concerned in decoying a young man to a low lodging near Lincoln's Inn Fields, where the unsuspecting youth was robbed and maltreated.

DEPENDANTS OF BEGGARS

THE dependants of beggars may be divided into screevers proper; i.e., writers of "slums and fakements" for those who live by "screeving," and referees, or those who give characters to professional beggars when references are required. Beggars are generally born and bred to the business. Their fathers and mothers were beggars before them, and they have an hereditary right to the calling. The exceptions to this rule are those who have fallen into mendicancy, and follow it from necessity, and those who have flown to it in a moment of distress, and finding it more lucrative than they supposed, adopted it from choice. Hence it follows that the majority are entirely destitute of education; and by education I mean the primary arts of reading and writing. Where there is demand there is supply, and the wants of mendicants who found their account in "pads," and "slums," and "fakements," created "screevers."

The antecedents of the screever are always more or less—and generally more—disreputable. He has been a fraudulent clerk imprisoned for embezzlement; or a highly respected treasurer to a philanthropic society, who has made off with the funds entrusted to him; or a petty forger, whose family have purchased silence, and "hushed up" a scandal; or, more frequently, that most dangerous of convicts, the half-educated convict—who has served his time or escaped his bonds.

Too proud to beg himself, or, more probably, too well-known to the police to dare face daylight; ignorant of any honest calling, or too idle to practise it; without courage to turn thief or informer; lazy, dissolute, and self-indulgent, the screever turns his little education to the worst of purposes, and prepares the forgery he leaves for the more fearless cadger to utter.

The following are specimens of the screever's work, copied from the original documents in the possession of Mr. Horsford, of the Mendicity Society:—

"Parish of Battersea;

County of Surrey.

"This memorial sheweth that Mr. Alexander Fyfe, a native of Port Glasgow N.B., and for several years carrying on the business of a NURSERY and SEEDSMAN in this parish, became security for his son in law, Andrew Talfour, of Bay Street, Port Glasgow, who in October last privately disposed of his effects and absconded to the colonies, leaving his wife and six children totally unprovided for and the said Mr. Alexander Fyfe responsible for the sum of £1,350; the sudden reverse of fortune together with other domestic afflictions so preyed on the mind of Mr. Fyfe that he is now an inmate of a LUNATIC ASYLUM.

"The said Mr. Fyfe together with his family have hitherto maintained the character of HONESTY and INDUSTRY in consideration of which I have been earnestly solicited by a few Benevolent persons to draw up this statement on behalf of the bereaved family. I have therefore taken on myself the responsibility of so doing trusting those whom Providence has given the means will lend their timely aid in rescuing a respectable family from the ruin that inevitably awaits them.

"Given under my Hand at the VESTRY in the aforesaid parish of Battersea and County of Surrey this Twenty-Fourth day of February in the year of Our Lord 1851."

John Thomas Freeman,   £3

Vestry Clerk.

J. S. Jenkinson £5	
Vicar of Battersea.	
Watson and Co. £5	
John Forster & Co. 5	
Revd. J. Twining 2	
Alderman J. Humphrey 5	
Sir George Pollock 5	
Southlands.	
Henry Mitton 2	
Wm. Downs 2	
Oak Wharf.	
Mrs. Broadley Wilson 1	
Sir Henry B. Houghton £5	
Mrs. Adml Colin Campbell 1 1	
Col. J. McDonall . . . . £5 paid.	
Anonymous 2	
Mrs. Col. Forbes £3	
Col. W. Mace paid 5	
P. H. Gillespie 5	
Minister of the Scotch Church	
Battersea Rise	
3rd March, 51	
Messrs. Moffat, Gillespie & Co. . . . . 5 pd."	

My readers will perceive that the above document is written in a semi-legal style, with a profuse amount of large capitals, and minute particularity in describing localities, though here and there an almost ostentatious indifference exists upon the same points.

DISTRESSED OPERATIVE BEGGARS

ALL beggars are ingenious enough to make capital of public events. They read the newspapers, judge the bent of popular sympathy, and decide on the "lay" to be adopted. The "Times" informs its readers that two or three hundred English navigators have been suddenly turned adrift in France. The native labourers object to the employment of aliens, and our stalwart countrymen have been subjected to insult as well as privation. The beggar's course is taken; he goes to Petticoat Lane, purchases a white smock frock, a purple or red plush waistcoat profusely ornamented with wooden buttons, a coloured cotton neckerchief, and a red nightcap. If procurable "in the Lane," he also buys a pair of coarse-ribbed grey worsted stockings, and boots whose enormous weight is increased by several pounds of iron nails in their thick soles; even then he is not perfect, he seeks a rag and bottle and old iron shop—your genuine artist-beggar never asks for what is new, he prefers the worn, the used, the ragged and the rusty—and bargains for a spade. The proprietor of the shop knows perfectly well that his customer requires an article for show, not service, and they part with a mutual grin, and the next day every street swarms with groups of distressed navigators. Popular feeling is on their side, and halfpence shower round them. Meanwhile the poor fellows for whom all this generous indignation is evoked are waiting in crowds at a French port till the British Consul passes them over to their native soil as paupers.

The same tactics are pursued with manufacturers. Beggars read the list of patents, and watch the effect of every fresh discovery in mechanics on the operatives of Lancashire and Yorkshire. A new machine is patented. So many hands are thrown out of work. So many beggars, who have never seen Lancashire, except when on the tramp, are heard in London. A strike takes place at several mills, pretended "hands" next day parade the streets. Even the variability of our climate is pressed into the "cadging" service; a frost locks up the rivers, and hardens the earth, rusty spades and gardening tools are in demand, and the indefatigable beggar takes the pavement in another "fancy dress." Every social shipwreck is watched and turned to account by these systematic land-wreckers, who have reduced false signals to a regular code, and beg by rule and line and chart and compass.

Starved-out Manufacturers

STARVED-OUT manufacturers parade in gangs of four and five, or with squalid wives and a few children. They wear paper-caps and white aprons with "bibs" to them, or a sort of cross-barred pinafore, called in the manufacturing districts a "chequer-brat." Sometimes they make a "pitch," that is, stand face to face, turning their backs upon a heartless world, and sing. The well-known ditty of

> "We are all the way from Manches-ter
> And we've got no work to do!"

set to the tune of, "Oh let us be joyful," was first introduced by this class of beggars. Or they will carry tapes, stay-laces, and papers of buttons, and throw imploring looks from side to side, and beg by implication. Or they will cock their chins up in the air, so as to display the unpleasantly prominent apples in their bony throats, and drone a psalm. When they go out "on the blob," they make a long oration, not in the Lancashire or Yorkshire dialects, but in a cockney voice, of a strong Whitechapel flavour. The substance of the speech varies but slightly from the "patter" of the hand loom weaver; indeed, the Nottingham "driz" or lace-man, the hand on strike, the distressed weaver, and the "operative" beggar, generally bear so strong a resemblance to each other, that they not only look like but sometimes positively are one and same person.

Unemployed Agriculturists and Frozen-out Gardeners

UNEMPLOYED Agriculturists and Frozen-out Gardeners are seen during a frost in gangs of from six to twenty. Two gangs generally "work" together, that is while one gang begs at one end of a street, a second gang begs at the other. Their mode of procedure, their "programme," is very simple. Upon the spades which they carry is chalked "frozen out!" or "starving!" and they enhance the effect of this "slum or fakement," by shouting out sturdily "Frozen out," "We're all frozen-out!" The gardeners differ from the agriculturists or "navvies" in their costume. They affect aprons and old straw hats, their manner is less demonstrative, and their tones less rusty and unmelodious. The "navvies" roar; the gardeners squeak. The navvies' petition is made loud and lustily, as by men used to work in clay and rock; the gardeners' voice is meek and mild, as of a gentle nature trained to tend on fruits and flowers. The young, bulky, sinewy beggar plays navvy; the shrivelled, gravelly, pottering, elderly cadger performs gardener.

There can be no doubt that in times of hardship many honest labourers are forced into the streets to beg. A poor hard-working man, whose children cry to him for food, can feel no scruple in soliciting charity—against such the writer of these pages would urge nothing; all credit to the motive that compels them unwillingly to ask alms; all honour to the feeling that prompts the listener to give. It is not the purpose of the author of this work to write down every mendicant an impostor, or every almsgiver a fool; on the contrary, he knows how much real distress, and how much real benevolence exist, and he would but step between the open hand of true charity and the itching palm of the professional beggar, who stands between the misery that asks and the philanthropy that would relieve.

The winter of 1860-61 was a fine harvest for the "frozen-out" impostors, some few of whom, happily, reaped the reward of their deserts in the police-courts. Three strong hearty men were brought up at one office; they said that they were starving, and they came from Horselydown; when searched six shillings and elevenpence were found upon them; they reiterated that they were starving and were out of work, on which the sitting magistrate kindly provided them with both food and employment, by sentencing them to seven days' hard labour.

The "profits" of the frozen-out gardener and agriculturist are very large, and generally quadruples the sum earned by honest labour. In the February of 1861, four of these "distressed navvies" went into a public-house to divide the "swag" they had procured by one day's shouting. Each had a handkerchief filled with bread and meat and cheese. They called for pots of porter and drank heartily, and when the reckoning was paid and the spoils equally divided, the share of each man was seven shillings.

The credulity of the public upon one point has often surprised me. A man comes out into the streets to say that he is starving, a few halfpence are thrown to him. If really hungry he would make for the nearest baker's shop; but no, he picks up the coppers, pockets them, and proclaims again that he is starving,

though he has the means of obtaining food in his fingers. Not
that this obvious anachronism stops the current of benevolence
or the chink of coin upon the stones—the fainting, famished
fellow walks leisurely up the street, and still bellows out in
notes of thunder, "I am starving!" If one of my readers will
try when faint and exhausted to produce the same tone in the
open air, he will realise the impossibility of shouting and starving
simultaneously.

Hand-Loom Weavers and Others Deprived of Their Living by Machinery

As has been before stated, the regular beggar seizes on the latest
pretext for a plausible tale of woe. Improvements in mechanics,
and consequent cheapness to the many, are usually the causes of
loss to the few. The sufferings of this minority is immediately
turned to account by veteran cadgers, who rush to their wardrobes of well-chosen rags, attire themselves in appropriate costume,
and ply their calling with the last grievance out. When unprovided
with "patter," they seek the literati of their class, and buy a
speech; this they partly commit to memory, and trust to their
own ingenuity to improvise any little touches that may prove
effective. Many "screevers, slum-scribblers and fakement-dodgers"
eke out a living by this sort of authorship. Real operatives seldom
stir from their own locality. The sympathy of their fellows, their
natural habits and the occasional relief afforded by the parish
bind them to their homes, and the "distressed weaver" is generally
a spurious metropolitan production. The following is a copy of
one of their prepared orations:
"My kind Christian Friends,
"We are poor working-men from —— which cannot obtain
bread by our labour, owing to the new alterations and inventions
which the master-manufacturers have introduced, which spares
them the cost of employing hands, and does the work by machinery instead. Yes, kind friends, machinery and steam-engines now
does the work, which formerly was done by our hands and work
and labour. Our masters have turned us off, and we are without
bread and knowing no other trade but that which we was born
and bred to, we are compelled to ask your kind assistance, for
which, be sure of it, we shall be ever grateful. As we have said,
masters now employ machinery and steam-engines instead of

men, forgetting that steam-engines have no families of wives or
children, and consequently are not called on to provide for them.
We are without bread to put into our mouths, also our wives
and children are the same. Foreign competition has drove our
masters to this step, and we working-men are the sufferers thereby.
Kind friends, drop your compassion on us; the smallest trifle will
be thankfully received, and God will bless you for the relief you
give to us. May you never know what it is to be as we are now,
drove from our work, and forced to come out into the streets to
beg your charity from door to door. Have pity on us, for our
situation is most wretched. Our wives and families are starving,
our children cry to us for bread, and we have none to give them.
Oh, my friends, look down on us with compassion. We are poor
working-men, weavers from ——— which cannot obtain bread
by our labour owing to the new inventions in machinery, which,
&c., &c.''

In concluding this section of our work, I would commend to
the notice of my readers the following observations on alms-
giving:—

The poor will never cease from the land. There always will be
exceptional excesses and outbreaks of distress that no plan could
have provided against, and there always will be those who stand
with open palm to receive, in the face of heaven, our tribute of
gratitude for our own happier lot. Yet there is a duty of the head
as well as of the heart, and we are bound as much to use our
reason as to minister of our abundance. The same heaven that
has rewarded our labours, and filled our garners or our coffers,
or at least, given us favour in the sight of merchants and bankers,
has given us also brains, and consequently a charge to employ
them. So we are bound to sift appeals, and consider how best to
direct our benevolence. Whoever thinks that charity consists in
mere giving, and that he has only to put his hand in his pocket,
or draw a cheque in favour of somebody who is very much in
want of money, and looks very grateful for favours to be received,
will find himself taught better, if not in the school of adversity,
at least by many a hard lesson of kindness thrown away, or perhaps very brutishly repaid. As animals have their habits, so there
is a large class of mankind whose single cleverness is that of
representing themselves as justly and naturally dependent on
the assistance of others, who look paupers from their birth, who
seek givers and forsake those who have given as naturally as a tree

sends its roots into new soil and deserts the exhausted. It is the office of reason—reason improved by experience—to teach us not to waste our own interest and our resources on beings that will be content to live on our bounty, and will never return a moral profit to our charitable industry. The great opportunities or the mighty powers that heaven may have given us, are never meant to be lavished on mere human animals who eat, drink and sleep, and whose only instinct is to find out a new caterer when the old one is exhausted.